Inside
Investment Banking
Second Edition

Inside
Investment Banking
Second Edition

Ernest Bloch

C. W. Gerstenberg Professor of Finance
New York University

DOW JONES-IRWIN
Homewood, Illinois   60430

Project editor: Jane Lightell
Production manager: Bette Ittersagen
Production services: Caliber Design Planning, Inc.
Jacket design: Tim Kaage
Compositor: Compset Inc.
Typeface: 11/13 Century Schoolbook
Printer: R. R. Donnelley & Sons

LIBRARY OF CONGRESS
Library of Congress Cataloging-in-Publication Data

Bloch, Ernest.
 Inside investment banking / Ernest Bloch.—2nd ed.
  p. cm.
 Includes bibliographical references and index.
 ISBN 1-556-23128-8
 1. Investment banking. 2. Investment banking—United States.
I. Title.
HG4534.B46 1989
332.66—dc19   88–17781
                  CIP

Printed in the United States of America

1 2 3 4 5 6 7 8 9 0 DO 5 4 3 2 1 0 9 8

**In memoriam
Henry Simon Bloch
Gustave Lehman Levy**

PREFACE
TO THE FIRST EDITION

This book grew out of necessity and opportunity. The necessity was forced on me when I began to teach a course on investment banking and could find no text on that subject. The opportunity came from that very necessity, for it was my good fortune to team-teach for six years an undergraduate seminar on investment banking with Mr. Gustave L. Levy, senior partner, Goldman, Sachs & Co. After Mr. Levy's untimely death in 1976, Mr. John C. Whitehead, senior partner, Goldman, Sachs & Co. continued the course. During the entire period the seminar was conducted, Mr. Jonathan L. Cohen, now a partner of Goldman, Sachs, was an active and creative participant. To all of them I owe an intellectual debt, and to this day Mr. Cohen remains my intellectual lender of last resort.

In the seminar that Gustave L. Levy and I ran, we made do with various reading materials, memoranda, newspaper and journal articles, and so on, but the students learned the most from Mr. Levy and from the partners and other financial experts he brought to class. By this book's dedication I want to thank Gus and to suggest that even after a decade, he remains a vivid memory to me as he does, I am sure, to many others.

During the past four years, I have been teaching a graduate lecture course. In running that course, the assistance of the Securities Industry Association, and particularly of Ms. Judith Cutler of Goldman, Sachs & Co. and of Messrs. Bruce S. Foerster of Paine Webber and Robert J. Kase of L. F. Rothschild, Unterberg, Towbin was very important, and their intellectual contributions to the course and to the book were essential.

The present version of the book is structured to discuss the many functions performed by investment banking firms. The book highlights the market-making functions of these firms, for that is the expertise they make available to their clients. Included in these functions are, for example, participations in large-scale and frequently innovative deals with institutional clients; mergers and acquisition; and the entire panoply of the new-issues process. The pressure of time precluded a discussion of the globalization of finance—that is, the spread of U.S. firms to foreign markets, and the increasingly large-scale entry of firms from abroad on the U.S. capital market.

The industry is a very dynamic one that, in the recent past, has shifted from a partnership type of organization to a corporate structure. And it is this very dynamism of the industry that makes it difficult to set it into the freeze-frame of the covers of a book. For this reason, we shall emphasize the innovative activities of investment bankers as well as their clients' more permanent needs for the services they provide. Indeed, some of the innovative activities of investment bankers are developed in some detail to indicate how these new activities are themselves part of the dynamism of market making; that as the industry promotes new types of deals, it is changing itself. In the discussion of mergers and acquisitions, the emphasis is on the industry's own activities as it participates in the merger game. And in the discussion of these innovations an essential source has been the research output of Salomon Brothers Inc., which the reader will find throughout the book. The permission to use these materials is gratefully acknowledged.

The plan of the book is to discuss the several market-making functions of investment banking in Part I and the new-issues process in Part II. Part III covers the public-policy issues regarding regulatory changes in the new-issues process (such as shelf registration), and Part IV deals with some investment management issues raised by the institutionalization of security markets. Finance and investment banking have developed a jargon all their own; to assist the reader a glossary of technical terms is provided at the end of the book.

In closing, I would like to acknowledge financial support from the Henry and Elaine Kaufman Foundation, Inc., and the NYU Schools of Business Research Fund. This is also an acknowledgment to the patience of our secretaries, Ms. Diane

Shand, Ms. Maureen George, Ms. Diana Greene, and Mrs. Selma Rabinowitz, for while their patience was often tested, it never broke. And finally, many thanks should go to my wife, Amy W. Bloch, whose drafting skills the reader will appreciate and whose general encouragement made this book possible.

Ernest Bloch
1986

PREFACE
TO THE SECOND EDITION

The first edition was written to provide a book to back up a course in investment banking. In the process of writing that book, I began to understand how the industry earns its substantial returns from the financing of new and different types of deals. In fact, the industry's business is the financing of change itself. Further, the pursuit and execution of innovative deals produced feedback effects on the firms that did the deals. It is that dynamic material that forms the basis for the second edition.

Just about one half of the book is new. In order of appearance the new chapters cover an analysis of the changed (and changing) investment banking industry, and the impact (easily exaggerated) of the crash of 1987. Two new chapters are devoted to financial innovation. These two chapters discuss first, the new security forms, and, second, the impact on financial markets and market participants of the new security types.

Because mergers and acquisitions and leveraged buyouts have become the major activity of a number of investment bankers, an entire part of the book is devoted to the market for "corporate control." That part also contains a new chapter on insider trading problems.

Among the other new materials in the book are an updating of the institutionalization of the securities markets, and the impact of that process on the industry. Finally, in a new last chapter, the process of innovation and the related rapid growth of the investment banking firms themselves is assessed. The book concludes that the industry being so committed to innovation and to the trading on rapidly changing markets is now, itself, subject to rapid and continuous change.

As in the first edition, this writer remains a heavy debtor to many: Bruce S. Foerster, Managing Director, Paine Webber; Ms. Carolyn H. Jackson, First Vice President, Banque Nationale de Paris; Richard C. Perry, Vice President, Goldman Sachs; Jon Rotenstreich, President, Torchmark Corporation; Dr. Henry Kaufman, President, Henry Kaufman & Co., Inc.; J. R. Lovejoy, General Partner, Lazard Frères; Robert Kase, Managing Director, L. F. Rothschild; Samuel G. Liss, Vice President, M. D. Youngblood, Vice President, and Jeffrey Hanna, Managing Director, all of Salomon Brothers; and Andrew Ellner, Vice President, First Boston Corporation. These busy practitioners have been patient with my questions, and many have shown interest in the organizing ideas—some of which even survive in this edition. My thanks go to all those talented, busy, and patient people. My hope is that my debt/equity ratio has not risen unduly.

Further, my colleagues at NYU have provided an intellectual environment in which work is stimulated. My sometime co-author, and co-editor, Robert A. Schwartz continues to be a helpful reader and tough critic. My good friend and colleague, Ely Kushel, has read the text and, with a new colleague, Roy C. Smith, also provided helpful comments. The deans of the Schools of Business (in reverse alphabetical order, for a change), Richard R. West, Abraham L. Gitlow, and Daniel E. Diamond, as well as the successive chairmen of the Finance Department (Marti Subrahmanyam, Ingo Walter, Lawrence S. Ritter), have all helped to provide an environment in which ideas and research can flourish. My students who have read through and commented on preliminary drafts of chapters (old and new) and Ms. Selma Rabinowitz, who cheerfully typed all of them, all have my thanks. And Mrs. Amy W. Bloch, who drafted several versions of the charts in the book, is owed more than I can say.

I also want to take this occasion to memorialize Henry Simon Bloch, my cousin, and a partner of E. M. Warburg, Pincus & Co., Inc. During his life, Henry was a wonderful friend whose cheerfulness and deep interest in the interests of others remained with him even during his last difficult years. Many of us will remember him and miss him.

Ernest Bloch
1988

CONTENTS

Return from Risk Arbitrage. Investment Bankers: Other Activities in Corporate Restructuring: *Investment Banker Fees Once Again.* The Merger Fee as an Insurance Premium: *Demand for Advice.*

10 Insider Trading Problems   *180*

Recent Surge in Insider Activity. Recent Case Law: Individual Insiders: *Chiarella (1980). Dirks (1983). Misappropriation Theory. Legislative Actions. The SEC Actions. Institutional Insider Trading. Some Conclusions, and Extensions to Commercial Banking.*

Part III   New Issues Flotation   *197*

11   The Venture Capitalist   *202*

The Venture Capital Process: *The Organization of Venture Capital Funds.* Venture Capital Financing of a New Firm: Bioengineering. Moving into the World of Finance: *Venture Capital. Brief Digression on Convertible Preferred.* The IPO: The End of Another Beginning: *The Investment Banking Function.*

12   The New Issue Underwriter: How to Price that
      Market-Making Service   *213*

New Issue Market Making. The Information Set for a New Issue. Price Action for a New Stock Issue: *Preoffering Price Action. Pricing Debates. Underpricing Once Again: An Investment Banker's IPO.*

13   The Nuts and Bolts of an Initial Public Offering   *226*

Preparation. First Steps in Finance from, and Information for, Outsiders. Purpose of Public Financing. Decisions, Decisions . . . Preparations. The Legal Side. Execution: *The Underwriting Problem Summarized. The Adjusted Present Value Rule.* Dealing with the Underwriters. The Underwriter's Side. Security Analysis Versus Valuation of a Firm. The Time Line of an IPO. Schematic Time Schedule for Public Offering of Common Stock.

14   New Issue Underwriting as Insurance to the
      Issuer   *248*

Waiting Risk. Pricing Risk. The Demand for Risk Shifting. Supply of Risk Shifting by Underwriters through Diversification, Marketing, Hedging, and Institutional Sales: *Diversification. Marketing. Hedging.*

Institutional Sales.   Pricing Services: *New Issues Pricing.*   *Valuation of an IPO.*   Valuing Informatics: A Case Study: *Avoidance of Flotation Risks: Management's Point of View.*   *"Privileged Subscription" for Rights Issues and Standby "Insurance."*   Some Conclusions: Underwriting and Its Risks.

PART I

MARKET MAKING

1

INTRODUCTION

Investment bankers perform two closely interrelated functions:

1. In the *primary* market, they *float* new securities for cash.
2. In the *secondary* market for existing securities, they assist buyers and sellers by acting as brokers or dealers.

It is the first function, the sale of a new issue to raise cash, that most people think of when the subject of investment banking comes up. The problem of pricing and distributing a new issue— that is, a security that has never been traded—is most important to the corporate issuer because it sets the firm's cost of capital. At the same time, U.S. law restricts the issuance of publicly traded corporate securities to investment bankers. The price of the new stock or the interest rate on the new bond (and its other characteristics, such as maturity) must necessarily be related to the prices and other characteristics of comparable (existing) securities currently trading in the secondary markets. Setting the appropriate price and nonprice terms on a new issue is the all-important information step in the investment banking process. That process, in turn, must be based on active and large-scale trading in the secondary market—hence the necessary linkage between the two.

More recently, in the 1980s, investment bankers and others have developed new products by repackaging already existing securities. This type of market making produces financial innovations and new types of securities, and raises funds for the asset holders with far greater ease and lower cost than direct sale. Innovating bankers can place the new securities with investors because they have the expertise in finding investors and in structuring and pricing the new securities so they can be readily sold. Another major line of business is mergers and acquisitions (M&A), and the financing of that activity. In the 1980s, the innovative use of junk bonds was a major factor in the record surge of M&A activity.

In discussing the purposes and functions of investment bankers, this book concentrates on three major themes. The first of these, as noted, is innovation. The second is market making, which requires a set of trading skills that involve finding institutional buyers for large-scale sales and (less frequently) assembling large-scale blocks of securities for a potential purchaser. These trading skills are maintained and tested in secondary markets where existing securities trade on a continuous basis. Because investors' large-scale sales are not predictably matched by other investors' desires to buy on the same large scale at the desired price, the market maker must often take a substantial position, and, accordingly, he must be backed by an equally substantial amount of capital. Not many brokers can be dealers because the risk capital required is greater than most brokerage firms can raise.

The third theme is new-issues finance, perhaps the most significant subset of the overall market making process. I will deal with the problems of new-issues finance in some detail because that is the market area in which investment bankers provide the information skills, as well as the trading skills, that give them their unique position in the American capital market.

In the last part of the book I discuss the other implications of institutionalization for American financial markets. As noted above, this situation requires not only larger trades and larger capital positions by market makers, but it may require as well another way of looking at market theory. For example, the prevailing theory of corporate governance (known as agency theory) assumes conflict between the firm's stockholders and its management. But what if the stock is held by institutional portfolio managers who use indexing as a portfolio management technique? What are their interests in corporate governance?

Finally, beyond looking at the market-making activities of investment bankers, this book will examine the industry structure of investment banking.

THE MARKET PROCESS

The dealer, or market-making, function involves placing capital at risk and carrying financial inventories. For those firms that play a leadership role in the industry, it involves performing these services *on a large scale*. As noted, one of the special functions performed by investment bankers is the placement of new issues on the market. However, other financial institutions that are not called investment bankers also engage in new-issues financing. For example, many commercial banks are syndicate managers for new issues of municipal securities (also called tax exempts) or are involved in new-money flotation of U.S. government securities. In addition, banks and insurance companies (as well as investment bankers) place new issues of corporate securities directly with institutional investors.

Under the 1930s Glass–Steagall Act, U.S. commercial banks were not permitted to underwrite new issues of corporate stocks, although they began to underwrite some corporate debt issues in the 1960s. Nor were banks permitted to act in the secondary corporate markets as dealers in stocks, although they were permitted to act as agents for customers. Perhaps the most significant new-issues function performed by commercial banks in the 1970s and 1980s is the flotation of industrial development bonds. Technically, these are municipal issues, but they are specifically designed to finance industrial—that is, corporate—projects.

Under SEC regulations well-established investment banking firms can engage in every type of underwriting and trading. Today they have entered the new satellite markets such as options and futures, international activities, and asset management.

Not only do investment bankers offer multiple financial services, but different firms in the industry offer different combinations of these services. The investment banking industry, moreover, is more adaptable and flexible than most of its competition to substantial outside shocks and market changes. Among these, the data processing revolution permitted the industry to raise its equity trading capacity roughly 10-fold during the period 1968 to 1984.

In discussing the scale of the industry, one important aspect is industry leadership—specifically, the handful of companies called special-bracket firms.[1] One (or more) of these firms is usually the syndicate leader in every major flotation. In addition these firms are considered an elite group that plays a similar leadership role in takeovers, mergers, and acquisitions. Is that leadership position based on the results of objective performance tests in specific industry outputs? With the exception of data concerning underwriting leadership by types of security (e.g., corporate bonds, municipal issues, etc.), few output measures are generally available.

Still, the perception that some firms have certain specialties that they do particularly well persists, in part because those services are identified with certain well-known individuals. For the major firms, market expectations are that they will participate in a leadership role in all of the basic outputs of investment bankers. For the next group of firms, one or more areas will tend to represent a predominant factor.

Nevertheless, *all* investment banking firms, large and small, do some of the same things.[2] All of them engage in new-issue underwriting, private placements, and block trading; in bond swaps and principal transactions; and in brokerage activities for individual and institutional clients. Finally, at this writing, other financial industries, notably commercial banks and insurance firms, are increasingly entering (and for the banks, reentering after 50 years) some of the same brokerage/investment banking areas. Everything is getting more complicated.

A QUICK GLANCE AT HISTORY

A little more than a half century ago, a speculative frenzy on all financial markets was followed by the great Wall Street crash of 1929 and the Great Depression of the 1930s. In that decade Congress passed a great deal of, it hoped, remedial legislation.

---

[1] These are, in no special order, Merrill Lynch, Goldman Sachs, Salomon Brothers, First Boston, and Morgan Stanley.

[2] This is roughly equivalent to the argument that the average country club hacker and John McEnroe practice their serves. The statement is true; the results are very different.

In 1947, many of the investment bankers that survived the Depression were hit by an antitrust complaint filed by the Department of Justice under the Sherman Act. The government brought suit against 17 major investment banking firms and the Investment Bankers Association (IBA) (see Table 1–1 for a list of the firms involved)[3] charging monopolization of the securities business and, most notably, of about two-thirds (69 percent) of publicly offered syndicates. The case came to trial in late 1950 before Judge Medina, sitting without a jury. After a lengthy trial, Judge Medina dismissed the charges in September 1953 on the grounds of insufficient evidence.[4]

Following that trial the investment banking and related broker–dealer industries suffered from further disruption in the organization and regulation of the financial system:

1. A surge in corporate (as well as state and local) debt financing in the 1960s and 1970s.
2. A surge in stock-market prices and volume until 1968 and subsequent dislocation of trading capacity.
3. A rise in inflationary finance from 1968 to 1981.
4. A sharp rise in volatility of security prices and rates of return and the advent of negotiated commissions.
5. As a result, a sharp increase in price volatility in secondary and primary markets even as commission rates receded (at least in equity markets).

But the industry has a rather unusual capacity to respond to market, technological, and regulatory shocks. In part, this may be due to the relatively small number of major firms in the industry and their manageable size (see Chapter 2). The industry has also survived the disappearance of more than half the firms deemed to be major underwriters in 1950.

---

[3]Compare this list to Table 4–8 in Chapter 4 to identify survivors among today's major firms.

[4]For an interesting discussion of the trial and the issues and personalities involved see V. P. Carrosso, *Investment Banking in America* (Cambridge, Mass.: Harvard University Press, 1970).

TABLE 1–1

**Concentration of Control in the Investment Banking Business:
Security Issues Managed* January 1, 1938, to April 30, 1947 (In Millions)**

	Issues Registered with SEC	Rail Issues (Exclusive of Equipment Trust Issues)	Total Issues Managed	Percent of All Issues
Morgan Stanley & Co.	2,783.6	578.8	3,362.4	16.1%
First Boston Corporation†	2,592.4	133.6	2,726.0	13.1
Dillon, Read & Co., Inc.	1,460.1	26.0	1,486.1	7.1
Kuhn, Loeb & Co.	762.1	618.0	1,380.1	6.6
Blyth & Co.	838.9	63.3	902.2	4.3
Smith, Barney & Co.	804.0	—	804.0	3.9
Lehman Brothers	604.3	36.0	640.3	3.1
Harriman, Ripley & Co., Inc.	611.6	6.7	618.3	3.0
Glore, Forgan & Co.	418.7	—	418.7	2.0
Kidder, Peabody & Co.	364.0	28.9	392.9	1.9
Stone & Webster Securities Corporation	352.1	—	352.1	1.7
Goldman, Sachs & Co.	287.8	—	287.8	1.4
Harris, Hall & Co. (Incorporated)	240.6	—	240.6	1.2
White, Weld & Co.	233.5	4.8	238.3	1.1
Eastman, Dillon & Co.	212.0	—	212.0	1.0
Union Securities Corporation	181.8	—	181.8	0.9
Drexel & Co.	90.2	23.4	113.6	0.5
Total—17 defendant banking firms	12,837.7	1,519.5	14,357.2	68.9
Total—1 nondefendant investment banking firm	2,097.7	1,050.3	3,148.0	15.1
Total—257 nondefendant investment banking firms	3,190.8	146.2	3,337.0	16.0
Total—275 investment banking firms	18,126.2	2,716.0	20,842.2	100.0

*Co-managed issues shown pro rata for each co-manager.
†Includes issues managed by Mellon Securities Corporation.

Source: *U.S.* v. *Henry S. Morgan et al.*, "Copy of Complaint," 49.

THE ANTITRUST CASE

Judge Medina held it "preposterous" that investment banking firms had "entered into a combination, conspiracy, and agreement to restrain and monopolize the securities business of the United States" at the time of World War I.[5] To the contrary, he concluded, the pyramidal shape of syndicate organization was a characteristic structure for performing the new-issue management in the United States and abroad since the 19th century. Medina suggested that the market-making needs that shifted somewhat with each issue gave the process its peculiar organizational structure.

Broadly put, Medina's argument is that the flotation mechanics are not a specific technical process (as, say, the formulation of a patent medicine) but a combination of security valuation and price forecasting techniques and market-making and management skills that he described as the sum of many different "banking services." In Medina's words, these services were "the product of a gradual evolution to meet specific economic problems created by demands for capital which arose as the result of the increasing industrialization of the country and the growth of a widely dispersed investor class."

Hayes et al.[6] argue that the 1930s legislation (the Exchange Act, Securities Act, and Glass–Steagall) in combination with the relatively small volume of business done then led to more competitive offerings, to narrower spreads, and, in turn, to greater concentration of lead position in syndicates by established firms. Hayes[7] then quotes Carrosso's data and comments as follows: In the four and a half years between January 1, 1934, and June 30, 1938, 40 investment banking houses headed 94.6 percent of all managed issues in terms of value and held 82.6 percent in terms of value of all underwriting participations. The real point,

---

[5]U.S. District Court, Southern District of New York (Civil no. 43–757), *United States* v. *Henry S. Morgan et al.*, pp. 350 ff.

[6]S.C. Hayes III, A. M. Spence, and D. V. P. Marks, *Competition in the Investment Banking Industry* (Cambridge, Mass.: Harvard University Press, 1983), especially pp. 22 ff.

[7]Ibid., p. 23.

though was not whether the pyramid still existed but whether it was being misused."

Hayes et al. further point out that the pyramidal structure of syndicate management and the persistence of a small group of lead firms seemed to support the popular (and populist) folklore that an "anticompetitive money trust" existed and persisted. Hayes argues further that such beliefs were *not* supported by evidence of secret plots or back-room collusion. Instead they grew out of a perception of "professional incompetence, irresponsibility, and out-and-out fraud" that characterized a well-publicized group of broker–dealers and led to the legislation of the 1930s. Because these criminal and venal acts were individual and unorganized, the chosen regulatory remedy—full disclosure—reflects the notion that the broker–dealer community can be relied on to control an excess of organized greed. (Similar misfeasance and malfeasance were discovered in the banking system, although there the chosen regulatory remedy took on a different, and confidential, aspect.)

COMPETITION FOR SYNDICATE BUSINESS: POSTWAR FINANCE

During World War II and the immediate postwar period, the new-issues business was slow, owing partly to the liquid financial position of the corporate sector and partly to its strong cash flow. To some extent a geographic dispersion of financial power away from New York also began. As a result, many new firms began to enter the distribution business, especially as members of syndicate selling groups.

The adjustment of the major investment banking firms started off quietly in the 1950s, when new-issue financing contributed only a small share to financing of corporate real investment. At that time a few old-line, lead underwriters did the main originating work; they expended little effort on either distribution (retail or institutional) or secondary market making. Specialization was the name of the game; retail ("wire") firms were included in syndicates exclusively as members of the selling group. To overstate the case somewhat, the large, old, mainly

New York-based originating firms were corporate underwriters and advisers to issuers; the distributing (selling) firms were newer, smaller brokerage firms that emphasized relations with security buyers (at new issue).

Everyone could see that the big profits at new issue accrued to syndicate leaders (originating firms), whose management fee came to 20 percent off the top of gross spread (as it still does today). Further, large syndicate leaders also earned substantial underwriting fees by taking down large portions of new offerings and placing them with large institutional buyers. Private placements to the same buyers were also a substantial source of new business. During the 1950s and the early 1960s, moreover, the comparative stability of the financial markets held down the riskiness of the underwriting process, thereby giving originating firms an especially good base for their total profits. This situation did not escape the attention of distributing firms in the syndicate process—especially when these firms became more prosperous and acquired more capital with the bull market of the 1960s.

The 1960s

In fact, the very prosperity of the stock market began to open cracks in the system from the brokerage/distribution side of the new-issue process. To begin with, the "paper crisis" overwhelmed the record-keeping and transaction capacity of the New York Stock Exchange, resulting in the bankruptcy and forced merger of some firms. Further, the fact that many brokerage firms were organized as partnerships turned out to be a weak link in the chain of trading relationships. Some older partners thought the sharp price drops in equities in the late 1960s and the breakdown of market processes were all too reminiscent of the Great Depression. Fearing a similar collapse, they withdrew from the business and took their money out of the firms. For many of the firms suffering from flight capital, this set of events brought the very debacle the departing partners were eager to avoid for themselves. This situation also led a number of firms to broaden their capital base by going public. By reorganizing as corporations, such firms as Bache, Merrill Lynch, Dean

Witter, E. F. Hutton, Paine Webber, and Shearson Hayden Stone brought in a more stable capital base as well as a larger volume of public (and permanent) capital.

INFLATIONARY FINANCE

The 1970s opened with the back-office crisis on the New York Stock Exchange and a transition to negotiated—that is, expectations of lower—stock trading commissions. In addition, the decade brought on in full force the problems and opportunities of inflation finance and the associated price volatility of securities. Underwriting became a riskier game while market-making expertise in the secondary market became a more significant component of all securities-related activities. Institutional traders, for example, needed and wanted capacity to swap large blocks of bonds. The ability to place securities—either in inventory or with an institutional client—made many institutional and retail firms increasingly valuable as syndicate members to old-line syndicate originators and managers. Their value rose further as the financial environment became riskier and more difficult.

And, as the increasingly more strategic role of distributors became apparent to the firms themselves, they developed their own capacity to manage syndicates. Corporate financial officers and new-business representatives of the most eager major-bracket firms saw that something had fundamentally changed. With more active competition and less tradition in syndicate leadership, greater competition to run syndicates might lead to better performance for new issues. The traditional tie between a corporation and a specific investment broker was broken. On the buying side of the market, the capacity to deal on a large scale was increasingly in demand by institutional investors. As a result of such jockeying, substantial readjustments of major-bracket firms occurred between the beginning and the end of the decade as shown by Hayes.[8] (See Table 1–2.)

---

[8]S. L. Hayes III, "The Transformation of Investment Banking," *Harvard Business Review,* January–February 1979, p. 165.

TABLE 1–2
Equity Underwriting Syndicate Positions: 1971 versus 1978

1971	*1978*
Special bracket:	
Dillon, Read & Co. Inc.	—
The First Boston Corporation	The First Boston Corporation
Kuhn, Loeb & Co.	—
Merrill Lynch, Pierce, Fenner & Smith, Inc.	Merrill Lynch, Pierce, Fenner & Smith, Inc.
Morgan Stanley & Co. Incorporated	Morgan Stanley & Co. Incorporated
Salomon Brothers	Salomon Brothers
	Goldman Sachs & Co.
Major bracket:	
Blyth & Co., Inc.	Bache Halsey Stuart Shields Incorporated
Drexel Harriman Ripley Incorporated	Blyth Eastman Dillon & Co. Incorporated
Du Pont Glore Forgan Incorporated	Dillon, Read & Co. Inc.
Eastman Dillon, Union Securities & Co.	Donaldson, Lufkin & Jenrette Securities Corporation
Goldman, Sachs & Co.	Drexel Burnham Lambert Incorporated
Halsey, Stuart & Co. Inc.	E. F. Hutton & Company Inc.
Hornblower & Weeks—Hemphill, Noyes	Kidder, Peabody & Co. Incorporated
Kidder, Peabody & Co. Incorporated	Lazard Frères & Co.
Lazard Frères & Co.	
	Lehman Brothers Kuhn Loeb Incorporated
Lehman Brothers Incorporated	Loeb Rhoades, Hornblower & Co.
Loeb, Rhoades & Co.	Paine, Webber, Jackson & Curtis Incorporated
Paine, Webber, Jackson & Curtis	Smith Barney, Harris Upham & Co. Incorporated
Smith, Barney & Co. Incorporated	Warburg Paribas Becker Incorporated
Stone & Webster Securities Corporation	Wertheim & Co., Inc.
Wertheim & Co.	
White, Weld & Co.	Dean Witter Reynolds Inc.
Dean Witter & Co. Incorporated	
Major out of order:	
Bache & Co. Incorporated	Bear, Stearns & Co.
Paribas Corporation	L. F. Rothschild, Unterberg, Towbin
	Shearson Hayden Stone Inc.
Mezzanine bracket:	Oppenheimer & Co. Incorporated
	Thomson McKinnon Securities Inc.

TABLE 1–2 (continued)

1971	1978
Submajor bracket:	
Bear, Stearns & Co.	Ladenburg Thalmann & Co. Inc.
A. G. Becker & Co. Incorporated	Moseley, Hallgarten & Estabrook Inc.
CBWL—Hayden, Stone Inc.	
Clark, Dodge & Co. Incorporated	
Dominick & Dominick Incorporated	
Equitable Securities, Morton & Co. Incorporated	
Hallgarten & Co.	
Harris, Upham & Co. Incorporated	
E. F. Hutton & Company Inc.	
W. E. Hutton & Co.	
Ladenburg, Thalmann & Co.	
F. S. Moseley & Co.	
John Nuveen & Co. (Incorporated)	
R. W. Pressprich & Co. Incorporated	
Reynolds & Co.	
L. F. Rothschild & Co.	
Shearson, Hammill & Co. Incorporated	
Shields & Company	
F. S. Smithers & Co., Inc.	
Spencer Trask & Co., Incorporated	
G. H. Walker & Co.	
Walston & Co. Inc.	
Wood, Struthers & Winthrop Inc.	

Source: S. L. Hayes III, "The Transformation of Investment Banking," *Harvard Business Review,* January-February 1979, p. 165.

Meanwhile the forces of competition were pressing in on all firms by the move from fixed to negotiated brokerage commissions for equity trading. Although May Day 1975 was the date when all brokerage commissions became subject to negotiation, pressure from Congress and the SEC had pushed institutional-sized trades into negotiation of commission as early as 1971 and into some other forms of informal negotiation (through give ups) even earlier.[9]

---

[9]For further discussion, see SEC's *Institutional Investor Study Report,* 82d Congress, 1st Session, Washington, D.C.: U.S. Government Printing Office, 1971.

A FEW CONCLUSIONS

The investment banking business is often called dynamic and for good reason. With a few exceptions the group of leading firms has involved a changing cast of characters—namely, those firms that managed to adjust best and fastest to a substantial set of shocks. One shock was the retooling of the major market place, the NYSE. The Exchange, once a paper-based retail operation with a daily trading volume of 15 million shares, was threatened with collapse and required to close one trading day a week. Today the electronic market has traded 500 million shares a day, or 30 times the volume of the late 1960s, without major interruption. At the same time the broker-dealer firms that in part competed with and in part supplemented floor trading by upstairs block trading made that rise possible because average trade size was rising with growing institutionalization of the market.

Finally, large-scale institutionalization moved into the new issues market, and the SEC proposed its shelf-registration rule. But because that issue has many ramifications and raises many other questions, it will be discussed separately in Part IV.

2

INVESTMENT BANKING AS
MARKET MAKING
IN THE REAL WORLD

Over the past decade academic research in finance has developed concepts that help explain market performance and, going deeper, the actions of market makers. To understand market functioning, it is necessary to understand how a security's price is influenced by the market process.

The efficient-market hypothesis is now widely accepted. While security markets are essential to permit trading between sellers and buyers, the security price information produced by the markets permits analysts to assess how new company information influences price formation. That by-product of securities markets, namely, price information, has recently been studied in some depth. Scholars doing research on price formation have examined how a market maker in a structured market—be he (or she) a floor trader, a specialist, a banker in a call market, and so on—is interposed between buyer and seller. If the market for each security does *not* clear automatically at one price, the market maker can supply securities out of his inventory or add the market's excess to his inventory. He adds a service (for a fee) to provide liquidity—or market pricing continuity. That fee makes the buy/sell market prices different from each other and different from a single equilibrium price.

The nature of the service(s) offered, their pricing, and the industrial organization of that service industry are discussed under such terms as *auction markets, specialist systems, call markets, banking systems*, and *investment banking*. Put differently, an examination of market making helps in understanding the structure of real-world pricing as opposed to assumptions of perfect competition and a single equilibrium price.

In its most general sense, a market permits investors to adjust portfolios efficiently to meet changing objectives.[1] Some traders want to change portfolios because they believe that new information has changed the relative value of one security (information traders). Since neither the initial trading incentive nor the trade parameters of any buy/sell pair of transactions are necessarily the same, the existence of market makers provides continuity of trading with presumably smaller price swings. These services are often subsumed under the term *market liquidity*. In the U.S. secondary markets for stocks, such as the New York Stock Exchange (NYSE), specialists behave as "passive stabilizers." That is, they do not gear their decisions to anticipated price changes but to actual price changes. They buy when there is excess supply (net sell orders) and sell on "upticks" (incremental price increases). Because such behavior occurs in over 90 percent of all transactions, the NYSE concluded that the system provides a "fair and orderly market."[2]

These specialist market makers have a privileged position in that they observe customer limit orders in their "book"—their schedule of buy or sell orders at specified prices that have yet to be filled.[3] This added information suggests that market makers can protect themselves against accumulating excess inventory by lowering the bid price after a purchase. It has been argued that what is called price stabilization by the NYSE and others is a by-product of profit maximization by dealers since unregulated NASDAQ market makers behave the same way as regulated NYSE specialists.[4] Because of the large volume of trades

---

[1]The following is based on an article by H. R. Stoll, "Alternative Views of Market Making" (Working paper no. 84–113, Vanderbilt University, 1984).

[2]NYSE, "The Quality of the New York Stock Exchange Market Place in 1979," March 6, 1980 (Report of Quality Markets Committee, NYSE).

[3]This is the practical equivalent of supply-and-demand schedules.

[4]H. R. Stoll, "Dealer Inventory Behavior: An Empirical Investigation of NASDAQ Stocks," *Journal of Financial and Quantitative Analysis,* September 1976, pp. 359–80.

and the large number of traders, most observers believe that specialists cannot move "equilibrium" market price up or down and that their function is to narrow price variances over time rather than to push prices in one direction or another. (Block trading is covered in Chapter 18.)

Market-making arrangements thus provide a service called immediacy or liquidity to all asset holders. Immediate purchase or sale capacity, even in size and at little price variance, represents a service for traders who can view the cost of this service as a share of the bid/ask spread. And the seller does not deal directly with the buyer even in a single round-lot transaction, nor does he receive the price paid by the buyer.

A NOTE ON TECHNOLOGICAL CHANGE

Although the institutional processes described here have been called by the same names for many years, data processing technology has revolutionized securities trading. For example, the great shift of equity trading from an emphasis on individual trading in the 1960s to institutional transactions in the 1980s required, first, instant communication, and, second, the capacity to execute large-scale trades just as quickly. In turn, market makers needed the capacity to accept offers, hit bids, and do it in size. It follows that market makers for institutions must have substantial capital resources to participate, and, since this is where the action is, smaller market makers are likely to have a more difficult time.

Another by-product of the electronics revolution is the fact that the market can exist wherever a market maker has a terminal or CRT. Even though the NYSE will record (or "print") the outcome of each completed trade in registered stock, the actual transaction may have occurred away from the NYSE floor ("upstairs").

In addition, large-scale market makers must be able to manage large-scale portfolios that represent the unsold counterpart of institutional trades, to lay off the associated risks, to provide the services to clients that will generate fees, and to avoid major losses on unhedged positions. Because information on large-scale trades is available instantaneously, trading departments of investment banking firms have acquired more personnel, absorbed more capital, and gained in relative importance.

Some large-scale trades are automatically "crossed" (purchase and sales price are the same) within a firm or on the exchange floor. Since both seller and buyer pay commission, the trades—after transaction costs—are *not* made at the same effective prices even though the tape will indicate a trade done at identical prices.

TYPES OF MARKET MAKING

Three different market structures have been developed to trade securities, and they can be adapted to the trading of any security type. In order of declining familiarity, these are:

1. Brokered trading.
2. Dealer trading.
3. Market making.

Brokered Trading

This approach to securities trading involves a buyer's agent and a seller's agent, both typically trading on an exchange. Brokered markets are supported by a bureaucracy of floor personnel in charge of (1) transacting securities, (2) recording and publishing price and volume information, and (3) reconciling cash flows and other transaction-related mechanics. (See Figure 2–1A.) All of these activities are regulated by the exchanges and other units called self-regulatory organizations (SROs). The exchanges and all securities brokers and dealers must belong to an umbrella organization called the National Association of Securities Dealers (NASD). Because the SEC has delegated many of its regulatory powers to the NASD and the exchanges, these units are called self-regulatory organizations.

FIGURE 2–1
Security Transaction Processes

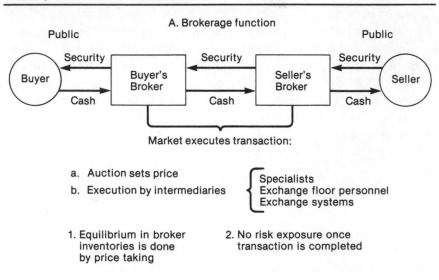

A professional trading *as an agent* is a price taker, and all broker inventories in the market will be set by the same price-taking decision as those of other investors. Brokers incur no inventory risks for the completed agency transactions.

Dealer Markets

When acting as a *dealer,* the market participant sets a bid-and-ask price for each security he offers to trade: He is the price maker. When his bid is hit, he buys a security from the seller (a broker, an institution, and so forth) with cash. His asset position is now less liquid (more securities, less cash) and riskier. He may want to readjust the entire bid/ask structure of his assets to lighten the security inventory (or reduce his risks); that is, he lowers ask and bid prices.

If, on the other hand, the dealer lays off systematic or market risks in satellite markets, such as financial futures markets, the risk-reducing downward shifts in inventory pricing may not

FIGURE 2–1 (*continued*)

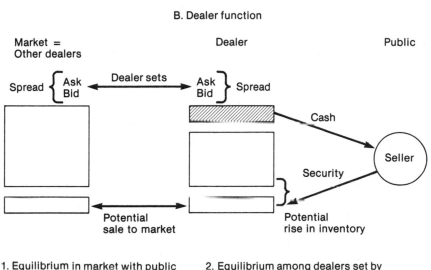

B. Dealer function

1. Equilibrium in market with public set by Bid/Ask price making

2. Equilibrium among dealers set by same Bid/Ask price making

take place. On the income side, however, a fee has been charged to lay off the risk implicit in the larger securities inventory. (See Figure 2–1B.)

Market Making

Many underwriters in initial public offerings act as market makers for some time after the issue is sold to the public and after the closing of the underwriting. In fact, the position of market maker represents the entire market structure on the other side of any trade by a seller of the security or by most buyers. Even when more than one market maker is active in the same security, it takes time for the market to acquire sufficient depth before price-making policies shift toward price taking as the major market process. A deep and wide market is required, one that carries the entire panoply of floor traders, specialists, and so on

FIGURE 2–1 (*concluded*)

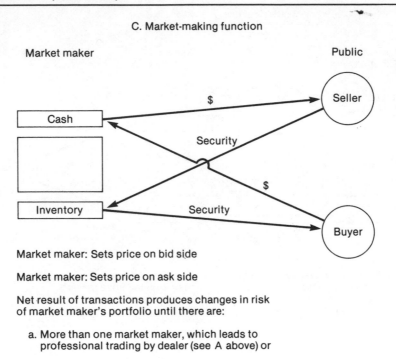

C. Market-making function

Market maker: Sets price on bid side

Market maker: Sets price on ask side

Net result of transactions produces changes in risk
of market maker's portfolio until there are:

    a. More than one market maker, which leads to
       professional trading by dealer (see A above) or

    b. Registration on exchange (see B above)

to facilitate routine agency trading on a price-taking basis. (See
Figure 2–1C.)

    Even in broad and deep markets such as the NYSE, certain
large transactions can overwhelm the process. Very large sell
offers require the arrangement of an "upstairs deal" by a trading
unit acting as a dealer. Once completed, the block trade (as it is
called) is recorded by the NYSE floor bureaucracy and prints on
the tape. Yet the pricing and transacting of a block trade are
done on a dealer basis, with the block trader often winding up
the deal—like any other dealer—with a larger inventory than
before. (The NYSE defines a block trade as a transaction consisting of a minimum of 10,000 shares.)

    Figure 2–2 illustrates the preceding analysis. The area
marked by a grid represents the brokered trading that takes
place on exchange floors. The market maker trading as a follow-

FIGURE 2–2
Comparative Market Structures

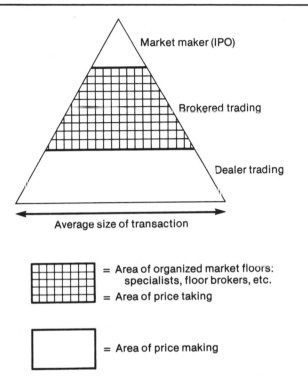

up to an initial public offering—usually in small units per trade—is usually an investment banker. In the brokered trading markets, investment bankers and brokers perform essentially the same functions, with the exception of the block trades noted above.

Dealer trading is what is often called over-the-counter (OTC) trading. In the OTC stock markets, the improvements in communications processes and recent (1984) regulatory changes have produced a mechanism that may approach the brokered trading process (at least in its mechanical aspects). The bond markets, on the other hand, imply OTC market making on a large scale with large amounts of risky inventories being positioned by dealers such as investment bankers and commercial banks—but not usually by brokers.

In Figure 2–2, therefore, institutionally oriented firms are active (although to a lesser extent) at the top and most active at the bottom of the pyramid, while retail-oriented firms are most active at the top and in the middle (compare with Chapter 4). This classification is not exclusive, but it does suggest that emphasis of trading practices can be used to distinguish retail-oriented from institutional-type firms.

SOME CONCLUSIONS

The purpose of the several different trading systems may be the same: (1) to earn a rate of return acceptable to the trading firm, (2) to perform a service for clients, (3) to develop a continuous information set that assists the investment banker or broker–dealer firm in pricing any security at new issue or at other times, and (4) to establish trading relationships with institutional-sized buyers and sellers. Volume dealing is a major factor that distinguishes dealers from brokers. This trading capacity, however, goes beyond mere size.

3

THE INVESTMENT BANKING INDUSTRY: SIZE AND STRUCTURE

INTRODUCTION

Little quantitative information is readily available about the investment banking industry's size or the structure of its current outputs. Few people appreciate the fact that up to the 1980s this was a cottage industry located on the island of Manhattan and concentrated primarily in the area around Wall Street. This section provides quantitative estimates based on comparable and consistent Securities and Exchange Commission (SEC) data.[1]

INVESTMENT BANKING FIRMS: SOME PARAMETERS

In its role as regulator of broker–dealer firms engaged in providing secondary-market trading services (under the Securities Exchange Act of 1934), the SEC classifies firms by trading function and location of head office. Altogether some 5,700 firms reports to SEC via FOCUS reports; less than half (about 2,500) do business directly with the public. As Table 3–1 indicates, among the 2,473 firms reporting to the SEC, only the first 21 firms are in-

---

[1]The data to be discussed are compiled by the SEC primarily from an analysis of FOCUS reports, which are regulatory reports filed by broker–dealers with self-regulatory organizations (such as the organized exchanges) or the SEC. Over 5,700 broker–dealers filed such reports in 1981, the latest full-year data available.

TABLE 3–1

The U.S. Securities Industry and Its Major Components by Number, Assets, and Equity Capital, 1981 (Dollars in Millions)

	Number of Firms	Total Assets	Equity Capital
NYSE member firms:			
National full line	11	$ 36,004	$2,600
Large investment banking	10	58,042	1,881
New York based	35	7,334	395
NYSE regional	126	9,252	872
Other NYSE carrying	65	10,563	1,230
NYSE introducing	206	1,160	344
Non-NYSE firms:			
Securities brokers	272	1,206	151
Securities dealers	315	2,844	657
Other non-NYSE carrying	226	2,326	303
Non-NYSE introducing	1,207	1,068	415
Total firms doing a public business	2,473	$129,799	$8,847

Source: SEC, *The Securities Industry in 1981* (Washington, D.C.: 1982).

volved primarily in investment banking. The national full-time firms are those (such as Merrill Lynch) that have an extensive network of branch offices. Firms included under "large investment banking" are engaged mainly in large-scale underwriting and trading (for example, Salomon Brothers). The terms *clearing* or *carrying* mean that such firms "cleared" securities transactions (for themselves and/or other firms) or maintained possession or control of customers' cash or securities (as, for example, through margin accounts). Most of the remaining New York Stock Exchange (NYSE) members that carry customer accounts are classified as New York-based firms if their head office is located in New York City or NYSE regional firms if the head office is outside New York City. NYSE introducing firms are members who neither clear nor carry securities for customers; the unclassified group are NYSE members who carry public customer accounts but fall outside the other classifications.

Firms classified as large investment banking houses by the SEC in consultation with the Securities Industries Association (SIA), a trade association, constitute a small industry even within the financial-services universe. At the end of 1981 (the latest date for which complete data are available), total industry assets were about $94 billion—roughly equal to the size of a single large money-center bank (i.e., Bank of America).

Financial transactions considered investment banking are not conducted exclusively by the two groups mentioned; many broker–dealer firms are involved in such activities. But if we group all broker–dealer firms that do business with the public, that group's total assets at year-end 1981 were about $130 billion, a total just slightly larger than Citicorp's, the nation's largest single bank holding company. (See Table 3–1.)

The most easily identifiable activity of investment bankers is the flotation of new issues, although other financial industries (for example, commercial banks) are involved in new-issues financing as well. Investment bankers also perform typical broker–dealer transactions in secondary markets (many of these transactions require special handling because of their large scale).

What, then, is investment banking? To paraphrase a famous quote, investment banking is what investment bankers do. And because the increasingly volatile price and interest-rate environments compel quickness of decision and response in financial markets, investment bankers have learned (1) how to use satellite markets to lay off risks and (2) that innovation in products, markets, and services may provide an important, even if temporary, boost to their own rates of return. This proposition may help to explain the stimulus to innovation and the quick (and defensive) response of other firms in the industry to the innovation of any pioneer, thereby producing a series of competitive readjustments in a set of firms that could conventionally (and probably erroneously) be thought of as an oligopoly. More on this later.

THE SEC CLASSIFICATION OF INDUSTRY GROUPS AND SIZE COMPARISONS

All classifying schemes, although useful, are somewhat arbitrary. Accordingly, the following section peels down the statistical onion, hopefully without tears.

The analysis begins with data for what the SEC calls carrying/clearing firms. These are firms that both:

1. Do business with the public.
2. Are members of an organized exchange.

This means that excluded are all firms that are not exchange members as well as those exchange members that do not do business with the public (such as exchange-floor traders or specialists) and all member firms that do not clear, or carry, customer accounts.

The investment banking industry is rather concentrated (refer to Table 3–1). Following the SEC's classification, in terms of total assets, the 11 national full-line firms,[2] and the 10 large investment banking houses together aggregate $94 billion of the total $130 billion security-business universe. Put slightly differently, the assets of 21 firms out of 2,473 (or fewer than 1 percent by number) constitute about 70 percent of the security industry's total assets. Within that group of 21 firms, the assets of the 10 investment banking houses alone add up to almost half the assets (those of the 11 national full-line firms add up to about 30 percent) of the securities industry as defined. If only for that reason, the investment banking industry bears separate examination.

WHICH ARE THE MAJOR FIRMS?

The SEC classification system uses size of the firm, type of business done, and location of the firm to establish subsets of the industry. The 11 national full-line firms are large broker–dealer firms that are involved in all aspects of the securities business and that have a nationwide network of branch offices. The 10 large investment banking houses are large firms that are known mainly as syndicate managers or leaders (other than those that operate extensive branch networks and are therefore placed in the first group). Most of the remaining NYSE members that do

---

[2]In the past these firms were identified as "national wire houses" because of the private wires that connected their many retail-oriented branch offices.

TABLE 3–2

Comparisons of Primary Revenue Items among Three Major Groups of Firms Engaged in Investment Banking, 1981 (Dollars in Millions)

	Full Line	Investment Banking Houses	NYSE Regionals
Security commissions:			
Listed equities	$1,753	$ 567	$ 646
Other	673	95	333
Total	2,426	662	979
Margin interest (income)	1,707	232	503
Profits from underwriting	722	318	324
Gains (losses) trading A/C:			
Debt	1,070	1,672	192
Other	376	370	210
Total	1,446	2,042	402
Other securities related*	1,000	1,327	265
Residual	1,056	1,065	229
Total revenues	$8,357	$5,646	$2,702
Pre-tax profit margins†	6.9%	15.4%	11.5%
Pre-tax returns to equity capital‡	24.0%	54.3%	37.5%

*Includes merger and takeover service revenues.
†Ratio of pre-tax income (income after partners' compensation but before taxes) to total revenues.
‡Pre-tax income as a percent of average of four quarters of ownership equity capital.

Source: SEC, *The Securities Industry in 1981* (Washington, D.C.: 1982), Table III-1 and Appendix C-1, 2, 4.

a public business are placed into a group called New York-based firms if their main office is in New York City or into NYSE regional firms if their main office is located outside of New York City.

MAJOR REVENUE COMPONENTS

Pre-tax revenue components indicate the variety of outputs and/or services produced by major firms doing investment banking. Based on the data in Table 3–2, several preconceptions may need adjusting. For example, figures on revenues from under-

TABLE 3–3
Distribution of Trading Gains in Debt Securities among Carrying Firms in 1981

	Number of Firms	Percent of Gains	
Large investment banking houses	10	49.4%	} 81%
National full-line firms	11	31.6	
Non-NYSE regional firms	315	7.8	
NYSE regional firms	126	5.7	
Other carrying firms	598	5.5	
All carrying firms doing a public business in 1980, 1981	1,060	100.0%	

Source: SEC, *The Securities Industry in 1981* (Washington, D.C.: 1982).

writing (that is, revenues from new-issue flotations) show that full-line firms earned twice as much from that source, and even NYSE regionals earned more than the large investment banking houses. More surprising, in 1981, before the NYSE bull market pushed up trading volume, the large investment banking houses earned twice as much from securities commissions as they did from underwriting. And, along with margin interest revenues, underwriting profits constituted one of the smaller components of total revenues (about 6 percent). By far the largest single source of revenue was trading gains, especially from debt issues (including U.S. government securities); revenues from such services as mergers and takeovers came in second. Indeed, the large investment houses did better on trading account than full-line firms (whose assets are larger), although the latter are involved in more retail-oriented trading situations. That retail orientation, finally, is also reflected in the full-line firms' relatively large earnings from margin interest.[3]

Considering the relationship of these earnings (pre-tax) either to total revenues or to equity capital, the large investment banking houses show up particularly well. First, their profit

---

[3]See also discussion of more recent data in Chapter 4, especially income statement data for Morgan Stanley.

TABLE 3–4

Distribution of Gains from Market Making in OTC Equity Securities among Carrying Firms in 1981

	Number of Employees		
	In Thousands	Percent	Percent of Gains
National full line firms	96	47.8%	46.7%
Large investment banking houses	18	9.2	10.0	56.7%
NYSE regional firms	29	14.4	22.5
Non-NYSE securities dealers	8	4.0	11.9
Other carrying firms	49	24.6	8.9
All carrying firms doing a public business in 1980, 1981	200	100.0%	100.0%

Source: U.S. Securities and Exchange Commission, FOCUS report, prepared by Directorate of Economic and Policy Analysis.

margins were better than twice those of full-line firms and about half again as good as those of NYSE regionals. Returns to equity were about 3.5 times profit margins, as were those of the other two sets of firms. Finally, these 1981 results for investment banking houses were the same as the 1980 results, a consistency record not achieved by the other two sets of firms.[4]

Taking revenue data a step further, the SEC has separated out the distribution of trading gains from debt issues and from market-making activities in over the counter (OTC) equities. As Table 3–3 indicates, better than four fifths of the industry's debt gains came from the two major sets of firms, with the large investment bankers counting for about half of the industry's total.

On the other hand, about half of market-making gains from OTC equity securities—a much more labor-intensive activity—

---

[4]Pre-tax margins and returns to equity (in percent) for 1980:

	Full Line	Investment Banking Houses	NYSE Regionals
Pre-tax margins	10.8%	17.6%	15.0%
Returns to equity	43.1	52.9	52.7

TABLE 3–5
Securities Industry Combined Balance Sheet* (Dollars in Billions)

	December 31	
	1974	1984
Assets		
Cash	$ 0.6	$ 3.5
Receivables	9.1	56.3
Securities purchased under agreements to resell	—	104.4
Securities and spot commodities owned	8.3	100.6
Other assets	1.8	11.2
Total assets	$19.8	$276.0
Liabilities and stockholders' equity		
Bank loans payable	$ 8.3	$ 25.1
Payables	5.1	41.7
Securities sold under repurchase agreements	—	130.1
Securities sold short	0.6	44.3
Other current liabilities and mortgages	2.6	18.1
Subordinated debt	0.9	3.9
Stockholders' equity	2.3	12.8
Total liabilities and stockholders' equity	$19.8	$276.0

*Data are for approximately 400 corporate entities that both deal with the public and are members of the New York Stock Exchange.

Source: Securities Industry Association.

were earned by full-line firms (using about an equal proportion of the industry's employees), with investment bankers providing about one tenth of the total industry, based on a comparable employees share. (See Table 3–4.)

The NYSE-member regional firms contribute the second most important OTC earnings share (better than a fifth) with only one seventh the number of employees. Finally, all the other carrying firms (598), employing about one fifth of the personnel, produced less than one tenth the gains of the industry's OTC market making. The foregoing suggests the conclusion that even in a labor-intensive output like OTC market making, there may be significant differences in productivity (and/or scale economies) as well as other factors.

The large investment banking houses were the major earners of other securities-related income, which includes earnings

TABLE 3–6
Aggregate Equity in Selected Financial Sectors, Year-Ends
(Dollars in Billions)

Sector	1984	1983	1982	1981	1980
All insured commercial					
banks	$143.4*	$152.8	$133.8	$129.6	$114.2
17 Largest BHCs	42.4	38.1	33.8	29.8	26.8
Securities firms	12.8	11.7	9.0	6.7	5.4
Investment banks†	4.0	3.5	2.7	1.9	1.3
National full-line firms†	4.7	4.5	3.4	2.6	2.1
All others†	4.1	3.7	2.9	2.2	2.0
Life insurance	47.8	46.4	41.5	37.4	34.4
Stockholder-owned	30.3	29.1	25.1	22.4	20.2
Mutual	17.5	17.3	16.4	15.0	14.2
Property and casualty					
insurance	74.8	76.9	72.2	64.1	62.4
Stockholder-owned	53.3	55.4	53.3	47.5	47.5
Mutual	21.5	21.5	18.9	16.6	14.9
Insurance brokerage					
Six large firms	.8	1.0	1.0	1.1	1.0

*Data for 1984 not comparable to those for earlier dates.
†Inter-year data not comparable due to reclassifications.

from merger and takeover fees. These 10 firms garnered better than one third of the industry's income, with the 11 full-line firms making up another third. The more than 99 percent of all other firms together produced only about the last third of such service earnings.

An historical perspective of the industry's recent rapid growth can be gained from an examination of the 10-year period 1974 to 1984. From asset/liability footings of less than $20 billion in 1974 (Table 3–5), the industry's size rose by a factor of 14, to $276 billion in 1984 (for discussion of the composition of the asset/liability structures see Chapter 4).[5] And for the major

[5]Tables 3–5 through 3–7 are drawn from a staff study done at the Federal Reserve Bank of New York, *Recent Trends in Commercial Bank Profitability,* New York, 1987, esp. chapter 14, "The Performance of Bank Competitors," by R. H. Mead and K. A. O'Neil.

TABLE 3–7
Large Investment Banks Condensed Balance Sheet Data 1980–1984
(Billions of Dollars)

	1980	1981	1982	1983	1984
Assets					
Cash	$ 0.1	$ 0.2	$ 0.5	$ 0.2	$ 0.2
Receivables	8.5	7.2	11.2	16.2	12.6
Securities purchased under agreements to resell	15.3	25.5	36.8	48.8	63.2
Securities and spot commodities owned	16.7	23.7	41.8	41.5	65.8
Other assets	0.8	1.4	1.7	2.4	3.1
Total assets	$41.4	$58.0	$92.0	$109.1	$144.9
Liabilities and stockholders' equity					
Bank loans payable	$ 2.4	$ 4.3	$ 4.4	$ 6.8	$ 10.3
Payables	7.1	5.5	8.0	10.9	10.2
Securities sold under repurchase agreements	20.3	31.6	52.7	55.3	83.2
Securities sold short	8.8	12.5	20.9	27.9	32.1
Other current liabilities and mortgages	1.3	1.9	2.8	3.9	4.1
Subordinated Debt	0.2	0.3	0.5	0.8	1.0
Stockholders' Equity	1.3	1.9	2.7	3.5	4.0
Total liabilities and stockholders' equity	$41.4	$58.0	$92.0	$109.1	$144.9

Source: Securities Industry Association.

subset of the industry, the large investment banks, the enormous growth in the 4-year period 1980 to 1984 was by a factor of more than 3 (see Table 3–6 and 3–7). The aggregate equity of these investment banking firms in that period also rose by about a factor of 3, while the equity of the 17 largest bank holding companies rose by a bit more than one half, from $26.8 billion to $42.4 billion. The enormous growth rate of the industry from its cottage industry roots through 1986 will be discussed in some detail in the next chapter.

4

THE INVESTMENT BANKING BUSINESS IN THE MID-1980s

The U.S. financial markets represent an important international resource. The volume of secondary transactions that is efficiently processed provides real-time information on the *price* of capital. In parallel the large-scale availability of funds on the primary markets makes the United States an important *source* of new money for investment in the United States and in the rest of the world. In secondary trading markets the transaction volume on U.S. fixed income markets dwarfs that done on any other marketplace, and even though trading activity on equity markets abroad rivals U.S. equity volume, the U.S. share still constitutes about 40 percent of worldwide volume totals. That level of importance in the world's capital markets has been sustained in spite of the reduced share of the United States in the world's output of goods and services, and in spite of the shift, in less than one decade, from world creditor to world debtor status. Why should trading and new-issue volume hold up so well?

The strategic component in maintaining a high volume of financial transactions on any market is human capital. The trading expertise that is an integral part of existing transaction mechanisms and linkages, the information and execution machinery, and the credit support relationships all contribute the necessary critical mass to make the system operational. Indeed, the momentum carried by such systems alone can maintain transaction volume even after the national economy that gave rise to that system lags behind other, competing economies. The most striking example of this situation is the trading volume produced by the City in London. It remains today Europe's prime financial market even though the United Kingdom is no longer Europe's preeminent economic power. Human capital is the strategic variable that integrates the other elements of a trading system.

A further point to consider is that within any marketplace, large or small, each financial firm requires a sufficient amount of financial capital to provide the bona fides to its trading partners. It is important to recall that in the financial markets the execution of equity trades on secondary markets involves a forward transaction supported by freely available credit. It is often said that financial markets are driven by information; it is frequently forgotten that the routine provision of credit is essential for execution.

This point is supported by the analysis of the industry's asset structure. As Figure 4–1 indicates,[1] a quite stable—and large—proportion of industry assets consists of receivables and the provision of short-term credit to other asset holders in the market [through reverse repurchase agreements (RPs)]. For the 11 years shown in the charts the amounts so invested come to nearly two thirds of assets. About 30 percent—the only other significant asset position—consists of securities (and commodity positions) owned directly by firms in the industry.

Figure 4–2, showing industry liabilities, is equally instructive: Again two thirds represent bank loans and RPs. About one third of liabilities consists of payables and short positions. Finally, and most revealingly, equity represents about 5% of total liabilities. Leverage is thus about 19:1—that is, about $19 of financing for each $1 of equity. A corollary of this proposition is that entry into the business, even on a relatively substantial scale, is not as difficult, say, as entry into other financial industries (e.g., banking). The foregoing also illustrates that only a small share of industry assets are *fixed* assets; as we shall develop in detail in discussions of income statements below, there is only one large item of net expense, namely, payrolls. In consequence, our analysis of firm data below will find the following:

---

[1]These charts are taken from Federal Reserve Bank of New York *Recent Trends in Commercial Bank Profitability,* 1986, especially Chapter 14, charts A1a and A1b.

FIGURE 4–1
Securities Industry Composition of Assets

Percent of Assets

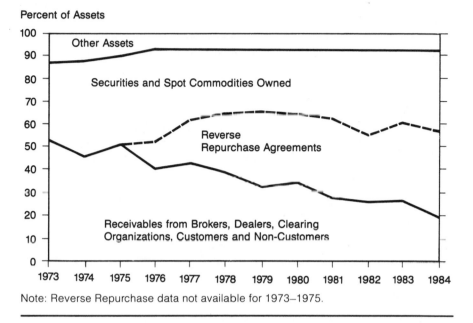

Note: Reverse Repurchase data not available for 1973–1975.

Source: Securities Industry Association.

1. Because of the large volume of payables/receivables, and their financing, the interest expense item on income statements will be just about offset by the interest (and dividends) revenue item; the two are a wash for each major firm.
2. There is one large expense item: payrolls.
3. In a period of expansion, the need for human capital sets up competitive bidding for talent. Not only will compensation rates skyrocket, but the equivalent of talent warehousing (if not hoarding) may further add to labor market pressures. Conversely, in a period of contraction, payrolls will be significantly cut because: (i) they are a large item and/or (ii) there had been prior expansion of payrolls.

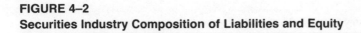

FIGURE 4–2
Securities Industry Composition of Liabilities and Equity

Percent of Liabilities and Equity

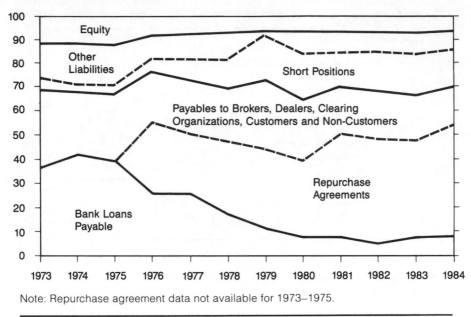

Note: Repurchase agreement data not available for 1973–1975.

Source: Securities Industry Association.

4. The demand for the other scarce resource, *financial* capital, will be met by infusions of outside funds when growth in activity [as well as pressure from exchange and Securities and Exchange Commission (SEC) rules] force that requirement.

The experience of U.S. investment banking firms exemplifies these principles. In the mid-1980s, the U.S. capital markets experienced transactions on a scale and at a volume far larger than heretofore. New types of securities were traded and the financial institutions that made all the markets go grew at an enormous rate. Among these institutions, the U.S. investment bankers transacted more, innovated at a more frantic pace, and grew faster than ever before. From their relatively modest size in the 1970s, they became large-scale firms after the early

1980s. While all the major firms grew by several magnitudes, they grew, as before, each in its own way.

Likewise, most firms, each in its own way, began to retrench early in 1987. Sometime before the events of October, a brief surge in interest rates in spring had led to some substantial losses in fixed income positions among the leading firms. And all of these firms experienced declines in their rates of return and their stock prices. For example, Salomon Brothers began a structural reorganization in the summer of 1987. This included, first, the disposition of its entire tax-exempt operation (after a $100 million loss in the spring of 1987). Second, it dropped its entire commercial paper business. In late summer it sold a 12 percent equity interest in the firm to Warren Buffett as a means of avoiding the undesired attentions of Ronald Perelman. Choosing Salomon as an example at the point of retrenchment is useful: through the mid-1980s Salomon had been the paradigm of the all-purpose investment banker with a powerful trading base in most major markets.

The melancholy events that led to sharp personnel reductions and to other forms of reorganization among these firms will be discussed below, and in other chapters. Before doing so, however, it is important to discuss the prior *growth* phase among these firms. This will be done in the next section.

THE GOOD OLD DAYS: 1983 TO 1986

Table 4–1 shows the growth of the work force of five institutional firms and of two full-line firms between 1983 and 1986. In those three years, the institutional (and one of the full-line) firms had about *doubled* their work forces. The largest firm did not grow in toto, but its internal changes were substantial (see below for further discussion).

It should be recalled that the data developed in Chapter 3 indicated that the industry's rapid growth rate did not start in 1983, but began in the 1970s. This rapid growth continued through the period of accelerating inflation of the late 1970s and early 1980s, a period of high volatility in financial markets. Growth continued as well during subsequent deceleration of in-

TABLE 4–1
Employee Count at Major Investment Banking Firms, Selected Years

	1986	1983
Drexel Burnham Lambert	10,172	5,310
Goldman Sachs	6,049	3,251
Salomon Bros	6,000	2,878
First Boston	4,500*	2,248
Morgan Stanley	5,322	2,413
Merrill Lynch	47,900	44,200
Shearson Lehman	26,300	13,465

*Add about 1,000 for Credit Suisse/First Boston.

Source: S. G. Liss, "Fundamentals Do Count," April 30, 1987, pp. 2–3. Copyright © 1987 by Salomon Brothers Inc.

flation and volatility in the mid-1980s. And because that rapid growth rate would be remarkable at any time and for any industry, it is all the more remarkable for continuing through several recessions. This should not be interpreted as suggesting that the industry is "recession-proof." Instead consider that any service industry with only a small ratio of fixed costs to total costs can quickly respond to a demand surge by hiring human capital. The reverse is true as well: a reduction in demand for services, or any other pressure to downsize, can be dealt with just as quickly, as we shall see below.

Beyond workforce growth in the 1983 to 1986 period, the rise of broker/dealer capital was even more remarkable. For, in the *two*-year period shown below (Table 4–2), all but one of the firms doubled their capital, while some *tripled* their capital. How could they achieve such rapid growth rates? The short answer is that some of them raised new money by going public—that is, by selling equity in an initial public offering (IPO). Others were taken over by large nonfinancial firms, thereby receiving a large injection of capital from a new (single) owner rather than from the public. The two large firms that still maintain a partnership organization (Goldman Sachs and Drexel Burnham Lambert) leveraged their capital structures by raising debt on a large scale.

As the "short" answer suggests, each of these firms dealt

TABLE 4–2
Total Capital* at Major Investment Banking Firms, Selected Years
(In Millions of Dollars)

	1986	1985	1984
Drexel Burnham Lambert	1,626	929	504
Goldman Sachs	1,951	1,201	859
Salomon Bros	3,209	2,230	1,577
First Boston	1,051	843	527
Morgan Stanley	901	455	355
Merrill Lynch	2,942	2,224	1,488
Shearson Lehman	3,122	2,741	1,915

*Broker–dealer capital (equity plus debt); omits consolidation with holding company.

Source: S. G. Liss, "The Issue of Capital Adequacy," April 10, 1987, pp. 1–3. Copyright © 1987 by Salomon Brothers Inc.

with its capital problem in its own way. To give an appropriate structure to this story, three representative firms will now be examined. The three—Morgan Stanley, Merrill Lynch, and Drexel Burnham Lambert—are offered as three different approaches to the "how" and the "why" of investment banking growth.

MORGAN STANLEY: AN INSTITUTIONAL FIRM GOES PUBLIC

For firms doing an investment banking business with large clients and large (institutional) customers, the demand for more capital to back up transactions kept growing in the 1980s. The shelf-registration process involved, by definition, the largest corporate firms that require "instant syndicates" for very large flotations that may, in fact, be "bought deals."[2] In addition, a presence in major markets abroad requires further capital investments (both human and financial) in London and Tokyo, as does the simultaneous need to backstop at home innovative

---

[2]For further discussion of these issues see Chapter 17.

deals in, say, mortgage-back securities. Last, and perhaps most important, the bridge financing deals for takeovers and mergers represent an insatiable maw for added capital. All of these factors were present to a greater or lesser degree for the flotation of new capital by institutional firms in the mid-1980s, and an analysis of Morgan Stanley's own IPO is an important anatomy lesson.[3] Consider, first, Morgan Stanley's income statement (taken from 1988 prospectus) for the years 1983 to 1987 (Table 4–3).

The largest *revenue* item, as well as the largest *expense* item, is interest (and dividends). The two rows of interest data (revenue and expense) for the years 1983 to 1987 indicate that they are about a wash for each year, with a small positive revenue residual. This is so because investment banking firms are dealers, whose major asset is an inventory of security position (and related items) that is financed by repurchase agreements, receivables, and brokers' loans; interest and dividend revenues, payables, and reverse RPs from these positions finance the carry cost.

The next largest revenue item is "investment banking." It appears to be a very large item, but I will contend that it is relatively small. How can this be? After all, the figures appear to be quite sizable. Defer that discussion for a moment. The only other two remaining revenue items are principal transactions: capital gains less losses on security positions, and commissions.

Table 4–4 separates the structure of "investment banking" into its two components. It shows that the smallest revenue item of the two is what we think of first, namely, underwriting revenues from flotation of new issues. In 1984 and 1985, for example, financial advisory revenues exceeded new-issue income by almost 3:1; in 1986 and 1987 "financial advisory" was nearly twice underwriting revenue. Thus the recasting of Morgan Stanley's total revenues for 1985 to 1987 indicates that new-issue under-

---

[3]For a discussion of the Morgan Stanley IPO see Chapter 12; the 1988 prospectus, data from which are used here, covers a secondary equity issue (for discussion, see below).

writing represents a rather modest element in the total, falling somewhat short of security commission earnings for two years out of three (see Table 4–5).[4] On the other hand, merger and acquisition (M&A) revenues and income from principal (i.e., trading) transactions combined to produce more than half of (restated) revenue totals; underwriting constitutes less than one fifth of reconstituted total revenues.

I would like to summarize here my analysis (from Part 2 of this book) of why M&A advisory is such a large revenue item for special bracket firms such as Morgan Stanley. First, it is mainly the special bracket firms that have large revenues from M&A. This is so because boards of directors of clients involved in takeovers or mergers as the acquiring firm, and/or the target firm, recognize that they have only one procedural defense against litigation from their stockholders: that defense is the use of fairness (that is, price per share) opinions provided by special bracket investment bankers. In effect, these directors say to their stockholders that the price per share received (or the price paid) was based on the opinion of one of the best and most successful M&A advisory firms available. Why is this believed to be the case? Because these are the firms that are continuously involved in pricing the largest merger and takeover [or leveraged buyout (LBO)] deals, as well as in the financing—including bridge loans that are financed by investment bankers' own capital—that makes the deals possible. This combined pricing and flotation expertise is necessarily based on the investment bankers' continuous experience as traders and dealers on a large scale in existing issues. Basic to that pricing—and bridge loans—is the trading and distribution capacity of special bracket firms acting as risk-taking dealers in trading existing securities. Consider that a substantial entry into M&A requires a number (if not all) of the following:

---

[4]For 1987, the Prospectus mentions a $75.5 million underwriting *loss* in connection with the British Petroleum stock issue. For further discussion of that underwriting see Chapter 14.

TABLE 4–3
Morgan Stanley Prospectus: May 13, 1988 (In Millions of Dollars)

	Year Ended December 31,				
	1987	1986	1985	1984	1983
Income statement:[1]					
Revenues:					
Investment banking	$ 711	$ 656	$ 424	$ 267	$ 212
Principal transactions	633	473	243	122	78
Commissions	297	216	154	130	131
Interest and dividends	1,421	1,063	938	795	415
Asset management	72	49	35	25	21
Other	13	6	1	2	1
Total revenues	3,148	2,463	1,795	1,340	860
Expenses:					
Interest	1,380	1,035	900	748	391
Employee compensation and benefits	885	695	421	305	254
Occupancy and equipment rental	138	109	79	52	38
Brokerage, clearing and exchange fees	84	70	45	31	23
Communications	73	54	39	29	20
Business development	66	53	36	25	18
Professional services	67	48	30	14	10
Other	91	77	61	30	20
Total expenses	2,784	2,141	1,612	1,235	773
Income before income taxes	364	323	183	106	86
Provision for income taxes	133	121	77	45	35
Net income	$ 231	$ 201	$ 106	$ 61	$ 51

Balance Sheet:[2]				
Total assets	$29,663	$29,190	$15,794	$13,054	$7,442
Total capital	1,694	1,178	486	374	290
Stockholders' equity	1,137	798	314	238	207
Long-term borrowings[3]	556	381	173	136	84

[1]Totals may not add up exactly due to rounding of figures.
[2]Does not include commitments and contingencies.
[3]Excludes current portion of long-term borrowings.

TABLE 4–4

Morgan Stanley Prospectus (Continued): The Material Components of the Company's Investment Banking Revenues for the Five Years Ended December 31, 1987 (In Thousands of Dollars)

A. Investment Banking

	Year Ended December 31				
	1987	1986	1985	1984	1983
Underwriting and financing activities*	$251,133	$249,998	$123,189	$ 66,734	$105,698
Financial advisory activities†	459,664	405,929	300,326	200,136	106,549
Total	$710,797	$655,927	$423,515	$266,870	$212,247

B. Principal Transactions and Commissions

	1987	1986	1985	1984	1983
Principal transactions					
Fixed income	$283,870	$327,251	$132,639	$ 83,184	$ 59,930
Equity	259,776	95,593	78,184	23,907	11,925
Foreign exchange, commodities and other	89,283	50,335	32,217	14,612	6,530
Total	$632,929	$473,179	$243,040	$121,703	$ 78,385
Brokerage commissions:					
Fixed income	$ 9,091	$ 5,763	$ 3,830	$ 1,251	$ 598
Equity and other	288,178	210,472	150,530	128,878	130,535
Total	$297,269	$216,235	$154,360	$130,129	$131,133

*Includes the full amount of underwriting discounts and commissions with respect to underwritings by the company.
†Includes revenues from the company's real estate advisory and brokerage activities.

TABLE 4–5
Morgan Stanley's Revenue Data, Adjusted, 1985–1987 (In Millions of Dollars)

	1987	1986	1985
Advisory (M&A)	$ 460	$ 406	$300
Underwriting	251	250	123
Principal transactions	632	473	243
Commissions	297	216	154
Interest (net)	41	28	38
Asset management	72	49	35
Other	13	6	1
	$1,766	$1,428	$894
Memo A/C (expenses)			
Employee compensation	$ 885	$ 695	$421

Source: Prospectus, *Morgan Stanley Group Inc.*, May 13, 1988.

1. A presence in the new-issue junk bond flotation market (e.g., to refinance bridge loans).
2. A presence in new-issue corporate bond (and equity) flotations.
3. A presence and capacity to do very large-scale bridge loans or merchant banking related to mergers and takeovers.[5]

All of the above also require a substantial presence in the secondary dealer markets that help to support these primary market activities. To be sure, the term "special bracket" (or "bulge bracket") refers specifically to the position on a tombstone ad or a share of a syndicated flotation. In the most fundamental sense it is the capacity to price and to trade in any market, primary or secondary, that represents leadership in this industry. That capacity helps to attract the capital that backstops and underwrites the process, including the process of innovation.

The capital thus attracted includes human capital as well.

---

[5]This "merchant banking" activity is, perhaps, the ultimate step in "market making." For, in the process of closing a merger or takeover deal, the investment banker as advisor may now have to put its capital where its advice is. More specifically, Morgan Stanley in 1986 helped Kohlberg, Kravis, Roberts & Co. in a $3.6 billion buyout of Owens-Illinois by providing a $600 million bridge loan.

A quick glance at the bottom of Table 4–5, which includes compensation and benefits as a memo account, indicates that that expense accounted for about one half of income (as adjusted). Further, it is possible to calculate the average compensation by dividing the compensation expense by the number of employees. Average compensation per employee exceeds $100,000 for 1985 and $140,000 for 1987. There is no reason to assume that, for competing major firms, the average compensation package would be significantly different from these amounts.

THE MORGAN STANLEY SECONDARY OFFERING OF MAY 13, 1988

On that day (Friday) Morgan Stanley's managing directors and principals[6] made a secondary stock offering for a total of 2,170,364 shares, of which 960,464 were offered to the public, and 1,209,900 were repurchased by Morgan Stanley. The offering was priced at the closing New York price on May 12, 1988, at $63⅜ per share. In effect, the stock sale not only did not produce new money for Morgan Stanley, but its repurchase of stock would, dollar for dollar, reduce the funds available to the firm. All of the funds produced by the offering—whether for sale to the public, or to Morgan Stanley—went directly to the selling stockholders. The secondary offering could be made because the required two years had elapsed since the March 1986 IPO for "inside" buyers of Morgan Stanley stock.[7] It is useful at this stage to make one further point: lest this sale be viewed as a bailout (by Morgan executives) the prospectus is careful to point out that these same sellers will, after the closing of the offering, still hold more than 34% of Morgan Stanley's stock (down from 41.2%).[8]

As usual, the Morgan Stanley prospectus (Figure 4–3) pre-

---

[6]And, to a minor extent, a few family members of that group.

[7]Such buyers are "restricted" from sale under Rule 144 of Securities Act.

[8]That last percentage is, in part, *boosted* by the arithmetic of the transaction: After repurchase, the number of shares outstanding is *reduced* from 24,832,013 shares to 23,622,113 shares.

FIGURE 4–3

PROSPECTUS

960,464 Shares
Morgan Stanley Group Inc.
COMMON STOCK

All 960,464 Shares of Common Stock are being sold by stockholders of the Company. Of such Shares, 760,464 Shares are being offered in the United States and Canada by the U.S. Underwriters, and 200,000 Shares are being offered outside the United States and Canada by the International Underwriters. See "Underwriters". The Company will not receive any proceeds from the sale of the Shares offered hereby. See "Selling Stockholders". The Company's Common Stock is listed on the New York, Boston, Midwest and Pacific Stock Exchanges. On May 12, 1988, the last reported sale price of the Common Stock on the New York Stock Exchange was $63¾ per share. See "Price Range of Common Stock and Dividends".

Simultaneously with the purchase of the Shares by the Underwriters, the Company will, subject to certain conditions, purchase 1,209,900 shares of Common Stock (the "Purchase Shares") from Selling Stockholders at a price equal to the Price to Public less the Underwriting Discounts and Commissions. See "Prospectus Summary".

THESE SECURITIES HAVE NOT BEEN APPROVED OR DISAPPROVED BY THE SECURITIES AND EXCHANGE COMMISSION NOR HAS THE COMMISSION PASSED UPON THE ACCURACY OR ADEQUACY OF THIS PROSPECTUS. ANY REPRESENTATION TO THE CONTRARY IS A CRIMINAL OFFENSE.

PRICE $63¾ A SHARE

	Price to Public	Underwriting Discounts and Commissions(1)	Proceeds to Selling Stockholders(2)
Per Share	$63.375	$1.59	$61.785
Total(3)	$60,869,406	$1,527,138	$59,342,268

(1) See "Underwriters" for information relating to indemnification arrangements among the Underwriters, the Company and the Selling Stockholders.

(2) Does not include proceeds to be received by Selling Stockholders in connection with the sale by such Selling Stockholders to the Company of the Purchase Shares. Estimated expenses of $450,000 will be payable by the Company.

(3) The Selling Stockholders have granted to the U.S. Underwriters an option, exercisable prior to the Closing Date for the offering, to purchase up to an aggregate of 144,000 additional Shares (the "Over-allotment Shares") at the Price to Public less the Underwriting Discounts and Commissions, solely to cover over-allotments, if any. If the U.S. Underwriters exercise such option in full, the total Price to Public, Underwriting Discounts and Commissions and Proceeds to Selling Stockholders will be $69,995,406, $1,756,098 and $68,239,308, respectively. See "Underwriters". The number of Over-allotment Shares (if any) purchased pursuant to such option will reduce by an equal number the number of Purchase Shares to be purchased by the Company.

The Shares are offered, subject to prior sale, when, as and if accepted by the Underwriters named herein and subject to approval of certain legal matters by Davis Polk & Wardwell, counsel for the Underwriters. It is expected that delivery of the certificates for the Shares will be made on or about May 20, 1988, at the offices of Morgan Stanley & Co. Incorporated, New York, New York, against payment therefor in New York funds.

MORGAN STANLEY & CO.
Incorporated

BEAR, STEARNS & CO. INC.

THE FIRST BOSTON CORPORATION

GOLDMAN, SACHS & CO.

MERRILL LYNCH CAPITAL MARKETS

SALOMON BROTHERS INC

SHEARSON LEHMAN HUTTON INC.

May 13, 1988

sented at the time of the public offering offers a fascinating glimpse into the activities of this major investment banker. It was those prospectus data that were discussed above. The surge in "principal" transactions in 1987, especially in the *equity* portion, is attributed in the prospectus to the following three types of activities (none is separately quantified):

1. Block trading.
2. Program trading.[9]
3. Risk arbitrage.

It is noteworthy, as shown in Table 4–5, that for 1987, the unusually high total "principal" revenues were derived from equity transactions; that income was nearly three times as high as the 1985 to 1986 average. This surge in equity revenues occurred in spite of the October crash, although the heavy trading volume of equities in 1987 can explain that year's jump in *commission* earnings.

In sum, the Morgan Stanley secondary achieved two objectives, only one of which was stated directly in the prospectus. That first objective was to permit Morgan Stanley's management group to sell some of their previously restricted stock shortly after the legally required restriction period had passed. The less obvious objective was to *reduce* the number of shares outstanding. That last objective might be interpreted as a classic corporate finance move that raises the proportionate share of ownership of the remaining stockholders. Beyond that goal, the retirement of some 1.2 million shares might also be viewed as an attempt to reduce the "fixed" (or equity) sector of the capital structure if there is an expectation that, because a lower rate of financing activity may be expected, less capital will be required. Even after that repurchase of shares, Morgan Stanley carries an amount of capital many times larger than the minimum required by the capital rules of SEC (rule 15c3-3) and other regulators. In its analysis (p. 30 of the prospectus) Morgan Stanley

---

[9]The prospectus states that this type of transaction is done as agent and as principal; Morgan Stanley "recently announced that it had discontinued proprietary stock index arbitrage trading." (p. 21 of Prospectus.)

indicates that it carries about a $.5 billion *excess* capital over the minimum required. Finally, with respect to the nearly 25 million shares outstanding (as of May 1988), those outstandings are little more than a tenth of the 200 million shares that are authorized.

MERRILL LYNCH: BIG AND STILL IN TRANSITION

Merrill Lynch has been the largest U.S. stock brokerage firm for a long time. Because stock trading was, for an equally long time, a marketplace for individuals, Merrill Lynch has always emphasized the retail end of financial transactions (see Table 4–6). Because this emphasis has required a force of retail personnel several magnitudes larger than that of its more institutionally oriented competitors, that aspect of the business has remained in place. Merrill's growth on the capital markets side of investment banking of, say, 500 to 1,000 professionals in the mid-1980s, would in Merrill's case be difficult to detect in a crowd of

TABLE 4–6
Merrill Lynch Revenue Data 1986 and 1984 (In Millions of Dollars and Percentages)

	1986		1984	
	$	%	$	%
Commissions	1,646	33	1,217	31
Principal transaction	785	17	561	14
Investment banking*	617	12	582	14
Real estate	542	11	462	13
Insurance	295	6	171	5
Asset management	294	6	—	
Net interest	283	6	343	8
Other	324	9	592†	14
Total	4,786	100	3,928	100

*Includes M&A.
†Investment income + gain from sale of corporate headquarters.

45,000. Instead, that change is reflected in the doubling of capital between 1984 and 1986.[10]

At the same time, Merrill showed some early innovative characteristics. Long before any of its competitors, the firm went public and had its shares listed on the New York Stock Exchange (NYSE) in 1971 (yes, 1971). To be sure, at that time, only Merrill was large enough to qualify for a significant stock issue (all the other "special bracket" firms were too small to even consider an IPO, much less floating one).

In the meantime, during the 1970s, Merrill innovated a number of retail-oriented activities. It broadened its appeal to retail customers by the development of the CMA account to supplement brokerage services with the close substitute to a bank deposit account, and its development of a "nonbank bank" to support such transactions. However, with nearly 500 brokerage offices and a retail network of more than 10,000 financial consultants, Merrill has probably the largest fixed-cost personnel to total costs ratio of any of its competitors. Accordingly, net income is vulnerable to occasional periods of slowdown in activity (notably in 1984).

An important policy move by Merrill to develop its capital market capabilities has been its development of the LBO business. First, its large capital base provided the deep pockets to help finance equity positions in LBOs. Second, that large capital position also helped to finance the related bridge loans (see next section). Indeed as early as 1981 Merrill Lynch developed a unit called Merrill Lynch Capital Partners to finance LBOs and other corporate reorganizations with the partners as well as the firm's capital. From 1981 through mid-1987 Merrill has financed and sponsored LBOs totalling better than $15.1 billion.[11]

Like those of its competitors, startup costs in London and

---

[10]In spite of these shifts, Merrill's commission income remains about one third of (adjusted) total revenues. Compare this share to that of Morgan Stanley, where commissions accounted for about one sixth of adjusted total revenues (see Table 4–5).

[11]See L. P. Cohen, "Merrill Lynch Leads Wall Street's Buyout Business," *Wall Street Journal,* August 5, 1987.

Tokyo (as well as in Canada and Australia) have eaten into revenues in the mid-1980s. At the same time, Merrill has divested its real estate operations, perhaps to help finance its shift to more institutionally oriented investment banking activities. These changes have helped to build capacity in M&A, including bridge financing, and in institutional trading.

DREXEL BURNHAM LAMBERT: FROM JUNK BONDS TO SPECIAL BRACKET FIRM

Drexel dominates the junk bond market after having developed it practically alono (see Chapter 6 for further discussion of junk bond financing). Drexel makes a market in some 1,800 high-yield issues and provides that market with liquidity. In this fashion, the innovator (Drexel) has induced the special bracket firms to follow it into the market, and by their participation, Drexel has improved the market's depth. At the same time, it has expanded into the more conventional types of business of other firms—such as U.S. Government securities, mortgage backs, etc.

As a well capitalized private firm Drexel's financial structure in 1987 was in line with industry practice even though its output is more specialized than that of most of its competitors. A comparison of Drexel's 1987 balance sheet at year end shows a strong resemblance to that of Dean Witter (or, for example, Morgan Stanley) (Table 4–7). Like the asset and liability charts indicated (see Figures 4–1 and 4–2) Drexel has financed about half of its liabilities with RPs and shows half of its assets in the form of "resale agreements" (i.e., reverse RPs). A rough equality of RPs and reverse RPs (in Table 4–7 these are called "resale" agreements) prevails for the other firms as well, and each of these financing mechanisms constitutes about one half of total assets (or liabilities). This pattern also explains the near equality of interest (and dividend) revenues and expenses shown by the Morgan Stanley income statements, which holds for the other firms as well.

Finally, the balance sheet data indicate that, while Drexel's

TABLE 4–7
Balance Sheets, Year-End 1987 (In Millions of Dollars)

	Goldman Sachs & Co.	Drexel Burnham Lambert Inc.	Dean Witter, Reynolds Inc.	Bear, Stearns & Co.	First Boston Corp.	Morgan Stanley & Co.
Assets						
Cash	100	136	131	57	24	384
Cash segregated under regulations	233	207	327	1,382	1,310	627
Securities owned (at market)						
U.S. Government and federal agencies	11,113	810	1,558	3,731	5,977	2,521
Municipal debt	526	—	347	111	791	226
BAs, CDs, Com. paper	674	818	234	—	892	299
Corporate debt	4,494	1,662	285	1,401	2,397	871
Equities	—	491	85	—	—	1,142
Other	—	—	—	—	—	36
Total securities owned	17,257	3,781	2,509	5,243	10,057	5,095
Resale agreements	21,567	6,238	6,305	15,260	21,112	15,454
Receivable from clients	2,058	1,259	1,969	2,839	1,191	743
Receivable from brokers, dealers	2,212	1,964	1,576	4,357	—	2,948
Fixed assets	—	—	136	4	204	47
Other	471	320	399	163	46	207
Goodwill	—	—	212	—	—	—
Total assets	43,898	13,905	13,637	29,306	34,476	25,504

Liabilities						
Bank loans	—	840	588	681	1,795	147
Repurchase agreements	24,978	6,547	6,437	11,791	25,243	15,882
Drafts and checks payable	—	—	264	190	—	—
Securities sold (at market)						
U.S. Government and federal agencies	—	378	1,169	7,077	—	2,368
Municipal	—	—	19	9	—	—
Corporate	—	332	157	1,873	—	292
Equities	—	167	186	—	—	807
Exchangeable securities	—	—	—	—	—	239
Total securities sold (at market)	12,204	877	1,532	8,959	2,463	3,706
Payable to clients	2,498	914	1,109	4,489	1,461	1,065
Payable to brokers and dealers	619	1,580	1,714	1,545	—	1,856
Other	700	1,407	255	226	—	1,314
Accrued compensation	—	—	262	164	1,960	437
Dividends and interest payable	—	—	97	—	318	—
Income taxes payable	497	—	—	—	42	—
Payable to parent	—	—	34	—	8	—
Subordinated liabilities	746	522	583	307	453	400
Stockholders' equity	1,656	1,218	761	955	731	697
Total capital	2,402	1,740	1,344	1,262	1,184	1,097

capital is smaller than Goldman's and larger than Dean Witter's, the similarities are greater than the differences.

THE LAST DECADE IN INVESTMENT BANKING: A BRIEF REVIEW

Between the mid-1970s and the mid-1980s the major investment banking firms successfully dealt with major changes to become a much more important financial industry than before, as follows:

1. Cottage industry adjusts after 1975 to negotiated NYSE commissions and to:
2. Data processing revolution: from paper processing to electronics that permits:
3. Shift to institutional and larger scale retail transactions that led to:
4. Need to refinance firm structures: going from partnership to corporate firm. This is necessary to provide capital to support the required expansion to trade at institutional size.
5. Globalization of finance: shifts to London and Tokyo also requires more capital. This also stimulates:
6. Competition from foreign-based investment bankers located in New York, as well as London and Tokyo and elsewhere.
7. Overarching all of these stages is the need to maintain market share in new flotations (Table 4–8), by developing new products, and trading the new products. Competition also drives each firm to imitate the innovations of others.
8. All of the above require more:

   Risk-taking
   Personnel
   Capital

   as each of prior seven developments becomes important to a leading firm, and then becomes the industry standard.

TABLE 4–8
Leading Underwriters of Corporate Issues, 1985

Corporate Underwriters	Flotation Amounts (In Billions of Dollars)	Position
Salomon Brothers	$26.4	1
First Boston	20.3	2
Merrill Lynch	16.6	3
Goldman Sachs	15.7	4
Drexel Burnham Lambert	11.5	5
Morgan Stanley	10.0	6
Shearson Lehman Brothers	9.9	7
Kidder Peabody	4.1	8
Paine Webber	3.2	9
Smith Barney, Harris Upham	2.1	10

Source: *Institutional Investor,* March 1986, p. 155

At another level of firm development, the rapid growth in size of the unit begins to dictate organizational structure. Recall that in 1980—a mere eight years ago—the personnel of the typical large institutional firm comprised about 2,000 employees,[12] while retail firms carried about 10,000.[13] By 1986, the numbers at representative institutional firms had about tripled, while the numbers at retail firms had risen by about 50 percent. The explosive growth of personnel—and the related need for added capital—has to be seen in the context of a rise in the number and diversity of innovative and increasingly more complex types of securities and hedging policies.

Perhaps the most persuasive argument that supports the innovator/imitator cycle of investment banking development can be derived from the structural changes in the organization of the

---

[12]Goldman, Salomon, Bear Stearns, Morgan Stanley, First Boston.

[13]Shearson Lehman, Paine Webber; Merrill's count was then about 32,000. These numbers are larger because of the large force of client-contact personnel which include about 11,000 at Merrill, 7,200 at Dean Witter, and about 5,000 at Shearson Lehman.

TABLE 4–9
Acquired or Publicly Held Firms

Current Name of Firm	Date	Change in Status
Prudential-Bache Securities	March 1981	Takeover
Shearson Lehman Brothers	June 1981*	Takeover
	May 1984†	Takeover
Dean Witter Reynolds	December 1981	Takeover
Salomon Brothers	March 1982	Takeover
Rooney, Pace Group	October 1983	Went public
Jefferies Group	October 1983	Went public
L. F. Rothschild	March 1986	Went public
Bear Stearns	October 1985	Went public
	May 1986	Went public
Alex Brown & Sons	February 1986	Went public
Morgan Stanley	March 1986	Went public
Kidder Peabody	May 1986	Takeover

*Shearson Loeb Rhodes absorbed by American Express.
†Lehman Brothers Kuhn Loeb absorbed by American Express.

industry. For over and above the need for added capital to support innovative markets, the institutionalization of *all* securities markets has led to the need for financial firms to deal in size—and to deal in size the firms need capital in size. They have achieved this in the 1980s by infusions of funds from other firms (called takeovers in Table 4–9) or by going public.[14] And as Table 4–9 indicates, among the special bracket firms only Drexel and Goldman Sachs & Co. remains organized as a partnership at year end 1987.

The rise in participation in the junk bond market by special bracket firms was driven from the other side of the market, namely, the borrowers. For example, large amounts of cash are required following takeovers or other forms of corporate reorganization. The need to finance clients with more risky forms of

---

[14]It may be hard to remember that Merrill Lynch was the first NYSE member whose stock was listed, on July 27, 1971.

debt might not be unrelated to the concern that lucrative M&A fees might be lost if appropriate financing could not be made available to client firms. Indeed, this connection with the M&A department is so important to special bracket firms that all now offer their own capital to support bridge financing. That form of merchant banking is probably more risky than junk bond flotations—although, as the next section will suggest, those two services are interrelated.

BRIDGE FINANCING: WHAT IS IT? WHY IS IT DONE?

In major corporate takeovers or other forms of corporate reorganization (LBOs, mergers, acquisitions) there is often a time lag between the closing of the deal—that is, the agreement on the price, completing the documentation, the legal conveyance of property for cash, etc.—and the final financial arrangement that develops the more permanent, longer term security issue that finances the reorganization. The reason for this two-step financing is that the flotation of new securities (say, junk bonds) to more permanently finance a deal between $500 million and $1 to $2 billion is not in the best interest of the buyer until after the deal has closed.[15] It does not make sense to finance early because, among other reasons, the flotation cost and carrying the net interest cost of new debt (if the transaction should fail to close) would be prohibitive even if it were possible.[16] Still more significantly, the buyer's bargaining position might be weakened with respect to the price to be paid if the seller knows that the

---

[15]This does not preclude the potential buyer from negotiating a commitment or "letter of intent" from a junk bond underwriter to float a substantial new issue once the deal closes.

[16]Further, in any prospectus, the *purpose* of the financing is spelled out in the "use of the proceeds" section. If such financing was raised *prior to* the closing of the deal, the size of the deal would not be known. Nor would all of the pieces of the sometimes complex financing package be in place. Under those uncertainties the indenture would be difficult to write.

clock is running on the buyer's expensive junk bonds, and especially if the acquirer is competing with other buyers.

If, then, flotation can take place only *after* the deal closes, that flotation process must develop financials for a prospectus, get SEC approval for flotation, and ensure that new debt fits into the overall financing package such as, e.g., constraints in indentures of other securities sold, private placements, etc. Finally, to ensure flotation success, the syndicate and/or buying group needs to be organized. Suppose that the time period needed to crank up a flotation takes about a month.

That means that interim financing is needed so the buyer can make the payment for the company he is committed to buy by the closing of the deal. That implies raising short-term loans; most often, such loans, including bridge financing, are arranged by the investment banker who was the advisor during the negotiations for the deal. By being involved in the bridge financing the (advisor) investment banker stands to ensure that he will be the underwriter chosen for the junk bond flotation. To sum up, for the investment banker the provision of bridge financing keeps in house the financing fees of the deal as follows:

1. Fairness opinion and other consultation fees earned during negotiations.
2. Bridge financing fees.
3. Underwriting fees and commissions.

Just prior to the worldwide sharp decline in stock prices on October 19, 1987, the House Ways and Means Committee reported a new tax proposal (which has been withdrawn since) that threatened the valuation of potential takeover stocks. And while that policy is said to have played a role in the Black Monday scenario, it also put at greater risk some M&A deals in the making. Subsequent declines in the junk bond market added to the perceived risks in M&A deals.[17]

---

[17]Delays in financing occurred in the Southland deal that was finalized only on December 8, 1987. As a result, the rate of return on the deal was reduced.

SUCCESS AND ITS DISCONTENTS: OR, HOW DO YOU MANAGE?

This chapter has discussed the transition of the major investment banker from a partnership structure of some 1,500 professionals to a corporation three to four times as large.[18] That transition took place in the 1980s. Whatever the legal form of organization of the major firms, that multiplication of personnel led to a more complex level of management. The management problem was complicated further by the enormous surge in institutional transactions, innovative security types, and in the associated trading and hedging techniques performed by many of the newly hired personnel. When the avalanche of mergers, takeovers, LBOs and bridge loans is mixed in with all of the above, effective management must develop new conflict resolution and asset allocation skills to maintain the firm's capacity to do deals effectively.

The changes described above have at times involved several management problems that were resolved, in some cases, only after much internal conflict, and in one case at least, a major firm's takeover by another.[19] In part, the story of transition from partnership to corporate form, which is related to the need for added financial capital from the outside, is also the story of a more conscious and deliberate centralization of the decision-making process, and of control systems made necessary by the physical expansion of the firm. The internal politics of the control system are another story, however.

Consider a senior partner in the 1970s who is also a member of the firm's management committee. The strategy planning for the firm as a whole, the related decisions regarding capital allocation within the firm (both financial and human), and the control of his department and that of other departments are all integrated: *they take place in his head.* And the overall manage-

---

[18]To be sure, Merrill carried a corporate structure since 1971, and Goldman remains a partnership.

[19]See Ken Auletta, *Greed and Glory on Wall Street,* New York, Random House, 1986.

ment of the firm is coordinated among the half dozen members of the management committee, all of whose heads are similarly organized.

Now switch these same people into a corporate setup that is several times the size of the partnership, scattered over many floors and across several buildings. Add to that the analytical complexities of trading the new products, and the pressures of maximizing stockholder wealth. Finally, superimpose a conscious effort by the chief executive officer to develop an administrative bureaucracy that can execute policy decisions in the realms of the remaining (former) partners. Even in the best of times, when business is booming, that type of exercise is fraught with a struggle that is never totally resolved. Any leveling off of the rate of rise in total revenues to the firm will begin a new conflict that may involve cutbacks in personnel and other forms of capital for some departments of the firm. At that point some firms reproduce by fission. That is when some of the (former) partners attempt to recapitulate the old days by forming boutiques.[20]

Are we seeing here a rebirth of the specialized partnership to serve certain clients (say, LBO, or M&A)? Perhaps so. But in many respects these changes are a byproduct of the managerial revolution that, in this instance, followed a conscious attempt to manage the much larger investment banking units. That quantitative change implies a qualitative change as well, for the shift to more conscious corporate control is just another symbol of growth and success. The last chapter of this book argues that the changes brought in the aftermath of the October 1987 crash represent another signpost in the process of continuous change, rather than a great divide between "success" and the lesser rates of return that accompany the down phase of any cyclical industry.

---

[20]The term "boutique" is Wall Street jargon for a single-purpose financial firm. In the 1980s, the M&A boutique compares with the full-service investment banking firm whose retail analog would be a department store.

5

THE STOCK MARKET CRASH OF 1987 AND ITS AFTERMATH: MARKET MAKING IN CRISIS

A major conclusion of the *Brady Report*[1] is that the several markets on which financial institutions trade and invest have, by their trading, investment, and hedging activities become *one market*. In the words of that Report, "From an economic viewpoint, what have been traditionally seen as separate markets—the markets for stocks, stock index futures, and stock options—are in fact one market. Under ordinary circumstances, these marketplaces moved sympathetically, linked by financial instruments, trading strategies, market participants and clearing and credit mechanisms. To a large extent, the problems of mid-October [1987] can be traced to the failure of these market segments to act as one."

In that context, consider the typical major investment banking firm in mid-1987: In the space of the preceding 2 to 3 years it had doubled its size, first, by doubling personnel, and second, by doubling its capital.[2] It had accomplished the latter by going public, or by outside institutional investment in its debt and equity. For the typical large investment banker, its $1 to $1.5 billion of capital in 1987 was the foundation for an asset position

[1]*Report of the Presidential Task Force on Market Mechanisms*, U.S. Government Printing Office, 1988, p. VI. This document will be referenced as the "Brady Report," after Nicholas F. Brady, its chairman.
[2]See Chapter 4 for further discussion and data.

of $40+ billion, and that enormous leverage was financed mainly by borrowing on the money market.

Indirect support for this leverage was provided as well by the 1,000 to 2,000 professionals who worked in recently expanded new areas of arbitrage, risk analysis, and hedging rather than in the more traditional departments where corporate securities were analyzed, originated, and traded. In that sense the new research and analytical capabilities of the staff helped each firm to feel more comfortable about its leveraged position. In practice risk was also controlled by market requirements: asset portfolios of marketable securities were marked to market, or hedged.

Finally, investment policy was conducted with the knowledge that, on average, the equivalent of the entire firm's assets was turned over *daily* in trading activities. What could go wrong? Plenty. And the frustrating problem was that what could go wrong was essentially beyond the control of the major firms, their analysts, and their traders. That was not only scary, but beyond what anyone could have anticipated.

WHAT HAPPENED?

On Monday, October 19, 1987, about half a trillion dollars of corporate equity out of a nearly $4 trillion total U.S. market value was extinguished in one 7-hour trading day in New York. Similarly large avalanches in valuation occurred in all of the world's equity markets. Thus the large investments made in human and financial capital and in the latest technology devoted to information processing, analysis, hedging, and even in market execution were shown to be ineffective if not helpless in crisis. How could this happen?

The consensus of market observers suggests that, like any other major catastrophe, the crisis can be said to have been driven by many forces. It would, of course, be neat to isolate one or two of these. Yet, given the fairly narrow perspective that is necessarily the byproduct of the division of labor and interests among market participants, each group has its own view of culprit and victim. A favorite early target, for example, was the process of program trading.[3]

An unfortunate obstacle to the search for a single, or even a simple, explanation of any catastrophe (as opposed to a mere crisis) is the confusion that attends it. It is difficult to isolate variables—or marketplaces—that necessarily interact. Further, the participants involved in a subset of the catastrophe will perceive only the narrow confusion that attends their own disasters, or their own particular marketplace [e.g., the New York Stock Exchange (NYSE)]. Nevertheless, we attempt, below, to give some coherence to the sequence of events from mid-October 1987 [Dow Jones Industrials (DJI) near 2,500] to the first week of November (DJI below 2,000). The two most critical days were October 19 and 20; on each day volume on NYSE exceeded 600 million shares;[4] Table 5–1 indicates that in the four weeks between the close of October 9 and November 6 the Dow lost better than 21 percent of its value.

To arrive at a perception of the events to be described an unsettling premise should be accepted: The component events of the crash can be better understood if the confusions and emotions of the time are not ignored but kept as important parts of the explanation.[5] In that context recall that expectations of investors in the mid-summer weeks of 1987 might have been based on generally rising prices, and perhaps rationalized by optimistic earnings projections and economic forecasts. The Tokyo stock exchange was then trading at a price/earnings (P/E) mul-

---

[3]The fact that major price breaks prior to the NYSE opening on October 19 had occurred on some foreign equity markets that do *not* use that technique has not reduced the fervor of those arguing that position.

[4]It is difficult to recall that in 1980, on the then record trading day, the NYSE traded 84 million shares—a mere 13% of those magnitudes.

[5]In a National Bureau of Economic Research working paper, based on survey evidence collected immediately after the October 19 crash, Prof. Robert J. Shiller argues that: (1) A growing literature calls into question the "efficient markets" theory and that (2) "there is statistical evidence that suggests the stock market may have a life of its own to some extent, unrelated to economic fundamentals." This is not the place to get into that argument, but see *National Bureau of Economic Research,* Working Paper No. 2446, "Investor Behavior in the October 1987 Stock Market Crash: Survey Evidence."

TABLE 5–1
Dow Jones Industrial Index and NYSE Trading Volume
October 12, 1987–November 6, 1987

Day	Dow Jones Industrial Index	Point Change from Previous Close	Percentage Change from Previous Close	Number of Shares Traded (millions)
Mon Oct 12	2,471.44	−10.77	−0.43	141.9
Tues Oct 13	2,508.16	+36.72	+1.49	172.9
Wed Oct 14	2,412.70	−95.46	−3.81	207.4
Thur Oct 15	2,355.09	−57.61	−2.39	263.2
Fri Oct 16	2,246.74	−108.35	−4.60	338.5
Mon Oct 19	1,738.74	−508.00	−22.61	604.3
Tues Oct 20	1,841.01	+102.27	+5.88	608.1
Wed Oct 21	2,027.85	+186.84	+10.15	449.4
Thur Oct 22	1,950.43	−77.42	−3.82	392.2
Fri Oct 23	1,950.76	+.33	+0.02	245.6
Mon Oct 26	1,793.93	−156.83	−8.04	308.8
Tues Oct 27	1,846.49	+52.56	+2.93	260.2
Wed Oct 28	1,846.82	+0.33	+0.02	279.4
Thur Oct 29	1,938.33	+91.51	+4.96	258.1
Fri Oct 30	1,993.53	+55.20	+2.85	303.4
Mon Nov 2	2,014.09	+20.56	+1.03	176.0
Tues Nov 3	1,963.53	−50.56	−2.51	227.8
Wed Nov 4	1,945.29	−18.24	−0.93	202.5
Thur Nov 5	1,985.41	+40.12	+2.06	226.0
Fri Nov 6	1,959.05	−26.36	−1.33	228.3
Change from Oct 12 close		−512.39	−20.73	

earnings (P/E) multiple of 80; on NYSE, the P/E ratio stood at 21.[6]

The NYSE had been thought of as an active and liquid marketplace with growth potential, buttressed by many safety features and supported by hedging vehicles. On October 19, that same market experienced a chain reaction out of control. The president of the NYSE referred to a nuclear accident when he

---

[6]It is useful to recall that the longer-term average P/E multiple on NYSE is about 12.

called the events of Black Monday a "near melt-down." That comparison is apt, for similar to nuclear accidents, those events revealed that what were thought to be safety devices designed to offset company and market risks turned perversely into accelerators for the selling panic. That change of events can be described as a melodrama with a prologue and two acts—so far.[7]

THE DRAMA

The Stage Set

The stock market crash as theater can best be understood as playing on a one-market set with several stage levels (as an analog to the Brady Report). Within that set, each of the component marketplaces [e.g., NYSE, Chicago Board of Trade (CBOT)] represents one, separate, level. Nevertheless, the dramatic events take place on the same stage at the same time although different scripts are acted on each level. And on each of the levels there are some actors who are conscious of the other levels, while other actors play as if the drama was only on their own level.

This variety of interactions on financial markets can be seen most readily by a discussion of index arbitrage (or "program trading"). Arbitrage is, quite simply, the purchase of an item where it is cheap and the sale (or sale of a close substitute) where it is expensive. If a particular grade of aluminum sells for $9,000 a ton in market A and for $8,800 a ton in market B, and if transportation costs between A and B are less than $200 a ton it pays to buy B aluminum and sell A aluminum until the two prices come closer together. What is called the "law of one price" could be related to the outcome of that "arbitrage effect."

Now suppose that the price of a stock index futures contract exceeds the price of a stock portfolio set up to mimic that con-

---

[7]The following is based on a number of excellent articles in the *Wall Street Journal* and the *New York Times*. Their authors were Randall Smith, Steve Swartz, George Anders, James Stewart, and Daniel Hertzberg from the *Wall Street Journal,* and James Sterngold and other members of the Business Section of the *Times.* In addition, the Brady Report, or more formally, *Report of The Presidential Task Force on Market Mechanisms,* January 1988, is an invaluable source.

tract [say the Standard & Poor 400 (S&P 400)]. Suppose further that the price difference exceeds the difference of the present values of the carry costs of these two substitute assets (this is the analog of the transport cost differential). The "index arbitrageur" (like the "aluminum arbitrageur") attempts to profit from that difference between the two market prices: his action will drive up the price of the cheaper item (where he buys) and lower the price in the more expensive (where he sells). On our stage set, the simultaneous purchase of futures contracts and selling of stock portfolios closes the "price gap" between the two markets. On each level of the stage set, the sellers and buyers in each market believe that they have concluded a routine, local, transaction even though the arbitrageur has in fact made them *one market* (as the Brady Report puts it). The "program trading" technique comes into play by the use of a particular NYSE trading mechanism [designated order turnaround (DOT) or Super DOT] that will, when put into action, purchase pre-*programmed* amounts of some scores of stocks to mimic the S&P 400 index; hence the term "program" trading.

Sales of such "program" stock portfolios occur when futures contracts sell at a discount to equity value, and futures are purchased by arbitrageurs. As with any arbitrage, the arb wants to lock in the spread to make a profit. And that profit will be free from the vagaries and volatility of market activities—most of the time. It will *not* be available when the necessary local-market counterpart to the desired trade is unavailable. In that process, market dislocation on one level of the stage set may be transferred to the other levels by the lack of arbitraging facilities.

Prologue: Prices Begin to Break

On October 14 (the Wednesday prior to Black Monday) the House Ways and Means Committee majority proposed a tax on takeovers—that action shook the values of a number of major stocks. On the same day, the August trade deficit figures suggested disappointing results, thereby raising the fear of higher interest rates (and lower security prices). That same Wednesday, the Dow Industrial average fell by more than 95 points, a record (up to then). The next day the Dow fell another 58 points, and on Friday by still another 108 points, the second *new* record reached in three days. In those three days *prior* to Black Monday, the Dow lost more than 260 points. From its peak level of August 25, it had fallen by 17 percent. Prior to the opening in New York on Monday, October 19, selling pressure from abroad was very heavy: It began in Tokyo, moved to London, and to all other financial markets in Europe.

Act 1: The New York Stock Exchange on October 19

As is now well known, on that day, Black Monday, the Dow fell by 508 points. All reports of that day describe events on the floor in terms of emotional reactions: Panic, Fear, Terror. One specialist would be reminded of his combat experience during World War II. The following will discuss the major players in the drama of the crash.[8]

---

[8]The paragraphs below quote from "Notes and Comments" by Richard Preston in *The New Yorker* of November 2, 1987, pp. 33–34, and describe the emotional context of the panic. (© 1987 The New Yorker Magazine, Inc. Reprinted by permission.)

At four o'clock, closing time, the [NYSE] building shuddered as brokers ran every which way to complete their last trades, and a bell went off. On Broad Street, in front of the exchange, a crowd had gathered around the members' entrance, just as on October 29, 1929. We expected to hear noise and shouting, but the crowd was quiet, alert, expectant, like those Roman mobs described by Tacitus, waiting for someone to be torn apart before their eyes. All attention was focused on the members' entrance but nobody came out for a while. Then a few clerks in blue jackets appeared. "That mother took a plunge," a clerk said. "I don't know what is going on."

"Scotty, how are ya?" said one clerk to another. "Brain dead," Scotty answered.

"Tokyo starts in four hours. I hope they crash and burn, like we did."

A young man in a tan jacket, an institutional wire clerk, described what he had seen. He said he worked in a room called the Garage, beside the main trading floor. In the Garage, clerks and traders sit in front of computer screens and, taking telephone orders from all over the world, buy and sell huge blocks of stock. He said, "Half the Dow stocks couldn't open for trading this morning. They didn't open for an hour or more. We were frozen in front of our screens. There were just no bids. I.B.M., General Electric, Merck—some of the biggest blue-chip stocks on the Dow, and we couldn't open them!" He inhaled from a cigarette that consisted of an ash attached to a filter. "I did some trades on Merck today," he said. "You know what a downtick is? When a stock goes down an eighth of a point, a quarter of a point? I was watching Merck on my screen, and it started trading on downticks four points at a time. Then it downticked eight points."

Mutual Funds

On the morning of October 19, most mutual funds, even those that carried a cash cushion to redeem tendered shares, began to add to sell pressures as customers pressed them for cash at any redemption price.[9]

Portfolio Insurance

This mechanism is designed to permit institutional investors (mostly pension funds) to develop long-term portfolios by offsetting short-term price fluctuations mainly by hedges in the futures market. To prevent undesired sales of stock, these institutions need *buyers* of futures. But as futures prices began to collapse even faster than stocks on Monday, many portfolio *insurers* (e.g., potential futures buyers) pulled out of the market. This forced even those institutional investors interested in *buying* insurance (that is, selling futures) to forgo that device, and to *sell stocks* instead. Further, the sharp declines in the Chicago Board of Trade futures index added, by itself, a signal for further sell pressures on NYSE. On the NYSE floor, the delayed openings of some bellwether stocks (e.g., IBM, Merck) even while futures contracts of the S&P 500 were still trading caused some professional traders to doubt whether the system could, in fact, be operating properly. After all, the stocks that had not yet opened were a substantial portion of the index that *was* trading. The doubts of the pros added to the sense of panic.

Block Traders

The very large blocks of stock that institutional sellers were then placing for sale were some of the issues that were delayed

---

[9]A number of complaints have been made to NYSE and the SEC by holders of mutual fund shares that telephone communication with mutual funds on October 19 was nearly impossible. The funds claimed that their lines were clogged with sell orders. These complaints were different from, albeit parallel with, complaints by direct investors that brokers and market makers refused to receive orders on that day by suspending telephone communications.

in opening and that, technically, were caught in the down-drafts of the indexes (even if the separate stocks had not yet opened for trading). That uncertainty, following the several preceding days of sharp price declines and the tax threat to values of take-over stocks, induced upstairs traders at investment banks to offer these stocks directly to the marketplace. It should be recalled that the investment bankers are thinly capitalized (the asset to capital ratio is 20 or more) so that the customary placement of a share of the block trade into their own portfolio would have created an added threat to capital adequacy. Indeed, some even took clues on bidding from (more rapidly dropping) futures markets rather than from (the late, possibly misleading) prior stock quotes. All of the above added to sales pressures directly.

Specialists

Specialists are not supposed to offset a market crash—and in any case, they are too thinly capitalized to do so. Many of them have but $40 to $60 *million* of buying power even though they are exempt from the Fed's margin rules. Their basic function is to smooth out random price fluctuations. On October 19, a number of specialists were overwhelmed by the costs of standing in the way of the sell avalanche and were ultimately taken over by better-capitalized securities firms.

Index Arbitrage

Over and above the institutional traffic, the flood of retail orders began to swamp the super DOT computer system that, at the printer end, provides information to specialists.[10] To avoid system collapse, the data traffic to printers was partly suppressed. Program traders could have, in theory, locked in substantial

---

[10]For index arbitrageurs, gaps between stock prices and futures prices have to be executed precisely and immediately before the gap vanishes. The DOT or super DOT systems permit arbs to trade a basket of $30 million of stocks, which mimic a stock index, in a few minutes. Without DOT, the arbitrage cannot be executed effectively or profitably. And to that extent the potentially stabilizing mechanisms that arbitrage could have provided were lost.

profits by buying "cheap" futures, and selling stocks. But in a market clogged by information delays and a bottlenecked transaction computer, execution could occur only after some uncertain time delay. In that circumstance the arb knew that the very motivation for a transaction, a locked-in gain, could evaporate before execution, and could even turn into a substantial loss. Further, the exchange's short selling rules (a short sale can be executed only on an uptick or zero-plus tick) created another technical obstacle to possibly off-setting trades. In sum, a number of regulatory and mechanical bottlenecks prevented the execution of whatever (modest) offsets that arbitrage execution could have provided to the panic.

At the close on October 19, more than 600 million shares had been traded, as noted, and the Dow had lost nearly one quarter of the value that it had at the start of that day. A number of specialist firms were dismayed to find that their losses had absorbed all of their capital, and that they were technically out of business. Those specialist firms that could still hope to open on Tuesday knew, late Monday night, that to continue to operate even in a stable environment they needed to borrow very large sums because, on Monday, they had been the only buyers in the marketplace. Near midnight, on Monday, a number of New York money center banks refused to make loan commitments to market participants, especially specialists. These same banks were lenders as well to investment banking firms, to arbitrageurs, and to government securities dealers. To all potential bank borrowers the answer was the same: no *un*secured loans were being made. Thus Act 1 closed with a bang: There was a realistic fear that if the credit stopped in a forward market such as NYSE, so would trading. In a market in which a number of routine processes were already in question, ready access to credit was essential to permit the routine sales (and purchase) agreements to be honored with the usual five-day payment delay.

Act 2: The Terror Intensifies—and Recedes

As the perception of the potential credit crunch widened from market participants to the New York banks and to the Federal

Reserve, the new Chairman of the Federal Reserve Board, Alan Greenspan, and the president of the New York Federal Reserve Bank, E. Gerald Corrigan, recognized that there was a potential of the market crash widening as in 1929 and the 1930s to a wholesale collapse of financial institutions.

One contributing factor was clearly in their control: credit availability. The Fed issued an unusual policy statement (dated October 20) that indicated its ". . . readiness to serve as a source of liquidity to support the economic and financial system." In that policy they were following Bagehot's classic recommendation to central bankers: "In crisis, discount liberally."

Accordingly President Corrigan called on the New York banks to make credit available to market participants, adding his bank's willingness to support that credit policy. If an overall crisis should occur it should not be brought on by a lack of credit or liquidity.

Even with that open credit support, the aftermath of Monday's NYSE crash continued into Tuesday morning. Many specialists would not open their stocks unless buyers were available. About two thirds of their $3 billion of buying capacity had been swallowed up by their swollen inventories of (so far unsalable) stocks. As a result, many stocks opened 1 to 2 hours late, albeit with generally higher prices. When the Dow index was finally quoted it was an extraordinary 200 points higher. As soon as the specialists perceived the upsurge they began to sell into that opportunity as much of their enormous inventory as they could—and thus quickly turned an upsurge into another sell panic. Buyers vanished as quickly as they had appeared. Stock index futures plunged once again.

Serious consideration was then given by many to close trading on the NYSE. According to the *Wall Street Journal*,[11] one blue-chip index of 20 stocks, the "Major Market Index" (MMI) continued to trade: the futures of the MMI index trade on the CBOT, and the options trade on the Amex. Options trading of MMI was halted on Amex on Tuesday when half of the stocks in

---

[11]See J. B. Stewart and D. Hertzberg "Terrible Tuesday," *Wall Street Journal*, November 2, 1987, p. 1.

that index had not opened on NYSE (the rules permit a stop to options trading when 20% or more of underlying stocks don't trade). The CBOT continued to trade the futures because 17 of the stocks continued to trade, albeit sporadically, on *regional* exchanges. And, meanwhile, traders of the "little-used" MMI on CBOT were, for that reason, "not flooded with sell orders. And there was the fierce long-standing rivalry between the Board of Trade and the New York Exchange, a rivalry that has given rise to a generally defiant attitude at the Board of Trade toward any action adopted by the Big Board."[12]

Just after noon that same day executives of NYSE were meeting to decide whether or not to close in the midst of another crisis of uncertainty and disarray. At that point the MMI futures contract, the "only major index still trading staged the most powerful rally in its history." Its rise was "from a discount (to cash market) of nearly 60 points to a premium of about 12 points. Because each point represents about five in the (Dow Jones) industrial average the rally was the equivalent of a lightning-like 360 point rise in the Dow. Some believe that this extraordinary move set the stage for the salvation of the world's markets."[13]

The article goes on to speculate that this rally might in fact have been manipulated by a few sophisticated speculators. In any case that rally was supported by announcements shortly after noon by a number of major industrial firms of stock buy-backs of their own shares. These buy-backs had been suggested by calls to corporate clients on the part of major investment bankers.[14] Honeywell, ITT, Allegis, four regional Bell companies,

---

[12]*Wall Street Journal,* "Terrible Tuesday," op. cit., p. 23. Reprinted from The Wall Street Journal (Barron's), © Dow Jones & Company, Inc. 1987. ALL RIGHTS RESERVED.

[13]Ibid.

[14]The major institutional trading group on the NYSE has changed once again. While few will argue today that individual traders remain a major force, and many understand that today institutional traders are the main actors, what is not yet understood totally is that the institutions have changed: The trading volume of mutual funds and pension funds is still great, but the increasing weight of corporations acquiring corporate equities (their own, and those of other firms) is not as yet as widely appreciated as it should be.

and USX were major buyers among the industrials. Among financial firms Citicorp and Shearson Lehman followed suit.

As buy orders began to be noticed some major stocks on NYSE (especially those that form part of MMI) began to open after 1 P.M. Such stocks as Merck and IBM began the parade, and by 2 P.M. all MMI stocks had opened. Shortly thereafter, MMI options were opened again on Amex and trading in nearly all stocks began. At the close, the Dow had *risen* by 102 points. Volume was once more immense, at 608 million shares.[15] Tragedy had been averted by the credit support of the Fed and the provident performance of a little-known futures index. The theater metaphor is useful—the "deus ex machina" performed its work. But no one knew whether the drama had ended.[16]

WHAT CAN WE LEARN?

The events described above represent a challenge for market participants.

1. What does the drama mean?
2. Whatever its meaning, how will, or should, or can, financial institutions react to crisis in future?
3. And how will the systems developed by enormous investments in talent and technology perform in a future crisis (or crises)?
4. Should there be regulatory changes?

Taking the last point first, the writers of the Brady Report recommend a number of changes that could imply substantive changes for the financial markets. Among the major proposals made the following are noteworthy:

---

[15]In the *full year,* 1955, about 650 million shares were traded on NYSE. That was the first *year* since the 1930s when total *annual* volume reached the level of either crash day, October 19 or 20. Subsequent to 1955, it took about a decade, to 1964, before a *full year's* trading (1,237 million shares) equaled the volume reached in the two days, October 19 and 20. It is worth recalling that on October 29, 1929, the day of *that* crash, about 16.4 million shares were traded.

[16]Analogous to Pirandello's play, "Six Characters in Search of an Author," the stock market drama in October 1987 might be called "Several Acts in Search of an Ending."

1. Circuit Breaker mechanisms (e.g., price limits and coordinated trading halts) for equity markets.
2. Margins on the several markets should be coordinated to "control speculation and financial leverage."
3. One agency to "coordinate" regulations of the several but related financial markets.
4. "Unified" clearing systems that cross marketplaces.
5. Information systems that monitor transactions and conditions in "related markets."

To be sure, many of these proposals will require further discussion and debate, and several will require new legislation. This ensures that transactors on the financial markets will continue to live in interesting times.

INVESTMENT BANKING MANAGEMENT

The stock market crash has been interpreted as a major break as well in the fortunes of investment bankers. And for many of them it was that. But even prior to October 1987, many of these firms sensed a worsening of the atmosphere. Firms such as, for example, First Boston, Salomon, Shearson, and Merrill experienced significant drops in their own stock price between early 1987 and September 1987. This does not deny that the October crash did not imply a further decline—as it did, in fact. Table 5–2 indicates that the year-to-year change in share prices of investment banking firms underwent valuation declines from nearly a third (Morgan Stanley) to as much as two thirds (E. F. Hutton). Meanwhile, over the same period, the Dow Jones Industrial Average *rose* slightly, as did some other equity averages (the NASDAQ—National Association of Securities Dealers Automatic Quote—average declined by 10%, however).[17]

---

[17]The SEC's study of the market break reported that in October 1987 the 15 largest investment banking firms (and wire houses) lost nearly $700 million, with two of the firms losing about $210 million each. The study indicates that "between October 14 and October 30, 1987, the firms reported combined losses of approximately $796.5 million in their equity positions." (p. 5–4) At the month end, most of the 15 firms carried less than 5% of their assets in the form of equity holdings.

TABLE 5–2
**Share Prices of Broker/Dealers in October 1987 and October 1986,
and Percentage Changes* (Dollars Per Share and Percent)**

	Share Price		Percent Change
	Oct. 30, 1987	Oct. 30, 1986	
Morgan Stanley	53	77	−31
A. G. Edwards	18	28	−33
Bear Stearns	12	18	−34
Alex Brown	10	17	−41
Merrill Lynch	25	42	−41
Quick & Reilly	12	21	−42
First Boston	25	50	−49
Salomon, Inc	20	42	−53
Paine Webber	17	38	−55
L. F. Rothschild	6	15	−61
E. F. Hutton	17	50	−66
Dow Jones Industrials	1994	1876	+6%

*In order of price declines.

Source: *Wall Street Journal*

These data make clear that the market's perception and valuation of market makers (and not just the NYSE specialists) has been substantially changed. And these firms during that period first felt it necessary to raise capital from other financial investors, notably Japanese firms. In addition, even during the early part of 1987, these firms began substantially to reduce current outlays by personnel layoffs, mergers, and other forms of reorganization.

Figure 5–1 is designed to give a longer-term perspective to the investment bankers' management problems. The first thing to observe is that these firms have, historically, undergone wide fluctuations in rates of return. The source cited indicates that the investment bankers' rates of return dominate the entire securities industry's returns on equity.[18] And it is the latter returns

---

[18]See Federal Reserve Bank of New York, *Recent Trends in Commercial Bank Profitability* Federal Reserve Bank of New York, 1987, esp. chapter 14.

FIGURE 5–1
Return on Equity in Two Financial Industries

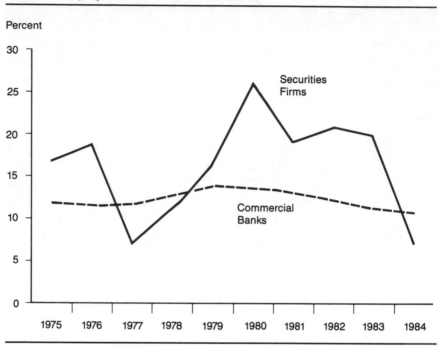

Sources: Federal Reserve Bulletin; Securities Industry Association.

that must serve as a proxy for equity valuation for most of the period. This is so because stock price data are not obtainable since, among the majors, all but Merrill Lynch were still organized as partnerships prior to 1980.[19] As the chart indicates, in the years 1975 to 1984 the securities industry experienced three peak years in returns to equity (of about 19%, 26%, and 21%) and two deep trough years (of 7% each). Meanwhile the commercial banking industry's returns on equity moved smoothly within a range of 12% to 14%. Considering only the drop in equity returns for investment bankers to the two trough

---

[19]See Tables 4–7 and 4–8.

years, the securities industry can be seen to have experienced year-to-year declines of more than 60%. This prior experience helps to place the 1986–87 drop in equity values in some historical perspective: It is reasonable to argue that the return volatility of securities firms about the stable returns to commercial banks in the 1970s and early 1980s could be considered to contain a premium to offset a risk factor similar to that experienced in 1986–87. The higher average *secular* return to investment banking industry (about 17 percent for 1975–84) could then be expected to incorporate that premium for risk. Most seasoned Wall Streeters know in their bones that the valuations of market makers will fluctuate.

The managing directors, partners, and boards of directors of these same firms have learned that the increasingly integrated transactions on the several financial markets now compel a more directed management style. The entrepreneurial management styles of the early 1980s had given wide scope to separate departments in the firm. Further, the relatively high rates of return had permitted these departments to grow very rapidly. When these firms were of moderate size (say, with 2,000 personnel each) the informal supervisory system characteristic of partnerships could suffice. But, ironically, the very success of that methodology produced a doubling and a tripling of firm size, of the scale of the average trade, and of the portfolio assets that were at risk and that had to be hedged.[20]

Seen from the other side of the market the institutionalization of trading has raised the risks to the traders. And because the magnitude of the average trade has surged with institutionalization of the markets, and because the investment banking firms have grown in scale to suit, any mistake became more costly. Prevention implies tighter control. At their much larger corporate size, the new control bureaucracies then constrain the

---

[20]A hidden problem in this context derives from the high real estate values of New York City. As the firms grew in size, they expanded onto additional floors of the same building, or into different buildings. The direct partnership-type relationships (and informal control possibilities) tended to get lost in the scatter of personnel and facilities.

clever traders and arbitrageurs and merger and acquisitions (M&A) specialists that helped the firm to grow to its present size. If these specialists choose not to operate under the new control systems, they opt out. The crash of 1987 only made more dramatic what the better managed firms already knew, but were not forced to recall until October 1987.

6

MARKET MAKING
BY INNOVATION

In finance, the capacities to innovate and to take risks often go together. Innovation represents a special sort of risk taking, namely, the willingness to underwrite and trade a new type of security even though its return variance is as yet untested in a market setting. It is by engaging in new markets and in floating a novel or unusual type of security that the innovative firm and its personnel gain experience in trading, in hedging, and in portfolio management—in short, in innovative finance. The innovator also pressures his competitors: because competitors feel compelled *not* to lose market share they eventually tend to follow suit into the innovative territory. By this process the firms in the new markets perform a symbiotic service for each other, as follows:

1. Wider participation (among competitors) helps to develop depth and breadth in secondary markets.
2. In the primary market, competitive entry is feasible only by narrowing spreads over comparable Treasury issues for customers (issuers) and clients (buyers) relative to prior security arrangements.
3. The innovative deal becomes a routine transaction in day-to-day market making as these spreads converge toward the average rate of return for market deals of similar risk.

What has come to be called "securitization" is a core feature of financial innovation in the 1980s. Often securitization means the repackaging of traditional financial assets into a new form.

For the innovator the idea for a new product emerges from the perception of a market inefficiency that (prior to innovation) had involved a significantly higher borrowing cost for an issuer. In turn, that higher cost provided a margin for inserting a (lower cost) innovative issue, while still providing a profit margin to the innovator as well as a more attractive return to the newly attracted investor. In that approach, innovative finance generates a double irony, as follows:

1. The innovative practitioner and his imitators (or competitors) will, by providing their new products, reduce the price differentials and inefficiencies among new and old securities: The inefficiency is thus removed.
2. The theoretician who typically assumes away market inefficiencies will, thereby, miss the very rationale for the innovative product. Ultimately, however, he will be able to point to the elimination of the inefficiency (through the innovative product). His "simplifying" assumption will turn out to have been appropriate. But the "simplifying" assumption in fact misses the rationale for many changes that have occurred on the financial markets. In that sense he will miss as well exactly those innovations that have substantially changed those financial markets in which inefficiencies have stimulated change such as, e.g., the mortgage market.

In the overall innovation and securitization game, investment bankers were pioneers. This was a logical role for them because they were accustomed to taking new risks in their trading activities as dealers, underwriters, and market makers, as well as in managing inventory. In compensation for such risk-taking, investment bankers acquire continuous information with respect to market pricing (information on trades) and demand (the portfolio needs of their clients). By analyzing client requirements, they may discover some as yet unmet parameters for issues that will better satisfy the current portfolio requirements of an institutional money manager. At the same time, these new types of issues might provide the issuer with a lower cost of capital just because the innovative characteristics of the new issue can more directly meet the buyer's portfolio needs and hence can be sold at a premium.

This chapter will discuss in some detail how investment bankers innovate: how they invent a new security; how they develop a new market; and how a particular firm—namely Drexel—by doing both can move up in industry ranking to the top.

DEEP-DISCOUNT BONDS AND OTHER VARIANTS

When interest rates rose very sharply after 1979, nearly the entire supply of outstanding debt began to sell at a discount. At that time a number of analysts and some corporate officials considered the feasibility of selling new-issues bonds at a substantial discount (from par). Among some issues sold in 1981 were bonds with 30 percent to 40 percent discounts below par and with coupons significantly below current yields to maturity; for bondholders, the rate of return came in part from the rise in the value of the bond based on the accrual of "noncash" interest. Firms such as IBM, Alcoa, ITT, and J. C. Penney issued this type of debt. In June 1981 an issue of 10-year notes sold by General Motors Acceptance Corporation (GMAC) went all the way to a zero coupon, where the bondholder's income would come totally from accruals of interest on the original purchase price until, at maturity in 1991, the GMAC bonds would be paid off at par.

This type of issue was partly supported by preferential tax treatment for the borrower and not (as some early commentators mistakenly supposed) by preferential capital-gains tax treatment of the incremental value for the lenders. The latter was never granted. The best way to explain the tax treatment of the borrower is by the example shown below.

A Zero Coupon Prototype

The implicit rate of return on an issue price at $252.50 per 10 year bond is 14.8 percent; this is, of course, another way of indicating that the present value of $1,000 in 10 years, discounted at 14.8 percent, is equal to $252.50.[1] The lender's position can be evaluated as follows.

In the first year, the bonds appreciate by 14.8 percent; their value (per bond) increases by $0.148 \times \$252.50 = \$37.30$; at the end of the first year, the bond will be worth $\$252.50 + \$37.30 = \$289.80$. In the second year, the value goes up by $0.148 \times \$289.80$, or $42.80; and so on (see Table 6–1).

The aggregate change in future value (FV) ($747.50) is added to purchase price ($252.50) to get par, or $1,000.

In 1981 the Internal Revenue Service took the position that even though GMAC would have no cash interest outflow until year 10, it nevertheless was accruing obligations to make such payments; accordingly, interest deductions for tax purposes could be taken. The amount then permitted for tax write-off was the total sum of interest to be paid ($747.50) divided by 10, or $74.75 per note per year. A comparison of the second and third columns of Table 6–1 indicates that the accrual of interest falls short of allowable tax write-offs for the first six years of a note's maturity, while the last four years show the reverse (deductions lower than accruals). All else the same, the present value of the borrower's tax deductions (net accruals) are clearly maximized in that process, thereby further lowering the after-tax cost of capital to the borrower.

This type of present value "tax loss" to the IRS should be offset to some extent by tax collections from lenders (note holders). It quickly became apparent, however, that those institutional investors who were in low (or zero) tax brackets were the major buyers of these issues. Further, investors quickly became aware that zeros were the only securities available that carried *assured* reinvestment rates for interest earnings, thereby guaranteeing yields for the life of the security. In an environment of volatile rates and, worse, volatile short/long rate relationships, that assurance was especially valuable to institutional investors

---

[1] The value using 14 percent as a discount factor (DF) is equal to $269.70; using 15 percent as a DF, the value equals $247.20. Interpolation will not be precise because accruals are semiannual.

TABLE 6–1
Zero Coupon Bond Cash Flows, 10-Year Issue

	Lender's Position		Borrower's Position
Year	Present Value at Start of Year	Change in Future Value During Year	(Allowable Annual Tax Write-Off = 10% of Interest Total)
1	$252.50	$ 37.30	$ 74.75
2	280.80	42.80	74.75
3	332.50	49.10	74.75
4	381.60	56.30	74.75
5	437.90	64.60	74.75
6	502.50	74.10	74.75
7	576.60	85.10	74.75
8	661.70	97.60	74.75
9	759.40	112.00	74.75
10	871.40	128.60	74.75
Total		$747.50	$747.50

seeking to meet contractual cash flows in the future (for example, pension funds). The fact that these very same investors carried no current tax liabilities made the acquisition of these issues all the more attractive. Finally, the development of Individual Retirement Accounts (IRAs) and the liberalization of Keogh plans further added to the demand for zero coupon bonds.

Synthetic Zeros: Conversions of Government Securities

Beginning in August 1982, Salomon Brothers and, subsequently, other investment bankers began to issue Certificates of Accrual on Treasury Securities (CATS), which represented the repackaging of coupon-bearing U.S. Treasury issues into a more tradable form. This was done by "stripping" the Treasury securities of their coupons, with each dated semiannual coupon and the principal of the security held by Morgan Guaranty Trust Company of New York as the custodian on behalf of the owners of the CATS.

Suppose that Salomon "stripped" $200 million of a 10 per-

TABLE 6–2
Stripping a 10 Percent, $200 Million Issue with 15 Years Maturity

	Period		Millions of Dollars
Interest date	1	(3 months hence)	10
	2	(9 months hence)	10
	3	(15 months hence)	10
	—		—
	—		—
	—		—
	30	(15 years hence)	10
Maturity date		(15 years hence)	200

cent issue of securities that had a 15-year maturity (see Table 6–2). This means that for each six-month interest date, $10 million of CATS could be sold.

Current interest rates in the capital market may show 90-day Treasury bill yields (the equivalent of the first CATS in the table) to be different from 10 percent; the same may be true for all the maturities up to 15 years. Nevertheless, the discount factor applied to the rate of return from the several issues of CATS will reflect the market yields for the relevant maturity. Of course, the two yields—that on CATS and the yield to maturity (YTM) of a Treasury issue of equivalent maturity—will *not* be the same. This is because the yield to maturity of a Treasury issue, which is based on the current price, implies an assumed reinvestment of interest cash flows equal to the YTM rate. On the other hand, the reinvestment rate of each issue of CATS beyond the first year implies an *assured* rate of reinvestment since each issue of CATS—that is, each set of stripped coupons of a given date and the principal as well—has now been converted to the equivalent of a zero coupon bond. In that sense, from the packager's point of view, CATS represent a more marketable set of securities. These securities, in turn, are more marketable because some buyers will pay an additional premium for tax and other advantages conferred by the equivalent of a zero coupon issue.

The Next Step: STRIPS

In 1985 the U.S. Treasury got into the act by introducing the Separate Trading of Registered Interest and Principal of Securities, or STRIPS. Under that program "selected Treasury securities may be maintained in the book-entry system operated by the Federal Reserve banks in a manner that permits separate trading and ownership of interest and principal payments."[2] The only difference between this program and the physical "stripping" of existing Treasury issues by investment bankers is that those bondholders who have access to a book-entry account at any Federal Reserve bank may, for the designated issues, ask the Fed to "strip" interest components from the issue; the Fed does not charge for that service.

The Treasury set a unit size of $1,000 for a set of STRIPS. Further, to originate STRIPS, a bondholder must have enough bonds to obtain $1,000 units. For example, if interest rates are at 10 percent and interest is paid semiannually, at least $20,000 of bonds are needed to produce the minimum unit of $1,000 per interest date.

At the inception of the program, a number of 10-year notes (maturing in 1995) were made eligible for the origination of STRIPS. The interesting aspect of this process is that a successful innovation may induce a borrower (here the U.S. government) to further facilitate the process, presumably because the cost of capital may be reduced and because a new technology (a computerized book-entry system at the Fed) makes it easy to trade.

INTEREST-RATE SWAPS

Asset swaps have been a familiar part of the finance landscape for as long as large-scale bond trades have taken place. In a typical asset swap a financial institution trades in one set of bonds

---

[2]From offering circular of the U.S. Treasury.

with a bond dealer for another set and then pays or receives from the dealer the difference in the two agreed-on value totals. This constitutes a swap of assets.

Interest-rate swaps, on the other hand, are a partial misnomer because no swap of title takes place. And even though they deal with the cash flows of liabilities (or debts) rather than assets, the actual indebtedness obligations of the two sets of borrowers *does not change.* The only things that are swapped are the debt-service obligations that the two borrowers must continue to make to their lenders in order to remain in good standing.

At first blush this sounds like a strange arrangement. Why is it done? The simplest answer lies in the law of comparative advantage.[3] Figure 6–1 indicates that a high quality (AA) rated borrower (say, a U.S. bank) could raise seven-year money at a fixed interest rate of 9.8% or short-term money at LIBOR (London interbank offered rate) currently at 7¼% + 25 basis points. At the point in time given in the figure assume this to be 7.5% overall. The lower quality (BBB) rated institution [say, a U.S. savings and loan (S&L)] could raise, at short term, floating funds at LIBOR + 75 basis points, for a total cost of 8%, and seven-year note (fixed rate) at 11 percent. The AA bank has an absolute cost advantage in both markets because of its high credit rating. With the perception of investors that risk premiums should rise with maturity, that absolute advantage for the AA borrower rises from ½ percentage point at the short floater maturity to 1.2 percentage points at the seven-year maturity. At the seven-year maturity the *relative* cost advantage is thus more than twice that at the floater (or six-month) maturity. This is just another way of suggesting that the BBB borrower would minimize his comparative cost *dis*advantage at the floater end, while the bank maximizes its comparative advantage at the fixed end. And this sets up the rationale for the liability swap: the S&L borrows at the floater end and swaps that set of pay-

---

[3]The discussion below is based on an insightful presentation by S. D. Felgran, "Interest Rate Swaps: Use, Risk, and Prices" in Federal Reserve Bank of Boston, *New England Economic Review,* Nov./Dec. 1987, pp. 22–32.

FIGURE 6–1

Assessing Comparative Borrowing Costs by Quality and by Effective Maturity

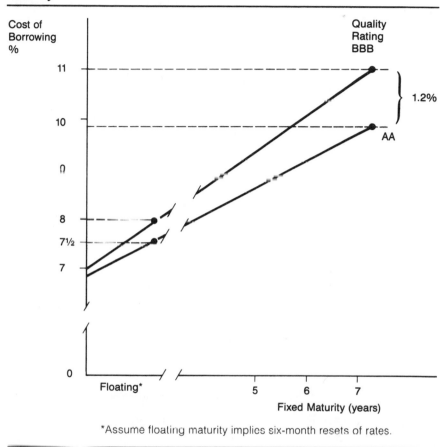

*Assume floating maturity implies six-month resets of rates.

ments for the bank's fixed-income interest rates; the AA bank would have borrowed in the market where its comparative cost advantage was the greatest.

This view of the deal is a partial one. What makes the S&L's decision ultimately rational is that its basic intermediation business already comprises a mismatch of short-term (deposit) liabilities with its fixed-rate mortgage portfolio. Suppose that the S&L swaps out of rate-sensitive, short-term deposits (or more technically, out of money market deposit liabilities, or MMDL) for the fixed-rate interest payments on the seven-year bond raised by the bank. Suppose that an appropriate share of the S&L's fixed-rate mortgage portfolio yields 13 percent. By concluding the swap, the S&L gets out of the present maturity mismatch by the dollar amount of the swap. This means that long-term average revenue (based on the mortgage portfolio) will be larger than the fixed cost of financing liabilities. As a result, the S&L not only immunizes itself from possible costly increases in marginal cost (MMDL rising above 13 percent) but, in addition, locks in a net return of 2 percent, neglecting taxes.

The section below examines a swap described by the Philadelphia Fed.[4]

Swap Mechanics

The upper panel of Figure 6–2 shows the parties to the swap, going from left to right:

1. The bank, with a seven-year 11 percent liability (fixed) and expectations of acquiring short-term, variable-rate assets.
2. The intermediary, or swap arranger, namely, an investment banker who collects a fee for his trouble.
3. The S&L, with assets in the form of a fixed-rate mortgage portfolio averaging 13 percent net return and variable-rate liabilities (based on T-bill rate).

The intermediary, or arranger, is charged with calculating the costs to each of the swappers. For the fixed-rate payer, for example, cost may include not only the coupon rate of the bond but the annualized (over seven years) new-issue costs of issuing the bond and whatever other costs are required to produce an "all-in" rate acceptable to the long-term borrower. For the counterparty, all of these fees must, of course, be acceptable before the swap is consummated; that last point may include, for example, a short-term rate higher than (or lower than) LIBOR. For

---

[4]Jan G. Loeys, "Interest Rate Swaps: A New Tool for Managing Risks," *Business Review,* Federal Reserve Bank of Philadelphia, May–June 1985, pp. 17–25.

FIGURE 6–2
How the Swap Works

Bank		S&L
Assets: Loans yield LIBOR + ½%	Pays LIBOR → Collects 11% →	Assets: Fixed-rate mortgages: 13%
Liabilities: 7-year bond at 11%	Investment banker (intermediary) ← Pays 11% Receives LIBOR	Liabilities: MMDL at T-bill + ½%

		Net Payment Flows			
(1)	*(2)*	*(4)*	*(5)*	*(7)*	*(0)*
				Net Payment:	*Net Payment:*
		Floating-Rate	*Fixed-Rate*	*Bank to S&L*	*S&L to Bank*
Date	*LIBOR*	*Payment**	*Payment*	*(4 > 5)*	*(5 > 4)*
May 1983	8.98%	$4,540,000	$5,500,000	0	$ 960,000
Nov 1983	8.43	4,215,000	5,500,000	0	1,285,000
May 1984	11.54	5,770,000	5,500,000	$27,000	
Nov 1984	9.92	4,960,000	5,500,000	0	540,000
Nov 1985	8.44	4,220,000	5,500,000	0	1,280,000

*LIBOR at six-month rate (LIBOR × $50 million).
Note: LIBOR is London Interbank offer rate, or the cost at which banks lend funds to each other in the London money market.

the sake of simplicity, the swap is set at $100 million net; the fixed rate is set at 11 percent paid semiannually; and the floating rate is set at the monthly average of LIBOR during the two semiannual payment months.

In the period shown, which saw a general decline in interest rates as inflationary pressures receded, the fixed-rate payer made just a single payment to the floating-rate payer, while the floating-rate payer made four payments. Lest this arrangement be considered unfair to the S&L, recall that the S&L has locked in a $2 million per year gross return over and above the implied 11 percent fixed rate while at the same time largely covering its own risk exposure regarding the spread between short-term and long-term rates.

Why would the commercial bank engage in this game? The

bank expects to be able continuously to make commercial and industrial (short-term) loans of acceptable risks in an amount similar to the par value of the original bond and at a rate equal to LIBOR + 50 basis points. Because the bank is compensated (by swapper) for the cost differential between short-term rate and fixed rate borrowing, the bank is in fact arbitraging between LIBOR (cost) and LIBOR + 50 basis points (return).

Attesting to the success of the swap market is its enormous expansion from its inception in 1982 to over $300 billion by year-end 1986, "an 84 percent increase over the prior year."[5] Similarly high growth rates are shown by data covering U.S. banks as intermediaries in the swap market: the top 10 U.S. banks by asset size comprise 9 of the 10 largest swap intermediaries among banks. In fact, because swaps are off-balance sheet items, central banks have raised the question that the narrow spreads being collected by the banks (and others) may be too small to cover the credit risk exposure of intermediaries.[6]

Swap Arbitrage

The preceding discussion covered arbitrage transactions between two relatively separate financial markets. Both swap parties were able to lower borrowing costs because the "price" of debt in one market is higher. Yet, the very action of setting up arbitrage will, inevitably, bring the two "prices" closer together, thereby cutting into arbitrage gains: added demand in low-cost market raises its (relative) "price"; reduced direct demand in high cost market will lower it. The two markets never quite come together because of the transaction cost of swaps, and the cost of risk.

Transaction costs, however, also are subject to compression as more and more swap originators begin to compete more aggressively and as they develop a secondary market in swaps. Indeed as other forms of swaps such as, for example, currency

---

[5]International Swap Dealers Association Inc., press release May 4, 1987, cited on p. 32 of Felgran, op. cit.

[6]In Table 6–3 the concept of "notional" value equals the principal of the two debt liabilities being swapped.

TABLE 6-3
Top 25 U.S. Banks by Notional Value of Swaps Outstanding (Thousands)

June 1987 Rank					
By Notional Value	By Asset Size	Bank	Notional Value June 1987	Notional Value Dec. 1986	Notional Value Dec. 1985
1	1	Citibank	$90,638,000	$66,071,000	$33,380,000
2	5	Chemical Bank	67,253,000	35,531,000	16,051,133
3	7	Bankers Trust	66,838,183	51,565,862	23,541,000
4	6	Manufacturers Hanover Trust	52,550,000	37,956,000	22,413,601
5	4	Morgan Guaranty Trust	50,730,600	40,193,800	21,450,700
6	3	Chase Manhattan Bank	40,051,644	21,948,194	9,994,300
7	8	Security Pacific National Bank	28,457,392	14,739,495	1,328,598
8	9	First National Bank of Chicago	19,381,043	17,722,840	8,458,000
9	2	Bank of America	14,172,000	11,489,000	7,367,000
10	15	First Interstate Bank	13,782,489	11,343,601	7,176,760
11	13	Marine Midland Bank	10,739,480	4,242,480	3,154,600
12	11	Mellon Bank	6,529,518	5,956,720	2,440,046
13	14	Irving Trust	4,898,851	2,437,141	502,400
14	10	Continental Illinois	4,615,319	4,923,875	3,322,362
15	16	Bank of New York	4,534,529	3,573,540	1,216,076
16	19	Bank of New England	2,319,680	1,412,192	312,333
17	22	Philadelphia National Bank	2,281,844	1,210,426	684,000
18	23	Harris Trust	2,117,715	2,109,170	1,603,700
19	20	Citibank South Dakota	2,100,000	945,000	0
20	21	Seattle–First National Bank	1,325,362	1,799,569	754,300
21	12	Bank of Boston	1,819,239	1,931,948	1,482,270
22	24	Comerica Bank—Detroit	1,540,716	1,565,716	1,168,000
23	26	Bank One Columbus	524,790	1,362,790	1,607,280
24	25	National City Bank	344,218	1,229,218	658,400
25	18	NCNB—North Carolina	228,709	689,942	10,000

Source: Board of Governors of the Federal Reserve System, Combined Call and Income File. 1987 data from call reports filed June 30, 1987. Other data from yearend call reports.

swaps (between different countries' exchange rates) and tax and regulatory arbitrage (between different countries' tax rates and regulations) begin, some very large foreign financial institutions, such as the world's largest banks, get into the game. These transactors have driven down profit spreads for intermediaries to very low levels—say, to a level between 10 and 20 basis points in 1986 to 1987.[7]

Developments in the swap market, like other successful financial innovations that promote more competitive markets, reflect a 4–I sequence:

1. Innovation.
2. Imitation (more competitors).
3. Institutionalization (larger-scale deals).
4. Internationalization (largest transactors in the world participate everywhere).

Broadly speaking, the imitators gain entry into the new market by lowering the cost to borrowers in "higher" market and/or raising costs in "lower." With institutionalization come the large deals in secondary as well as in primary markets that can help to rationalize the narrower spreads to intermediaries. And this broadening and deepening of the markets further helps to make transactions routine, and reduces perception of risk. Finally, the internationalization of the swap market (using foreign exchange swaps) brings in the largest transactors and also develops 24-hour trading as the swap "book" circulates around the world.

That internationalization through the 4–I process is not necessarily costless. The clearest gainers are the borrowers who, in fact, improve their "terms of trade." For the "market makers," namely the banks, the collection of 10 to 20 basis points per deal is, to be sure, not a major money maker. From the individual bank's point of view, the swap service is a useful entry point into other financial services for major clients. As a financial loss leader, the swap book may be a useful marketing device for a bank.[8]

---

[7]See Felgran, op. cit.

[8]The fact that swaps are "off-balance sheet" items may be seen as an additional advantage by some banks.

From the point of view of the lenders of last resort, the central banks, a different message is delivered. Concerns regarding capital adequacy have surfaced in a number of contexts, including the swap market. The Fed and the Bank of England agreed that, on *interest* swaps, a minimum of ½% per year should be retained as an equivalent offset to credit risk; this is a much lower offset than the proposal for *currency* swaps, which include a 5% flat rate *plus* a 1% per year retention against credit risk.

This analysis of the swap market has taken the discussion beyond the U.S. market. Within the U.S. market another innovative product, junk bonds, has followed the same sequence and, thereby, promoted competitive pressures for U.S. investment bankers as well as commercial banks. Drexel, Burnham, Lambert was the innovator in the junk bond market. The discussion of that market is another illustration of an innovation that, if it is successful, leads to a symbiosis[9] in market development.

INNOVATING HIGH-YIELD DEBT:
THE JUNK BOND MARKET

During the early 1980s, as the bond markets continued to experience wide rate gyrations, and many innovative financing techniques became routine, another innovative financing tool began to make inroads into the capital market, namely, junk bonds. This is called "innovative" even though low-rated debt has been found in the marketplace since debt has been rated. Junk bonds are those bonds rated below Moody's Baa, the lowest "investment grade." The idea that junk debt *at new issue* can be (1) an effective source of funding and (2) a high-return investment vehicle is behind the innovative success story of Drexel, Burnham, Lambert. The importance of that innovation can be perceived from Table 6–4 which indicates that in 1986, junk bonds constituted nearly one fifth of total corporate bond outstandings, rising from a modest 4% just seven years earlier. And

---

[9]Symbiosis is a term used in biology to describe a condition in which two (or more) organisms coexist, while sharing the same sources of food and shelter in the same environment in a mutually beneficial relationship.

TABLE 6–4
Corporate Straight Debt Outstanding: Total and Low Rated, 1979–1986
(In Billions of Dollars and Percent)

Year	1 Total	2 Low-Rated	3 Share of Low-Rated 2/1 (%)
1986	$505	$93	18
1985	420	59	14
1984	358	42	12
1983	319	28	9
1982	286	19	7
1981	255	17	7
1980	265	15	6
1979	270	11	4

Source: E. I. Altman, *The Anatomy of the High-Yield Debt Market: 1986 Update.* Morgan Stanley, April 1987, p. 2.

this has *not* been the product of wholesale downratings, but mainly from new-issue flotations. What are junk bonds, and why is their importance increasing?

In the words of one major rating agency (Moody's), ". . . bonds which are rated Ba are judged to have speculative elements; their future cannot be considered as well assured. . ." With respect to the next lower rating, ". . . bonds which are rated B generally lack characteristics of the desirable investment."[10] The other major rater, Standard & Poor's indicates that all bonds rated BB or less are ". . . predominantly speculative with respect to capacity to pay interest and repay principal. . ."[11] Clearly this is not meant to be sales copy for such issues.

On the other hand, investors who can diversify both among junk bond issues and across the quality spectrum can realize significant improvement over risk-free rates of return. They can do this even after discounting expected total return for the added, speculative risk.[12] (In mid-1987 junk bond yields ex-

---

[10]*Moody's Bond Record,* Moody's Investor Service, January 1984, p. 1.
[11]*Standard & Poor's Bond Guide,* Standard & Poor Corporation, July 1985, p. 10.
[12]The following is based on a study by E. S. Mulhare, "Junk bond market's resiliency," *Credit Review,* Standard & Poors, June 15, 1987.

ceeded Treasury yields of equivalent maturity by more than 400 basis points.) There are, in effect, some pricing inefficiencies in the bond market in which "investment grade" issues appear to be priced too aggressively relative to those that are not. This may still be the case even after two major recent disturbances, namely the insider trading scandals and some spectacular defaults in 1986. But because even mainstream asset managers feel the pressure of performance measures, junk bond portfolios with high total returns will seem very attractive.

Meanwhile, on the supply side the bonds keep coming, thereby holding up total return. One part of that supply surge is generated by the wave of corporate buyouts and takeovers, and other forms of restructuring, on the part of well-known firms. Household names like Beatrice Company and R. H. Macy have issued junk bonds as part of restructuring themselves; in addition, middle-range firms such as former divisions of Goodyear Tire and of Times Mirror Co. have issued debt under their own names (Motor Wheel Co. and Graphic Controls Co.). Funding restructurings on the wholesale or retail level has been based on junk bond issues.

Indeed, Standard & Poor's industrial bond rating distribution as of May 1987 indicates that out of its rating universe of 893 firms nearly 500—or more than half—fell into the junk bond category (see Table 6–5). As the table shows, BB is the median category. The innovative nature of junk-bond financing in the mid-1980s can be illustrated further by the fact that in 1982 the median group had been "A"-rated. It should be recalled, however, that measured by the dollar volume of debt issues or outstandings, investment-grade debt is far more important (see Table 6–4).

On the other hand, the fact is that new firms, or firms experiencing a spurt of growth in new, risky industries, have the same need for funds that they had when they were financed by venture capitalists or others. And this is the point where investment bankers (other than Drexel) perceived that an entry into the junk bond market for rapid-growth and risky firms might give them an opening to provide more conventional investment banking services when the borrowing firm reached a more secure maturity.

As Table 6–6 suggests, starting with 1984, the junk bond

TABLE 6–5
Industrial Rating Distribution*

Rating Category	No. of Companies
AAA	16
AA	71
A	171
BBB	138
BB	169
B	293
CCC	35
Total issuers	893

*Distribution as of mid-May 1987. Affiliated issuers counted as one company.

Source: E. Mulhare, op. cit.

TABLE 6–6
Financing Sources of Corporations: Business Loans versus Junk Bonds
1981–1986 (In Billions of Dollars; Yearly Change in Amounts Outstanding)

	Business Loans	Junk Bonds	Net Open Market Paper*
1981	53.8	2.3	16.9
1982	43.4	1.1	−6.5
1983	22.9	9.7	2.6
1984	73.6	13.5	23.1
1985	33.7	17.5	13.5
1986	40.8	32.8	8.1

*Issued by corporations only.

Source: E. I. Altman, *1986 Update*, op. cit. Table 6-4.

market became a significant competitor for bank loans in supplying funds to corporations. By 1985 and 1986, indeed, that competition supplied a volume of funds that corresponded to an equivalent of one half to three quarters of incremental bank loans (that is, increases in loans outstanding) to all forms of business. And as the third column of Table 6–6 shows, the volume of commercial paper outstanding that had served as the classic substitute for business loans also tended to recede in the mid-1980s with the surge of junk bond finances.[13]

Junk bond finance illustrates the development initiated by a particular investment banking firm, and its most important imitators, namely, the rest of the industry. As the industry succeeds it will take some business away from the previously dominant supplier of funds—in this case the business loans supplied by commercial banks. This phenomenon of an innovation leading to inter-industry competition will become even more strategically significant when innovative mortgage finance is discussed. Whereas that latter competition ultimately pitted investment bankers against S&Ls, the junk bond competition pits investment bankers against commercial bankers in a way heretofore neither discussed nor especially well understood. But more on this below.

With hindsight, the logic of any financial innovation is always quickly understood: the two requisites are (1) a need for funds that meets (2) a demand for the security that raises the funds. The early recognition of the logic makes the innovator; its success breeds imitation. That logic will now be assessed.

Market Entry by Investment Bankers

Investment bankers have a comparative advantage in building the foundation of any financial innovation: they know how to organize and how to trade in secondary markets. For example, as an essential support to the new-issue flotation of junk bonds, Drexel offered market-making services for the long pull to all of its customers. Recall that the major investors and traders in bond markets are institutions whose fiduciary obligations place

---

[13]The point being made here is that some firms in the corporate universe may now substitute junk bonds for *additional* bank loans. The monitoring role of banks will not necessarily be eliminated by the issuance of junk bonds, however. As long as banks make loans to a junk-bond borrower, their monitoring function continues at least to the extent that a share of the bank's assets are now at (greater?) risk with the new junk bond issue outstanding. Alternatively, to the extent that a bank issues a letter of credit to support a client's bond issue, other creditors *rent* that monitoring mechanism.

TABLE 6–7

New Issue Statistics by Lead Underwriter: 1982–1986 (In Millions of Dollars)

Underwriter	1986				1985			
	Amount	%	Number	%	Amount	%	Number	%
Drexel Burnham Lambert	15,775	45.86	82	35.04	7,239	49.71	83	44.15
Merrill Lynch	3,782	10.95	25	10.68	666	4.57	9	4.79
Morgan Stanley	2,817	8.16	15	6.28	1,050	7.21	13	6.91
Salomon Brothers	2,814	8.15	16	6.41	1,464	10.06	13	6.91
Shearson Lehman	1,903	5.51	11	4.60	708	4.86	8	4.26
First Boston	1,650	4.78	11	4.60	640	4.39	9	
Goldman Sachs	1,228	3.56	9	3.77	615	4.22	5	2.66
Bear Stearns	1,145	3.32	14	5.86	456	3.13	7	3.72
Kidder Peabody	880	2.55	7	2.93	—	—	—	—
Paine Webber	545	1.58	4	2.93	206	1.41	2	1.06
E.F. Hutton	370	1.07	5	2.09	280	1.92	2	1.06
Prudential-Bache	357	1.03	4	1.67	435	2.99	8	4.26
Donaldson, Lufkin & Jenrette Inc.	338	0.98	7	2.93	—	—	—	—
Others	864	2.50	24	9.62	804	5.52	29	15.43
Total	34,117		234		14,562		188	

Source: Morgan Stanley, op. cit.

quality constraints on portfolio decisions. Because junk bonds must compete with investment grade issues to be attractive to institutional portfolios, the capacity to trade them in size in secondary markets is an essential prerequisite for the institutional market. It was well understood that junk bonds offered attractive rates of return. A number of well publicized studies[14] indicated that, even in a risk-adjusted basis, such rates of return had, for some time, exceeded rates of return on investment grade, or Treasury issues. Less well understood was that the sufficient condition for an institutional investment committee of, say, an insurance company to take a flyer on junk bonds was the ability to get out of the decision without too much damage. *That* was the Drexel innovation.

As more and more institutional investors were attracted to

---

[14]See E. I. Altman and Scott Nammacher, *Investing In Junk Bonds,* John Wiley, New York, 1987 and sources cited there on pp. 247–250.

1984				1983				1982			
Amount	%	Number	%	Amount	%	Number	%	Amount	%	Number	%
10,358	69.28	67	54.03	4,346	58.60	46	53.49	1,544	55.18	28	58.33
530	3.54	4	3.23	427	5.76	5	5.81	699	24.99	7	14.58
310	2.13	5	4.03	80	1.08	1	1.16	—	—	—	—
865	5.79	9	7.26	423	5.70	4	4.05	—			
718	4.80	8	6.45	230	3.10	1	1.16	25	0.89	1	2.08
390	2.61	5	4.03	325	4.38	3	3.49	—	—	—	—
100	0.67	1	0.81	125	1.69	1	1.16	—	—	—	
360	2.41	4	3.23	380	5.12	5	5.81	35	1.25	1	2.08
—	—	—	—	—	—	—	—	—	—	—	—
66	0.43	1	0.81	235	3.17	3	3.49	225	8.04	1	2.08
145	0.97	3	2.42	100	1.66	2	2.33	83	2.95	2	4.17
950	6.35	13	10.48	275	3.71	6	6.98	40	1.43	1	2.08
—		—		—		—		—		—	
152	1.02	4	3.23	381	5.14	9	10.47	147	5.27	7	14.58
14,952		124		7,417		86		2,798		48	

this process, and particularly when interest rates began to decline after 1982, financial institutions were increasingly more willing to invest in "high-yield" issues. That was also the time during which new studies emerged that supported claims of the relative rate-of-return attractiveness—even after risk adjustment—of the high-yield bond portfolios. And last—but not least—pressures from institutional clients pressed each of the special bracket firms into becoming managers of junk bond flotations. Further, to give credibility to these syndicate leadership positions these same (increasingly less reluctant) investment bankers had to boost their own secondary market capability. That's how the junk bond market was helped to grow. And as Table 6–7 suggests, in 1986 the five largest bulge bracket firms led new-issue syndicates that constituted about 45% of new junk bond money, an amount about equal to the flotations volume of Drexel alone. In 1982, four of these special bracket firms had floated no junk bonds at all.

Another factor that encourages participation in new issue market by major investment banking firms was the wide new-issue spreads carried by even well-known names. As the recent prospectus covers show (see Appendix) these spreads still range between 2.36% and 3.75% for such bond issues at a time when the new-issue spreads of investment grade bonds were between one fifth and one tenth that size.[15]

The fact that the largest merger wave in U.S. history is contemporaneous with the surge of junk bond financing gave rise to the argument that such securities financed mainly hostile takeovers. To be sure, some junk bonds were so used.[16] But most of the funds raised went to new firms, or to ailing firms, whose only alternative source of funds had been commercial bank loans or trade credit.

Drexel has shown in a recent study that most U.S. firms with assets of $25 million or more are, in fact, below investment grade. Most of these firms are small, but some larger firms with low bond ratings are companies that have fallen on hard times; some of these down-rated bonds are called "fallen angels." In some four states (New Hampshire, Vermont, Colorado, and Alaska) not a single firm carries an investment-grade rating.

Finally, as a result of all of the above, Drexel has shouldered its way into the bulge bracket group. In looking at the rankings produced by Investment Dealers Digest or Institutional Investor, Drexel is now by any measure a special bracket firm. The fact that it leveraged its position on the fulcrum of its preeminence in the junk bond market is supported by the argument that its imitators—the other special bracket firms—needed Drexel to help make the secondary market work. At the same time, Drexel understood that a special bracket firm has to develop market shares in most of the traditional investment banking products. And this Drexel has done.

---

[15]For discussion of gross spreads on new issues see Chapters 14 and 15.

[16]Because nearly all special bracket firms now offer bridge financing to finance takeovers means that each investment banker's capital is now at disposal of bidding firms. Such financing is more immediately available to bidding firm than the proceeds from any flotation—junk or nonjunk.

REMAKING THE MARKET: INNOVATIVE GAINS TO USERS

In general, the greater the original inefficiency, the greater the original margin, the more competitors will follow, and hence the broader and deeper the new market will be. Market making by innovation is exactly that: in hindsight, the market can develop because, at inception, the cost of inefficiency to market users leaves a wide enough margin for the innovator and his imitators.

By the same efficient process, the old market's activity is drawn away. And while the original innovative firm may experience a reduction in profit margins per new issue or per trade, it is offset by volume. Further, imitators will offset those lessened returns (per unit) to originator by the risk reduction implicit in the deepening marketplace. For the old, displaced producers no such compensation exists.

LAST BUT NOT LEAST: THE BANKS

For an *un*threatened industry, the commercial banks, the partial substitution of junk bonds for bank loans that was discussed above is, from the point of view of the commercial banks, another example in which innovative finance is precluded *for them* at least in part by Glass–Steagall. Worse yet, the junk bond substitutes for bank loans competes away from the banks a significant share of the one product—namely business loans—that the regulatory segregation implicit in the Glass–Steagall Act had set aside for banks as their specialty product. The banks' claims for repeal of that act are usually framed very differently— namely, the need for a level playing field for public underwriting of new investment-grade corporate securities. If Glass–Steagall is set aside, one must wonder whether bank supervisors, or the Federal Deposit Insurance Corporation would be totally comfortable with (1) bank underwriting of junk bonds, and with (2) the banks' support system for such flotations that requires the large-scale dealing and positioning by banks of these issues in the secondary markets.

The preceding chapters indicated that in an increasingly transaction-oriented market, those institutions most comfortable with performance of dealer functions have done best. Deregulation and innovation provided the environment in which the most competitive firms, including investment bankers, were able to benefit. In that sense, *de*regulation, like regulation, may have a differential incidence on those being deregulated.

APPENDIX FIGURE 6–A1

PROSPECTUS

$500,000,000

Holiday Inns, Inc.

11% Subordinated Debentures due 1999

(Interest payable on April 1 and October 1)

The 11% Subordinated Debentures due 1999 (the "Debentures") are being issued by Holiday Inns, Inc. (the "Company") in connection with the proposed recapitalization (the "Recapitalization") of the parent of the Company, Holiday Corporation ("Holiday"), pursuant to which Holiday will distribute a cash dividend aggregating $1.55 billion to its stockholders. See "Plan of Recapitalization." The Recapitalization was approved by Holiday's stockholders at a special meeting held on February 27, 1987. However, not all conditions to the Recapitalization have been satisfied or waived, and they may not be satisfied or waived prior to the closing of this offering. It is possible that the Debentures will be sold and that the Recapitalization will not occur thereafter. Concurrently with this offering, the Company is offering $900 million principal amount of 10½% Senior Notes due 1994 (the "Senior Notes"). See "Financing of the Recapitalization."

The Debentures will be sold pursuant to delayed delivery contracts and will be delivered against payment therefor, subject to postponement under certain circumstances, on March 30, 1987 if certain conditions have been satisfied or waived. The Company will pay 0.625% of the aggregate principal amount of the Debentures to the purchasers upon delivery of executed delayed delivery contracts. See "Underwriting and Delayed Delivery Contracts."

The Debentures will be redeemable at the option of the Company, in whole or in part, at any time after April 1, 1990 at the redemption prices set forth herein, together with accrued interest, except that no such redemption may be made prior to April 1, 1992 from borrowings having an effective interest cost of less than 11% per annum. Annual mandatory redemption payments commencing April 1, 1997 are calculated to retire 60% of the principal amount of the Debentures prior to maturity.

The Debentures will be subordinated to all of the Company's Senior Debt (as defined), and will be effectively subordinated to the indebtedness of the Company's subsidiaries. If the Recapitalization is completed, immediately thereafter the Company will have Senior Debt and indebtedness of subsidiaries estimated at $2.4 billion. The Debentures will be guaranteed on a subordinated basis by Holiday, which if the Recapitalization is completed will have Senior Debt and indebtedness of subsidiaries (other than the Debentures) estimated at $2.5 billion immediately thereafter.

The Debentures will be listed on the New York Stock Exchange.

See "Risk Factors" for a description of certain risk factors to be considered by investors.

THESE SECURITIES HAVE NOT BEEN APPROVED OR DISAPPROVED BY THE SECURITIES AND EXCHANGE COMMISSION NOR HAS THE COMMISSION PASSED UPON THE ACCURACY OR ADEQUACY OF THIS PROSPECTUS. ANY REPRESENTATION TO THE CONTRARY IS A CRIMINAL OFFENSE.

THE ATTORNEY GENERAL OF THE STATE OF NEW YORK HAS NOT PASSED UPON OR ENDORSED THE MERITS OF THIS OFFERING. ANY REPRESENTATION TO THE CONTRARY IS UNLAWFUL.

NEITHER THE NEVADA GAMING COMMISSION NOR THE NEW JERSEY CASINO CONTROL COMMISSION HAS PASSED UPON THE ACCURACY OR ADEQUACY OF THIS PROSPECTUS.

	Price to Public	Underwriting Discount(1)	Proceeds to the Company(2)
Per Debenture	100%	3.75%	96.25%
Total	$500,000,000	$18,750,000	$481,250,000

(1) The Company and Holiday have agreed to indemnify the Underwriters against certain liabilities, including liabilities under the Securities Act of 1933. See "Underwriting and Delayed Delivery Contracts."

(2) Before deducting expenses of the Company estimated at $1,500,000.

The Debentures are being offered by Drexel Burnham Lambert Incorporated and Goldman, Sachs & Co., subject to prior sale and approval of certain legal matters by counsel, for delivery pursuant to delayed delivery contracts. It is expected that delivery of the executed delayed delivery contracts will be made on or about March 12, 1987 at the offices of Drexel Burnham Lambert Incorporated, 60 Broad Street, New York, New York.

Drexel Burnham Lambert   Goldman, Sachs & Co.
INCORPORATED

March 5, 1987

APPENDIX FIGURE 6–A2

PROSPECTUS

$400,000,000

R.H. Macy & Co., Inc.

★

14½% Senior Subordinated Debentures due 1998

R. H. Macy & Co., Inc. ("Macy") is the surviving corporation of the merger (the "Merger") of Macy Merger Corp. ("Merger Corp."), an indirect wholly-owned subsidiary of Macy Acquiring Corp. ("Acquiring Corp."), with and into Macy. Merger Corp. and Acquiring Corp. were formed to effect the acquisition of Macy. The Merger was consummated on July 15, 1986. The effective time of the Merger is hereinafter referred to as the "Effective Time". Macy prior to the Merger is sometimes referred to as "Old Macy" and Macy subsequent to the Merger is sometimes referred to as "New Macy". General Electric Credit Corporation ("GECC" or the "Selling Securityholder") purchased the 14½% Senior Subordinated Debentures due 1998 (the "Debentures") at the Effective Time and is offering such Debentures for sale to the public. See "THE MERGER". The Debentures are guaranteed by Acquiring Corp. on a senior subordinated basis. See "DESCRIPTION OF THE DEBENTURES—Guarantee".

See "RISK FACTORS" for a description of certain risks which should be considered by investors.

THESE SECURITIES HAVE NOT BEEN APPROVED OR DISAPPROVED BY THE SECURITIES AND EXCHANGE COMMISSION NOR HAS THE COMMISSION PASSED UPON THE ACCURACY OR ADEQUACY OF THIS PROSPECTUS. ANY REPRESENTATION TO THE CONTRARY IS A CRIMINAL OFFENSE.

	Initial Public Offering Price(1)	Underwriting Discounts(2)	Proceeds to Selling Securityholder(3)(4)
Per Senior Subordinated Debenture	106.00%	2.36%	103.64%
Total......................................	$424,000,000	$10,000,000	$414,000,000

(1) Plus accrued interest from July 15, 1986.

(2) Acquiring Corp. and New Macy have agreed to indemnify the Underwriters and GECC against certain liabilities, including liabilities under the Securities Act of 1933. See "UNDERWRITING".

(3) The Selling Securityholder purchased $400,000,000 principal amount of the Debentures in connection with the Merger. New Macy received all of the proceeds from such purchase. New Macy will not receive any proceeds from this Offering.

(4) The Selling Securityholder may be deemed to be an "underwriter" within the meaning of the Securities Act of 1933. See "SELLING SECURITYHOLDER".

The Debentures will be offered severally by the Underwriters, subject to receipt and acceptance by them and subject to their right to reject any order in whole or in part. It is expected that the Debentures will be ready for delivery in fully registered form at the office of Goldman, Sachs & Co., New York, New York, on or about July 24, 1986.

Goldman, Sachs & Co.   Kidder, Peabody & Co.
Incorporated

The date of this Prospectus is July 17, 1986

APPENDIX FIGURE 6–A3

$55,000,000

Queen City Broadcasting of New York, Inc.

13½% Subordinated Debentures due August 1, 1999

**Guaranteed on a Subordinated Basis as to
Payment of Principal, Premium, if any, and Interest by**

Queen City Broadcasting, Inc.

The Debentures are being issued by Queen City Broadcasting of New York, Inc. (the "Company"). Payment is guaranteed on a subordinated basis by the Company's parent corporation, Queen City Broadcasting, Inc. ("Queen City"). Interest on the Debentures is payable on February 1 and August 1 of each year, commencing February 1, 1988. The Debentures may not be redeemed prior to August 1, 1992; thereafter, they may be redeemed in whole or in part at the option of the Company at any time at the redemption prices set forth herein. The Company is also required to redeem $40,000,000 principal amount of Debentures ($10,000,000 on January 2, 1996, $15,000,000 on August 1, 1997 and $15,000,000 on August 1, 1998) through a sinking fund which is intended to retire approximately 73% of the Debentures prior to maturity. The Debentures and Guarantees will be subordinated in right of payment to all of the Company's and Queen City's Senior Indebtedness (as defined). See "Description of Debentures and Guarantees".

For a discussion of certain matters which should be considered in evaluating an Investment in the Debentures, see "Risk Factors".

THESE SECURITIES HAVE NOT BEEN APPROVED OR DISAPPROVED BY THE SECURITIES AND EXCHANGE COMMISSION NOR HAS THE COMMISSION PASSED UPON THE ACCURACY OR ADEQUACY OF THIS PROSPECTUS. ANY REPRESENTATION TO THE CONTRARY IS A CRIMINAL OFFENSE.

	Initial Public Offering Price(1)	Underwriting Discount(2)	Proceeds to Company(1)(3)
Per Debenture	100%	3.25%	96.75%
Total	$55,000,000	$1,787,500	$53,212,500

(1) Plus accrued interest from August 1, 1987.

(2) The Company and Queen City have agreed to indemnify Goldman, Sachs & Co. against certain liabilities, including liabilities under the Securities Act of 1933.

(3) Before deducting estimated expenses of $350,000 payable by the Company.

The Debentures are offered by Goldman, Sachs & Co. subject to receipt and acceptance by them and subject to their right to reject any order in whole or in part. It is expected that the Debentures will be ready for delivery at the offices of Goldman, Sachs & Co., New York, New York, on or about August 24, 1987.

Goldman, Sachs & Co.

The date of this Prospectus is August 17, 1987.

7

THE MACRO SIDE OF THE INNOVATION PROCESS: HOW MARKETS CHANGE

By far the largest type of non-federal debt obligation issued each year in the U.S. capital market is the residential mortgage (see Figure 7–1). This is the product of the high social approval carried by home ownership, as well as its political popularity. The many housing acts passed by the Congress since the Great Depression of the 1930s attest to all of the above. The evident need to keep on fixing the mortgage market also reveals the complexities of a national policy process attempting to provide financial accommodation to a basically local instrument—a residential mortgage. The Housing and Urban Development Act of 1968[1] was one of the early attempts specifically designed to improve mortgage financing, as it followed in the wake of a surge in interest rates and other financial disturbances of the credit crunch year 1966.[2]

---

[1]House of Representatives, *Housing and Urban Development Act of 1968,* 90th Congress, 2nd Session, Report No. 1785.

[2]The following is based partly on E. Bloch, "The Setting of Standards of Supervision for Savings and Loan Associations," in I. Friend, ed., *Study of the Savings and Loan Industrsy,* Federal Home Loan Bank Board, 1969, pp. 1620–73 and on E. Bloch, "Moving Mortgage Finance into the Capital Market: GNMAs and Other Mortgage-Backed Issues," Salomon Brothers Center Working Paper, November 1980.

FIGURE 7–1
Long-Term Borrowing: Private Domestic Nonfinancial Sectors

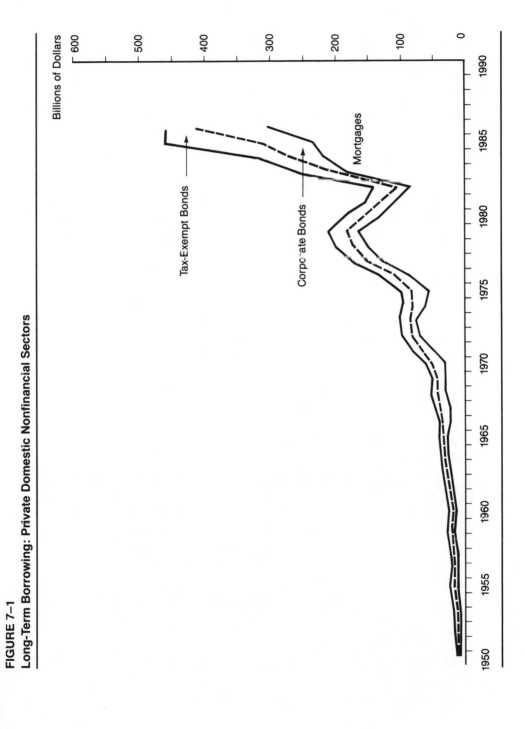

THE 1968 LEGISLATION

Several House and Senate bills were combined into the "Housing and Urban Development Act of 1968." Among the items included was a specific set of quantified housing goals (Title XVI), along with the requirement that the president report annually to the Congress, for a decade, on the ". . . realization of the goal. . ." according to the Conference Report.[3]

With respect to financing policy, the Act included Title VIII, "Secondary Mortgage Market," whose purposes, as given in the Conference Report,[4] included the organization of the "Government National Mortgage Association" (GNMA, Ginny May) that would be part of the Government [Housing and Urban Development (HUD)], and would retain the assets and liabilities of the previously existing corporation (FNMA).

But most important, in Section 804, subsection (d) was added "to provide a greater degree of liquidity to the mortgage investment market and an additional means of financing its operations . . . Accordingly the corporation is authorized to set aside any mortgages held . . . under this section and . . . to issue and sell securities based upon the mortgages so set aside. Securities issued . . . may be in the form of debt obligations or trust certificates of beneficial interest . . . Mortgages set aside . . . shall at all times be adequate to enable the corporation to make timely principal and interest payments on the securities . . ."[5]

In the original House Report[6] the Committee on Banking and Currency had shrewdly observed that these (GNMA-guaranteed) securities ". . . could have a greater liquidity than the mortgages backing them and can be expected to attract sources of investment funds which do not ordinarily invest in the mortgage market, such as pension funds and retirement funds." In the *Second Annual Report* by the President on the National Housing Goal in 1970 no such prescience was shown, however.

---

[3]Op. cit., p. 138.
[4]Op. cit., p. 66, sec. 801.
[5]Op. cit., pp. 73–74.
[6]90th Congress, 2nd Session, House Report No. 1585, June 25, 1968, p. 70.

In estimating the volume of GNMA pools "it is expected that $1 billion of these new securities will be sold in 1970. This annual level of security sales is projected for each of the years 1971–78."[7]

In fact, a generation later (at this writing in 1988), the GNMA passthrough program set up in 1968 is still influencing the structure of mortgage finance. During the 1960s and early 1970s it appeared to be a supplement to the savings and loan association (S&L) process by providing a federally managed structure for the intermediation process of the savings and loan industry. That passthrough structure served to mobilize funds from a national financial market beyond each of the (more limited) local savings markets. The market changes that occurred then, and in the 1980s, have fundamentally changed the method by privatizing it.

HOUSING FINANCE PROBLEMS AND FINANCIAL INTERMEDIATION

The financing side of housing has attracted governmental attention in nearly all countries. The problem is complicated by the financial instrument used, namely, the mortgage. It is an ancient legal device, already well established in Roman times, and, in spite of some awkward financial aspects, has undergone relatively little change on the legal side. What makes it financially awkward is the necessarily *local* nature of the characteristics that give it value, such as location (e.g., with respect to social amenities); (regional) differences in creditors' rights during slow pay or foreclosure; the fact that monthly amortization payments reduce the size of the debt, and thus complicate the valuation process further; and other legal and economic characteristics peculiar to the site of housing so financed.[8]

---

[7] *Second Annual Report,* 1970, p. 100.

[8] The legal instrument conveys a property and provides a security for payment of debt. By using a residence as collateral, households with relatively little equity can acquire funds large enough to purchase a residence valued at several times their net

These technical differences also help to explain why the use of local financial intermediaries to finance and service mortgages has been found convenient: (1) The acquaintance of local intermediaries with local conditions (either as unit firms in some states, or through branches) tends to reduce credit risk through information. (2) Support to these local institutions was provided by nationally based funding schemes such as GNMA and/or the Federal Home Loan Bank System (FHLBS).

These government support actions make possible the following (seeming) paradox: while mortgages constitute the largest single type of private financial instrument of this country's capital market, the ratio of direct trading of mortgages in secondary markets to the amount of outstanding mortgages is in all probability the lowest of any type of debt. This combination of inefficient markets, large size, and high social value attached to housing and residential construction has resulted in a good deal of tinkering with the process of financial intermediation—that is, with the policies that affect the institutions that originate, finance, and hold mortgages. Only in more recent times has there been any success in developing policy substitutes for improving the trading characteristics of the mortgage instrument itself.

The major factor behind the early legislative and administrative policy tinkering is the vulnerability of mortgage-lending institutions to disintermediation. That loss of funds follows when (money) market interest rates rise above savings-deposit rates. At such times, by supervisory regulation, financial intermediaries were not permitted to raise deposit rates (the best-known is the Fed's Regulation Q). But more fundamentally, these intermediaries could not have afforded to meet the market

---

worth or annual income. Although debt service terms have become more flexible over time those terms for the majority of residential mortgages involve equal monthly installments over the life of the loan. Level payments at the beginning consist mainly of interest, and at the end, mostly of amortization. In practice, however, relatively few mortgages are held to maturity. Most are refinanced (or repaid to lender) prior to contract maturity. Such refinancing may result from a change in residence (due to death, divorce, or a move to another area), or from the default of debtor. See Appendix 1 for discussion of prepayments.

rates of the 1970s and early 1980s because the average revenue rate of their (aged) mortgage portfolios fell below the marginal cost (which may also come close to average cost) of their current and volatile savings deposits.

This is not the place to give a detailed discussion of the problems of the S&L industry today. Data issued by the Federal Home Loan Bank Board[9] show a continuous decline in *number* of insured institutions between 1970 and 1986 (from 4,365 to 3,220), and while their net income averaged a positive $2.2 billion per year in the 1970s, that average dropped to a net annual average *loss* of $60 million in the 1980s.

To the extent that nationwide government institutions such as the Federal Home Loan Banks support member S&L intermediaries and offer assistance following disintermediation emergencies, a national savings market can, at least indirectly, begin to support an (essentially) local financial institution that finances and services local mortgages.[10] The rise in allocational efficiency thus obtained supplements institutional intermediation by a modest broadening of the reach of savings mobilization through federal intervention.

SECURITY INTERMEDIATION

The development of GNMA passthrough permitted a more general shift in the mortgage financing process away from local deposit-type intermediaries to the capital market where any financial investor, including the intermediary, has the opportunity to pick up a mortgage-backed security. This broadens allocational efficiency for mortage financing by the addition of a nationally

---

[9]See *Combined Financial Statements 1986,* especially Tables I to VII, Washington, D.C., 1987.

[10]Mortgage "servicing" includes the gathering in of monthly debt service payments and can go as far as the management and disposal of real estate in the event of slow pay and/or foreclosure. In all of these local administrative tasks there are obvious elements of (local) economies of scale.

available security that can trade on a national or an institutional market.

To underwrite this change, at the beginning, an additional institution called a "mortgage banker" enters the process. That institution is important to *security* intermediation (as contrasted with S&L intermediation) because it is needed to assemble and package the mortgages initially, and subsequently to provide a facility for collecting (monthly) interest and amortization payments and transmitting that debt service through to (GNMA) debt holders. In technical terms this is called "servicing" a mortgage portfolio. Since the large-scale issuance of GNMA securities has become routine, mortgage bankers have used the capital markets not only to place their output of assembled mortgage passthrough securities, but also to finance mortgage inventory.[11]

In addition, the very marketability of the GNMA-type issue not only opens wider markets at *new* issue, but the marketability of "seasoned" (i.e., partly amortized) securities further provides a secondary market, thereby developing liquidity and pricing continuity. The existence of GNMA dealers, investment bankers, and the competitive markets that they make also provides the issuers of all mortgages with more price information along with greater transaction efficiency.

Finally, and perhaps most importantly, the availability and marketability of GNMA passthroughs of substantial size permitted institutional investors to consider seriously, and for the first time, an instrument that finances residential mortgages. To be sure, a number of institutional investors had always invested in whole loans (i.e., large-scale mortgages, or bundles of relatively homogeneous residential loans). The introduction of the new instrument made feasible the financing of any (packaged) mortgage loan by the largest and fastest-growing pool of institutional funds in the U.S. capital market.

---

[11]Mortgage bankers may be organized as exclusively local institutions, but most of the large firms in the industry are nationwide in scope, with many local offices. In one sense, mortgage bankers perform as *nationwide* institutions in finance in a manner *not* permitted by legislation that governs the typical mortgage investor (e.g., a financial intermediary) such as a bank or nonbank institution.

What was not understood at the time was that the very attractiveness of the government-underwritten passthroughs began to shift savings flows more or less permanently away from the S&L intermediaries. These flows were switched into direct investments, namely, GNMAs, and subsequently into their improved mortgage-backed innovations.

Structural Characteristics of Mortgage Passthrough Securities

The pooling of mortgages for refinancing via a passthrough security is technically a sale of assets by the originator to the packager; at the same time the packager resells a set of "undivided" interests in the pool to the investor. The latter point means that each buyer acquires cash flows from the "securitized" mortgages of interest and amortization as well as prepayments equal to his proportionate share in the pool. For his efforts the packager collects a "servicing fee" deducted from the "proportionate" share of all cash flows that are "passed through" to the investor every month. The fact that GNMA passthroughs were supported not only by federal backing to the securities (they were backed by "full faith and credit" of the United States) but that each of the original pools consisted of Federal Housing Authority (FHA) (government-insured) and Veterans' Administration (VA) (government-guaranteed) mortgages helped to open up the market by eliminating any vestige of credit risk. Subsequent to the original type of passthrough (called GNMA I), some modifications were made to improve the availability of this type of refinancing to smaller issuers, shorter terms (than 30 years), graduated payment mortgages, etc.[12]

Since the early 1970s, some other federal housing agencies have entered this market, namely, the Federal Home Loan Mortgage Corporation ("Freddy Mac") and the Federal National

---

[12]For a detailed discussion of various types of passthroughs see K. H. Sullivan, B. Collins, D. A. Smilow, "Mortgage Pass-Through Securities" in F. Fabozzi and I. M. Pollack, eds., *The Handbook of Fixed Income Securities,* 2nd ed., Dow-Jones Irwin, Homewood, Illinois, 1987, pp. 383–403.

Mortgage Corporation ("Fanny May"). Table 7–1 summarizes the characteristics of these various types of passthroughs, including the mortgage types included and their maturities, the minimum pool size, etc. The minimum purchase size per passthrough at original issue was $25,000. with increments of $5,000 for Ginny May and Fanny May issues. For Freddy Mac issues only $25,000 pieces were available.

Because these issues are *passthroughs,* they pay *monthly* cash flows.[13] The idea behind the selling of only *large* pieces was to reduce the competitive aspect of these securities pulling *retail* savings away from the savings institutions. At that time it was believed that excess competition for savings with those institutions (e.g., S&Ls) would have a counterproductive impact on their capacity to originate mortgages, and thus cut into the financing rate of residential construction.

In view of the fact that the GNMA passthroughs carry no credit risk, their rates of return to investors are frequently compared to yields on U.S. Government securities. Two profound differences exist between the yield characteristics of these two types of securities: First, interest payments on Treasuries are semiannual whereas passthroughs pay monthly interest (and amortization); this tends to raise passthrough rates of return. Second, not only are Treasuries essentially noncallable, but the increasing monthly amortization payments and the nonpredictable rate of prepayments make passthroughs much shorter issues than would be implied by a securitized portfolio of 30-year mortgages purchased at new issue. This shortening of maturities, and shortening them via prepayment of mortgages especially when interest rates fall, tends to reduce the capital gains potential of passthroughs relative to Treasuries. Putting this proposition in a secondary market context, a move by passthrough issues to a premium (owing to a drop in interest rates) would, at best, be limited and even short-circuited because mort-

---

[13]These securities are called "fully modified passthroughs" because they carry guarantees of timely payment of both interest and principal.

TABLE 7–1
Agency Passthrough Programs

	GNMA I	GNMA II	FHLMC	FNMA
Issuer	FHA-approved lender	FHA-approved lender(s) (single-issuer and multiple-issuer pools)	FHLMC	FNMA
Underlying mortgages	FHA/VA	FHA/VA	Conventional or FHA/VA	Conventional or FHA/VA
Guarantee	Full and timely payment of principal and interest	Full and timely payment of principal and interest	Full and timely payment of interest and eventual full payment of principal, or full and timely payment of principal and interest (separate programs)	Full and timely payment of principal and interest
Guarantor	GNMA (full faith and credit of U.S. Government)	GNMA (full faith and credit of U.S. Government)	FHLMC	FNMA
Monthly payment	Multiple checks, one for each certificate*	One check per investor for all holdings*	Federal funds	Federal funds
Delivery	Physical (definitive) certificate; settlement in federal funds*	Physical (definitive) certificate; settlement in federal funds*	Book-entry through Federal Reserve banks; settlement in federal funds	Book-entry through Federal Reserve banks; settlement in federal funds
Days to first payment	45	50	75	54
Denomination	$25,000 minimum, $5,000 increment	$25,000 minimum, $5,000 increment	$25,000 minimum	$25,000 minimum, $5,000 increment

*Conversion to book-entry system through Mortage-Backed Securities Clearing Corp. (MBSCC) now under way. Monthly payments and settlement after conversion are expected to be made in Federal funds.

gage borrowers tend systematically to prepay when rates fall by some significant, but not unusual, amounts.[14]

On the other hand, slowing prepayment rates when interest rates are rising (and when long-term debt issues are falling in price) will tend to extend capital losses in a way similar to Treasuries of like maturity. An understanding of this prepayment option is crucially important to an understanding of the securitized mortgage market. (See Appendix 1.)

Passthrough Problems

Once passthrough securities became a familiar instrument in the financial market, their excellent credit rating as well as higher rates of return, when compared to Treasuries, made them attractive to conservative institutional investors. Clearly, the ability to trade in the secondary markets made such instruments preferable to the mortgages themselves for institutional investors. The relative preference of passthroughs over Treasuries, however, was problematic. At first, rules of thumb were used to take account of the unpredictable prepayment schedule of, say, mortgages issued with original maturities of 30 years. That rule was to assume an effective life of 12 years for passthroughs (based on 30-year mortgages) to quote mortgage yields. That 12-year convention was based on the FHA experience through the 1960s. By the 1970s the rise in interest rates, and particularly the rise in rate variances, led to somewhat earlier—and even less predictable—rates of prepayments.

Any rate cycle would lead to rapid prepayments, especially if the reverse slope of the peak was a steep one. And since, from an investor's point of view, prepayment rates are the function of not only unpredictable future interest rates, but also of the even less predictable exercise of mortgagees' put options, that rule of

---

[14]This also assumes that there are no special technical obstacles to refinancing individual mortgages. But recall that lenders prefer higher mortgage earnings to lower; one might assume at best a deliberate speed in the processing of mortgage refinancings. In any case, a clustering of refinancing decisions at particular times would present peak-load rationing difficulties on the personnel side alone.

thumb standard of 12 years could fall to periods as short as five or six years.

In secondary markets premium passthroughs (that is, packaged mortgages with above-market contract rates) would have a much more rapid paydown than discount purchases; and the same argument goes for shallow versus deep discount acquisitions if rates continued to fall. In the face of rising rate variance, the built-in unpredictability, as well as the nonhomogeneous size of the (partly paid down) passthrough, defeated to some extent the advantages that had permitted efficient trading of passthroughs in secondary markets.

NEXT STEPS IN SECURITIZATION: THE COLLATERALIZED MORTGAGE OBLIGATION (CMO)

Following one of the most turbulent episodes of interest-rate volatility in the early 1980s, the first CMO was issued by another government agency, the Federal Home Loan Mortgage Corporation (FHLMC, or "Freddy Mac") in June 1983.[15] Fundamentally, the CMO mortgage component on the *input* side is similar to the passthrough: it is a portfolio of mortgages (or even a set of passthroughs) that is to be securitized. Where the CMO differs is on the *output,* or investor-oriented, side.

In a passthrough, each investor receives a proportionate share of all cash flows such as principal, interest, and prepayments (net of the servicing fee). If the investor buys 10% of a passthrough issue he gets one tenth of all of the above as payments are made. And, as emphasized in the preceding section, these prepayments may produce much shorter maturities, and hence different yields, than expected by each of the investors.

The CMO restructures investor cash flows by maturity group, or *tranche.* By and large, the typical CMO channels

---

[15]Recall that the first mortgage passthrough was also issued by a federal agency, namely, GNMA.

amortization and/or prepayments to retire each of the group of CMO bonds (or *tranches*) in sequence; in contrast, the pass-through treats all investors equally. Under one typical arrangement the CMO *short-term* investor would be the first to receive (beyond interest) all of the amortization and prepayment cash flows; in some issues only one class of investor at a time would receive principal payments, depending on the stipulations contained in the CMO prospectus (see Figure 7–2).* The first Freddy Mac CMO carried *tranche* maturities of 5 years to 25 years, with an expected maturity range (due to prepayments) of 3 to 21 years. The shorter *tranches* carry less interest rate risk and, by shifting earliest prepayments exclusively to them, this gives longer tranches some degree of call protection (at least when compared to passthroughs). By thus decreasing yield uncertainty, while maintaining protection from credit risk, total demand for such issues, and by extension, for securitized mortgage finance, was increased by this type of financial innovation.

This process had two effects:

1. It raised effective demand for mortgages, thereby increasing total availability of credit for housing. It probably also lowered rates below what they would have been otherwise, thereby qualifying more lower-income families for more housing.
2. It reduced demand for intermediation-related finance for housing by shifting more investors to the direct investment market, namely CMOs.

The importance of the second point may emerge when one considers that, prior to the introduction of CMOs, that market-place had been dominated by 15- to 30-year (original maturity) passthroughs. The uncertainties associated with unpredictable effective maturities of these issues, as well as their longer term maturities, made them less than attractive to a significant number of substantial fixed-income investors. A much broader array

---

*For source of Figure 7–2, see "Introduction to Mortgages and Mortgage Backed Securities," K. Jeanne Person, September 1987. Copyright © 1987 by Salomon Brothers Inc.

FIGURE 7–2
CMO Cash Flows (Home Mac Mortgage Securities, Series 1987-1;
125% PSA,* in Millions of Dollars)

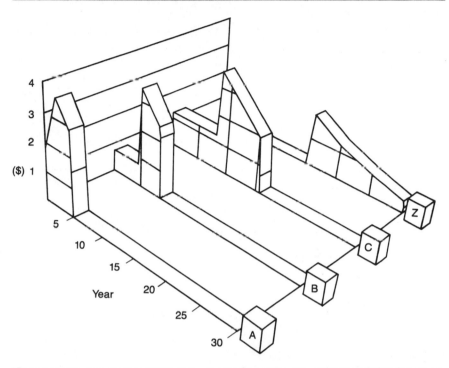

*Prepayments assumed at 125% of the Public Securities Administration (PSA) Standard.

of investors were attracted by the shorter life CMO tranches be
cause they offered more predictable timing in return of principal
(as well as higher yields than Treasuries); this also implied easier resale in secondary market. That particular innovation thus
produced more competitive pressure in the markets for savings
inflows, the absolutely essential raw material for the S&L industry. But the greater surge of investment funds into the mortgage financing market at the investment end generated a kind
of reverse of Say's law: mortgage origination was probably stimulated by the increased demand for the investment product at
the end of the CMO chain.

Indeed, the demand for investment product continued to grow. Gross CMO issuance grew from less than $5 billion in 1983 to nearly $50 billion in 1986, and to an annual rate of about $80 billion in the first quarter of 1987.

The typical CMO structure of cash flows is laid out in Figure 7–3. To avoid clutter, only the essential components are presented and only the simplest type of issue is illustrated. It will

FIGURE 7–3
A: Cash Flow Diagram for CMO.

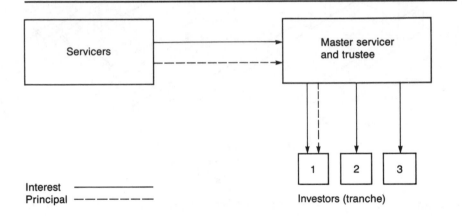

B: After First *Tranche* Is Retired.

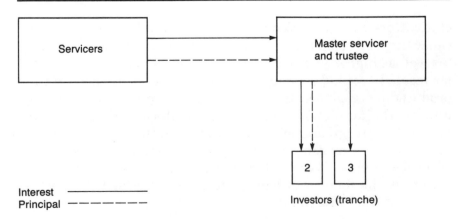

be assumed in the schematic below that there are only three classes of investors.[16]

As Figure 7–3A suggests, a number of servicers in the field transfer the cash flows generated by the collateral mortgages (or the collateral passthroughs) of the CMO to the master servicer and trustee. Many CMOs were set up to transfer prepayments to sequential tranches: for example, *tranche 1* would receive *all* principal payments until fully paid off; following its elimination, all prepayments would then be routed to *tranche 2* until it was fully refunded; all residual cash flows would then be routed to *tranche 3*.

This rather simple process provided little beyond a segmentation of the cash flows that a passthrough would generate, and thus attracted only a modest increment to the typical set of passthrough investors. To improve attractiveness to investors, packagers began to offer add-ons, such as a minimum repayment schedule that might exceed that expected, or guaranteed, by the underlying collateral: it is, in fact, a sinking fund feature.

Table 7–2 illustrates the mechanics of a guaranteed minimum sinking fund in which issuers/packagers have approximated the cash flows that would have been generated by a high-quality, sinking fund bond. In period 1, sinking fund requires transfer to investors of $1,000. Because mortgage collateral generated cash flows of only $500 (column 2), the issuer had to lend the $500 difference. In period 2, collateral payment ($900) equaled guarantee ($900), thus leaving the $500 "loan" unchanged. In period 3, a $100 principal shortfall raised issuer's "loan" to $600. In period 4, a $200 "excess" return of principal was applied to return the issuer's advances. In period 5, a $1,400 return of principal was applied, first, to the issuer's advance ($400), thereby cleaning up that account. The remaining $1,000 could then be applied to any subsequent CMO *tranche*, like any other prepayment. For the packager, the (lending) service thus provided carries a cost that, from his point of view, should at least be met, if not exceeded, by the better return generated by

---

[16]This illustration is based on G. J. Parseghian, "Collateralized Mortgage Obligations," in Fabozzi and Pollack, eds., op. cit. pp. 404–21.

TABLE 7–2
Sinking Fund Support to Investors*

Period	(1) Principal Guaranteed to Bondholders	(2) Cash Flow Generated by Collateral in Excess of That Needed for Interest	(3) (2) − (1) Excess (+) or Shortfall (−)	(4) Advance Required by Issuer	(5) Return of Advances	(6) (3) − (5) Excess Paid to Bondholders
1	$1,000	$ 500	$ −500	$500	0	NA
2	900	900	0	0	0	0
3	800	700	−100	100	0	NA
4	700	900	200	0	200	0
5	600	2,000	1,400	0	400	1,000

*Provided by issuer/packager.

124

this issue. Partly, that return could come from a rating quality improvement related to the guarantee feature of the sinking fund.

Other variations on the theme of replicating conventional credit instruments with CMO *tranches* were the use of issuer cash flow management and/or supplements to *accrual bonds* (the equivalent of zero coupon bonds) which are frequently called "Z" *tranches*. Since *interest payment* on these *tranches* is deferred to maturity, it is, in fact, these investors who now provide the "loan add-on" service that in the "sinking-fund" *tranche* was provided by the issuer/packager. To be sure, the issuer is still liable for providing the cash flows needed to fulfill his obligations. If the issuer needs added funds he may, of course, use whatever assets he may have as collateral for financing (temporary) needs for funds. The development of a money-market-related supplement to the CMO market will be discussed below.

Another strategic factor in raising the demand by investors for mortgage-backed issues is the capacity of underwriters of CMOs to trade them in the secondary market. By thus offering liquidity to investors, investment bankers enhance their activity as underwriters and traders in this specialized marketplace.

Transactions in secondary market are not hard to arrange once valuation problems are solved. This is so because CMOs carry AAA credit ratings, first, because they may be backed by mortgage passthroughs enhanced by federal agency guarantees. Second, if insured by private agencies, pool insurance is taken to guarantee timely payment, and a second private insurance policy guarantees all loans that carry loan/value ratios above a certain level. Those AAA ratings, moreover, are deemed to be more secure than those on corporate bonds because quality on CMO issues reflects a collateralized structure (see Figure 7–4) that makes the issuer's (or sponsor's) credit quality irrelevant.[17] As the underlying securities pay down as time passes, credit

---

[17]This also derives from the freestanding organization of CMO issuers. These are mostly single-purpose finance subsidiaries that are incorporated for the sole purpose of issuing CMOs. The mortgage collateral is held by a third-party custodial bank. In fact, CMO ratings are typically better than those of their issuer-sponsors.

FIGURE 7–4
Generic CMO Structure

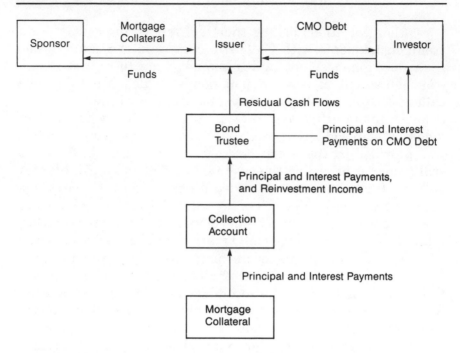

quality is not going to change. For the typical CMO investor, those issues are likely to carry less credit risk, and have in the past carried better yields, than similarly rated corporates. It should be emphasized in this investor context that the ability to trade CMOs—even if it is rarely exercised—presents a substantial benefit to the typical portfolio manager.

Whatever the perceptions of market participants, the effect of the securitization process was to provide a competitive substitute for the S&L direct investment (or warehousing) process.

A study by Kenneth T. Rosen[18] indicates that, while the *se-*

---

[18]*Securitization and the Mortgage Market.* Copyright © 1987 by Salomon Brothers Inc. August 1987. This paper was originally given at the annual conference of the Federal Home Loan Bank of San Francisco in December 1986.

TABLE 7–3
Flow of Securitized Single-Family Mortgages, 1975–First Quarter 1987 (In Billions of Dollars)

	1–4 Family Mfg. Orig.	Gross Securitized Mfg. Flow*	Securitized Seasoned Loans	Percent of Mfg. Flow Securitized†	Publicly Offered Passthrough Issuance			
					GNMA	FNMA	FHLMC	Conventional
1975	$ 7.8	$ 7.9	—	10.1	$ 7.4	—	$ 0.5	—
1976	113	⁻4.8	—	13.1	13.8	—	1.0	—
1977	162	21.7	—	13.4	17.4	—	4.1	$0.2
1978	185	21.8	—	11.8	15.4	—	5.7	0.7
1979	187	29.1	—	15.6	24.9	—	3.8	0.4
1980	134	23.3	—	17.4	20.6	—	2.5	0.2
1981	98	18.6	$ 4.2E	14.7	14.3	$ 0.7	3.5	0.1
1982	97	54.4	34.5E	20.5	16.0	14.0	24.2	0.2
1983	202	84.8	14.8E	34.7	50.5	13.3	19.5	1.5
1984	204	60.3	21.3E	19.1	27.9	13.5	18.7	0.2
1985	246	110.8	28.4E	33.5	45.9	23.6	38.9	2.4
1986	443	263.2	65.0E	44.7	98.2	60.6	97.8	6.6
1987‡	104	75.1	19.1E	53.8	31.1	⁻5.7	25.1	3.2

*Summation of issuance of publicly offered GNMA, FNMA, FHLMC, and conventional mortgage passthroughs.
†Gross securitized mortage flow less seasoned loans, divided by 1–4 family mortgage originations.
‡Through the first quarter of 1987.
E, Estimate.

Sources: U.S. Department of Housing and Urban Development, Board of Governors of the Federal Reserve, GNMA, FNMA, FHLMC, and Securities Data Corporation.

TABLE 7–4
Savings Institutions' Secondary Market and Borrowing Activity,
1975–First Quarter 1987 (In Billions of Dollars)

	Purchases of Mortgages	Sales of Mortgages	Net Sales	Net Change FHLB Advances	Other Borrowings
1975	8.5	5.2	(3.3)	(0.4)	(0.1)
1976	12.8	8.4	(4.4)	(1.8)	0.2
1977	14.5	13.8	(0.7)	4.2	4.4
1978	11.0	15.5	4.5	12.1	2.9
1979	12.0	18.3	6.3	8.5	3.9
1980	13.0	15.9	2.9	6.7	2.9
1981	10.5	12.6	2.1	15.9	8.7
1982	23.3	53.4	30.1	0.9	7.6
1983	45.8	55.4	9.6	(6.7)	7.3
1984	64.2	63.8	(0.4)	15.0	24.0
1985	62.4	104.6	42.2	13.2	7.7
1986	69.0	170.2	101.2	15.7	23.7
1987*	15.3	34.5	19.2	(2.8)	6.7

*Through the first quarter of 1987.

Source: Federal Home Loan Bank Board.

TABLE 7–5
Issuers of CMOs, January 86–June 87 (In Billions of Dollars)

	Amount	Percentage of Total
Investment banks	47.4	56.7
FHLMC	2.7	3.2
Home builders	14.6	17.5
Mortgage bankers	9.9	11.9
Insurance companies	1.5	1.8
Thrifts	7.3	8.7
Commercial banks	0.2	0.2
Total issuance	83.6	100.0

TABLE 7–6
Major Institutional Investors Buying CMOs, 1986*

Tranche	Thrifts (%)	Commercial Banks (%)	Insurance Companies (%)	Pension Funds (%)
Class A	8.7	24.3	11.2	44.5
Class B	13.0	21.0	19.3	39.0
Class C	5.2	5.8	20.9	56.0
Class D	10.2	0.5	21.8	46.0

*Based on Salomon Brothers Inc trade data. Classes reflect maturity at issuance.

curitized share of 1-4 family mortages held between 11% and 14% through 1978, that proportion surged to reach one fifth by 1982, one third by 1983, and about one half in the period 1986 to 1987 (see Table 7–3).

The problems posed to savings institutions, and particularly the S&Ls, is shown by Table 7–4. Consider the net product of the cash flows of savings institutions for the residential mortgage market as a whole. The key column is the third, which indicates heavy net sales out of portfolio since 1981, reaching over $100 billion in 1986.

In Table 7–5, the major issuers of securitized mortgages in the recent past (1986–1987) in the form of CMOs are shown. As discussed above, investment bankers account for more than half of these issues, with mortgage bankers and builders contributing another 30%. The share accounted for by thrifts comes to less than 9%. Table 7–6 indicates that CMOs *do* attract mainly the large institutional investors: pension funds and insurance companies, with commercial banks mainly interested in the shorter-term *tranches*. It is, of course, the need of investment bankers to maintain their market share with institutional investors that induces the imitators to follow the innovators, thereby helping the symbiotic development of new primary markets and their necessary complements, the secondary markets.

STRIPPED MORTGAGE-BACK ISSUES

Taking a leaf from the technique of stripping Treasury securities, investment bankers in 1987 began to separate, in "strips," *monthly* interest cash flows from scheduled and prepaid *principal* cash flows. And like the stripping of Treasuries, this recasting of cash flows was designed to increase value, thereby raising total demand. This added demand can be assessed as follows:

The investor in any mortgage security (not yet stripped) takes a long position in an annuity that is subject to a mortgage borrower's call option: he is in a short position on the call. Many institutional investors find the option feature especially unattractive, hence the idea that the value of the annuity position could be enhanced by selling off the call position. Because that call position also has value to other investors, the combined values are higher than the passthroughs or the CMO *tranches* from which they were created.

The innovation provided by the strips was a tricky one, as some traders and issuers were to find out—to their sorrow—in spring 1987. The trickiness in price performance of interest-only (IOs) and of principal-only (POs) strips depends in a crucial way on prepayments of underlying mortgage collateral. The strips are in fact bets on the prepayment rate. To support valuation analysis, underwriters and traders have had to develop a model of prepayment responses to rate changes.[19] Below, the Salomon Brothers model will be used. Based on that model, price responses of IOs and POs can be projected.[20] As Figure 7–5 indicates, at point 0 (16 April 1987) the FNMA 9% passthroughs are valued at about 100, which represents the sum of IOs and POs. The model is then used to project a rise in forecasted prepayment rate (lower panel of chart in percent of forecast), should

---

[19]See Appendix 1 for a discussion of mortgage prepayment concepts and the analytical difficulties in developing a model for such forecasts.

[20]This discussion is based on M. Waldman, M. Gordon, T. A. Zimmerman, and K. Person, "Interest Only and Principal Only Strips." Copyright © 1987 by Salomon Brothers Inc., May 1987.

FIGURE 7–5
Projected Price Paths—FNMA 9% IOs and POs (16 Apr 87)

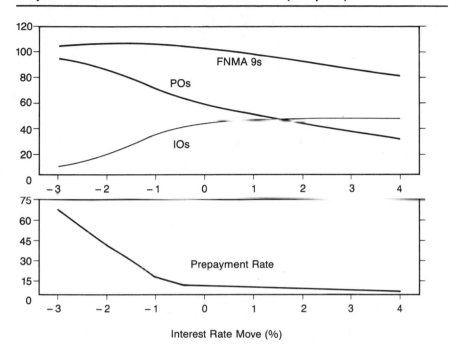

Interest Rate Move (%)

future rates drop. Further, that prepayment rate has an inflec-
tion point toward acceleration as rates drop by more than 1 percentage point below the 16 April level. Let us now examine a
bit more closely how the two types of strips perform as rates
change.

The first cut intuition would suggest that, should rates fall
(and bond prices rise), then *interest*-only (IO) strips should rise
in price even faster. But that intuition is wrong because it does
not take account of the induced surge in prepayments, and hence
in the reduction in number of mortgages outstanding. That reduction in future cash flows from *interest* payments will be borne
entirely by the investors who brought claims on *interest only*

strips.[21] In short, those investors have made a bet (a short position on call feature) that future interest rates will produce a lower prepayment rate than the current price implies: they are betting on the equivalent of rate stability, or a rate *rise*.

It is worth underlining that the present value of IO strips is influenced *not* by the discount factor applied to expected cash flows but to the actual occurrence of these cash flows. It is the prepayment of the underlying mortgage collateral that drives the price of the IO and PO strips, and in opposite directions.

A *rise* in interest rates will lower expectations of prepayments, and thus *raise* the value of IO strips, and the prices of IOs will respond positively to a rise in rates. Another way of putting that argument is that the rise in rates increases the size of anticipated interest cash flows (in nominal terms) and this factor more than outweighs the negative impact on present value.

By contrast the value of POs is raised by a decline in rates—that is, by a *rise* in prepayments. This phenomenon is, in some ways, easier to explain. Consider that at point 0 the price of PO = X, or the present value of scheduled amortization payments plus the modest amount of anticipated prepayments (at current interest rates). Assume now that rates fall, and the *pre*payments rise. That means that, instead of waiting for cash flows to the investor coming mostly from slow buildup of amortization flows, there is now a sudden upsurge of cash flows from prepayments. It should be remembered that when a mortgage prepays, it is redeemed at par and in full. Because a substantial amount of capital is received back much earlier than anticipated, the present value of the PO cash flow is much improved. Beyond this, the (now) lesser residual is discounted at a lower rate, thereby further enhancing its value.

---

[21]The following is quoted from Prospectus Supplement of *Fannie Mae Stripped Mortgage Securities* (Dated January 23, 1987) in which "Stripped Coupon" refers to what was called "IO" above; the PO is called "Stripped Bond." On p. S-15 of the prospectus supplement the following language appears: "With respect to a Stripped Coupon, prepayment of principal on the underlying Mortgage Loans will *preclude* receipt of all or a portion of the payments that would have been received if such Mortgage Loans had paid in accordance with their scheduled payments." (Emphasis supplied.)

A useful insight into the innovation process can be derived from the arbitrage profits (or excess returns) that the issuers of strips can generate. In any market equilibrium, the total value of the IO + PO strips should equal the value of the underlying collateral, the FNMA passthrough issue.[22] But in February 1987, for example, the sum of the prices of FNMA strips substantially exceeded the price of the underlying issue (FNMA Trust 1 which was then valued at about $750 million); it is the excess return to the innovator that explains why the issue was stripped. The example to follow is priced (like bonds) in percent of par. If the prices of the two components equals the price of the underlying issue there is not much point or revenue in stripping. Now consider the situation in late January through early February 1987:

February 1987

Price of IO strip issued @	58.16
PO strip issued @	48.00
Total value	106.16

Late January

Trust 1 security price @	102.19
Possible profit:	3.97

It is this arbitrage-return potential that provided the incentive to strip the FNMA mortgage backs. As these profits dwindled, the volume of IO/PO stripping was sharply reduced (see Figures 7–6 and 7–7). As these figures indicate, the monthly volume of strips fell below $1 billion after April 1987 as combined valuation of strips receded to a level of about 100 basis points above the mortgage, or less (after June). The excess return to innovators was just about eliminated in a period of less than half a year.

The much enhanced price sensitivity to interest rate

---

[22]This discussion is based on M. D. Youngblood's analysis in "Disequilibrium in the Mortgage Securities Market: Arbitrage Opportunities in Mortgage STRIPS." Copyright © 1988 by Salomon Brothers Inc., January 22, 1988.

FIGURE 7–6
Monthly New Issue Volume of Mortgage STRIPs, Feb–Dec 1987
(In Billions of Dollars)

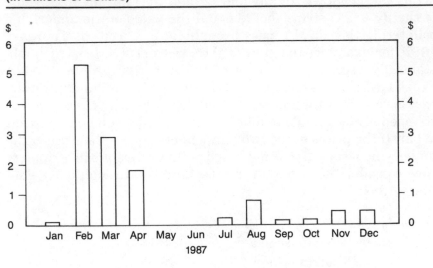

changes makes strips useful hedge vehicles with respect to interest-rate movements, or prepayment movements. The main issuers have been FNMA and FHLMC; the lead managers of these
issues have been primarily the special bracket investment bankers and other first-tier firms. All of the investment banking
firms in this area have substantially built up their research and
trading capabilities for mortgage-backed securities. An informal
survey by this writer suggests that the volume of daily trading
is large:

Estimated *daily* trading volume, CMOs = $300 million.

Estimated *daily* trading volume, GNMAs = $4 billion.

These data suggest that in each month's trading about one
fourth of outstandings turn over.

A significant share of that substantial trading volume in
mortgage backs may also be attributed to the money-market as-

FIGURE 7–7
Prices and Spread of FNMA 9.0% MBS and FNMA SMBS Trust 6,
Apr 87–Jan 88

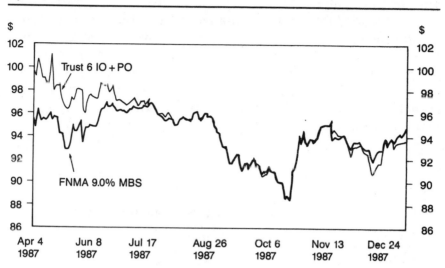

pect of that market: as a logical finishing move to complete the CMO market menu, a repurchase market has recently (in 1987) been developed for CMOs that are rated AA or better and are registered with the SEC.[23] Recent changes in the regulations of the NYSE have ". . . reduced the minimum security margin that broker–dealers must require of the reverse repurchase agreements on collateralized mortgage obligations (CMOs). . ."[24] These changes make possible a maximum loan/value ratio of 95% (replacing 75%) when based on current market value.[25] The present overcollateralization level is comparable to that re-

---

[23]The following is based on M. D. Youngblood, Ph.D., "CMO Repurchase Agreements," *Salomon Brothers, Inc.*, New York, 1987.

[24]Op. cit., p. 1.

[25]Current market "haircuts" on U.S. Treasuries vary from 1 to 5%.

quired on Federal agency passthroughs and, according to Dr. Youngblood, ". . . should encourage active financing of CMOs with broker dealers."[26]

This added flexibility in financing techniques and/or ability to add to total income by institutional investors thus further helps to bring the CMO into the investment market mainstream. On the one side, this broadens the flow of funds into the mortgage market; on the other side, mortgage rates are now increasingly subject to all the financial pressures that impinge on capital and money markets.[27]

CONCLUDING REMARKS

In Chapter 6, a 4-I construct of financial innovation was proposed:

Innovation
Imitation
Institutionalization
Internationalization

A combination of the second and fourth "I" saw the light of day when Great Britain, Canada, and Australia developed, respectively, the following securities:

1. Sterling Mortgage-Backed Floating-Rate Notes.
2. Canadian Mortgage and Housing Corporation Insured Mortgages.
3. Australian Mortgage Backed Bonds.

In each case, the new security filled an unmet housing finance need, partly supported by government guarantees and insurance.

---

[26]Op. cit.

[27]See S. A. Gabriel, "Housing and Mortgage Markets: The Post-1982 Expansion," *Federal Reserve Bulletin,* December, 1987, especially chart 9, p. 901. As noted in that study, during the mid-to-late 1970s only 20 percent of change in 10-year Treasury yields was mirrored in mortgage rates within a week. By 1986–87, nearly 80 percent of Treasury yield changes was reflected in mortgage rates within a week.

For the United States, the emphasis developed in this chapter was placed on the transmutation of mortgage collateral into capital market securities by investment bankers. As these innovators gained experience their new securities have progressively mimicked conventional debt instruments, and with increasing success. Beyond merely supplementing the mechanics of financial intermediation by an innovative capital-market instrument, that instrument has now been transformed into a more tradable form of debt. No doubt, this tends to increase the flow rate of investible funds into financing housing especially as the increased institutionalization of the economy's investible funds can be so accommodated. But this set of events has other, perhaps unintended, side effects.

Most immediately, the substitution of privatized capital market mechanics—primarily managed by investment bankers—has sharply increased the volatility of mortgage rates. In the past, mortgage rates would adjust to changes in Treasury rates with a lag, and with damped interest rate sensitivity. At this writing, however, mortgage rates have become as sensitive to market changes as other securities. There is no point in arguing whether this is good or bad. It just is.

At the same time it must be observed that participation in this newly volatile market requires a powerful capacity to analyze the values and to trade these complex new instruments. And that capacity must be of a magnitude to permit institutional-size participation and market making. This also implies taking substantial risks.[28]

One of the less discussed by-products of the latest revolution in mortgage finance has been the inter-industry competition by innovation. In the more competitive environment of the 1970s and 1980s, GNMA, FNNMA, and FHLMC—all Federal agencies—pioneered the changes in innovative mortgage backs that led to the improved flows into financing residential mortgages that followed. These changes should not blind us to the by-product produced by these innovations: the pressure thus placed on

---

[28]Newspaper reports indicating losses of $400 million or more by investment bankers in mortgage-backed securities and some derivative issues surfaced in the second quarter of 1987.

the average intermediary (e.g., the S&Ls) whose specialized service capacities could not be adapted to the volatile and risky new world. And attempts at governmentally sponsored asset deregulation, while maintaining insurance of liabilities, has led to classic moral hazard problems (e.g., the Texas S&Ls).

In late 1987 another variable was added to financial markets by a regulatory change. Permission was given to loosen up the Glass–Steagall Act by allowing some commercial banks to underwrite mortgage-backed issues. Whether an additional set of players will further change the mortgage-back markets remains to be seen. What is clear is that the innovative process instituted by federal agencies and underwritten (largely) by investment bankers has increasingly shifted the center of gravity of the mortgage market away from the intermediation process. The active part of the mortgage market is now a market-based process. The capacity of traders in the market for a variety of passthrough, CMO, and stripped issues has changed market characteristics for good.

APPENDIX 1

Two Necessary Digressions

The Prepayment Problem

The prepayment rate on mortgage portfolios is unpredictable not only because interest rate prediction itself is an imperfect art. There is, in addition, a random component to the prepayment process, which will be assessed first. That set of events stems from the vagaries of fortune of the average homeowner complicated by the due-on-sale constraints that may apply to the mortgage contract itself in a number of cases.

Consider a representative 1,000 homeowners in the United States. Per unit time there will be a fairly predictable set of deaths and divorces, and a somewhat less predictable set of job-related relocations, etc.[1] But a still *less predictable* derivative of the above set of events will result in the sale of the home: for example, following a divorce, one of the partners may continue to reside in the home, or neither may— only in the latter case will a home sale follow. Or a similar set of events may follow from the death of a member of the household, or even from the relocation of one of the partners. In some of the cases where a sale does take place, the mortgage may not have been subject to a "due on sale" restriction. For that subset, only those homes on which mortgage rates at time of sale were lower would an accurate projection of the rate of sales make such a projection a useful instrument for forecasting the random part of the prepayment stream.

With respect to the systematic, or interest-rate related share of the prepayment stream, the homeowner faces the effect of the typical put option. That put option may carry a premium—called the prepayment fee—or it may not. In any case that option is worth to the homeowner the algebraic sum of the following:

    a. Gross gain = present value of interest savings after rates have fallen below the contract rate on the mortgage
    less:
    b. Gross costs = legal fees related to the refinancing; fees charged by lender (including "points" and the tax treatment of these points); prepayment fees on replacement mortgage, if any.

---

[1]Such relocations may be related, for example, to waves of mergers and reorganizations.

At any point in time, the information relative to (b) can be known to each homeowner with certainty. The value of (a) is, necessarily, a function of homeowner's expectations relative to future interest rate developments. And, indeed, once prepayment and refinancing of a mortgage can be shown to carry a positive net present value, the homeowner trades off expectations of still larger possible gains for the risk of missing the market prior to consummation. And the more volatile interest rates, the greater the gain/risk tradeoff, and hence the less predictable will be homeowner reactions to a given interest-rate change. In the end, forecasting the combination of random and systemic prepayments is not yet an art that is totally understood. The Public Securities Association (PSA) Standard Prepayment Model has replaced the FHA model even though both models are essentially an averaging out of historical experience. The prepayment assumptions applied to rate calculations are then specified relative to PSA experience such as, e.g., 100% PSA = PSA model; or 50% PSA: one half expected prepayments relative to PSA model.

Underwriting Risks[2]: Mortgage Commitments

Mortgage lenders engage in a process that is similar to securities underwriting by investment bankers in a fundamental way: they take on the market risk for floating the issue in an environment of changing market rates. A review of the mortgage commitment process bears this out:

1. The mortgage lender (say, an S&L) receives an application from a potential customer.
2. Lender then investigates
   a. Property value
   b. Applicant's credit   } = due diligence
3. If everything is acceptable lender then:
4. Gives applicant a written commitment to lend money on accepted terms such as:
   a. Interest rate.
   b. Prepay schedules.
   c. Expiration of commitment (typical limit = 60 days)

---

[2]For a general discussion of the underwriting of corporate securities, and related risks, see Chapter 14.

Once the loan is made, the lender may resell the new mortgage (e.g., to GNMA), and his profit then is based on the spread between effective price based on commitment (which represents an option similar to a security underwriting) and the price obtained on resale. In securities underwriting that difference is called a "gross spread." It will also be noted that the borrower's mortgage commitment, like any other put option, will not be exercised if rates decline prior to exercise point *unless* lender permits execution at the lower rate.

In sum, the lender is in the same position of any underwriter of long term bonds when the borrower has the benefit of shelf registration. If mortgage rates rise, the commitment becomes an increasingly valuable option to the borrower that is very likely to be exercised, and an increasingly costly risk to lender. If rates stay the same, or drop, the option risk disappears. Nevertheless, in both cases, the lender faces market risks during the period that elapses between mortgage closing and its resale. The latter is, of course, the analog to security flotation risk. Mortgage lenders, like all underwriters, have had to learn how to hedge these risks as mortgage rate volatility has risen.

APPENDIX 2

Maturity Measures for CMOs[1]

Given the unpredictability of prepayments, no CMOs trade on the basis of their stated, or even projected, maturities. Instead such issues trade on basis of Weighted Average Life (WAL). It is useful to keep in mind the following maturity concepts:

1. *Stated Final Maturity:* A period is assigned to each class (or *tranche*) of bonds under conservative prepay assumptions assigned by the rating agencies. In most cases this assumes amortization flows, but no prepayments. The conservative investor would therefore, use this concept only if he wished to compute *maximum* anticipated maturity of *tranche*.

---

[1]This set of definitions is based on "Introduction to Mortgages and Mortgage Backed Securities," K. Jeanne Person, September 1987. Copyright © 1987 by Salomon Brothers Inc.

2. *Projected Final Maturity* uses some reasonable prepayment assumption (over *stated final maturity* concept). This is more realistic than (1). Within each issue of CMO bonds, the fixed cash flow, interest only period of each *tranche* is determined by the final maturity of previous *tranche*. For this reason, investors in *tranches* other than the first will want to know projected final maturity of *tranche* immediately preceding their own.
3. *WAL*. Using some specific prepayment assumption, WAL calculates the average time needed to receipt of principal, weighted by size of each principal payment.
4. *Duration* is the average time to receipt of cash flows weighed by their present value. This widely used measure calculates the sensitivity of the security's market value to changes in the discount factor used. For a CMO *tranche* whose prepayment rate shifts systematically (but not precisely) with interest-rate shifts, the calculated duration can be only a first step in calculating market risk.

APPENDIX 3

REMICs

The most recent approach to mortgage (re) finance is a new legal device called a "Real Estate Mortgage Conduit" (or REMIC). This approach was established by Subtitle H of the Tax Reform Act of 1986. The REMIC would be a separate legal entity for tax purposes into which issuers could "sell" mortgage assets and that, in turn, can issue mortgage-backed securities. It is not a taxable entity if it is used as a conduit for passing mortgage payments to holders of mortgage-backed securities. And finally, the sale of mortgages to the REMIC would remove those assets from the issuer's portfolio—unlike the experience with the CMO. In that sense, the REMIC would make it easier for an intermediary to meet (increased) capital requirements if imposed by a regulator.

FINANCIAL INNOVATION AND THE CAPITAL MARKETS TODAY

The five preceding chapters have attempted to build a structure within which the general activities and the innovative actions of investment bankers can be assessed. To conclude this section it is useful to develop a few magnitudes within which these firms operate.

As the accompanying table indicates, the 1987 size of the equity market (at $3 trillion market value) and of the mortgage market ($2.8 trillion) are the two largest marketplaces. The government securities market, including agency issues comes to (only!) about $2 trillion; it should be noted that this number *excludes* the federal debt held by U.S. government entities, such as the Social Security system.[1] It must also be underlined that

---

[1]Consider trading volume on the equity market that, by market *valuation* is the largest single security-type outstanding. Suppose that the average stock is priced at $40 per share (the average price per share in 1986 was about $37). Then a 200 million share day transacts about $8 billion. Even a 500 million share day transacts no more than $20 billion at that price, whereas the U.S. government securities market *routinely* transacts $100 billion per average day.

Capital Markets Data (In Billions of Dollars) 1982–1987

	1987	1986	1985	1984	1983	1982
Size of the Capital Markets, 1982–1987						
Mortgage	2,848.5	2,578.0	2,279.9	2,047.2	1,837.8	1,654.3
Corp bonds	1,023.3	917.1	806.3	691.6	599.6	549.9
Government (Treasury & Agency)	1,987.8	1,857.4	1,666.8	1,433.3	1,262.4	1,094.0
Corp equity	3,019.9	2,948.0	2,584.3	2,021.5	2,021.8	1,720.9
Tax-exempt	776.3	754.1	701.6	577.2	510.2	468.0
Composition of the Mortgage Market, 1982–1987						
1–4 Family mortgage	1,836.4	1,645.1	1,445.7	1,298.8	1,177.1	1,059.6
Multi mortgage	276.6	253.3	220.3	191.2	166.0	151.9
Comm mortgage	648.9	583.6	509.6	447.0	383.5	334.2
Farm mortgage	86.6	96.0	104.3	110.3	111.2	108.6
Securitization of Residential Mortgage Debt, 1982–1987						
Residential debt						
No. Securitized	681.0	534.7	372.0	290.7	246.2	178.0
No. Nonsecuritized	1,432.0	1,363.7	1,294.0	1,199.3	1,096.9	1,033.5
Outstanding Passthrough Securities, 1982–1987						
Total	681.0	534.7	372.0	290.7	246.2	178.0
No. GNMA	311.0	260.9	212.1	180.0	159.8	118.9
No. FHLMC	218.0	168.6	100.5	70.9	58.0	42.9
No. FNMA	136.0	97.2	55.0	36.2	25.1	14.5
No. Conventional	16.0	8.0	4.4	3.6	3.3	1.7

the *transactions* volume in the $2 trillion federal and agency is-
sues, at about $100 billion per average day, is by far the largest
of all the secondary securities markets shown. Corporate bonds
(at $1 trillion) and tax exempts (at $¾ trillion) are the last two
items on this list.

One last point should be made: within the enormous aggregate, and the rapid growth, of mortgage outstandings the securitization rate has itself moved up rapidly from 1982 to 1987: in
the first year shown, the securitization rate was about 15%,
more than doubling to about one third of a much larger total in
the following 5 years. The innovative actions of investment
bankers have clearly made a difference; and the largest market
in which these actions could have been illustrated is the mortgage market.

Further, some of the innovations discussed in the chapters
above such as, e.g., junk bonds, substantially facilitated the
surge in corporate reorganizations. This set of innovations became an essential counterpart to the growth in the market for
corporate control, which will be discussed in the next part. For
these issues and the related merchant banking activities (see
Chapter 4) constituted the rationale for developing the large-
scale, full service investment banking firms that form the foundation of the industry at this writing. And yet, the very success
of these enterprises has fundamentally changed them: the days
of informal, consensus-type management are over. Further, a
number of senior personnel impatient with the new, more constrained rules in the larger firms have opted out to form their
own, specialized, investment banking boutiques.

The last two chapters of Part 1 were designed to show the
power of innovative finance and its success to change the capital
markets, and the firms themselves. Finally, as the last chapter
of the next section is intended to illustrate, the enormous temptations thrown up by the explosion of the markets for corporate
reorganization led a number of well-known operators into insider trading, and ultimately to jail.

PART II

THE MARKET FOR CORPORATE CONTROL

In the era of the corporate takeover the bidder's moves toward the target firm are often perceived by the latter as a form of warfare. While that perception is understandable, it should be at least equally well understood that in the context of a financial market, the acquisition of a certain company's shares on an institutional scale, or on a control-size scale, is no more than a difference of degree. Further, because mergers, acquisitions, takeovers, and other forms of trading corporate control of even the largest firms are now everyday events, the notion that they are exceptional events flies in the face of experience.

That there can be a wide gulf between the eagerness of a bidder and the lack of awareness of a target has been noted in a somewhat different, but equally intense context:

It is a truth universally acknowledged, that a single man in possession of a good fortune must be in want of a wife.

However little known the feelings or views of such a man may be on his first entering a neighborhood, this truth is so well fixed in the minds of the surrounding families, that he is considered as the rightful property of some one or other of their daughters.[1]

For the target firm's management, and for the bidder's management as well, the stakes are enormous. And for the investment bankers, the stakes may mount, especially if a direct investment in a bridge loan is committed to the deal. As the size of the deals done in the eighties has risen routinely to multibillion dollar levels, both the size of the returns, and the risks taken by the participants, have zoomed.

Finally, in a market driven by information and powered by a record number of transactions, the temptations to trade illegally on inside information have risen as well. As a result, the number of Securities and Exchange Commission (SEC) actions brought in the 1980s over a period of less than a decade equalled the number initiated by the SEC in the prior 50 years since the approval of the Securities and Exchange Act. These issues will be developed in the next three chapters.

---

[1] The context is, of course, the marriage game of early nineteenth century England as described in the first two sentences of *Pride and Prejudice* by Jane Austen. The reader need only substitute "target" for "man" and "bidder" for "daughters."

8

MERGERS AND ACQUISITIONS I:
MARKET MAKING AS A CIRCUS

When descriptions of investment banking activities move from the business pages to the front pages of the newspaper and when one merger gives rise to at least three trade books full of insider details,[1] show biz and the merger business share more than the same nomenclature. Today publicity campaigns and image making are an integral part of the information maneuvering of giant corporations and the megabucks risked to finance mergers and takeovers. This chapter goes a bit deeper than the headlines—back to the business pages of the paper and to the not necessarily quieter environment of the professional literature.

The total volume of mergers and takeovers since 1980 has been unprecedented. The size of the largest mergers and takeovers keeps on increasing, and multibillion dollar acquisitions are now commonplace (see Table 8–1).

The concepts "mergers," "takeovers," and "acquisitions" all involve the absorption of one firm (the target firm) by another (the acquiring firm). *Merger* generally implies a less reluctant attitude on the part of the target firm; *takeover* usually implies an unfriendly bid for the target firm. Either approach, if successful, means disappearance of the target firm.

Curiously, financial analysts have no agreed-on theory to

---

[1]See A. Sloan, *Three Plus One Equals Billions* (Arbor House); H. Lampert, *Till Death Us Part* (New York: Harcourt Brace Jovanovich, 1983); and P. Hartz, *Merger* (Morrow, 1985).

TABLE 8–1
Ten Largest Merger and Acquisition (M&A) Transactions: 1986 and 1987

Date	Acquirer	Target	Value (In $ Millions)
June 29, 1987	British Petroleum	Standard Oil	7,565
Apr. 17, 1986	Kohlberg Kravis Roberts & Co.	Beatrice	6,250
June 9, 1986	General Electric	RCA	6,142
Jan. 24, 1986	Kohlberg Kravis Roberts & Co.	Safeway	5,335
Sept. 16, 1986	Burroughs	Sperry	4,432
Feb. 15, 1987	Thompson Co.	Southland	4,004
May 8, 1987	AV Holdings Corp.	Borg–Warner	3,764
March 24, 1987	Kohlberg Kravis Roberts & Co.	Owens-Illinois	3,688
Dec. 31, 1986	Campeau Corp.	Allied Stores	3,597
Jan. 3, 1986	Capital Cities Communications	American Broadcasting Co.	3,530

Source: M&A Data Base, *Mergers & Acquisitions*, Philadelphia.

explain merger activity.[2] Mergers (or takeovers) are undertaken by the acquiring firm in the expectation of significant gains. What is the nature of these gains?

DEFINING ECONOMIC COSTS AND GAINS[3]

If the acquiring firm A believes there is a net gain to be made by combining with firm B to make firm AB, that gain can be stated in present value (PV) terms as follows:

$$\text{GAIN} = \text{PV}_{AB} - (\text{PV}_A + \text{PV}_B)$$

Only if GAIN were positive, so that the present value of $\text{PV}_{AB} > \text{PV}_A + \text{PV}_B$, would a merger make sense. If it makes sense, B must still be acquired, and that acquisition will carry a price. Let's call that price (from A's point of view) COST. Assume, only for the sake of simplicity, that A buys B with cash rather than a package of securities. In that case the *cost* to A is as follows:

$$\text{COST} = \text{CASH} - \text{PV}_B$$

where CASH includes all the outlays (including transaction costs, legal fees, and so forth) needed to place PV_B within the

---

[2]The word most often used to explain the urge to merge is *synergy*—the new math of 2 + 2 = 5. Synergy implies that the combined two (or more) firms are worth more than their separate values due to (1) operating economies (of scale); (2) financial economies (or a lower cost of capital); (3) differential efficiency (target firm's management is inefficient); and (4) increased market power. The last item is illegal under the Sherman and Clayton antitrust statutes, but some mergers *not* challenged by the U.S. government nevertheless have increased market-share effects. All the other rationales may be socially desirable, and so may the proposition that the acquisition of assets by merger may be cheaper than new construction (this appears to be the efficiency argument in another guise). Yet each one of these propositions is subject to controversy, first, in the academic literature and, second, in the implementation of actual decisions.

[3]The following is based on R. Brealey and S. Myers, *Principles of Corporate Finance*, 2nd ed., (New York: McGraw-Hill, 1984), Chap. 31.

combined firm. In the end, the merger makes sense only if the following post-merger, NPV_M, is *positive:*

$$NPV_M = GAIN - COST$$
$$= PV_{AB} - (PV_A + PV_B) - (CASH - PV_B)$$

All the values in the preceding equations must be estimated by the acquiring firm in advance of any merger. On the assumption that markets can efficiently place values on securities, each of the variables also has to be estimated on a post-merger *announcement* basis for the target firm, as does the forecast of the present value of the (as yet unknown) cash flows of the combined enterprise. And finally, the acquiring firm must have enough faith in such forecasts to risk a substantial amount of funds.

Only on that basis can the acquiring firm's management be satisfied that some positive GAIN will follow. If the decision turns out to be a mistake, the acquiring firm's management not only loses prestige but may be dismissed by its board of directors and/or the stockholders and the now financially vulnerable acquiring firm may even become a takeover target itself.[4] As partial protection from the errors of excessive optimism, plain bad luck, or both, the managements of acquiring firms almost always retain an investment banking firm to estimate the relevant variables for the target firm and for itself. Investment bankers active in the merger game have a great deal of experience in making such estimates and enough expertise in trading blocks to assess both strategic as well as tactical price changes expected to take place in both the acquiring and the target firms' stock prices.

The prior equation is a clear statement of not only the GAIN that makes the deal possible but COST, which is primarily the premium payment to target firm B. Since firm A has retained an investment banker to help bring about a positive result for it, the management of firm B will do the same to maximize its stockholders' wealth. In fact, the presentation is based purposely on the separation of two questions:

1. The analysis of GAIN establishes prima facie rationale

---

[4]See the discussion of the Bendix–Martin Marietta merger fight below.

for A of whether merger should even be considered and of how much to bid.

2. The analysis of COST sets the division of GAIN between the target firm and the acquiring firm. Suppose that the estimate of pre-merger GAIN is positive. Suppose, further, that COST = GAIN; then all of the benefits of the merger go to the *target* firm.

To clarify, suppose the following relationships hold, pre-merger:

$$PV_A = \$2,000,000$$
$$PV_B = \$200,000$$
$$GAIN = +\$120,000$$

Separately, the values of firm A and B are $2 million and $200,000, respectively, so the sum of their separate values equals $2.2 million. A believes that by combining with B the joint firm (because of synergy, economies of scale, magic, and so on) would be worth *not* $2.2 million but $2,320,000. This gives the merger a present value (or a GAIN) of $120,000.

Suppose now that A buys B for $250,000 cash. Immediately, B's stockholders enjoy a 25 percent rise in the value of their former holdings—let's call this B's premium. If A's estimate of the merger is right, its stockholders, too, are ahead of the game:

$$NPV_M = \text{Value with merger} - \text{value pre-merger}$$
$$= (PV_{AB} - CASH) - PV_A$$
$$= (\$2,320,000 - \$250,000) - \$2,000,000$$
$$= +\$70,000 = \$120,000 - \$50,000$$
$$= GAIN - B\text{'s premium}$$

Remember, however, that B's premium is *fact,* whereas GAIN is entirely a function of A's ability to forecast accurately the present value of an uncertain future. (A's stockholders must make a similar forecast.)

TWO BIG MERGER CASES

In February 1984 Getty Oil, the 14th largest U.S. oil firm, was acquired by Texaco, the 4th largest, at a total price exceeding $10 billion. Prior to the merger, the descendants (and principal owners) of J. Paul Getty (the founder) were restless with their own management because Getty shares were selling at about $65 per share. First, the trustees of the Sarah C. Getty trust, together with Pennzoil Co., announced a plan to take the firm private through an offer to buy shares not yet controlled at a price of $112.50 per share. Texaco subsequently raised the ante with an offer of $125 per share. Getty's heirs clearly got a good deal.

That deal was so good for the Getty side that it may turn out to be quite bad from the Texaco side. Recall that, on January 2, 1984, Pennzoil had reached (in its perception) what it deemed a binding agreement with Getty to acquire three-sevenths of that firm. Within less than a week from that date, Texaco purchased *all* of the Getty stock at a price above that proposed by Pennzoil. As a further condition of the sale, Texaco took on the liability of Getty and its largest shareholders against possible suits by Pennzoil. When the latter firm sued for damages, Texaco became the sole defendant. Pennzoil won the suit, and Texaco's successive appeals have been rejected. Pennzoil was awarded judgments of:

$$\$ \ \ 7.5 \ \ \text{billion (actual damages)}$$
$$3.0 \ \ \text{billion (punitive damages)}$$
$$\underline{1.5} \ \ \text{billion (accrued interest)}$$

for a total of: $12.0 billion in November, 1985.

Ultimately, in April 1987, Texaco had to file for bankruptcy protection, and the two firms subsequently moved toward a settlement. In an interesting study of these events, and using stock price data for the two firms up to the Texaco bankruptcy date, D. M. Cutler and L. H. Summers[5] calculated that, while Texaco's value fell by nearly $2.7 billion, Pennzoil's gain came to no more than $770 million. The net loss for the two firms combined ($2.7 billion loss for Texaco less $0.8 billion gain for Pennzoil) thus comes to about $2 billion. Some readers may find it a comfort that, in the Cutler–Summers article, it is argued that the legal

---

[5]"The Costs of Conflict Resolution and Financial Distress: Evidence from the Texaco–Pennzoil Litigation," *NBER Working Paper* No. 2418, October 1987.

fees ". . . can still only explain 30 percent of the loss in [aggregate] value" (see pp. 12–13 of article).

Nearly all empirical studies find that one unequivocal result of mergers is that stockholders of the *target* firm clearly benefit.[6] In the Texaco–Getty takeover, the Getty stockholders doubled their wealth, and did so on consummation in early 1984. For Texaco and Pennzoil the results were not only delayed by four years of struggle and turmoil, but for Texaco it meant bankruptcy, the payment of about $3 billion of damages, plus enormous legal and other expenses. Texaco's payment was transferred to Pennzoil on April 7, 1988.

On the other side of the transfer, Pennzoil's receipt of $2.6 billion (after expenses) nearly doubled its prereceipt value of $3.2 billion. There were rumors that Pennzoil could be a bidder for one of several takeover candidates (such as Phillips Petroleum, Unocal, Amerada Hess, and Sun).[7] There were other rumors that Texaco could itself become a takeover *target*, and that cash-rich Pennzoil could become a *target* as well. Such are the ambiguities of *bidder* success in the takeover game.

By contrast, in another megamerger, that of Conoco in 1981, the stockholders in the target firm appeared to have chosen the less attractive alternative. Moreover, that takeover was hostile; Conoco's managers preferred that the firm remain a freestanding unit.

In 1981 Conoco had $11 billion of assets (book value) and was the 14th largest U.S. firm in terms of sales. It became a target for (1) Mobil (another oil company and the second largest U.S. firm), (2) Du Pont (the 15th largest U.S. firm), and (3) Seagram (a large Canadian firm). In size, the merger that was eventually consummated was as large as *total* merger activity in any prior year.

Prior to the bidding, Conoco's price was about $50 per share; Conoco's coal, oil, and gas reserves plus its plant and equipment were thought to far exceed their market or book values. Not sur-

---

[6]See, for example, P. Asquith, "Merger Bids, Uncertainty, and Stockholder Returns," *Journal of Financial Economics,* April 1983, pp. 51–83.

[7]See *The New York Times,* "Marketplace," April 7, 1988.

prisingly, in the bidding for Conoco, its stock price rose above $100 per share.

In the struggle for Conoco, the U.S. Department of Justice indicated that it would fight a merger with Mobil (a horizontal, or market-share, merger) but *not* a merger with Du Pont or Seagram. Thus, although Mobil made the highest bid ($115 per share), stockholders chose a Du Pont offer of about $95 per share. They made that decision because a Department of Justice objection to the Mobil merger might have stopped the process and dropped the Conoco price below Du Pont's $95 offer.

For Du Pont, the need to borrow to finance the takeover more than quadrupled its $1.6 billion debt, thereby causing it to lose its AAA bond rating—evidence that benefits to the acquiring firm are less than certain or may even be equivocal at best. Why, then, do the acquiring firms do it?

MERGER CALCULATIONS

Both of the previous case studies indicate that the target firm is the beneficiary of a share of the merger's GAIN. Following Brealey and Myers's approach again, and if the following relationships hold (with firm A the acquiring and firm B the target), suppose that the market values B firm differently before and after, the *announcement* of the merger.[8]

Outcome	Value of B's Stock
1. No merger	PV_B: Value per share of B as a separate unit
2. Merger occurs	PV_B: *Plus* some part of the GAIN from merger

Suppose the following numbers hold for outcome 1 above.

---

[8]R. Brealey and S. Myers, *Principles of Corporate Finance,* pp. 711–13.

	Firm A	Firm B
Market price per share	$75	$15
Number of shares	100,000	60,000
Market value of firm	$7,500,000	$900,000

Assume that firm A expects to pay a $300,000 premium, or a total of $1.2 million cash, for B. A's COST would be:

$$A's\ COST = (CASH - MV_B) + (MV_B - PV_B)$$
$$= \$300,000 + 0 = \$300,000$$

Now suppose that, instead of paying cash, A offers B's stockholders 16,000 shares of its own stock. Then A's estimated cost would be (less PV_B) as follows:

$$Estimated\ COST = 16,000 \times \$75 - \$900,000 = \$300,000$$

But there are three reasons why this might *not* be so:

1. B's value (as a separate unit) may not be $900,000.
2. A's value (as a separate unit) may not be $7,500,000.
3. Since, after the merger, B's stockholders now own a share of A, they also own a share of A's merger GAIN over and above their own GAIN.

The proportionate share of A owned by B's old stockholders (call this X) after the merger will be as follows even if the stock price estimates of the two firms turn out to be correct:

$$X = \frac{16,000}{100,000 + 16,000} = 0.138$$

Now assume that A's total GAIN from the merger is $400,000; then:

$$PV_{AB} = PV_A + PV_B + GAIN$$
$$= \$7,500,000 + \$900,000 + \$400,000$$
$$= \$8.8\ million$$

It follows that

$$\text{A's FINAL COST} = X(\text{PV}_{AB} - \text{PV}_B)$$
$$= 0.138 \ (\$8.8 \text{ million}) - \$900,000$$
$$= \$314,000$$

In effect, if the total GAIN is $400,000, then firm A, which began the whole game, receives for its stockholders only: $400,000 - $314,000 = $86,000. Again the target firm receives by far the largest value of the GAIN, and relative to pre-merger value, B's stockholders enjoy a more than one third capital gain, while A's stockholders get a bit more than a tenth.

The benefits accrued to the acquiring firm, which are long term in nature, are clearly much more difficult to calculate than those for the acquired firm. For that reason, while the market's view of A's present value may remain fairly stable, it may now represent a stable averaging of a much wider set of expectations than that which held prior to the merger.

ROLE OF INVESTMENT BANKERS

The specific case studies and examples noted above did not consider such problems for the *bidding firm* as:

1. Forecasting GAIN for some time in the future.
2. Planning and transactions costs associated with a tender proposal (friendly or unfriendly) or a merger. This also requires the preparation of legal and financial documents.
3. Estimate of probability (and/or cost) of potential for antitrust action by the Department of Justice or another relevant government agency (FTC, FCC, SEC, 50 states).
4. Estimates of prices per share of the target firm following the announcement of the takeover, merger, and so forth. This has a strategic impact on COST.
5. Estimates of prices per share of the bidding firm following the announcement. From the bidding firm's view, this will affect GAIN.
6. Estimates of types and amount of additional financing

needed to execute the deal (recall Du Pont's downgrading of debt quality).

The target firm will seek investment banking advice especially if the merger or takeover is neither sought nor wanted.[9] Defenses by unwilling firms often involve battles in which heavyweight corporations, as well as heavyweight investment bankers, engage in mutually taxing fights over financial and corporate control. One such example is the bizarre four-way fight in 1982 that began with an attempt by Bendix Corporation to take over Martin Marietta Corp.[10] At one stage it looked as if, in a so-called Pac-Man defense, Bendix might own 70 percent of Martin Marietta, while Martin Marietta (perhaps with the aid of United Technologies) might own 50 percent of Bendix. If that fight had gone to the finish, the outcome would have depended on who could vote whose shares first—a tangle that the courts would have spent some time to unravel. To avoid a stalemate, Allied Corporation was brought in as a white knight, entered a bid for Bendix, and acquired that firm for $1.8 billion, while Bendix and Martin Marietta swapped their holdings of each other's stock on the basis of market value. Further residual (and major) financial readjustments required further investment banking actions. The originator of the whole struggle, Bendix, disappeared,[11] while Martin Marietta maintained its independent status, albeit with almost $900 million of new debt raised to buy Bendix stock in its Pac-Man defense. In addition, Martin Marietta had to issue almost $350 million of new stock to buy back the shares that Allied had acquired during the struggle. (Chapter 18 in the section on block trading discusses Allied's disposal of a block of RCA shares previously owned by Bendix.)

---

[9]This brings up another role for investment bankers—finding a "white knight" for the target firm. A white knight is another corporation with which the target firm prefers to merge for many reasons (for example, better fit, hence better terms).

[10]For a complete discussion, see H. Lampert, *Till Death Do Us Part* (New York: Harcourt Brace Jovanovich, 1983).

[11]The former president of Bendix, William M. Agee, first accepted a senior, but not the top, position with Allied Corporation, a position from which he resigned in less than a year. When he left Allied (including membership on its board) he received a golden parachute worth $4.1 million.

The foregoing is a much-condensed version of a complex, if not Byzantine, struggle. Each transaction in the secondary markets required quick and effective execution of the equivalent of large-scale blocks. Bids and offers involved nearly hourly consultations with investment bankers on all sides regarding current pricing of present values of enormously large future cash flows.[12] Investment bankers can serve as important consultants prior to and during the process of decisions that may mean the survival or the disappearance of multibillion dollar firms.

Finally, the M&A departments of major investment bankers can execute deals; provide continuous consultations; and offer tactical and strategic advice regarding proxy fights, antitrust implications, and last—but not least—the new-money financing required during and after the battle. But before moving into that part of the operational activities of investment banking firms and their clients, an important issue must be resolved, namely, the valuation to merging firms of mergers, acquisitions, and tender offers. This is not a simple task.

MEASURING BENEFITS TO THE BIDDING FIRM

Modern studies of the benefits to acquirers and acquired firms use the same currency—price per share of the firm's stock. Nearly all studies of benefits to the bidding firms suggest that such benefits are much more difficult to perceive than those of the acquired firms. Rather than repeat these results, shown in many academic studies,[13] note the following analysis of GAIN

---

[12]For the record, the following firms and investment bankers were involved:

Firm	Investment Bankers
Bendix	Salomon Brothers, First Boston
Martin Marietta	Kidder, Peabody
United Technologies	Lazard Frères
Allied Corp.	Lehman Brothers

[13]The following discussion owes a good deal to an article by Baruch Lev, "Observations on the Merger Phenomenon and a Review of the Evidence," *Midland Corporate Finance Journal* 1, no. 4 (1983).

TABLE 8–2
Calculation of GAIN and Its Distribution Between Acquiring and Acquired Firms

		Share Price
I. Pre-merger		
1. Acquiring firm, PV_A	= $5 billion	$50
2. To be acquired firm, PV_B	= $1 billion	$50
II. Expected post-merger (GAIN	= $500 million)	
1. PV_A − $5 billion + 0.5 ($500 million)	= $5.25 billion	$52½
2. PV_B − $1 billion + 0.5 ($500 million)	= $1.25 billion	$62½
III. Actual post-merger		
1. PV_A − $5 billion + 0.25 ($500 million)	= $5.125 billion	$51¼
2. PV_B − $1 billion + 0.75 ($500 million)	= $1.375 billion	$68¾

and its distribution between the bidding firm and the acquired firm.

Consider, first, the impact on the acquirer's GAIN produced by mere difference in *size* between the two firms involved. On average, the acquiring firm is about five times the size of the acquired firm. Suppose, then, that a $5 billion firm seeks to acquire a $1 billion firm. The expected GAIN from the merger is $500 million, or a hefty 50 percent premium for the acquired firm, of which the acquiring firm originally expects to capture one half (or $250 million). Table 8–2 indicates in part I the pre-merger and in part II the *expected* post-merger situation for firm A, the acquiring firm. In fact, it is the expectations set forth in part II that induce firm A to begin the merger process.

But now suppose that, in the process of putting together the merger and its transaction and financing costs, the split of the GAIN becomes less favorable to the acquiring firm. Since it is difficult to stop any megabuck-sized process, the final distribution of the GAIN tends to shift further in favor of the acquired firm, leaving the results as shown in part III of the table.

Firm A winds up with a stock price about 3 percent higher than pre-merger, while firm B's stock price, at the merger's consummation, yields its stockholders a GAIN of nearly 38 percent. Because there is likely to be a good deal of random noise regarding the level of A's stock price, especially in the neighborhood of a merger owing to, say, the unwinding of arbitrage positions (see Chapter 9), some small price variance could be accounted for on purely technical grounds. The combined relative size effect and transaction factors could make it much more difficult to show a positive GAIN for the acquiring firm than for the acquired firm. And all of the above hold even without any assumption of green-mail, which affects only the GAIN of the acquiring (or surviving) firm.

Finally, the preceding valuation of the acquiring firm's price per share assumed away the effect on the stock price of raising the funds to finance the acquisition. Suppose that the acquisition had been financed by new borrowing, for that clearly has been the recent funding of choice for cash acquisitions. The consequent rise in the acquiring firm's debt/equity ratio could certainly explain at least some part of that firm's short-term slack performance in the stock market. Indeed, the closer the volume of new debt comes to the size of the acquisition, the more likely a rise in the combined firm's debt/asset ratio. In the short run, then, the bidding firm's stock price should show a relatively low GAIN, if any.

9

MERGERS AND ACQUISITIONS II: RISK ARBITRAGE AND MERGER MARKET MAKING AS INSURANCE

In the process of participating in the merger, acquisition, and takeover game, investment bankers perform many roles. The most obvious is as advisors, rendering fairness (of price) opinions to the target and bidding firms. Beyond advice, the market makers may provide at the close of any agreement several additional items from their overall service menu. Among these are bridge loans, which are designed to finance the successful bidder until permanent financing can be arranged. Frequently, the same investment banker will underwrite the new securities that more permanently finance that firm (e.g., junk bonds).[1] The major investment banking firms have organized their merger and acquisition (M&A) departments to provide an integrated service set that can go from the advisory to the underwriting of a new issue designed to raise the funds for, say, a takeover.

Market making may extend beyond direct involvement in the deal. The risk arbitrage department may trade the securities of any corporation that may have been "put in play" by other firms. Corporations "in play" may be willing, or unwilling, participants in deals such as mergers, takeovers, liquidation (par-

---

[1]For further discussion see Chapters 4 and 6.

tial), leveraged buyouts, and even recapitalizations that go as far as bankruptcy. The "risk arbitrage" department of an investment banker is given that name because, by making a market in such a deal, the investment banker is taking a security position that puts him at some risk (see below). To be sure, risk arbitrageurs do what they do because the expected, risk-adjusted return exceeds that on alternative investments. All the same, their actions bring security prices closer to where the deal can get done, thereby facilitating consummation.

RISK ARBITRAGE

Arbitrageurs take a position in the firms involved in a merger or a takeover. They are interested in the *AB deal,* not in becoming stockholders in A or B. In order to commit funds to the deal, they must be convinced that the deal will go through.[2]

The assessment made by the "arb" may be based on security analysis of the two firms' financial statements and on reports in Moody's and Standard & Poor's—all designed to evaluate the economic logic behind the combination. (This is the equivalent of an independent evaluation of what was called GAIN in the preceding chapter.) The arb may also attempt to get more information from the two firms. In Wyser-Pratte's words, "It is at this point that the curtain rises on one of the great comic operas of Wall Street... the [acquired firm] is normally totally cooperative, realizing that the arbitrageur can, by purchasing [its] stock, accumulate votes which will naturally be cast in favor of the merger. ... The [acquiring] firm is an entirely different matter. He will not be pleased that [his] ... stock may become the subject of constant short selling by arbitrageurs; he is thus often elusive in his responses."[3]

---

[2]The following is based in part on G. P. Wyser-Pratte, *Risk Arbitrage II* (Monograph 1982–3/4, Salomon Brothers Center, Graduate School of Business Administration, New York University, 1982).

[3]Ibid., pp. 8–9. This information gathering process has led a number of participants into a territory where they become insiders, and then begin to trade on that information illegally. See Chapter 10 below for further discussion of insider trading.

Arbs go long on the target firm and short on the acquiring firm. That way, the arb's hedged position is not at the mercy of the market (and its changing prices) but is at risk only with respect to the consummation of the deal (hence the term, *risk arbitrage*). At the consummation of the merger, the arb tenders his long stock in B, the acquired firm, like every other B stockholder, and with the proceeds (or the new shares received from the merger) covers his short in A. If the market falls during these negotiations, and even if his proceeds from B are less, he makes money on the short position. If the market rises, he makes on the long what he loses on his short. In the end, if the arb is *not* nimble enough to unwind his position should the merger unravel, he becomes an unwilling investor with a possible problem position in his short. The following example examines this process more closely.

THE RISK-ARBITRAGE DEAL

Suppose a merger is being contemplated by company A with company B. The bidder (A) expects to acquire the target (B) through a one-for-one exchange of stock: one share of A for one share of B. Prior to the announcement of A's intent, A's price is $30 per share, while B is trading at $20 per share. B's price had risen to $25 per share prior to the announcement of A's intent (and the associated, customary, and temporary suspension of trading in B's stock). Because, ultimately, the arbitrageur can acquire a share of A (price $30) with a share of B (pre-merger), he counts the $5 difference between B's price and A's as his potential gross profit. That $5 spread exists because B cannot be converted into A immediately; the arbitrageur's problem is to ensure that the spread is maintained until the merger is consummated. But the spread may narrow and/or disappear entirely:

1. As the merger becomes more likely.
2. As the time prior to merger shortens.
3. As market prices of A and B change owing to the market's vagaries.

Taking the latter point first, if A's price should fall toward $25, the spread could narrow and even vanish. Thus, as a first step, the arbitrageur sells short the number of shares he wants to acquire of A at $30 per share. As protection against the open-ended risk that A could rise sharply, the arbitrageur also buys the same number of shares of B long, thereby indirectly acquiring A at the merger price.[4]

Two possible sets of price changes might affect the relative values of A and B at the time of the merger's closing. Company A's price could drop prior to merger, or it could rise. Suppose A drops in price to $27 at the closing; in a share-for-share merger, B would then be worth $27 as well. By selling A short (at $30) and holding B at $25, the arbitrageur maintains his $5 spread as follows:

1. Sells B at $27 per share:

    Per share profit = $27 − $25 = $2

2. Buys A at $27 per share;
    covers $30 short at $27:

    Per share profit = $30 − $27 = $3
    Per share total profit   = $5

If, on the other hand, A's price rises to, say, $34 per share, then the price of B will also rise to $34 per share at closing. The capital gain from B (per share) will be $34 − $25 = $9. If that gain is subtracted from the loss of $4 per share on the short sale of A at $30 ($34 − $30 = 4), the gross spread of $5 still holds.

Even if the actual exchange of securities is more complicated than a one-for-one stock deal (as it usually is), the principle in structuring the arbitrage spread is the same: the target firm's securities are held long; the bidding firm's securities are sold short.

---

[4] A short sale involves borrowing the number of shares sold short (from a broker or an investment manager) and then returning those shares to the lender when the short sale is reversed.

CALCULATING THE RATE OF RETURN FROM
RISK ARBITRAGE[5]

Continue the assumption that B is merging into A and each share of B will get a share of A in an even exchange of stock. B is now selling at $25 per share while A is selling at $30 per share, and neither company is expected to pay a dividend prior to consummation.[6] Consummation will take place in four months, an important variable in the calculation of the annualized rate of return to the deal (see following calculations).

The arb's first analysis of the rate of return works as follows, at an annual rate:

Gross return on deal multiplied by annualized rates:[7]

$$\frac{\$30 - \$25}{\$25} \times 3 = 60 \text{ percent}$$

The short sale of A is necessarily part of this approach since new (post-merger) shares (call these A_n) are "created" by buying B long. This makes sense since the arb shorts the old $30 A stock and buys long the equivalent of A_n at $25 (that is, holds B long). Here is one of the technical problems of arbitrageurs. If there is a struggle for controlling the shares in a merger or a takeover, the arb may have trouble borrowing enough stock for a short position to set up the hedge counterpart of the arbitrage position he wants to achieve. On the other side of the deal, competitive forces tend to drive up the premium on B, thereby lowering the gross return on the deal.

Entirely apart from hedging the position with respect to changes in market-price levels, shorting the acquiring firm makes sense because, if the arb did not do so, an exchange of B stock for A, post-merger, might concentrate too many shares of the surviving firm in unwilling arb hands. In turn, the arb's interest in selling out that position might depress A's price follow-

---

[5]The example is adapted from Wyser-Pratte, *Risk Arbitrage II*, pp. 18–19.
[6]This is only a simplifying assumption.
[7]There are three periods of four months per year.

ing the merger's closing, not only cutting the acquiring firm's
GAIN further but also (and from arb's point of view, more importantly) cutting into the profit from the position.

Setting up and unwinding of arbitrage positions tends to
produce positive price effects on B, which is held long until closing; in that sense, arbitrage supports the acquired firm's GAIN.
Conversely, for the acquiring firm, the establishment of a short
position, and its subsequent unwinding, generates a great deal
of noise/signal price information especially at the time of consummation. The more contested the merger, the greater the size
of the noise/signal ratio. As Stewart Myers pointed out, "in
mergers, the ratio of 'noise' to 'signal' is very high."[8]

For the sake of simplicity the above analysis has been developed as if these price data were fixed or somehow known. In
reality, risk arbitrageurs make trading decisions on the basis of
"expected" values, that is, on the basis of probability-adjusted
prices. To simplify the decision making process somewhat, consider an arbitrageur's price calculations as follows:

$$EV = a(P_p) + (1 - a)(P_b)$$

where:

EV = expected value

a = % probability of success

P_p = premium price (deal is successful)

P_b = break-up price (deal falls apart)

Suppose a corporation's pre-deal price was $40 per share. Sup-
pose further that "a," or probability of success, was deemed to be
80%, and that premium to be paid was one half of pre-deal price;

---

[8]Stewart Myers, "The Evaluation of an Acquisition Target," *Midland Corporate Finance Journal* 1, no. 4, p. 39.

a further simplifying assumption is made that if the deal breaks up, the stock price reverts to pre-deal price.

Then:

$$EV = 0.8\,(\$40 + \$20) + (1 - 0.8)\,(\$40)$$
$$= \$58 + \$8 = \$66$$

Whether a given firm participates as a risk arbitrageur depends first, on the expected return. That return is dependent on, among other variables, the time expected to elapse between initiation of the arbitrageur's participation and the close of the deal. Second, the price expectations and probability coefficients if the deal works, or if the deal breaks up, are of the same order of importance. Third, the relationship of expected value to the arb's purchase price (relative to anticipated holding period) sets the expected return. Suppose that the arb participates only in announced deals, and enters them when the likelihood seems favorable (as the probabilities cited above suggest). Suppose that his average acquisition cost comes to $60.00, and that the deal is expected to be closed in two months. Then:

Gross dollar return	= $66 − $60 =	$6
Gross return rate	= $6/$60	= 10%
Return @ annual rate	= 10% × 6	= 60%

That annual rate is the result of multiplying the gross return rate by six since there are six two-month periods per year. All of the returns are before taxes.

Continued participation in such deals develops the required estimating skills and/or a network of specialists who can provide the required forecasts. Among other predictions, those involved in expected value forecasts require the ability to predict likelihoods of actions of regulators of the industry (if relevant), the action of management(s) involved, and many other factors; and most crucial, the impact of all of the above on relevant stock prices. If that set of skills is not available, or fails often enough, the risk arbitrageur will not stay in business very long.

Who are these arbs? According to Wyser-Pratte they are members of the best-known investment banking firms "who commit house capital . . . in the various forms of arbitrage." The list includes such outstanding firms as Shearson Lehman Brothers (in an earlier incarnation), Goldman Sachs, Morgan Stanley, and Salomon Brothers.[9] He is too modest to mention his own firm, Prudential Bache; Wyser-Pratte also indicates that First Boston and Merrill Lynch are important players in risk arbitrage. Also, because most arbitrage transactions are deal oriented rather than market oriented, other broker–dealer firms as well as individuals deemed to be "fringe players" try to participate in some deals. Nevertheless, Wyser-Pratte and others have argued that market shocks and problem deals tend to send the fringe players to the showers early. After all, the pros can afford to lose on some deals what they previously made on others. The occasional player will not be as effectively diversified in a cross-section of deals.

Finally, nonprofessional traders are at a substantial rate-of-return disadvantage relative to the pros. First, the amount of funds (nonborrowed) needed by New York Stock Exchange (NYSE) member firms to participate in a deal is far less (haircut on long position plus modest capital/liabilities ratio) compared to a 50 percent capital margin rule for individuals.[10] Further, for member firms there is no capital requirement on short positions, while the same (Regulation T) margin rule applies to all credit transactions for individuals. Whatever returns are earned are thus applied for individuals against a much larger capital position than for member firms; in addition, the out-of-pocket transaction costs to the member firms are probably significantly less. Wyser-Pratte argues that the risk-adjusted return advantage of professionals over individuals is about 8.5 times.[11] Even if it were only half as great, it would, at best, make nonprofessionals a minor element in risk arbitrage.

---

[9]Wyser-Pratte, *Risk Arbitrage II*, p. 4.

[10]Wyser-Pratte's data refer to an 80 percent margin rule (Federal Regulation T).

[11]Wyser-Pratte, *Risk Arbitrage II*, pp. 30–31.

INVESTMENT BANKERS: OTHER ACTIVITIES
IN CORPORATE RESTRUCTURING[12]

Investment bankers are substantially involved with client consultations on both sides of acquisitions and mergers, finding a white knight, and so forth. They also participate in risk arbitrage *on their own*. Only a few additional functions remain to be discussed: divestitures, going private, leveraged buyouts, and spin-offs. The first and last of these are, once again, examples of the new math: $5 - 1 = 5$, or more.

A divestiture is, pure and simple, a sale of assets for cash, where presumably the sale and its attendant improvement in balance-sheet liquidity make the firm more valuable than holding the (now sold) assets. In other words, the substitution of *cash* in the asset portfolio called the firm for the *assets* sold raises the firm's value.

All the other corporate restructuring policies mentioned imply no change in the value of the assets but claim a benefit from a restructuring of the right side of the balance sheet. For example, "going private" means the repurchase of shares from the market—not on a piecemeal basis but the entire outstanding stock issue—so that ownership is no longer public but is concentrated in a small private group typically centered on management. A spin-off is an internalized divestiture where a subsidiary is set up with its own separate shares which are then issued to the original stockholders. These stockholders may then decide on their own portfolio (or liquidity ratio) policies by selling the shares for cash or holding them in portfolio.

The going-private type of reorganization of the firm's capital structure is done to improve monitoring incentives for management by eliminating the separation of ownership and manage-

---

[12]This section is based in part on K. Schipper, "The Evidence on Divestitures, Going-Private Proposals and Spin-Offs," *Midland Corporate Finance Journal* 1, no. 4, pp. 51–55; and C. Ferenbach, "Leveraged Buyouts: A New Capital Market," *Midland Corporate Finance Journal* 1, no. 4, pp. 56–63.

ment. In other words, agency costs are eliminated by collapsing a public corporation into private ownership.

Leveraged buyouts (LBOs) are what they say they are: the new owners (that is, *the lenders*) buy out the current stockholders. A firm that might have had an equity/debt ratio of 9:1 turns that ratio upside down. Management may take a more significant position in the much reduced equity, while lenders may benefit from higher rates on the larger debt. Many of these deals were made during the high-interest-rate periods of the early 1980s. Such decisions were made easier for many lenders because of (1) long-standing credit relationships and (2) the substitution of a 14 percent buyout issue for a 9 percent bond.[13] On the risk analysis side, as long as a lender's portfolio remained effectively diversified among credit ratings as well as among industries, the higher coupons as well as the elimination of below-par bonds made the risks appear acceptable. Besides, many banks (and other lenders) became packagers of LBOs and actively sold such deals as agents, happily collecting the fees involved. Why would they demonstrate their lack of faith in the product by not investing in it? Investment banking firms proper also invested in such deals as well as working as packagers.

It is interesting to examine the quantitative importance of all of the above on common stock retirements. Mergers, acquisitions, going private, and LBOs all necessarily involve a gross reduction in some equity issues. This point is illustrated by a chart showing Federal Reserve's flow of funds data (Figure 9–1) which compares the net funds raised by corporations through bond issues (upper panel) with net funds generated by equity issues (lower panel). Considering, first, the equity side (lower panel), one observes that in the period up to about 1979 *net* equity funds raised ranged from neutral (or zero) to a mildly positive number (generally at a rate of less than $10 billion per year).

Starting with 1980, however, the quarterly equity numbers

---

[13]To the extent that these same lenders were concerned about marking to market some 9 percent bonds selling below par, that same decision appeared even more sensible.

FIGURE 9–1
Net Funds Raised by Nonfinancial Corporations

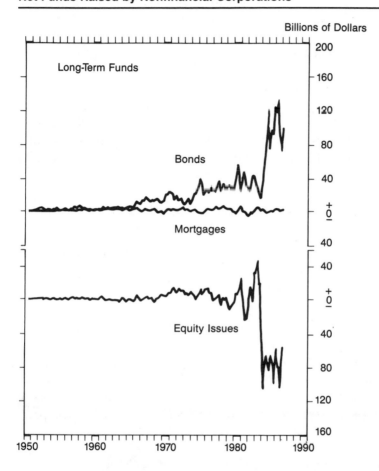

(at annual rates) began to gyrate wildly. New issues carried to *one* quarterly peak in excess of a $40 billion rate in 1983, but subsequently equity issues settled back to a net *retirement* rate of about $80 billion starting with 1984. Looking at the upper panel one notes a close parallel surge in new bond issues rising from an average of less than $40 billion prior to 1983 to average about $100 billion per year in the period since 1983. The parallel of the bond surge with stock *retirements* is very close: those equity retirements reflect the aftermath of the wave of mergers, acquisitions, LBOs, and other forms of corporate reorganization in which new debt was the primary source of funds for stock retirements.

Investment Banker Fees Once Again

All of these stock retirements and the issuing of new paper to finance acquisitions involve investment bankers not only as advisers to each of the parties involved but also as experts in pricing either the new securities or in setting a fair price on securities to be retired. Setting a price on a stock for a firm in a LBO or in going private is, in most respects, an analog to pricing a secondary or block trade.

This point regarding fee income was restated as follows in an article in the *New York Times* (April 5, 1988):

> The 11-week battle for control of Federated Department Stores Inc. will produce one of the biggest paydays Wall Street has ever seen. Investment banks and law firms expect to collect at least $200 million.

Table 9–1 shows the *Times'* estimate of the fees (in millions of dollars).

The market-making skills used by investment bankers in their routine activities can be transferred to mergers, acquisitions, divestitures, reorganizations, and risk arbitrage. One of the underappreciated examples of synergism in M&A is the pric-

TABLE 9–1
Estimated Fees Paid for Federated Department Stores Takeover, 1988 (In Millions of Dollars)

Banking Firm	Client	Fee
First Boston	Campeau	$49.0*
Drexel Burnham Lambert	R.H. Macy	25.0†
Kidder Peabody	R.H. Macy	25.0†
Shearson Lehman Hutton	Federated	19.8
Goldman, Sachs	Federated	17.8
Hellman & Friedman	Federated	16.3
Wasserstein, Perella	Campeau	10.0*

*Estimated (by New York Times).
†The total for *both* firms equals $25 million.

ing and operating skills investment bankers develop at their trading desks and put at the service of their merger clients.

THE MERGER FEE
AS AN INSURANCE PREMIUM

Early in 1985, in a suit involving the Trans-Union Corporation's directors, a Delaware court found that the latter had failed to "exercise informed business judgment" in selling the company. The directors agreed to a settlement in which shareholders were paid $23.5 million in damages. Insurance, the acquiring firm, *and the directors themselves* paid for the damage award. Later that same year, a Texas court rendered a $10.53 billion judgment for Pennzoil and against Texaco, following the Getty merger (for further discussion see Chapter 8). Partly in response to a flurry of stockholder suits, insurance companies have raised the premiums on corporate directors' liability coverage to "astronomical" levels—if they make it available at all. And finally, outside corporate directors are resigning, even while many directors' slots remain vacant.

These phenomena should be kept in mind when reviewing the large size of advisors' fees (for lawyers, investment bankers, and so forth) in recent megamergers, takeovers, and LBOs. The fairness opinions and other services purchased by corporate managers and directors from investment bankers, big-eight accounting firms, and merger lawyers should themselves be looked on as insurance premiums. Board members and managers buy that additional insurance because they believe it will protect them from legal attack from any parties to the deal (even if the attacks are ultimately unsuccessful). This demand for insurance has also been expanded because the "business-judgment rule" can no longer be assumed to provide an automatic or procedural legal defense. The merger wave was followed by expensive liability insurance settlements and still more costly increases in directors' liability insurance coverage.[14]

---

[14]The settlements referred to involved, among others, Chase Manhattan Corp. in a suit against its own officers who were connected with the purchase of loans from Penn

These developments have been in the making for some time and are reflected in the large fees paid to the major investment banking firms in merger and takeover cases. Managements and the boards of directors are buying insurance for themselves from the investment banking firms. The best way to see this is to separate the demand side from the supply side of these phenomena.[15]

Demand for Advice

A. *Attitudes*

Suppose a firm's board members and management find they are the target of an unwanted and unanticipated takeover bid. The first shock has worn off, the panic, anger, and other emotional reactions have been talked out. The next step is to evaluate an appropriate response with board and management participants who have had prior experience with such events. In most cases, and especially if a board member happens to be an investment banker, there will be a call for experts in the following areas:

1. Defense: poison pill, crown jewel sale, and so forth.
2. Implementation of defense and/or other strategies that are designed to lead to higher premiums on the target firm's stock.
3. Alternative reorganization: LBO and so forth.

For most of these activities, outside consultants will probably be brought in and *not necessarily because* board members have not had similar experience before.

Square Bank in Oklahoma. The same source cited more than tenfold increases in the direct cost of coverage for directors' liability as well as fourfold jump in deductibles and an "insertion of a dozen new exclusions" in the policies. (Source: L. Sloane, "Insurer-Management Rift Seen Growing," *The New York Times,* December 19, 1985.)

[15]"Fairness" opinions by investment bankers have come under more intense scrutiny as the merger boom continues. Whether or not these opinions are subject to stockholder suits, the argument proposed here is that the insurance purchased by corporate insiders from investment bankers appears appropriate to these insiders: it substitutes the investment banker as the defendant in litigation. See, "Suspect Opinions—If an Investment Bank says the Deal Is Fair It May or May Not Be," *Wall Street Journal,* March 10, 1988, p. 1.

Board members have an attitude that can be described in its simplest terms as a "negative agency" approach. Consider the following:

1. In the past, directors may have been insured against liability suits, but that insurance was never unlimited and is becoming less available.
2. Decisions that are made regarding the price of assets to be sold or the pricing of securities to be issued in an atmosphere of conflict and contested policies are not going to be easy. Nor are these pricing decisions necessarily related to currently published price data.
3. A good decision will be rewarded by the renewal of a director's contract at a decent (but not exorbitantly attractive) rate of return. A bad decision (in the perception of some litigious stockholder) may result in ruinous legal costs to any director even if the board's decision is ultimately upheld.

Because, in the absence of experts, board members are exposed to a risk of substantially greater losses than of potential gain, board members and management may opt for a call to lawyers and investment bankers. This attitude aspect of the demand side is reinforced by the second major element, namely, other people's money.

B. *Other People's Money*

In megamergers, target firms have been able to leverage enormous sums out of the bidding firms as premiums paid to stockholders. Moreover, the fact that the bidding firm is likely to have its investment bankers and lawyers as active participants in the negotiations will reinforce the demand side for similar services by the target firm. For the board members of the target firm, the payment of a $10.1 million fee for advice on a $1 billion deal can be justified as a transaction cost to the accepted limits for, say,

---

[16]These merger fees have been maintained at the level of the "Lehman rule" in spite of competitive factors, as will be argued below. For current competitive factors in setting flotation costs for new issues, see Chapter 17.

a new flotation.[16] Seen from the bidding firm, a similar cost can be rationalized by the same argument, especially if funds are raised by junk bond borrowing; the flotation costs for the latter are, of course, added to total transaction costs.

C. *The Supply Side*

It might be argued that investment bankers charge the large fees they do because they take on the risks of stockholder suits transferred to them by the boards that hire them. This is true in a general way. But it is hard to believe that, say, more than 1 in 10 mergers will generate an expensive suit. This portfolio approach reflects, of course, the possibility that investment bankers (or lawyers) diversify their risks in ways that board members or managers of a single firm cannot.

But if there is efficiency in that type of risk diversification, shouldn't competition bring down the cost of merger participation and consultation by other investment bankers eager to get into the game? Isn't this merger consultation arrangement analogous to the bidding for new issues that has driven down gross spreads?

The major difference here is the essentially confidential nature of merger advice and participation as opposed to the open competition for flotation of new issues (since shelf registration came on the scene) regarding gross spreads. Further, each merger or takeover conflict has elements that are not as readily converted to conventional bidding mechanics as are the rate (and nonrate) items of a new issue. Even innovative new issues carry wider gross spreads than those types of securities that have entered secondary trading.

Beyond all of the above are the elements of perceived quality differences among investment bankers. Such demand side elements (and negative agency attitudes) induce management to go with well-known, as opposed to newer, entrants even if the latter offer more competitive fees. In a crisis atmosphere when decisions must be made fast, whom do you consult: the person with experience or the new guy on the block offering a cheaper service, especially if you're risking litigation as a board member and "spending" someone else's money?

Investment bankers represent what may be the nation's largest *unregulated* insurance business. The insurance process is an important aspect of the new-issues business as well, but there the competition tends to reduce fees (with the exceptions to be noted).

10

INSIDER TRADING PROBLEMS

Most legislators, lawyers, regulators, and finance professionals agree on what insider trading can do to financial markets. The argument is that financial markets are driven by information, and in an academic formulation of this argument, it is hypothesized that market prices reflect the available information at the point of pricing a security. Suppose that some nonpublic or "inside" information were available that could significantly affect the security's price. If anyone acts on that information, the security's price is affected.

Most market participants argue that insider information is inequitable in that it gives an "unfair" advantage to those possessing it. As a corollary it is argued that an *unknown* component of unfair advantage makes security valuation that much more difficult. As a result, fears of mispricing may lead to a reduction in investors' confidence, and in their market participation. From a social policy point of view, many would argue, reduced participation would hurt the depth and breadth of markets.

The question then arises, Why the sudden attention to insider trading? The reason is simple: the opportunities to benefit (illegally) from such information dramatically increased with the merger wave of the 1980s. This proposition will be assessed in this chapter. Before we get into the actual examination of some well-publicized cases it is important to resolve the question, What constitutes "insider trading?"

It may be surprising to many that the agency in charge of

supervising the quality of markets, the Securities and Exchange Commission (SEC), has argued that legislative steps taken to control insider trading should *not* define what insider trading is. In part, this stems from the growth of case law developed in the years since the Securities Exchange Act (1934). More importantly, however, the SEC argues that the techniques of legislative definition might be so broad as to be difficult to interpret, or so narrow as to provide legal loopholes that market participants might be able to explore to excess.

This chapter will, first, present some parameters of the problem. It will then very briefly examine the issues in some recent relevant cases. Subsequently, the 1984 Act will be assessed, along with more recent discussions relating to the well-publicized actions brought by the SEC and the federal attorney for the Second District in New York. The chapter will close with an assessment of the special insider problems that affect multiservice firms such as investment bankers.

RECENT SURGE IN INSIDER ACTIVITY

In the early 1980s, the volume of activity in mergers and acquisitions (M&A) began to take off. In 1980, for example, fewer than 2,000 transactions were announced, but in the period 1981 to 1984 that number surged to an annual range between 2,400 and 2,500, and rose to 3,000 and 3,300, respectively, in the years 1985 to 1986. In value terms, the surge was even more dramatic: in the period 1981 to 1983 the amounts of the deal totals ranged between $50 and $80 billion per year. Deal volume subsequently more than doubled to between $175 and $180 billion annually in the years 1985 to 1987 (see Figure 10–1). How did M&A deals give rise to insider trading-type information? The answer is a simple one: as shown in Figure 10–2, merger premiums paid by the bidders to stockholders of the target company were better than one third of (pre-merger) market price. An insider could buy a $30 stock, hold it until a bid was announced, and then sell at between $40 and $45 per share. Since the volume of these

FIGURE 10–1
Aggregate Value of Announced Deals

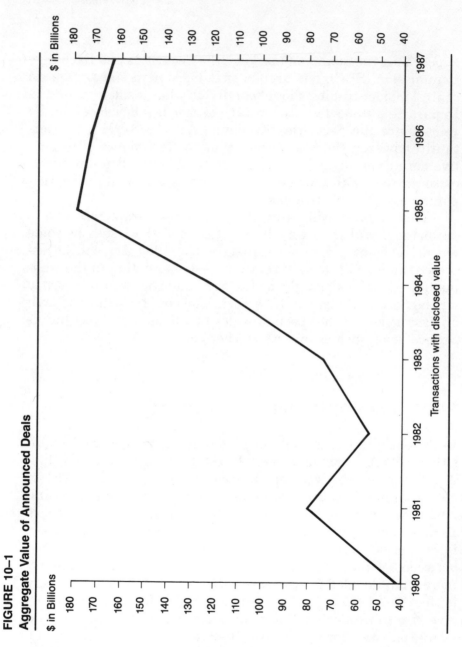

$ in Billions

Transactions with disclosed value

Source: W. T. Grimm & Co., *Mergerstat ® Review* and Lazard Frères.

FIGURE 10–2
Premiums Paid over Market

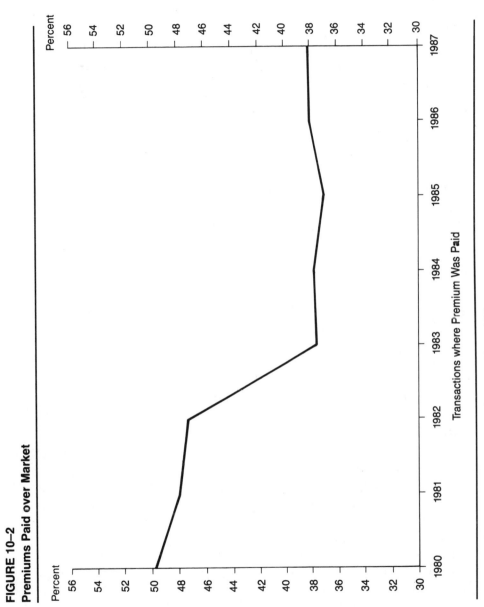

Transactions where Premium Was Paid

Source: W. T. Grimm & Co., *Mergerstat ® Review* and Lazard Frères.

transactions was sharply on the rise, as were all stock prices themselves, the temptations kept growing.

At this point a very important distinction should be made. The well-publicized cases brought by the SEC and the federal attorney for the Second District in New York referred to the criminal and civil liabilities of *individuals* (sometimes acting in conspiracy with other individuals). The individual insider trading cases, which will be discussesd first, are those that have made the front pages. There is another type of insider, however, whose actions are not as well known even though they are an organic part of the investment banking process. This type of institutional insider is the corporate finance professional or the M&A advisor who will be in the same firm as his fellow partners or professionals dealing with the investing public. The former set of pros are under wraps, obligated to keep faith with their clients, while the latter are under obligation to make public all available information to their customers. How do you deal with this *institutional* dilemma? See below.

RECENT CASE LAW: INDIVIDUAL INSIDERS

In pursuing insider trading cases, the SEC has used Section 10b and 10b-5 of the Securities Exchange Act of 1934, which prohibits "fraud" in connection with securities transactions. As the case law developed and was interpreted by the Supreme Court, the definition of "fraud" incorporated the common law notion that insiders owe a fiduciary duty to stockholders. Implicit in that version of agency theory is the notion that insiders by their actions should maximize stockholder wealth. Hence, a personal gain based on inside information implies a loss to the stockholders. Insiders have a duty to disclose or abstain from trading based on the relationship of "trust and confidence" between them and the stockholders. Further, that duty may be transferred to "tippees" who know of the tipper's breach of fiduciary duty. All such breaches of fiduciary duties (but *only* such breaches) are deemed to be "fraud" under Section 10(b). The major cases will now be briefly discussed.

Chiarella (1980)

In this case the Supreme Court reversed the criminal conviction of a financial printer who had successfully decoded the identity of takeover targets from the bidders' confidential tender offer materials, and then purchased stock of target companies. The Court held that mere possession of material nonpublic information brought no duty to disclose or to abstain. Instead, the Court focused on the *absence* of a fiduciary or agency relationship between (1) the printer and (2) the shareholders from whom he bought stock.

Dirks (1983)

The Supreme Court held that Dirks, an investment analyst who learned about massive fraud at *Equity Funding of America*, and who then informed his clients *before* the information became public, was not under any duty to *Equity Funding* shareholders to disclose or abstain. The case turned on the fact that Dirks's tipper, a former employee of *Equity Funding*, did not breach any fiduciary duties to stockholders by disclosing the fraud to Dirks since the tipper's intent was to expose illegal fraud and not the prospect of personal gain. In turn, Dirks could not be held liable for "participating after the fact" since a breach of law did not exist.

Misappropriation Theory

A person who has "misappropriated" nonpublic information from someone who expected him to keep that information confidential must refrain from trading. In this sense, misappropriation may range from outright theft of information to the conversion to personal advantage of information provided for some corporate purpose, or acquired in the context of another confidential relationship.

This theory was extended in the R. Foster Winans case

(1986)[1] in which the court let stand the convictions under Rule 10b-5 of three individuals who made prepublication trades based on advance knowledge of forthcoming "Heard on the Street" columns written by Winans and published in the *Wall Street Journal* (the Supreme Court split 4–4, thereby upholding the lower court conviction). Under that decision, the court observed that the "advance knowledge of the timing and content of these publications" allowed defendants to profit from their trading. The court declared that such conduct constituted "fraud and deceit as it would had Winans stolen material nonpublic information from traditional corporate insiders or quasi-insiders."[2]

Legislative Actions

As the volume of SEC actions increased in the early 1980s, and as some of the cases described were moved through the courts, the Congress began to act. The first legislation dealing directly with the insider problem was passed a half century after the Securities Exchange Act; it was called the *Insider Trading Sanctions Act of 1984* (or ITSA, P.L. 98-376, which became effective on August 10, 1984). It is useful, however, to recall the SEC's position prior to 1984. Up to then the SEC had only the provisions of the Securities and Exchange Act to rely on; Section 21(d) (1) of that Act permitted an injunction against any person who is "engaged, or is about to engage" in a violation of the Act. The SEC also had sought to force inside traders to disgorge profits (or remit funds equal to losses avoided) as a penalty. And finally, the development of derivative (that is, option) markets had made it easier and cheaper for violators to make large profits on violation of the law.[3] These profits, as well as inflation, had eroded the deterrent value of a $10,000 criminal fine. In effect,

---

[1]The Winans case extended the misappropriation theory. See *U.S. vs. Carpenter,* 791 F.2d 1024 (2d Circuit), *cert. granted.* 107 S. Ct. 666 (1986) in which the court affirmed convictions under Rule 10b-5 for the three individuals involved.

[2]U.S. vs. Carpenter; see citation above.

[3]In *SEC vs. Musella,* 578 F. Supp. 425 (S.D. N.Y. 1984), one group of defendants made $872,000 in profits on $92,000 in call options purchased a day before the announcement of a tender offer.

the SEC's use of the "obey the law" injunction or of the power to force disgorgement of ill-gotten gains merely placed the violator in the position that (aside from a modest penalty) he would have been in if he had obeyed the law.

In the 1984 Act (ITSA), the civil penalty payable to the U.S. Treasury was boosted to a maximum *three* times the "profit gained or loss avoided" on securities transactions "while in possession of material of nonpublic information" in violation of the Exchange Act, or of rules and regulations enacted on its basis.

It is interesting and important to note that, following the SEC's advice, Congress did *not* provide a statutory definition of insider trading. The SEC argued that existing case law provided "sufficient guidance" to market professionals without sacrificing the SEC's need for flexibility in meeting "unforeseen fact patterns." In addition, it was felt that a statutory definition could have been too broad and general to give guidance or so narrow as to create "statutory loopholes." Further, SEC rulemaking and adjudication could be used as substitutes for a definition while still leaving some flexibility; this was exemplified by SEC Rule 14e-3, which developed a specific definition of insider trading but only in a tender offer context.

The Act also made "aiders and abettors" liable for the civil penalty "if they communicate material nonpublic information." Further, the corporation for which an employee traded on material inside information could be held liable "under circumstances in which it would be appropriate to attribute the employee's action to the corporation."[4]

Finally, the *criminal* fine under the Act was raised from $10,000 to $100,000 [15 U.S.C. 78H(a)].

The SEC Actions

In recent years, as public perception of insider trading activities has increased, the SEC has sharply stepped up its efforts to detect and to prosecute insider trading. Testifying before a House

---

[4]See H. R. Rep. No. 355.

Committee[5] SEC Chairman John Shad stated that from fiscal year 1982 through fiscal 1985 the SEC had brought 77 insider trading enforcement actions. The same number of actions had been brought by SEC from its organization in 1934 through fiscal 1981. And SEC actions taken—as well as those brought by federal prosecutors—in 1986 and 1987 have shaken the Wall Street establishment. Further case developments may still be in process as information developed by those cooperating with the SEC and the prosecutors may lead to others. All of this activity has led to further legislative proposals during the 1987–88 Congress that may, in one form or another, extend ITSA by developing definitions for insider trading (although the SEC still opposes such attempts), and reducing court discretion in imposing large fines.

In May 1986, the SEC had brought its largest (in dollars) insider trading case to that date. The action was against Dennis Levine, a managing director at Drexel Burnham Lambert, several Panamanian corporations, and a Swiss national who was Levine's broker in a Bahamian subsidiary of a Swiss bank. The SEC alleged that since May 1980, Levine had made $12.6 million by trading in the stocks of at least 54 companies on the basis of material nonpublic information concerning mergers, tender offers, leveraged buyouts, and other changes in corporate control likely to enhance stock values. Since many of the deals from which Levine profited had not involved firms represented by Drexel, this suggested that Levine's information had come from others, especially from members of the risk arbitrage community. Levine ultimately pleaded guilty to one count of perjury, two counts of tax evasion, and one count of trading on inside information. He agreed to disgorge $11.6 million, and consented to an order barring him from the securities business for life. Even though he had faced a possible penalty of 20 years in prison on the four counts on which he pleaded guilty, his sentence was less than a tenth of that time in exchange for cooperation with authorities, which included naming names among the most respected firms in investment banking and arbitrage.

---

[5]Statement before the House Energy and Commerce Subcommittee, June 18, 1986.

In another action, the SEC brought proceedings against Ivan F. Boesky, Wall Street's leading arbitrageur, for violation of the antifraud provisions of the federal securities law. The SEC allegations included the charge that Boesky had traded the securities of at least seven U.S. companies based on material, non-public information concerning tender offers, mergers, and other corporate actions leading to higher prices of those stocks. According to the SEC, the source of that inside information was Dennis Levine. Boesky agreed to forgo a trial, to accept the entry of a judicial decree, and to pay over funds to the U.S. Treasury. Boesky settled the SEC civil enforcement proceeding by disgorging $50 million in trading profits, and paying another $50 million as a penalty. He also agreed to an order barring him from the securities industry for life, and pleaded guilty to one (unspecified) criminal charge. Within a week of the SEC's settlement the first of a number of civil law suits was filed against him for the purpose of recovering stockholder losses; if damage judgments are rendered against Boesky, these are to be paid out of the first $50 million disgorged by him. Boesky started serving time in prison in 1988.

Further actions may stem from the consent agreement made by Martin Siegel with the SEC in 1987.[6] Siegel had been at Kidder Peabody, but was co-head of mergers and acquisitions at Drexel Burnham Lambert at the time of the SEC action in February 1987. The SEC charged that Siegel had illegally provided confidential information to Boesky regarding takeovers for at least three years prior to SEC action. Siegel agreed to disgorge $4.25 million, including his partnership interest in Drexel. The Boesky/Siegel arrangement included the uses of passwords, and exchanges of briefcases full of cash. Information from Siegel to Boesky included merger and acquisition information regarding firms such as Carnation, Natomas, Bendix, and Getty Oil. Siegel also pled guilty regarding three members of the risk ar-

---

[6]In connection with the Siegel case, in June 1987, Kidder Peabody & Co. settled civil insider trading charges brought by the SEC. It agreed to disgorge some $13.7 million in illegal profits, and pay an ITSA fine of $11.7 million. This case may involve, to some degree, *institutional* insider trading although most of the breach of law apparently attached to the actions of Martin Siegel.

bitrage community working for Goldman Sachs, Kidder Peabody, and Merrill Lynch. The latter three cases are still in suspension at this writing.[7]

There have been further actions following these, but this summary is designed to be illustrative, not exhaustive. And while the stories of these individuals are instructive, the next section is more directly related to our purpose. The problem for a multi-service firm, such as an investment bank, is that it will be continuously accessing nonpublic and material information regarding a given firm in one department, and may be trading the *same* stocks in another department.

Institutional Insider Trading

An individual's insider trading activity, where intent to breach existing law and SEC rules is relatively clear, can be readily understood. The actions of an institution are much more complicated. Even the brief summary of the ambiguities of an individual's multiple fiduciary responsibilities (e.g., Dirks) can provide only a hint of the ambiguities and complexities for multiservice financial firms. This problem was recognized 25 years ago when the SEC in its *Special Study of the Securities Market* argued that:

> A striking phenomenon of the securities industry is the extent to which any one participant may engage in a variety of businesses or perform a variety of functions. A single firm with customers of many kinds and sizes may, and often does, combine some or all of the functions of underwriter, retailer of unlisted or listed securities, investment adviser to discretionary accounts, to others on a fee basis, and to one or more corporations. Its principals may invest or trade for their accounts in securities also dealt in for others. . . .
>
> . . . . Since each of these functions involves its own set of obligations to particular persons or groups of persons and since the self-interest of the broker-dealer may be involved in one or more,

---

[7]Arrests were made and indictments were brought, but these indictments were subsequently dismissed at the prosecution's request "without prejudice." The prosecution argued that these cases were the "tip of the iceberg," and that further actions would follow.

there are multifarious possibilities of conflict of obligation or interest in matters large and small. . . . Total elimination of all possibilities is obviously quite out of the question; theoretically it . . .
would have to involve fragmentation of the business to a point
where each investor would have his own broker who would not be
permitted to act for any other customer or for himself.[8]

Bringing this problem to the present, and even after the experience of the well-publicized insider trading pleas by Levine,
Boesky and others, the outgoing SEC chairman John Shad, argued in early 1987 *against* the required divestiture of risk arbitrage operations for investment banking firms that handle
mergers and acquisitions. He warned that such a decision would
have "tremendous adverse economic consequences" and said
that Wall Street businesses will "clean up their acts" without the
application of such draconian pressure. Senator William Proxmire (D-Wisconsin), Chairman of the Senate Banking Committee, had raised precisely this issue of prohibiting broker–dealers
from simultaneously conducting risk arbitrage and investment
banking activities.[9]

The institutional problem arises because one department of
the investment banker is required to keep new material information for a new XYZ bond issue confidential, behind a "Chinese
Wall," until the prospectus is published. At the same time another department may be acting as an agent for a buyer of XYZ
stock to whom all "new material information" should be given.
One statement of the first part of the problem reads as follows:

> Unless otherwise agreed, an agent is subject to a duty to the
> principal not to use or to communicate information confidentially
> given him by the principal or acquired by him during the course
> of or on account of his agency or in violation of his duties as agent,
> . . . on his own account or on behalf of another, . . . unless the
> information is a matter of general knowledge. *Restatement (Sec-
> ond) of Agency* S395 (1958).

---

[8] *SEC Special Study of the Securities Markets,* H. R. Doc. 95, 88th Congress, First
Session, Pt. 5 at 65–66 (1963).

[9] *Hearing Before Senate Banking Committee,* 100th Congress, First Session (March
4, 1987) (Statement of Senator Proxmire). It is instructive to compare the Proxmire
proposal to excerpt from the SEC *Special Study* above.

With respect to the *trading* clients, as opposed to the corporate clients to which investment banker may have an advisory (or "fiduciary") relationship, there are disclosure requirements that may run directly counter to the agency confidentiality constraint.[10] The SEC has developed a "shingle" theory regarding trading clients that sets the broad principle that any broker who hangs out a shingle must deal fairly with the trading public. The disclosure requirements under that theory are not completely clear. The Second Circuit rendered an often cited formulation of the shingle theory in *Hanly v. SEC:*

> A securities dealer occupies a special relationship to a buyer of securities in that by his position he implicitly represents he has an adequate basis for the opinions he renders. . . . He cannot recommend a security unless there is an *adequate and reasonable basis* for such recommendation. He must disclose facts which he knows and those which are reasonably ascertainable. By his recommendation he implies that a reasonable investigation has been made and that his recommendation rests on the conclusions based on such investigation.[11]

Investment bankers face difficult conflicts not yet resolved under existing law: the multi-service securities firm that obtains material nonpublic information about the issuer of publicly traded securities may find itself in a position where literal compliance with its disclosure obligations to its retail customers will render it guilty of impermissible "tipping" in violation of rule 10b-5; at the same time, a failure to so "tip" may render any recommendation it makes without "an adequate and reasonable basis" in light of all information about the issuer known to the firm.[12]

---

[10]There is another "institutional" conflict of interest between any broker/dealer and his institutional client called "front running." This involves a broker/dealer acting on his own behalf in the futures market after receiving an institutional-size equity order that, he believes, is large enough to move the market. The NYSE prohibited "front running" as of March 1988.

[11]415 F.2d 587, 596–97 (2d Circuit 1969). Footnotes are omitted, emphasis is supplied.

[12]Varn, *The Multi-Service Securities Firm and the Chinese Wall: A New Look in Light of the Federal Securities Code,* 63 Neb. Law Rev. 197, 246–48 (1984), p. 211.

In the attempt to keep separate (1) inside information flows generated by corporate clients from (2) trading clients, most firms have developed what is called a Chinese Wall between the inside information to which the investment banking firm has access and the market information made available to market makers. This well-known procedure may not solve information conflicts as shown by a case brought in 1972, Slade v. Shearson, Hammill & Co., Inc. [CCH Fed. Sec. L. Rep. 94,329 (1974)].[13]

In 1972 a stockholder (Slade) in a firm called Tidal Marine charged that the firm's investment bankers, Shearson, Hammill & Co., had permitted its registered representatives to promote Tidal's stock even though Shearson's investment banking department know that a large proportion of Tidal's fleet had been damaged. The registered reps were never told this news because Shearson, like many other Wall Street firms, had set up a Chinese Wall between the two departments.

This Shearson policy went so far as to preclude formal "buy" recommendations to be issued for securities of investment banking clients. But apparently, individual reps were permitted to research and freelance recommendations, including the stocks of investment banking clients.

When Shearson's investment banking department first heard the adverse news regarding Tidal, they tried to persuade Tidal to disclose the information to the public. When Tidal stonewalled this request, Shearson threatened to go to the regulators with the story. After that, Tidal disclosed the information to the SEC, and Shearson terminated its investment banking relationship with Tidal.

The original court in the case held that Shearson (or its reps) were prohibited from soliciting customers without disclosing all adverse information. Since disclosure might violate Shearson's confidential relationship with its investment banking client, its only alternative was to actively prohibit stock trading of client stocks through the use of a "restricted list" of stocks. The case went through a series of legal moves, ultimately being

---

[13]These paragraphs draw on N. Wolfson, *Conflicts of Interest: Investment Banking* (New York: Twentieth Century Fund, 1976), pp. 62–70.

remanded to the Second Circuit Court (see citation for description).[14] A brief excerpt from the remand order (517 F. 2d, pp. 401–402) gives some idea of the court's problem, as follows:

> Thus, it is plain that what we have here is not one legal question that has been certified, but a complexity of inter-locking questions the answers to which may vastly affect the operations of one of the most important financial businesses in the country, the securities business, as well as the investment public being protected and the various enterprises whose securities are being underwritten and traded. Inside information problems can arise in the context of a multiplicity of various functions performed by brokerage firms and in a multiplicity of factual contexts. These differing contexts may well involve different considerations and may require different solutions.
>
> It would be the height of judicial folly, we think, to attempt on an indeterminate factual record to make an abstract exposition that would adequately cover the various contexts and reach the proper overall results, however desirable this might be for the guidance of the business or however judicially challenging such an exposition might be. (Id. at 403.)

Since the case was settled on remand, it left unresolved the issues surrounding both the attribution of knowledge within investment banking firms and the efficacy of Chinese Walls, restricted lists, and other tactics in rebutting charges of insider trading lodged against them. The confusion concerning these issues stemming from the *Slade* decision has not been dispelled by the subsequent judicial and administrative teaching on the topic.

---

[14]*Slade v. Shearson, Hammill & Co., Inc.* [1973–74 Transfer Binder] Fed. Sec., L. Rep. (CCH) 94,329 (S.D.N.Y.) (denial of defendant's motion for partial summary judgment), *question certified* [1973–74 Transfer Binder] Fed. Sec. L. Rep (CCH) 94,439 (S.D.N.Y.), *remanded*, 517 F.2d 398 (2d Circuit 1974), *settlement approved*, 798 F.R.D. 309 (S.D.N.Y. 1978).

Some Conclusions, and Extensions to Commercial Banking

The dilemmas of institutional insiders may be further complicated by the use of a "restricted trade list." Such lists indicate the securities that, as an "insider," the investment banking firm will not trade. Anyone acquiring information, e.g., that stock XYZ is on a "restricted list," could use it, thereby receiving an inappropriate "tip" even though he is an outsider. Suppose, then, that a restricted list is *not* used; does that action (or inaction) leave open the risk of a recurrence of the *Slade* case? Which risk should the firm choose?

Extend now the same argument to commercial banks. Commercial banks, even when operating under somewhat eroded Glass–Steagall constraints, become the equivalent of corporate insiders through the client information obtained for their loan files and the data bases that are used for credit information. One of the corollaries of agency theory has been the notion that commercial banks serve as credit monitors for a group of creditors. One bank would be expected to monitor credit quality for other lenders if it had arranged, say, a private placement of longer term securities. The other lenders could be other banks, insurance companies, pension funds, etc. Since many of these lenders participate in other fixed income markets, as well as the equity market, when does the lead bank's monitoring function verge on the "tipping" function? This question, of course, extends to what the SEC pointed to 17 years ago in its *Institutional Investor Study Report,* albeit in a narrower context:

> Institutions must also consider the necessity of segregating information flows arising from a business relationship with a company as distinct from information received in an investor or shareholder capacity. Thus, a bank that receives detailed operating information from a company under the terms of a loan agreement may have to prevent that information from being utilized by the bank's trust department; if the information is material and nonpublic, its disclosure to the trust department investment officers might have the effect of contaminating any transaction in the

company's stock by the trust department during the period of non-disclosure.[15]

A question now occurs regarding the lead bank acting as a *monitor:* When does it inform the private placement members of new, material, *inside* information? Can it do this on the understanding that the "derivative tippees" will keep the new material under wraps from *their* trading departments? If more than three or four lenders are given this inside information, what are the probabilities that it will stay inside?

Second, if Glass–Steagall barriers are dropped further, and the banks develop security affiliates, how permissible is it for the affiliate to pass inside information to the "monitor" department for private placements (and vice versa)? This information transfer would *not* be used to gain a trading advantage in, say, the equity market, but to maintain fiduciary responsibilities regarding credit exposure. Would that "credit advantage" (say with respect to the outstanding commercial paper of the borrower) for the private placement group be considered insider trading? As financial markets become more integrated, these problems are likely to become compounded even as the use of information becomes more widespread. And the regulators will necessarily be placed in a position of playing catch-up.

---

[15]*SEC Institutional Investor Study Report,* H. R. Doc, No. 92–64, 92nd Congress, First Session, Pt. 5 at 2539 (1971).

PART III

NEW ISSUES FLOTATION

For many, the flotation of new issues is the quintessential investment banking activity. In the market-making context of this book it is an important product. All the same it is just another market-making action that carries some specialized attributes, but that employs routine market-making activities. In that environment, for example, large-scale trading in the secondary markets is a market making activity that may, at times, also support *primary* market actions.

To assess these actions it is useful, first, to lay out some parameters that refer to the corporate sector's financial requirements. It is useful to compare the sources of funds for corporate finance and the volume of new-money issues floated. Let's examine the total sources (which equal the uses) of funds of nonfinancial corporations as described by the Federal Reserve's flow-of-funds data. Table III–1 looks at a period covering six recent years to get some notion of the relative importance of internal sources—namely cash flow—and external sources. The latter consists of new-money equity and corporate debt—both long-term and short-term. Table III–1 shows that new debt far exceeds the importance of new equity even in the single year when corporate repurchase of equity does not make the volume of new-equity issues a negative number. Recall that this sector only covers nonfinancial firms.

TABLE III–1
Sources and Uses of Corporate Funds 1982–1987 (In Billions of Dollars)

	1982	1983	1984	1985	1986	1987‡
Debt*	97.4	69.8	209.5	172.4	161.4	127.6
Equity	−12.7	24.0	−82.4	−72.4	−86.4	−64.1
Total external sources	84.7	94.2	127.1	100.0	75.0	63.5
Total internal sources†	215.3	274.5	321.6	334.1	337.1	329.2
Plant and equipment spending§	267.9	261.0	309.3	330.3	322.0	327.3

*Includes all bank loans, open market paper, U.S. bonds, Eurobonds, and finance company loans. Excludes foreign equity investment.
†Sum of retained earnings after tax plus depreciation.
‡Partly estimated by Salomon Brothers.
§National Income Account basis.

Source: Federal Reserve Flow of Funds data and Salomon Brothers.

Table III–2 examines the net negative volume of new equity flotations a bit more closely. This second set of data includes financial firms, as well as other new sources of funds such as foreign buyers as well as managers' and stockholders' reinvestment plans. Even with this all-inclusive coverage, *gross* new equity flotations range between a bit below $30 billion and a bit above $65 billion. This compares with a volume of mainly merger-related purchases of equity securities (that is, the withdrawal of equity) which, since 1983 has exceeded $100 billion in each year. That is the explanation for the *net* purchase of equity from the marketplace of between $50 billion and $80 billion in the period 1984 to 1987 shown in Table III–2. In that period, equities were a *negative source* of funds.

In the following chapters, the new issue of debt securities will be emphasized for that reason. That should not be interpreted that no new equity funds were used by the corporate sector. A glance back at the overwhelmingly large volume of *internal* sources of funds, and the uses of funds for plant and equipment, for the corporate sector (shown in Table III–1) indi-

TABLE III–2

Corporate Stock Issues—Common and Preferred (Annual Issuance, Retirements, Net Issuance, and Net Purchases, in Billions of Dollars)

	1982	1983	1984	1985	1986	1987E
Gross New Cash Offerings						
Utility	9.8	7.9	2.9	3.3	3.2	3.6
Industrial	8.0	30.5	8.8	17.1	28.0	26.5
Finance	2.8	8.9	4.6	15.1	27.4	20.4
Div. Reinvesting, stock options, and foreign sales	9.8	9.8	9.1	10.8	9.0	8.2
Total cash offerings	30.4	57.1	25.4	46.3	67.7	58.6
Conversions of bonds	1.3	1.2	1.6	1.4	1.2	5.5
Debt for equity swaps	5.9	2.0	0.9	0.0	0.0	0.0
Merger exchanges for debt	15.7	5.4	11.3	9.8	11.5	5.7
Merger exchanges for cash	42.2	29.2	98.3	99.4	122.2	110.5
Net Issuance of Corporate Stock	−20.3	25.8	−81.7	−61.4	−64.9	−52.1

Source: *Prospects for Financial Markets in 1988,* H. Kaufman, J. Hannah, R.S. Salomon, Jr. Copyright © 1987 by Salomon Brothers Inc.

cates that in the United States the combination of tax factors and corporate policies regarding dividends permits the major corporations to generate the equivalent of new equity funds from within, rather than raising equity funds from the capital market. Finally, Figure III–1, which covers most of the postwar period, indicates that even looking just at *gross* new issues, the flotation of bonds (publicly offered or privately placed) is several magnitudes larger than (gross) equity flotations.

The initial chapters of this part cover the preliminaries, mechanics, and techniques involved in placing new issues in the capital markets. At the beginning we examine the preliminaries to, and the market-making process involved in, bringing a se-

FIGURE III–1
Corporate Security Issues: Gross Proceeds (Annual Totals)

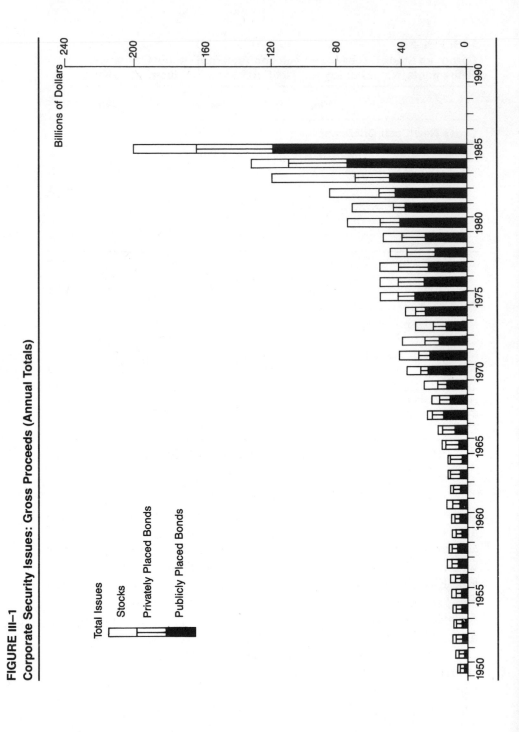

curity issue to market. An interesting approach to new security flotation is the notion of growing one's own initial public offering (IPO) through the financial equivalent of a plant nursery, namely, by venture capital investments. From there it is an easy transition (at least intellectually) to the IPO. All venture capital investments aspire to that goal. If, however, the stock market is not receptive to IPOs the venture capitalist may find himself committed to a longer term investment than he would prefer. For example, one of the byproducts of the October 1987 crash has been a sharp reduction in IPOs and an associated rise in capital committed to the venture sector of market making.

Following that discussion of pre-market financial nurturing we enter a discussion of the IPO. Whether the stock markets are receptive or not, the issuer (that is, the corporation) is brought directly into the market that determines its cost of capital for some time. The new-issue process can be made easier by market power as well as by market savvy. Accordingly, for the placement of large new issues, only the major investment banking firms in the industry play a significant role. This part then enters a general overview (Chapter 12) and goes on to describe how a corporation decides that a new issue should be sold (Chapter 13) and how the work is done (Chapters 14–15).

11

THE VENTURE CAPITALIST

Each of the world's major industrial powers has its own way of organizing the transition from scientific innovation into industrial production. In Japan, for example, big industry supports big science in house, on a large scale, and for the long pull. In the United States, scientific ideas are often nurtured through university laboratories by academic entrepreneurs. Often, the grantsmanship and management skills of these professors are harnessed in an increasingly more management-oriented environment that the venture capital firms can provide. This chapter will discuss how the process evolves toward the initial public offering (IPO) that converts experiment and prototype into a corporate enterprise and sales.

It should also be noted that low-tech as well as high-tech firms can be developed by venture capitalists. From the point of view of financing innovation, and bringing it to industrial-size production, the mix of science, entrepreneurship, and capitalism is a peculiarly American concoction. In that mix, finally, a number of investment banking firms and institutional investors are important participants.

THE VENTURE CAPITAL PROCESS

The term *venture capital* is an ancient one in finance, suggesting such state-of-the-art investments as the financing of the New England whaling fleet in the 19th century or the voyages of Captain Drake and other privateers in the 17th century. Even today the term implies risk, uncertainty, and hopes of a bonanza.

TABLE 11–1
Venture Capital Industry Total Pool of Capital Committed
(In Billions of Dollars)

	As of December 31,				
	1983	*1984*	*1985*	*1986*	*1987*
Private venture capital firms	8.2	11.8	14.2	18.1	22.8
Venture capital subsidiaries of large financial institutions and industrial corporations and non-SBIC public funds	2.5	2.9	3.4	3.9	4.0
Small business investment corporations (SBICs)	1.4	1.6	1.9	2.1	2.3
	12.1	16.3	19.5	24.1	29.0

Source: Venture Economics, Inc.

Venture capital investment is a useful institutional prerequisite to a new public offering. In addition, the process illustrates a peculiarly American phenomenon of the 1980s—a surge in private financial support for academic or scientific entrepreneurs. Venture capital financing has more than doubled over a three-year period in the mid-1980s. In the high-tech environment of, for example, genetic engineering or information-processing technology, a financing problem must be solved before a laboratory-volume activity can be moved into commercial production.

The Organization of Venture Capital Funds

Given the high risk of unpredictable cash flows, each venture is set up as a separate unit, subject to the vagaries of its own development. Until the public offering appears, there is no marketplace where any part of the investment can be sold or bought. The investors/organizers of each venture set themselves up as a freestanding partnership (or corporation). Such partnerships are run by the (active) general partner(s); the investors (as op-

posed to managers) are limited partners. (A few venture funds
are organized as publicly traded corporations.) This type of organization provides management continuity even if some limited partners decide to sell to other partners during the venture.
Capital funds can thus be looked on as mutual organizations
that reduce risks by diversification into multiple freestanding
ventures. This is an important factor since some studies show
that 40 percent of venture investments don't pay off. General
partners usually receive about 20 percent of the fund's gains as
income. They also share in the losses of the fund. Similarly, limited partners share gains and losses to the tune of about 80 percent.

Funds must make distributions annually to allow partners
to cover taxes. In addition, the general partner (manager) may
make other distributions—typically securities transferred to
limited partners rather than cash proceeds from security sales.
Such distributions do not generally produce taxable income for
partners or the partnership; they are only internal redistribu-
tions of assets. Tax liability follows only when such assets are
sold to outsiders.

VENTURE CAPITAL FINANCING OF
A NEW FIRM: BIOENGINEERING

In the 1970s and 1980s, the scientific basis for a new industry
was evolving in major university departments of biochemistry
and biomedical engineering. The industry was based on scientific developments derived from the analysis of DNA, improvements in the understanding of the body's genetic makeup and
immune system, and the development of products used to diag-
nose and treat a number of serious diseases. The overall name
for the manipulation of genetic traits is genetic engineering.

Genetic engineering is not a new industry. In agriculture,
breeding hybrid strains of corn, rice, and livestock is half a century old. Bacteria are now used in sanitary engineering and
mining. What is new is the *monoclonal antibody* technique,
among others, that permits the reorganization, or *recombina-*

tion, of bacterial DNA to perform a particular function; some call this development designer genes. A number of formidable technical and, subsequently, business problems are inherent in these schemes because bacteria mutate quickly. A gene perfectly designed for a particular task may change its characteristics in a week. And yet large-scale production is necessary for clinical testing and pilot production. Such large-scale requirements quickly forced scientists and technologists to realize that the volume of production needed for medical research exceeded the capacity of university laboratories.[1] They also recognized the possibility for creating substantial wealth by moving out of the laboratory and into an industry setting.[2]

MOVING INTO THE WORLD OF FINANCE

The scientist–engineer moving out of the sheltered environment of the university or corporate laboratory is usually far different from the stereotypical professor portrayed in the movies. Many have climbed career ladders as slippery and competitive as those found in the industrial world. Some have served on corporate boards of directors or in university administration. Others are academic entrepreneurs experienced in managing a group of highly trained and highly strung academics.

In the production start-up, some use their own financial resources (or those of friends and other investors); others have contacts with interested corporations or commercial banks. In the following discussion, these sources are listed in order of potentially increasing conflict of interest with the scientist–entrepreneur.

---

[1]All of this assumes that the host communities—including the scientific establishment—fear no major environmental problems. In some cases of DNA recombinant research and development, litigation has resulted in delays and constraints. For a recent treatment see M. Kennedy, *The University–Industrial Complex,* Yale, 1986.

[2]A similar scenario has developed in such areas as artificial intelligence and industrial development of computer hardware and software. For a more specific description, see Tracy Kidder, *The Soul of a New Machine* (Boston: Little, Brown, 1981).

Venture Capital

An entrepreneur's concern over losing scientific (or patent or process) control to the financial collaborator/potential competitor opens the door to the venture capitalist. The venture capitalist may present a conflict over corporate control some time down the road. But this problem is not obvious at the initial organizing step when the entrepreneur is facing a daily struggle to develop a costly production process without any inflows of funds from sales or any immediate prospects for such sales.

Seed Financing

Seed financing is provided to the entrepreneur to establish the feasibility of the concept; no marketing is done at this stage. The next step is *start-up financing*.

Start-Up Financing

This stage involves financing for product development and the initial marketing. At this stage a company may be formally organized or operating for less than one year. Although no product is yet sold commercially, in contemplation of such sales, the following are organized:

1. Key management group.
2. Business plan.
3. Marketing studies.

The end of the beginning comes with *first-stage financing*.

First-Stage Financing

At this point the firm has just about exhausted its initial capital; has developed a prototype that appears workable and salable; and is now ready to begin manufacturing and selling. In fact, the firm now begins its growth through *second-stage financing*.

Second-Stage Financing

Such funds provide working capital to finance goods in process, inventories, shipping, and accounts receivable. The firm needs enough funds to carry its net investment in current assets until the collection from receivables begins to reduce that aggregate investment substantially. The company is now much larger. Its output may be growing rapidly even though its rate of return may still be negative. However, hopes for profitable business development are reflected in progressively lower loss rates per unit of output. This development process leads directly to *third-stage financing*.

Third-Stage Financing

In this stage funds are provided for major expansion of the firm when its sales volume begins to take off and its income statement is near the break-even point or developing some positive (if modest) profits per unit. The financing helps to expand plant and equipment, broaden the marketing effort, and, if necessary, finance more working capital or product improvement.

Table 11–2 shows a schematic for High-Flying Technology Corporation. Note that it took about three years before the company could go public with a common stock offering.

The company's founders provided $3,000 of seed and start-up financing and acquired the common stock of the firm at 0.5 cents per share. The first round financing adds $1.5 million convertible preferred (Series A), while the second round adds another $5 million, once again through convertible preferred (Series B).

Brief Digression on Convertible Preferred

Why use convertible preference stock to finance first and second round (and subsequent rounds) of financing? As in many other problems in finance, the answer is taxes. Consider, for example,

TABLE 11–2
High-Flying Technology Corporation—Financing History

				Stage of Development		
	Seed	Start-up	First Round	Second Round	Mezzanine	IPO
Date	September 1980	January 1981	March 1982	September 1982	January 1983	June 1983
Money raised	Office space, living expenses	$3,000	$1,500,000	$5,000,000	$20,000,000	$100,000,000
Total valuation of company	—	$3,000	$1,750,000	$10,000,000	$80,000,000	$500,000,000
Security	—	Common stock	Series A convertible preferred	Series B convertible preferred	Series C convertible preferred	Common stock
Price per share	—	$0.005	$1.00	$4.00	$10.00	$15.00
Number of investors	—	Founders	3 + founders	10 + founders + employees	25 + founders + employees	General public

the tax problems of holders of common (rather than of convertible preferred) stock at $5 per share. If the original owners' and employees' 0.5 cents per share common is now valued at $5— without an easy market for the shares, moreover—they may face a devastating tax bill. They may have to make an elction under Section 83(b) of the Internal Revenue Code or risk recognition of an even larger "bargain stock" later under Section 83 as their stock vests.[3] Further, since the founders and venture capitalists are the only stockholders, there is no way to sell the shares without losing control of a potential bonanza. Worse yet, any distress sale to meet tax obligations will only drop the price (and price expectations) of the shares in a high-risk, high-potential gain situation.

Preferred stock also gives venture capitalists a preferred position in the event of liquidation (that is, failure). In the event of success, on the other hand, the legal provisions associated with senior securities (such as preferred) lies in the protection that may be written into the "term sheet" under which the new securities are sold. That protection involves provisions against dilution and for votes for the board of directors.[4] Finally, the specific terms of the several issues of preferred regarding rights to interest or cumulation of dividends or rights of repayment of investment frequently become an area of contention among the venture capitalists. As long as only one issue of preference stock is outstanding (Series A), no conflicts arise. However, features such as noncumulative dividends, proceeds at liquidation equal to investment, no mandatory redemption, voting rights equal to common stock, and no restrictive covenants must be made acceptable to the two (or more) sets of investors. Conversion to common will take place only when agreed-on financial targets are met.

---

[3]The preceding discussion is taken from M. J. Halloran, L. F. Benton, and J. R. Lovejoy, *Venture Capital and Public Offering Negotiation* (New York: Harcourt Brace Jovanovich, 1983), Supplement, pp. 253–54.

[4]Specifically, the number of shares of common issuable at conversion of preferred is adjusted upward by some formula if there are issuances by the firm of additional common at a price below the conversion price.

FIGURE 11–1
Venture Capital Financing

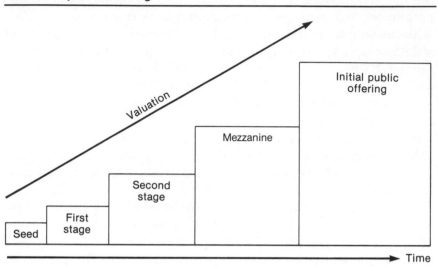

When Series B preferred is issued (or if nonconvertible debt is issued with warrants), a third party enters the contest.[5] Frequently, the terms required then become substantially more constraining, and the higher the price, the more constraining the terms. Figure 11–1 shows the venture financing strata necessary to build the firm's financial foundation *even prior* to the IPO.

The valuation levels shown for the firm represent proxies for market values. These values are derived by calculating the equity values as if each *tranche* of financing had been converted at the amount that will ultimately obtain just as the issue goes effective with an IPO.

This means that among the sellers of stock at the IPO will be the (prior) venture capitalists who may wish to reinvest their substantial gains in other ventures or in less risky opportuni-

---

[5]If nonconvertible debt is sold with warrants, the lenders are given the option to uncouple the potential for capital gain from the repayment of the loan.

ties. Of course, all of them will have a powerful interest in the pricing of the IPO because each incremental price improvement, no matter how small, represents (at least for some investors) a multiplicand over the original purchase price of each share of stock. If the venture capital department of the investment banking firm was one of the investors, it, likewise, will attempt to push the firm's syndicate department to price the new stock as richly as possible. Thus what might have appeared as a potential conflict of interest to the issuing firm may turn out to be a benefit in the pricing.

THE IPO: THE END OF ANOTHER BEGINNING

The culmination of the venture capital process is the IPO and, most specifically, the IPO price per share. For many limited partners this is the payoff for years of waiting—the time to decide whether to undertake a conversion to cash or to common stock. Those investors who sell out accept the new-issue price as the acceptable conversion price to cash for the preferred. Those investors who accept the exchange into common stock hope to gain more from holding the common than by selling off at the IPO and reinvesting the proceeds.

Consider the attitude toward new-issue pricing (or more specifically, *underpricing*) of the two sets of investors. Only the seller at the IPO would be immediately concerned about the new-issue price even though:

1. He is not concerned about new-issue reception in a fixed-price offering.
2. He is not concerned about the firm's cost of capital for new money.

In fact, if he believes that his funds should now be reinvested in other types of investments, he may accept a lesser new-issue price (as a fee for liquidity) to switch out more rapidly.

By contrast, the continuous investor in the new firm's common stock, having converted from the preferred held as a venture capitalist, may be persuaded that (a temporary?) dip in price at new issue may be his "acceptability fee" to access the market at a propitious time. He understands that the implicit rise in the firm's cost of capital (equal to per-share underpricing) implies lesser future gains as well as some dilution of control. And yet sophisticated investors accept these costs.

The Investment Banking Function

The venture capital process is market making; it is the financing that must occur before a market can be made for the securities in an IPO. Nevertheless, as noted above, these premarket financings are marketed in the form of venture capital partnerships or, in some instances, through a publicly traded venture capital fund. A few investment banking firms are active in this area. Venture capital financing is an important function that should be observed if only to assess how an embryonic corporate structure must be nurtured. That nurture, if successful, will then permit the issue of new common stock that brings the firm its independent life.

12

THE NEW ISSUE UNDERWRITER: HOW TO PRICE THAT MARKET-MAKING SERVICE

The participation by investment bankers in any market-making activity, even as traders, is a necessary prerequisite for the primary service offered to the issuer, namely, the ability to put an appropriate price on a new issue. This is not a simple matter. Beyond satisfying a number of regulatory constraints, the price must be high enough to be acceptable to the issuer and simultaneously low enough to be attractive to the marketplace.

To develop and maintain pricing skills, underwriters for new stock and bond issues are involved in secondary-market trading (and market making). In those markets, such underwriters–dealers compete with all other broker–dealers who trade exclusively in the secondary market and involve themselves in new issue flotations (as small syndicate members) only on occasion. From the point of view of managing a large investment banking firm, the secondary market is always an alternative to participation in the primary market. The underwriting firm thus has made a positive decision that, for a number of reasons, it will also participate in the primary market in that particular issue. At the same time, transactions in the primary market may include market making in a technical sense if, after the new issue is successfully launched, the investment banker continues to "make the market" in that issue.

For the initial public offering (IPO) of, say, a common stock, only two basic decisions are open to the issuing firm: (1) a negotiated "fixed price" per share offering of which the underwriter buys the entire issue or (2) a "best-efforts" deal in which the underwriter provides technical or marketing assistance only, leaving to the issuing firm all of the risk with respect to price per share and total proceeds. Under the rules of fair practice of the National Association of Securities Dealers (NASD) [a self-regulatory organization under the Securities and Exchange Commission (SEC)], the dealer cannot sell the shares at a price higher than that set forth in the prospectus. If at that price the issue does not sell (the issue is said to be priced above the market), the underwriter is stuck with unsold inventory; that position, of course, is not the object of underwriting.

NEW ISSUE MARKET MAKING

A syndicate is a group of underwriters assembled to float a new issue. The firm in charge of the syndicate is called the managing underwriter or manager. To avoid accumulating unsold shares in the syndicate, the managing underwriter typically places a stabilizing bid in the market at the offer price to the public and, if the offering goes well, may sell short some supply of the stock during the offering. (See below for further discussion of syndicate tactics.) There are, to be sure, competitively set prices for new offerings such as, for example, electric public utilities. In an IPO for a new stock, however, it would be difficult to set up two (or more) competitive syndicates.

After the offering is completed and the syndicate is dissolved with little or no residual shares left, the managing underwriter may continue to act as a formal market maker, that is, as a dealer in secondary markets, especially if the new issue has not traded previously. This means hitting all bids and making offers at stated prices.

By contrast, in the typical best-efforts deal for issuing a new stock, the company is on its own unless it has arranged for price stabilization with an underwriter—of course, for a fee. The issuing firm might consider supporting its own stock price during the offering period, but this is unlikely. The new issue is sold to meet the need for added financing—and if financing is needed to support the issue price, the very purpose of the new issue is defeated dollar for dollar. The issuing firm is not likely to have market contacts and trading connections as good as those of professional underwriters—it is not a market maker. All else the same, the lesser market-making efficiency of a corporate issuer requires more financial capacity to support the same price than would be needed by an underwriter. (These points will be discussed further below.)

THE INFORMATION SET FOR A NEW ISSUE

When a corporation decides to issue stock for initial sale to the public, it should provide potential buyers with information that makes the stock attractive or interesting for purchase. The new issue has to compete for the attention of investors with every better-known stock already trading. The buyer of an IPO doesn't buy the new stock to fill a conventional portfolio niche but, instead, has to be induced.

The need to attract information traders to IPOs is, of course, supported by the information requirements of the Securities Act of 1933, as amended. Legal sanctions force the investment banker to pursue energetically all material information from the issuer. This is called due diligence.

Further reasons induce the underwriter to pursue the information set with energy and effectiveness. If potential traders (individual or institutional) had better information than the underwriter in a fixed-price offering, they could short the new stock as it is issued or sell to the market maker after the offering is completed. This is another way of saying that the offering is mispriced. Copeland and Galai as well as Glosten and Milgrom have analyzed bid/ask spreads to offset adverse effects of information trading.[1] One defense of the underwriter against the ul-

---

[1]T. C. Copeland and D. Galai, "Information Effects on the Bid-Ask Spread," *Journal of Finance,* December 1983, pp. 1457–69; L. R. Glosten and P. Milgrom, "Bid/Ask and Transaction Prices in a Specialist Market with Heterogeneously Informed Traders" (Working paper, October 1982).

timate negative information trader—the issuer himself—is the hold-down of the share of the company that is sold by the owner–entrepreneur in the new offering. This could be put into a risk/issue-price analysis. An underwriter who is really concerned about excess risk from the new issue might walk away from the deal or insist on such a low issue price that it amounts to the same thing. Finally, the underwriter could shift the entire price risk to the seller by proposing a *best-efforts* underwriting.

Figure 12–1 illustrates these alternatives. The vertical axis indicates price per share (PPS), while the horizontal axis indicates the number of shares to be sold; the PPS multiplied by the number of shares to be sold equals the size of the offering. The function that relates PPS to the number of shares to be sold represents a forecast of market receptivity to the IPO. That function is concave to the origin because, as more shares are expected to be sold, the stock market's information traders are expected to become less interested in the issue. This is the case because potential buyers of untested issues have to be concerned that a bailout by the owner–entrepreneur might be taking place. The figure also shows two functions: the outer one represents the owner's expectations, which are more optimistic than the investment banker's.[2]

The first agreement that must be reached between owner and investment banker involves market receptivity. If they cannot agree, the owner moves to another banker, or the banker might make a counteroffer of a best-efforts deal, in which the owner himself takes on the flotation risks. Suppose that the owner accepts the investment banker's view. Then it becomes a case of financial engineering to decide on the PPS of the new issue and on the number of shares to be sold. In Figure 12–1 PPS is set at a, the number of shares is then set at L, and the owner's proceeds will be $a \times L$, less flotation costs.

---

[2]For a discussion of these issues and an empirical test of the attractiveness of (larger) owner retention in an IPO, see D. H. Downes and R. Heinkel, "Signaling and the Valuation of Unseasoned New Issues," *Journal of Finance,* March, 1982, pp. 1–10.

FIGURE 12–1
Optimal Size of IPO

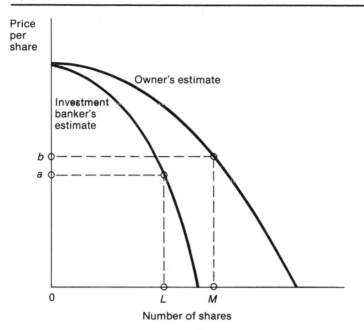

Number of shares

By contrast, if the owner insists on a best-efforts deal, based on the outer function, PPS will be set at b, the number of shares sold at M. The owner takes the risk of not selling many new shares for the chance to realize a much larger sum if the offering is successful. For the owner, accepting the lesser risks of a fixed-price underwriting, even though it may yield a lesser sum, may be a more attractive solution because few companies are sold in their entirety by a single IPO.[3] If, therefore, more growth is expected by the firm, and more new offerings of stock are expected

---

[3]In Chapter 14, the discussion of the *Informatics* case suggests that many IPOs may actually be done in more than one bite. To be sure, only the first issue is the IPO. Nevertheless, a second flotation will often follow the IPO within a year. This happens if the firm does well and the stock markets continue to be receptive. The last point is obviously the necessary condition for such an event.

to be made in the near future, the less necessary risks of an unsuccessful large IPO may also be taken into account by the owner because he might contemplate a second flotation and its potential reception even as he anticipates the initial public offering.[4] (Chapter 14 discusses the actual IPO of *Informatics,* its size, its pricing, and the follow-up flotation that took place.)

PRICE ACTION FOR A NEW STOCK ISSUE

To clarify the pricing problem assume that XYZ Co. issues some new stock for cash without preemptive rights—that is, shares are currently trading in some organized market (say American Stock Exchange), and the offering is a negotiated fixed-price underwriting.[5] Because the stock is trading currently, some of the problems of setting a value per share are avoided, although not entirely.

Preoffering Price Action

As negotiations proceed for the new issue, some current investors in XYZ stock will prefer to sell because a new supply of shares is expected to come to market. At the same time, stock market prices in general are subject to all the forces that continuously affect stock markets. Thus, XYZ's stock action cannot be said unequivocally to be subjected only to the price pressure of those stockholders who are apprehensive about the new stock sale. Nor is it possible to isolate empirically the price impact of those who will wait to buy the new issue from the secondary market rather than acquiring XYZ stock now. Nevertheless, assume that on balance the announcement effect of the new stock sale will drop the price. From the point of view of the issuer, that

---

[4]The *Morgan Stanley* IPO (see below) consisted of about 20 percent of the firm, and *Bear Stearns* floated a second issue about six months after its own IPO.

[5]This discussion is based, in part, on J. F. Childs, *Encyclopedia of Long-Term Financing and Capital Management* (Englewood Cliffs, N.J.: Prentice-Hall, 1976), Chap. 9.

price drop especially depends on the market's action at one particular time: the signing of the underwriting agreement that sets the offering price generally occurs following market closing on the day prior to the public offering of the underwriting. If that day happens to be a "down" day (even in a bull market, the price averages go down on some days), the presumptive "preoffering price pressure" could have been interpreted as having been greater than if it had been an "up" day.

At the final price meeting, a number of pricing parameters are set but they boil down to just two:

1. The per-share offering price to the public.
2. The per-share proceeds to the company.

The difference between the two is the *gross spread* that accrues to the underwriter(s)—that is, the gross compensation. In that sense, the gross spread is analogous to the bid/ask spread that prevails in secondary dealer markets and represents the compensation to market makers. It is a fee for service. But the gross spread cannot be exactly the same as the bid/ask spread in concept since, for the period of the underwriting, the offer price to the public and the proceeds to the firm are obliged to remain the same regardless of general market price changes.

Pricing Debates

The issuer (the XYZ Corporation) prefers as high a price as possible to maximize total proceeds for the firm. The underwriter, who is taking the risk of buying and then reselling the issue, would prefer a lower price to minimize selling risk. In most cases, during the preliminary discussions that precede the final price meeting and the signing of the underwriting agreement between issuer and underwriter, some limiting parameters are set.

Suppose the offering is "underpriced"—that is, the offering price to the public is set slightly below the closing market price that occurred just prior to the price meeting. To get the complete picture, let's review the data in Figure 12–2.

XYZ was trading at $100 a share prior to announcement of

FIGURE 12–2
Underpricing for a Direct Offering of Common Stock

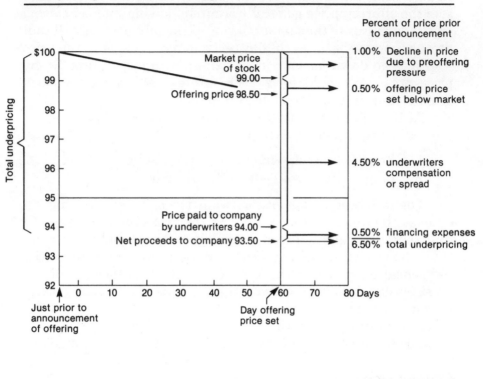

	Percentage of Price Prior of Announcement
Market price of stock just before announcement $100.00	
Decline in price due to preoffering pressure 1.00	1.00%
Market price on day offering price set 99.00	
Amount by which offering price is set under market 0.50	0.50
Offering price 98.50	
Underwriters' compensation or spread 4.50	4.50
Price paid to company by underwriters 94.00	
Corporate expenses 0.50	0.50
Net proceeds to company $ 93.50	6.50%

Source: J. F. Childs, *Encyclopedia of Long-Term Financing and Capital Management* (Englewood Cliffs, N.J.: Prentice-Hall, 1976).

the new flotation, and at the market's close prior to price meeting, the preoffering pressure dropped that price to $99 per share. The underpriced offer price to the public is set, by negotiation, at 98½, or one half point below the closing price on the day prior to the offering.

In addition to the cost to XYZ company of these pricing reductions, the net proceeds are reduced further by the gross spread of 4½ points per share which, when subtracted from the offer price (to the public) of 98½, give the corporation gross proceeds of $94 per share. From these proceeds XYZ must also subtract another one half point in the underwriting expenses charged to the company.[6] In effect the firm realized about 93½ per share from the new issue.[7]

The gross spread includes the following major items (stated in percent of the $4.50 gross spread):

1. Allowance for selling costs:[8] 60 percent.
2. Management fee for lead underwriter: 20 percent.
3. Allowance to cover underwriting:[9] 20 percent.

By far the largest share of the spread, the allowance for the selling cost (sometimes called selling allowance), permits syndicate members to sell the stock to the public at $98.50 per share but to buy it at the following purchase prices:

If the dealer is a member of the "preferred" group agreed on by the syndicate of underwriters, he may buy the stock with a per-share discount equal to the selling concession: at $98.50 − 0.6 ($4.50) = $95.80. That seller's spread will be equal to $2.70 per share. If the dealer is not a member of the preferred group, he will earn only one half of that spread (or $1.35 per share).

---

[6]These expenses include SEC fees, listing fees, federal revenue stamps, state taxes and fees, transfer agent's fees, and printing, legal, accounting, engineering, and other miscellaneous expenses.

[7]Further expenses charged to the issuer over and above the direct costs incurred during the registration period include charges for counsel, for accounting services, for other technical and printing costs, and so forth.

[8]Also includes "dealer concession."

[9]Of this, 5 percent is for underwriting expenses.

The major sales effort will be done by the first group; the second group is provided with some return not necessarily because they do a selling job but because, in accommodating their own clients, they are given a piece of the action called the dealer concession. In some sense, that distribution of the selling costs represents a substitute for selling commissions (or bid/ask spreads) on organized markets to the dealers (or brokers) who do the work.

The 20 percent of the gross spread called allowance for underwriting goes to the syndicate participants in proportion to their participation; the other 20 percent of the entire spread goes to the lead (or managing) underwriter right off the top of the gross spread to cover his costs for carrying the deal's major expenses—and risks.

Finally, from the issuer's point of view, any reduction of the per-share proceeds—whether by underpricing, by larger gross spread, or by expenses—clearly represents a flotation cost for the new issue. There appears to be a trade-off (neglecting tax effects) between (a) underpricing to the public and (b) a wider gross spread.

In that context, the issuer sees a wider underpricing as risk reducing for the underwriter, thereby suggesting a narrower gross spread (less return). In turn, the lead underwriter perceives a narrower gross spread as providing less sales encouragement to the syndicate members and to the other dealers who qualify for the selling allowance—and hence as riskier to the deal after it becomes effective. There is conflict in pricing any issue—even one that has a prior trading record on an exchange—and it must be resolved before a deal can go forward. For IPOs, that conflict can be more problematic since the basic parameter—the value per share—may itself be a subject of controversy. The fact that issues *do* go public indicates that even difficult conflict situations can be negotiated.

Underpricing Once Again:
An Investment Banker's IPO

In the many academic discussions of IPO underpricing one would like to see some discussion of how the industry treats its own.[10] One interesting example is the March 1986 offering when *Morgan Stanley,* one of the last major firms still organized as a partnership, changed to a corporate form of organization. As the prospectus cover in Figure 12–3 indicates, Morgan Stanley sold about 4½ million shares, or 20 percent of its authorized common stock that, at the offering price of 56½ per share, raised about a quarter of a billion dollars. The firm's management (managing directors and principals) own the remaining 80 percent of the common as well as all of the convertible preferred stock.

As in any other public offering, and in particular the stock of an investment banker who is also the lead underwriter of the syndicate selling the stock, the pricing of the new issue would carry certain conflicts of interest for that underwriter. In addition, as indicated earlier, the complex mix of activities and revenues and the cyclical nature of the risks of the investment banking business make the valuation of that type of firm especially tricky. Under the provisions of Schedule E to the bylaws of the NASD, to which all broker–dealers (such as Morgan Stanley) belong, the offering price "can be no higher than that recommended by a 'qualified independent underwriter' meeting certain standards."[11] The "qualified independent underwriter(s)" used were those (other than Morgan Stanley) listed on the prospectus' cover page.

Since all of the major investment banking firms were involved in pricing the new issue, the price should have been close

---

[10]See, for example, C. W. Smith, Jr., "Investment Banking and the Capital Acquisition Process," *Journal of Financial Economics,* Vol. 15 (1986), pp. 3–29 and sources cited there. See also, J. R. Ritter, "The Costs of Going Public," *Journal of Financial Economics,* Vol. 19 (1987), 269–81. Ritter found that *total* firm commitment costs (underpricing plus expenses) came to about 21% of proceeds.

[11]Citation is from Morgan Stanley prospectus, p. 55.

FIGURE 12–3

PROSPECTUS

4,500,000 Shares

Morgan Stanley Group Inc.

COMMON STOCK

All 4,500,000 Shares of Common Stock are being sold by the Company. Of such Shares, 2,900,000 Shares are being underwritten by U.S. Underwriters, and 1,600,000 Shares are being underwritten by International Underwriters. See "Underwriters". Prior to this offering, there has been no public market for the Common Stock. The initial public offering price has been determined by agreement between the Company and the Underwriters in accordance with the recommendation of "qualified independent underwriters", as required by the by-laws of the National Association of Securities Dealers, Inc. See "Underwriters" for a discussion of the factors considered in determining the offering price. The Company's Common Stock has been approved for listing on the New York Stock Exchange.

THESE SECURITIES HAVE NOT BEEN APPROVED OR DISAPPROVED BY THE SECURITIES AND EXCHANGE COMMISSION NOR HAS THE COMMISSION PASSED UPON THE ACCURACY OR ADEQUACY OF THIS PROSPECTUS. ANY REPRESENTATION TO THE CONTRARY IS A CRIMINAL OFFENSE.

PRICE $56½ A SHARE

	Price to Public(1)	Underwriting Discounts and Commissions(1)	Proceeds to Company(2)(3)
Per Share	$56.50	$2.95	$53.55
Total (4)	$252,922,500	$11,947,500	$240,975,000

(1) Up to 450,000 Shares are being reserved for sale to employees of the Company and their families at the initial public offering price less underwriting discounts and commissions. In determining total price to public and underwriting discounts and commissions, it is assumed that all of such reserved Shares will be sold to such persons. See "Underwriters".

(2) Before deduction of expenses payable by the Company estimated at $1,940,000.

(3) Morgan Stanley & Co. Incorporated and Morgan Stanley International, wholly owned subsidiaries of the Company, have committed to purchase, as a U.S. Underwriter and an International Underwriter, respectively, an aggregate of 10.4% of the Shares on the same basis and at the same price as all other U.S. Underwriters and International Underwriters. To the extent that part or all of such Shares are not resold by them at the initial public offering price, the funds derived by the Company from the offering will be reduced. See "Underwriters".

(4) The Company has granted to the U.S. Underwriters an option, exercisable within 30 days of the date hereof, to purchase up to 675,000 additional Shares at the price to public less underwriting discounts and commissions for the purpose of covering over-allotments, if any. If the U.S. Underwriters exercise such option in full, the total price to public, underwriting discounts and commissions and proceeds to Company will be $291,060,000, $13,938,750 and $277,121,250, respectively. See "Underwriters".

The Shares are offered, subject to prior sale, when, as and if accepted by the U.S. Underwriters named herein and the International Underwriters and subject to approval of certain legal matters by Davis Polk & Wardwell, counsel for the U.S. Underwriters. It is expected that the delivery of the certificates for the Shares will be made on or about March 31, 1986, at the offices of Morgan Stanley & Co. Incorporated, 55 Water Street, New York, New York, against payment therefor in New York funds.

MORGAN STANLEY & CO.
Incorporated

BEAR, STEARNS & CO. INC.

THE FIRST BOSTON CORPORATION

GOLDMAN, SACHS & CO.

MERRILL LYNCH CAPITAL MARKETS

SALOMON BROTHERS INC

SHEARSON LEHMAN BROTHERS INC.

March 21, 1986

to the market. What happened, however, was an egregious example of "underpricing": on the first day of trading (March 21, 1986), the stock moved to 70 a share, rising as high as 74¼ during the day and closing at 71¼ a share, up 14¾, or better than 26 percent higher than the offering price!

This performance raises a number of questions:

1. Is it especially difficult to price an investment banking issue? (Perhaps)
2. Is it possible that the six firms that were "qualified underwriters" purposely priced on the low side? (Unlikely)
3. Is it difficult to price *any* new issue? (Very)
4. Are all new issues of investment bankers underpriced? (Not by 26 percent)

Morgan Stanley's major financial data were given in Chapter 4 in Table 4–3 (taken from its 1988 prospectus). The structure of income and expense components shown there is similar to that of the industry generally. What may have made the stock particularly attractive to potential buyers was the ratio of pretax income to book-value equity: for 1985, for example, the book-value equity rate of return came to about 58 percent! This same information, of course, was available to the investment bankers who priced the stock. The jump in Morgan's new issue price illustrates both the difficulty in valuing any investment banking firm and in pricing any new issue.

13

THE NUTS AND BOLTS OF AN INITIAL PUBLIC OFFERING

PREPARATION

This chapter examines an initial public offering (IPO) by a firm, beginning with a view from within the firm.[1] The decision to go public must be made by the owner–manager–entrepreneur. The process of reaching that decision, in turn, is rife with conflicting interests and emotions. For openers, the only reason successful businesspeople consider sharing their businesses with others is that they have financing needs they are unable to meet with present resources. Often those needs are the result of a firm's success. First, rapid growth in sales requires more working capital; second, a move to a higher level of sales may require a larger production base in the form of plant and equipment. Even the resources of a wealthy individual owner and an understanding commercial banker (given regulatory constraints on loans to a single borrower) may be insufficient. But because these financing needs result from a firm's success, outsiders *will* be interested in providing financing.

An owner is thus faced with the dilemma of holding back the firm's growth or accepting outside financing. By bringing in more financing from the outside, the owner must share:

1. Potential growth in wealth.
2. Sole decision-making control.

---

[1]This chapter deals with a privately owned firm that is *not* financed by venture capitalists. For a discussion of venture capital, see Chapter 11.

Somewhere along the line, the owner perceives he is being constrained for lack of financing resources. He then has to consider the advantages of owning a smaller portion of a growing pie. If the owner–entrepreneur can be persuaded that the pie will grow enough, he will usually opt for added financing with outside funds.

FIRST STEPS IN FINANCE FROM, AND INFORMATION FOR, OUTSIDERS

The emerging firm can go in a number of directions for financing and professional advice when it changes scale from a single proprietorship. It can acquire partners who provide funding as well as some expertise (accountants, lawyers, professors of philosophy). These partners, who incur unlimited liability for the enterprise (as well as rights to all of its earnings), will demand up-to-date and complete accounting of the firm's affairs if only to protect their investments and limit their risks.

If, on the other hand, the firm began its life as a corporation, the bank officer in charge of making short-term loans will require all the usual statements of financial information as well. Finally, if the owner–entrepreneur receives financing from a venture capital firm, that firm, and especially the officer in charge of the account, will likewise require financial statements that reflect the corporation's present position.

All providers of outside funds before the IPO will want "full disclosure" of the corporation's affairs—even before it goes public—as a means of safeguarding their interests, limiting risks, and evaluating the value of their assets. Moreover, the partnership phase as well as the venture capital process may involve *group* company policy decisions rather than individual ones.

These sources of outside preparatory funding, while meeting the needs of one stage of company growth, will ultimately limit the size of the firm and its expansion, albeit on a larger scale than a single proprietorship. Conceptually, that limit is determined by the risk/return attitudes and portfolio decisions of a fairly small set of mainly professional investors. Moving to a still larger scale would require entry into the organized financial markets and the entire population of investors, broker–dealers, and regulators.

PURPOSE OF PUBLIC FINANCING

The successful sale of new equity to the public generates cash for two main purposes.

1. To buy a share of the firm from the original owner(s)—called a secondary offering.
2. For general corporate expansion purposes, called a primary financing.

In every case that is not an exclusively secondary offering, both purposes are achieved by going public. In every primary offering, purpose 2 has to be satisfied to some extent. In fact, only purpose 2 generates cash from the public to deal with the firm's financing needs by adding to working capital or by the acquisition of additional corporate assets. In short, it permits the successful corporation to grow. Beyond this, enlarging the equity base permits improved qualification for long-term borrowing in the form of a term loan, a private placement, or a bond issue. For all these reasons, the IPO of stocks may be a financial prerequisite for the economic takeoff of the firm beyond local resources even if subsequent financings are restricted to equity (more on this below).

Moving now to the financial market *after* the IPO has been sold, the mere fact that the stock is being traded makes it possible for all owners of the stock to gain liquidity by selling (or margining) the shares, including the sale sometime in the future of ownership position of the firm that remains. The expanded financial posture of the firm will not only help it become better known among local investors and lenders, but the financial information will also spread among a wider array of potential clients for the output of the firm. This serendipity may work particularly for firms that sell consumer goods or deal with a public that is in contact with financial markets.

But the very same advantage that spreads information through financial markets and generates publicity for the firm's output may be seen by some firm owners as a negative factor. The financial disclosure required under the Securities Act of 1933 may expose management salaries, transactions of key personnel (including the owner's relatives) within and without the firm, and other items that owner–managers may deem sensitive. Such disclosures are not often discussed in new-issue financing just because those problems get cleaned up early. The owner–entrepreneur may also be concerned about other items whose publication could be damaging. Among these are the firm's rate of return, its methods of operations, and its significant contracts. Owner–entrepreneurs often consider publication of such information as a gratuitous offering to competitors rather than as essential information required by law and by the necessity to attract potential new investors. Further, some entrepreneurs see constraints on managerial decision making (e.g., limitations on salary and fringe benefits to key personnel) as a problem when going public. Sole proprietors fear a slowdown in implementing decisions when they have to seek approval from a board of (partly outside) directors or from shareholders.

And finally, from the owner's perspective, a financial marketplace that efficiently monitors management performance through the processing of newly public information likewise interferes with effective management. Every decision now has implications for the firm's stock price. For example, a willingness to hold out in a strike or to persist with a price policy that may imply short-term losses to maximize long-term gains may be inhibited by stock price reactions and pressures from stockholders. Its takes a rare amount of character on the part of a chief executive to withstand such pressures, including those from company officials holding stock options.

In spite of these arguments, few large firms are *not* publicly held—that is, nearly all firms that expect to reach a certain size *do* go public at some time. Further, the oft-mentioned disadvantages of providing public information may reflect an executive's nostalgia for running a smaller firm.

DECISIONS, DECISIONS . . .

In seeking added financing, an owner–entrepreneur may meet a new business representative of an investment banking firm just because both are searching for what each has to offer the other. And at that point, a process of mutual education begins.

The new-business representative of an investment banking firm is trained to spot small corporations that can use the services of an investment banker. This means that the new-business people have to analyze the growing firm's financial potential and its financing needs. Ultimately, these estimates have to be translated into the number of shares to be sold at a determined price to set the dollar proceeds to the owner (to the extent that the offering is a secondary) and to the firm itself. If the firm's change of scale has some minimum requirement, the price/proceeds relationship must satisfy the needs of the firm for the IPO to proceed beyond the discussion stage. And on an even more fundamental level, some size parameters are likely to be required before an underwriter will consider a review of the firm's prospects.

An analysis of recent IPOs suggests that the first offerings of stock by corporations cluster about the following levels:

Sales of $15 to $20 million per year.

Net income of $1 million in most recent reporting year.

Annual growth rates of 30 to 50 percent, compounded, with reasonable expectations of meeting these projections for the next several years. To maximize interest by institutional investors, there should be realistic expectations of meeting sales projections of $50 to $100 million in the near future.[2]

On the other hand, many smaller firms have successfully issued IPOs. Such firms have certain characteristics that encourage underwriters (and, ultimately, investors) to accept the risk of floating a new issue for an unknown firm. Among these characteristics are:

---

[2]If current sales are at $20 million and a 50 percent annual growth rate is maintained, that minimum level could be approached in another two years.

1. A strong management team with an earlier track record of accomplishment.
2. Strong or leadership position in the industry or a technology supported by patent ownership.
3. Strong outlook for the market and the firm's market share based on 2.
4. Good product with strong possibility for growth between 33 percent and 50 percent per year.

These characteristics are necessary for new hi-tech issues. But some closely held, well-managed firms in less exciting or even routine activities that can promise good, stable, future rules of return also have used the IPO market to expand their financing base.

One final point must be made regarding the *timing* of an IPO. The per-share price of the stock is, among other variables, crucially dependent on expected future cash flows, on the desired size of the stock offering, and last—and never least—the current state of the stock market (the level of average stock prices as indicated by the level of say, the Standard & Poor 500 stock average). The higher the average or the higher the market's Price/Earnings (P/E) multiple, the higher the potential per-share price of the IPO. In short, even an IPO that is exceptionally interesting to investors and could get a good reception any time would still produce a better price per share in a strong stock market than in a weak one. Thus factors beyond the control of issuers or underwriters, to some extent, affect the size of proceeds from any issue. This fact is often difficult for owner–entrepreneurs to accept, especially if the stock market is moving downward just prior to the issue's pricing.

PREPARATIONS

If it is important to the success of any small business to establish good management techniques, including complete and up-to-date record keeping, it becomes doubly so when preparing to go public. In specific terms, the firm and its financial management can prepare for an IPO by producing reliable and analytically appropriate monthly financial statements from which quarterly data are easy to generate. This procedure leads executives of any firm—even one closely held—to make decisions that are based on analysis and control of current operations. When publication of these documents subsequently becomes a legal requirement, producing the documentation will be routine.

Financial statements that project a picture of growth and hold few surprises can be used by underwriters and syndicate members in selling stock. If those statements, when published, appear to reveal confidential data or, worse, some previously unknown problems, they will be harmful rather than helpful and may even result in cancellation of the offering.

THE LEGAL SIDE

Counsel to the firm about to go public should be familiar with the process, the required procedures, and the problems related to working with the SEC and the underwriters in an IPO registration. This work is complex and time-consuming, and there are severe penalties for presenting false or misleading statements. Moreover, there is a fine line between (1) full disclosure and (2) presenting data in a less-than-appropriate form that may not help the firm give a fair picture of itself in its prospectus. An error on the side of excess caution, while not leading to court action, may cost the firm by dropping its new-issue price. Experience in this work is essential.

In fact, counsel's first useful job is to determine whether the firm, as currently constituted, *can* go public. Among the organizational housekeeping chores may be the simplification of ownership and control structure. If, for example, the closely held firm is really (1) a number of corporations under common ownership, (2) a partnership, or (3) some other other combination of entities, simplifying the structure will produce an easier IPO (or, alternatively, a higher price per share). Counsel may then advise a merger, some liquidations, or simplification of company structure financed by ownership capital contributions. Similarly, an unnecessarily complex capital structure (including, say, preferred stock or special voting rights or preemptive rights provisions) or an unacceptably small (or excessively large) number of shares authorized may have to be dealt with. Finally, obsolete provisions in the corporate charter or bylaws may have to be changed. In short, many provisions in a closely held firm's organizational structure will be an unnecessary drag on the progress of a publicly held firm (or, once again, a potentially lower price per share in the IPO).

To move from the closet to the goldfish bowl, the firm must implement the information requirements of the Securities Act of 1933. Public disclosure, moreover, helps to generate interest in (or publicity for) the firm whose stock will be sold in the market. This means that *all* the information on the firm, if it is to help sell its stock at the best price, should provide answers rather than raise questions. Full disclosure includes:

1. Names of highly compensated employees and others, including relationships to owners, salary, and other benefits, and so on.
2. Shareholder rights beyond those of ordinary stockholders, including rights of first refusal. (These should be eliminated.)
3. Insider loans to company; company loans to insiders. (The latter should be repaid.)
4. Fairness of contracts (for example, leases) between company and insiders. (These should be appropriately documented, modified, or canceled.)
5. All employment contracts including stock options, pensions, and stock purchase plans. (These should be reviewed, arranged, or canceled.)

On the asset side, documentation and the marshaling of ownership should be clear, as should documentation on loans and leases as well as assessment of all default clauses to prevent the inadvertent occurrence of the latter during the offering. In fact, all the foregoing clarify and simplify the firm's valuation.

As part of the preliminaries that precede publication of its registration statement, the firm should prepare to have its accountants produce up to five years' worth of audited earnings statements if the underwriters require this (Form S-1 documents require audits for the last three years; Form S-18, two years). If unpleasant, unexpected surprises show up during this stage, the entire deal could be scrapped—after the firm has spent a good deal of nonrecoverable cash for professional services. Once again, if a firm routinely performs such analytical services as part of its prepublic activities, none of this need happen. And the underwriters' requirement for a five-year audited review of the firm's earnings performance is clearly a part of their risk-reducing, fiduciary responsibility.

Finally, the accountants' "comfort letters" to the underwriters that will attest to the dependability and accuracy of the financial information provided represent part of the underwriters' "reasonable investigation" of financial and accounting data. This subject will come up again in a discussion of the underwriters' "due-diligence" investigation.

EXECUTION

The Underwriting Problem Summarized

In one sense, the IPO procedure removes market imperfection and information insufficiency. Contrast this with the textbook world of Modigliani and Miller (M&M), in which methods of financing are irrelevant because all information is available and free and market adjustments are frictionless and immediate. In the M&M world, the net present values (NPV) of projects and firms are produced by simple exercises in capital budgeting:

1. Forecast a project's after-tax cash flows.
2. Assess a project's risk.
3. Project the cost of capital.[3]
4. Calculate, NPV by using discounted cash flow (DCF) methods and data from 1, 2, and 3.

Further, the aggregate value of the firm will be equal to the sum of all NPV's of currently owned assets, and that value is not

---

[3]More specifically, the expected rate of return available to investors by assets of the same risk classification traded in financial markets.

affected by the equity/debt ratio of the firm's capital structure, at least in one version of the M&M theory. And in that simple version of the theory, the NPV of a new project, however financed, could be calculated the same way.

The sale of an IPO cannot be assessed quite so simply because of lack of informational openness on which the M&M formulation depends. In fact, the closely held firm could be viewed as the theoretical opposite of the M&M world. Little, if any, information on firm value is published; no securities are valued in the market because none is traded; and in the end, the process of going public represents the presentation of the firm's information set to the market for the purpose of valuation *both by the firm and investors.*

The Adjusted Present Value Rule[4]

Suppose an entrepreneur wants to expand his firm through a primary issue by engaging in a $10 million project that is expected to provide a cash flow (after-tax) of $1.8 million per year for 10 years. Assume that the project's opportunity cost of capital (adjusted for the project's risk classification) is 12 percent. This is another way of arguing that investors are indifferent between buying the average (risky) market investment yielding 12 percent, or the IPO. For the new project, financed by IPO, the entrepreneur's calculation looks as follows (in millions of dollars).

$$\text{NPV} = -\$10 + \sum_{t=1}^{10} \frac{\$1.8}{(1.12)^t} = \$0.17$$

This means that NPV = $170,000. This also means, from the entrepreneur's point of view, that if the new-issue flotation cost of the IPO exceeds $170,000, he would *not* undertake the project. And since flotation costs usually range from 5 to 10 percent of the issue when all outlays are accounted for, that project would *not* be undertaken—if flotation costs of $500,000 to $1 million

---

[4]This discussion is based in part on R. Brealey and S. Myers, *Principles of Corporate Finance,* 2nd ed. (New York: McGraw-Hill, 1984), Chap. 19.

exceed the new NPV anticipated. In other words, after new-issue costs are met, NPV is negative.

It is not only in that sense that the special flotation costs make a naive analysis based on assumptions of efficient secondary-market trading inappropriate. Uncertainty associated with pricing the issue depends, not on some average rate of return, but on the one-time and unpredictable price level of stock averages at the moment of the price meeting for the flotation. Further, issue proceeds depend on the bargain that will be struck by the firm's owners and the underwriter(s). That price decision—which will be discussed at length in this and other chapters—involves two parties *only* in a fixed-price offering, and the same two parties are involved in pricing the flotation service even in a best-efforts underwriting.

DEALING WITH THE UNDERWRITERS

Issuers sometimes have difficulty accepting that their own stock price is significant for the firm not only at new issue. Only at new issue, to be sure, do the dollar proceeds accrue directly to the stock sellers. Yet the stock price, even after it trades on a local exchange, over the counter, or nationally, affects the fortunes of the firm because it influences the firm's cost of capital and, by extension, its investment policies with respect to real capital and other projects. Especially important are the market-making services provided by the investment banking firm after the IPO has been marketed. Until the investor base for the new stock has enough breadth and depth, the investment banker may be the major counterpart to all sell and/or buy orders so that some aspects of an underwriting process may, for all intents and purposes, be extended after the offering has been technically completed.

From the company's point of view, the need for a specific package of services to float the issue and provide post-issue trading capacity narrows the choice among potential underwriters. If the firm previously employed a venture capital firm, that connection may lead to a particular underwriter being used. As with other professional relationships offered on a competitive basis, a certain amount of exploratory discussions are necessary. Factors considered are:

A. For choice of new-issue underwriter:
   1. Reputation (especially with IPO underwriting).
   2. Distribution capability:
   Institutional.
   Individual.
   International.
   Regional.
   3. Experience: Review experience of IPOs in similar industries and for firms of corporate size.

B. After issue is sold:
   1. Market-making capacity: For how long and in what size will underwriter(s) continue to make a market? How good a dealer is the underwriter?
   2. Research capacity: How many analysts does the underwriter carry for the industry in which the IPO firm is active? How much of a following do these analysts have?
   3. Availability of financing advice by underwriter to firm: How helpful has the underwriter been to similar firms in developing new sources of financing; how well have the firms' stocks done subsequently?

Discussions with prior clients are essential in selecting an underwriter, even if these discussions involve competitors in the same industry. And discussions with competing underwriters are part of the game.

THE UNDERWRITER'S SIDE

The managing underwriter of an IPO syndicate incurs quasi-fiduciary responsibilities with respect to the members of the syndicate he has put together. He also incurs risk from underwriting the lion's share of the offering, and he may face further risks as a market maker by serving as the major *contra* trader for all buy-and-sell orders in the aftermarket. Finally, by incurring due-diligence liabilities under the Securities Act of 1933,

the lead underwriter has a powerful incentive to investigate
thoroughly the affairs of the firm about to issue its IPO.

SECURITY ANALYSIS VERSUS VALUATION OF A FIRM

It is tempting to view the underwriter's investigative function
as an analog to security analysis. There are similarities. Both
types of analyses attempt to forecast the future prospects of a
firm and the impact of these flows on the stock price.

The differences are the same as those between an efficient
and an inefficient market. The former reflects the efforts of
many stockholders and analysts who review and assess the information that each publicly held firm must issue to the SEC
and the public. Whenever that information induces owners (or
potential owners) to change their portfolios, the price effect of
such changes provides a continuous assessment of market valuation. By contrast, the investment banker looking at the affairs
of a firm on its way to a first public offering is placed into the
same situation as an appraiser. For assets that are not traded
continuously, a price valuation estimate is subject to opinion.
Market inefficiency, in fact, reflects that range, which, under a
different market structure, would be described by a relatively
wide bid/ask spread.

Further, that spread may also be related to data quality. A
firm with a lengthy history of stock-market exposure is unlikely
to have many substantive errors left in its financial statements.
A relatively new firm, on the other hand, has not undergone the
scrutiny of different accounting firms, security analysts, and
other experts. Instead, the lead underwriter must satisfy himself that his own investigative team, as well as the multiple-year
audited statements requested from the IPO firm properly and
fairly represent the firm's valuation. And in that evaluation, he
must maintain a balance between the optimism of one group eager to win the account and the skepticism of analysts who can
more readily see the negatives. That unknown balance (as contrasted with a market place) is another aspect of market inefficiency.

In the critical evaluation, the underwriter's investigation will consider:

Management:
  Experience.
  Depth.
  Leadership potential.
  Planning skills.
Product and industry:
  Quality of product.
  Competitors.
  Market segment.
  Growth potential.
  Expected life of product.
  Technology: Leader, follower?
  Research and Development: How close to the leader?
  How permanent is the industry?
Financial structure:
  How well are assets managed?
  How risky is credit rating; capital structure?
Earning capacity:
  History and growth of earnings.
  Upward trend?
  Compare to competitors.
Reputation:
  Are public, customer perception different from company's?
  Customer complaints, if any.
  Suppliers' complaints.
Use of proceeds:
  What proportion of offering is for corporate purposes?
  What proportion goes to selling stockholders?

That last element of the investigative process is a key variable to the underwriter and to eventual buyers of the firm's stock. If there is even a small possibility that the prime purpose of the stock issue is to transfer main ownership from selling stockholders–owners to the public, the notion could emerge that a "bailout" by present owners may be underway. Some underwriters are deterred from such an IPO. Others do not consider any but a best-efforts underwriting under such circumstances.

In appraising the company, each underwriter sets certain criteria to determine whether to offer the stock. For the underwriter, short-term benefits from the offering must be weighed against the risk of a tarnished reputation from underwriting a flop. In any case, underwriters spend several weeks or months investigating a firm. This includes some probing questioning of senior executives, key technical personnel, vendors, competitors, and clients of the company. In addition, underwriters may hold private meetings with the firm's accountants.

A SCHEMATIC TIME LINE FOR AN IPO

Once the two parties (issuer and underwriter) agree to go ahead with the deal, the schedule below describes the general process that will follow after the IPO firm (called Company below) has decided on its counsel and its printer (for documents).

Time Schedule

Required actions prior to public offering	Company selects counsel and printer.
	Company officers, directors, and managing underwriter make no statements about the proposed public offering without prior clearance from Company counsel and underwriters' counsel.
Nine weeks prior to offering date	Company, its accountants, and counsel begin assembling required data, including financial statements and exhibits, to be included in the registration statement.
	Company makes available to underwriters' counsel the Board of Directors' meeting

minutes for prior years and abstracts all important contracts for review by such counsel.

Company officer and Company counsel prepare and make available the first draft of the business, property, management's discussion of earnings, competition, and employee sections of Part I of the registration statement.

First draft of underwriting agreement to be available from underwriters' counsel.

Conference with managing underwriter, underwriters' counsel, and Company officers, counsel, and accountants to discuss the time schedule and initial document drafts.

Eight weeks prior to offering date

Board of Directors authorizes preparation of the registration statement and related documents.

Accountants prepare the audited financial statements for inclusion in the registration statement.

Company counsel begins preparation of Part II of the registration statement including exhibits.

Managing underwriter and underwriters' counsel begin preparing the first draft of the remaining sections of Part I of the registration statement, agreement among underwriters, underwriting agreement, underwriters' questionnaire, and underwriters' power of attorney.

Company counsel prepares questionnaires to be sent to officers and directors as to interest in material transactions.

Seven weeks
  prior to
  offering date
	Second draft of the registration statement and underwriting agreement to be available.

	Tour of principal Company facilities by managing underwriter and discussions with principal management personnel of the Company to assist managing underwriter in gaining a complete understanding of the Company.
	Conference with managing underwriter, underwriters' counsel, and Company officers, accountants, and counsel to discuss second draft of the registration statement and related documents.
	Reworked second draft of the registration statement and related documents sent to financial printer for page proof.

Six weeks
  prior to
  offering date
	Managing underwriter, underwriters' counsel, and Company officials, accountants, and counsel continue to work jointly on the preparation of the registration statement and related documents.

Five weeks
  prior to
  offering date
	Company counsel and underwriters' counsel jointly prepare appropriate resolutions for the Board of Directors' meeting to be held at the time of the initial filing of the registration statement.

	Managing underwriter submits a list of the prospective underwriters for review by the Company.

Four weeks
  prior to
  offering date
	Board of Directors (1) approves preparation, execution, and filing of the registration statement and all amendments thereto (ex-

cept the price amendment) and related matters; (2) authorizes qualification under state "Blue Sky" laws; (3) authorizes Company officers to negotiate with the managing underwriter as to the terms of the offering; and (4) takes any other action necessary.

Registration statement filed with SEC and a copy of the tentative time schedule delivered to the branch chief of the SEC who will review the registration statement and related documents forming a part of the registration statement.

Preliminary prospectuses printed in quantity.

Managing underwriter issues press and "broad tape" releases relating to the filing of the registration statement.

"Blue Sky" action is initiated by underwriters' counsel on behalf of the Company to register the proposed offering with various state security commissions.

Managing underwriter forms underwriting group and mails copies of the registration statement and related documents to members of such group.

Preliminary prospectuses broadly distributed to prospective underwriters, dealers, institutional investors, and individuals.

Company orders initial quantities of stock certificates.

Three weeks prior to offering date	Company counsel and underwriters' counsel prepare appropriate resolutions for the Board of Directors' meeting to be held at the time of the determination of offering terms and the filing of the price amendment to the registration statement.

Underwriters' due-diligence meeting held in New York City to discuss the registration statement with Company officers, accountants, and counsel.

Information meetings held in certain cities such as Chicago, Los Angeles, and San Francisco to acquaint underwriters and dealers with the Company and its management.

Two weeks prior to offering date	Executed underwriters' questionnaire forwarded to Company counsel.

Company counsel contacts SEC branch chief to confirm anticipated date of receipt of SEC comments on the registration statement.

Quarterly or "stub" financial statements made available, if applicable. |
| One week prior to offering date | Receive comments from SEC on the registration statement.

Managing underwriter, underwriters' counsel, and Company officers, accountants, and counsel correct deficiencies in the registration statement and, if necessary, file amendment no. 1 to the registration statement with SEC.

Preliminary prospectus distribution letter from managing underwriter sent to SEC along with letter requesting acceleration of the registration statement from managing underwriter and Company.

"Tombstone" advertising proofs prepared by managing underwriter for release on the day following the effective date of the registration statement. |

Company and managing underwriter prepare press release and "broad tape" release relating to the effectiveness of the registration statement and the public offering terms.

Week of offering	Managing underwriter meets with Company officers to negotiate terms of the offering.

Board of Directors (1) approves offering terms; (2) approves registration statement, including amendment no. 1 thereto, if any; ratifies actions of Company officers in executing and filing same; and authorizes Company officers to execute and file all further amendments and supplements thereto; (3) approves the form of underwriting agreement and authorizes Company officers to execute and deliver an underwriting agreement in substantially such form; (4) approves the indemnity agreement; (5) authorizes the issuance of the stock to be sold by the Company on proper documentation; and (6) authorizes all further actions as may be necessary to give effect to and facilitate the public offering.

Managing underwriter and Company officers, accountants, and counsel prepare pricing amendment to the registration statement including the underwriting agreement and agreement among underwriters.

Offering date (New York City)	Managing underwriter and Company execute the underwriting agreement.

Price amendment filed with SEC (after underwriters execute agreement among underwriters).

Company receives SEC order declaring the registration statement effective and so advises the managing underwriter.

Registration statement and the final prospectus forming a part thereof printed in quantity.

Underwriting agreement delivered to respective signators.

Underwriters' counsel transmits relevant information to "Blue Sky" authorities.

Managing underwriter commences public offering of the stock and so advises the Company

Managing underwriter releases "tombstone" advertisement for appearance on the day following the offering date and issues press release and "broad tape" release relating to the effectiveness of the registration statement and the public offering terms.

Day after offering date	"Tombstone" advertisement appears in selected newspapers throughout the United States.
Matters to be completed prior to closing	Managing underwriter provides registrar with the names in which the certificates are to be registered. Managing underwriter packages certificates for delivery.
Day before closing	Preliminary closing with underwriters and Company counsel.
Closing (one week after the offering date)	Payment for and delivery of shares sold. Documentation required from and by managing underwriter and Company delivered to appropriate parties in New York City.

Note: Special circumstances may require departures from the above outline, particularly as to the scheduling of Board of Directors' meetings, the period of time required to prepare audited financial statements and draft the description of business sections of the Registration Statement, and the period of time required by the SEC to review the Registration Statement subsequent to the initial filing. With regard to the SEC review of the Registration Statement, the above time schedule provides for a period of approximately four weeks from the date of initial filing to the effective date of the Registration Statement. This time period may vary depending upon the number of Registration Statements and Proxy Statements currently being processed by the SEC and certain other factors.

14

NEW ISSUE UNDERWRITING AS INSURANCE TO THE ISSUER

It is no accident that the word *underwriting* has similar meanings and connotations in insurance and investment banking. The insurance function provided by investment bankers has become more important as rates in the capital markets have become more volatile.[1]

Put differently, the management of a firm placing an issue of new common stock in the market is aware that the price per share when sold might be lower than it should be willing to accept because it implies negative net present value for funds raised ("flotation risk"). As one approach to minimizing flotation risk, the firm will purchase two types of services from investment bankers:

1. Pricing services.
2. Marketing (or market-making) services.

Based on expertise gained in continuous market participation, investment bankers set a realistic valuation on any new issue so that it can be sold. The second service, market making, refers to the capacity of underwriters to know who potential buyers are and to place the new issue at a price acceptable to both

---

[1]This insurance function has been pointed to in a general way by Mandelker and Raviv in "Investment Banking: An Economic Analysis of Optimal Underwriting Contracts," *Journal of Finance,* June 1977, pp. 683–94. Their emphasis on corporate risk avoidance generally is disputed by Mayers and Smith (see below). Further discussion in this chapter also suggests that risk avoidance by the issuing firms takes on quite a different form from that proposed by Mandelker and Raviv.

issuers and investors. This set of services and the conflicts that develop between issuer and investment banker can best be understood in the context of risk transfer from issuer to underwriter.

During the period when the issuer is waiting to go into the market or even waiting for Securities and Exchange Commission (SEC) approval for the issue to "go effective," changes in security market prices will either raise the expected price of the new issue or lower it. Such waiting risk is borne exclusively by the issuer.[2] Adding in other risks against which the issuer attempts to insure himself with an underwriter results in the following flotation risk:

(1) Waiting risk + (2) Pricing risk + (3) Marketing risk
= Flotation risk

Of these components, the first is the the least obvious.

WAITING RISK

The investment banker and corporate client may have a longstanding advisory relationship, especially prior to the initial public offering (IPO). Even after the decision to go public is made, it usually takes three to five months for the corporation and its investment banker, counsel, accountants, and other experts to prepare the registration statement and all the other documents that are necessary before the IPO is declared effective. To calculate the risk to the firm (XYZ) during that waiting period, assume that at the beginning of the period price levels in the stock market imply a price/earnings (P/E) multiple of 20 for the stocks of the corporations with characteristics similar to XYZ's. If market prices decline and reduce that multiple to 15 times several months later, XYZ may postpone the offering. In that case, the waiting risk has turned out to be too great.

A second type of waiting risk that affects the cash offers of new issues of large corporations was virtually eliminated by

---

[2]Shelf registration (SEC Rule 415) will be discussed in the next part.

SEC Rule 415 (the shelf-registration rule) and its predecessor in the development of "instant bond issues," the S-16 form. Prior to Rule 415, for any new corporate issue—stock or bond—to be declared effective by the SEC, there was a three- to four-week wait between the time the registration statement was submitted and the SEC's release of securities for trading. That waiting risk was eliminated by the SEC's change in policy, and at this writing, the issues that qualify may be declared effective in *two days* or less, sharply reducing the waiting risk for large, seasoned issuers.

This policy change has had a policy by-product (probably not foreseen at the time) that affected pricing risk as well.

When a new issue is decided on, the corporate client may require competitive bidding (a public utility holding company is obligated to do so by law), or the issue price may be negotiated. Since shelf registration, corporations can choose the *timing* of their new issues. And firms that qualify for shelf registration can ask for pricing services (bids) from more than one investment banker. In effect, this gives these corporations the equivalent of a competitively set pricing service even though the formal rituals of competitive bidding mechanisms are not performed.[3]

With the continuing experience of shelf registration, the most sophisticated and most active issuers in 1980s have gone as far as completing all of the prospectus mechanics up to and including having a note or bond issue *declared effective* by the SEC. The document declared effective will contain all but the *pricing* terms. At that point, waiting risk is totally eliminated since the issue can go at a moment's notice. This does not mean, however, that all issuing risks are eliminated. In effect, issuers trade off waiting risk for market-timing risk. The issuer's management must decide when to go and they have to take the heat

---

[3]The Dutch-auction scheme used by some corporations represents still another mechanism for developing a competitive pricing process. For further discussion of new-issue flotations under Rule 415, see S. Bhagat, "The Evidence of Shelf Registration," *Midland Corporate Finance Journal* 2, no. 1 (Spring 1984), pp. 6–12. For discussion of competitive bidding mechanics, see Chapter 15.

if, in a period of volatile rates and markets, they picked the wrong phase of the cycle.

In volatile markets, all issues are subject to such timing risks. Under the present (1988) mechanics of shelf-registration issues, the manager who decides to go can be identified. In earlier days, random events during the waiting period could be blamed. The new rules may make the issuer more conscious of pricing problems and more prone to lay them off on the underwriters.

PRICING RISK

The purchase of the pricing service is designed to minimize pricing risks:

1. Improper pricing in a stable market.
2. Proper pricing overwhelmed by an unstable market.

Improper pricing refers to the problem of setting an IPO price on a firm whose securities have not traded (if privately held) or are not traded as widely (if registered, say, on a local exchange) as they are expected to be after the new issue is sold. The major pricing service purchased, therefore, is a transactions price that comes closer to an equilibrium price than the bid/ask spread prior to the time the issue is traded. Put bluntly, the pricing service the company wants is a price as high as possible that will still appeal to the market. If the price is too high, the issue won't sell after it is underwritten, and a significant portion of securities will have to be sold at a sharp discount to the offering price. By that time, the firm has received its cash proceeds—the slow or discounted security sales will be a loss only for the underwriters. It is often said that a firm will not be as happy with a slow flotation than if its issue had done well.[4] That notion,

---

[4]A conflict in attitudes may develop between: (1) old (or selling) stockholders, who would clearly benefit from getting as high a price as possible from the market and (2) the new stockholders who, like everyone else, prefer a low purchase price.

however, may be one of the many Wall Street adages whose truth is appreciated mostly in lower Manhattan. The alternative, and a better known one, is the notion that new issues tend to be underpriced; a number of studies suggest that underpricing improves market reception and reduces underwriting risks to investment bankers, all for the obvious reasons.

The second pricing risk refers to those exogenously determined price changes that depress stock market prices occasionally (for example, a rise in the Federal Reserve discount rate). Because a newly priced issue then carries a price fixed to the public on its prospectus (as long as syndicate restraints prevail) that is above its prior relationship to the market, it will be difficult to sell. By that time, as noted, the flotation risk of an underwritten issue would be carried by the underwriters and not by the issuing company.

THE DEMAND FOR RISK SHIFTING

The demand for risk shifting by large corporations can no longer be discussed in terms of general risk avoidance. Instead, the theory emphasizes the impact of insurance on maximization of stockholder wealth.[5] Stockholders—that is, holders of stock portfolios—can generally eliminate corporation-specific risks by portfolio diversification. As Mayers and Smith put it, a corporation's purchase of insurance is no guarantee of stock price improvement since ". . . the purchase of insurance by firms at actuarially unfair rates would represent a negative net present value project, reducing stockholder wealth."[6] They go on to argue that closely held corporations, on the other hand, like individuals, have an incentive for risk avoidance in general. They prefer a less risky average outcome to a range of less predictable out-

---

[5]The following derives insights from the modern literature on insurance, especially, D. Mayers and C. W. Smith, Jr., "On the Corporate Demand for Insurance," *Journal of Business* 55 no. 2 (1982), pp. 281–96.

[6]Ibid., p. 282.

comes that may be higher or lower than the average. Likewise, for the one large stockholder in a firm, the diversification type of wealth self-insurance is not directly feasible. In order to diversify his wealth, he must first sell a share of his company. Consequently, like any other insurance buyer (individual or corporate), he acquires flotation insurance—that is, insurance against an "accident" for his IPO by having his new issue underwritten.

That isn't the end of the insurance story, however. Consider the asymmetry in the capacity to bear risks between even large firms that may face an occasional (or rare) accident in their own new-issue flotation and those firms (called insurance companies or, in our special example, investment bankers) that specialize in dealing with potential accidents. Insurance specialists deal with a large number of policies and a more predictable set of accident-related claims per unit of time. As a result they get the benefit of:

1. Better actuarial predictability of *aggregate* accident costs.
2. Improved claims management and settlement
3. More effective spreading of the costs and burdens of accidents among the insured population.

Finally, a number of factors tend to hold down the "loading fee"—that is, the difference between the premiums paid by policyholders and the insurance companies' aggregate payoff after an accident. First, as the loading fee rises, fewer corporations will be interested in buying insurance services. Second, this potential decline in demand will be met by a supply that becomes increasingly competitive among the insurance firms offering risk protection.

Investment bankers have a comparative advantage in risk bearing. Most of the Fortune 500 firms, which enter the financial markets fairly regularly to float bond issues and, less frequently, stock issues, have found that the flotation of new issues carries an insurable risk that investment bankers have a comparative advantage in covering for a number of reasons.

SUPPLY OF RISK SHIFTING BY UNDERWRITERS THROUGH DIVERSIFICATION, MARKETING, HEDGING, AND INSTITUTIONAL SALES

Diversification

1. Most large new issues are sold by syndicates. This spreads the total risk in any one flotation among the participating underwriters according to the size of each firm's participation or as spelled out in the underwriting agreement.

2. On the same day that the managing underwriter is carrying the largest single share of risk in any given flotation, he is also participating in other flotations already open for trading or about to. To that extent, any single flotation risk exposure may be diversified throughout the new-issues market (a sort of portfolio effect).

3. In the days following, all these underwriters will be participating in other new offerings, thereby diversifying flotation risks through time.

Marketing

Marketing reduces flotation risk as follows: the syndicate manager will "build a book" prior to the time the issue becomes effective. Further, after the offering is made effective, the over-allotment of securities to syndicate members and others and the price stabilization actions undertaken by the syndicate manager during the flotation period are all designed to improve reception of the new issue (or reduce underwriting risks). Under the present legal constraints of the Securities Act of 1933, only the underwriter can so support the offering. The underwriter has an *absolute* advantage in providing this service.[7] The issuing firm is prohibited from market stabilization of its own securities at new issue or thereafter for many valid reasons.

---

[7] He also has a liability regarding due-diligence efforts with respect to material information misstated or omitted in the prospectus and so forth.

The chart below illustrates how these risks may be perceived by the issuer (XYZ Corporation) and its investment bankers. To simplify the example, assume XYZ stock sold on the American Stock Exchange at $100 per share prior to the announcement of a new issue. In the three weeks after the announcement of the new issue that is accompanied by the distribution of the red-herring prospectus, the firm expects the stock price to rise $5 per share, to remain the same, or to drop by $5.[8]

Stock Price Change	A	B
Rise by $5	50%	35%
Stable	15	15
Down $5	35	50

In case A, waiting risk is favorable; there is a bull market. In case B, waiting risk is not favorable; there is most likely a bear market. XYZ Corporation projects that, with net proceeds of $95 per share, there is small net positive risk-adjusted present value for the project to be financed. With a gross spread of $6 per share, even in a bull market, if the stock price drops to $95 in the market during the waiting period, the issue will be postponed at best, or canceled. If the price remains at $100 during the waiting period and then drops during the pricing day to $99, XYZ will fight hard for a higher price to the public (that is *no* underpricing) or for a narrower spread (for example, price to public, $99; gross spread, $4; net proceeds, $95), or it will insist on a postponement.

From the underwriter's point of view, if the expected worst-case price drop during the marketing (or syndicate) period is $3 per share, a narrower ($4) spread at a $99 price that could decline to $96 when the syndicate breaks does not necessarily imply an immediate out-of-pocket loss since proceeds to XYZ are $95. If, however, out of pocket costs exceed $1 per share, the

---

[8]The red-herring prospectus contains all the information of the new-issue prospectus except for the price and size of the new issue.

underwriter will incur a loss. It is to avoid the equivalent of these losses that the issuing firm engages an underwriter in the first place.

Hedging

After a syndicate dissolution, any unsold securities in excess of the supply desired by the underwriter represent the outcome of an unforeseen (and risky) market event. For the syndicate operation involved, it would constitute a "loss event," but the securities can be placed in the portfolio of the investment banking firm or sold subsequently in the normal course of business. In any case, because these "leftovers" represent only a part of the underwriter's unsold share of any offering (other syndicate members also absorb their share), they are easier to hedge or diversify than the equivalent total leftover, following its own flotation, by the issuing firm.

Institutional Sales

While the concept of institutional sales may not appear to be directly related to the new-issue process, the capacity of investment bankers to deal on a large scale in secondary markets generates economies of scale for primary-market trading or the placement of securities generally. Knowledge of the market and its major institutional buyers helps investment bankers place large pieces of large new issues whatever the aggregate current volume of new issues. In fact, many new issues are largely presold to institutions prior to the formal offering. The usefulness of these contacts in placing new issues represents a type of scale economy that is not easy to achieve except by continuous market participation; moreover, it is difficult to measure. For that reason, the underwriter's market contacts tend to be ignored in discussions of flotation risk. After all, the continuous exercise of placing large blocks and of pricing skills (in large-scale buying and selling) provides relative stability (or narrow bid/ask spreads) in market pricing as well as generating transferable expertise to new-issues pricing.

For all of these reasons, investment bankers have "sold" their risk services to new issuers, and for all underwritten securities, corporations have effectively shifted new-issue risks to the underwriters.

After any issue is proposed for sale, the flotation may be executed in an open market or by negotiation. In more familiar jargon, the competitive process is called a public offering, while the negotiated flotation scheme is called a private placement. For a private placement, the negotiations for pricing and for flotation schemes are collapsed into one process.[9]

PRICING SERVICES

For investment banking firms and particularly for special-bracket firms (or lead underwriters generally), the sale of pricing services extends into many areas. For example, the sale of pricing expertise may occur by itself in consultations with firms that acquire other companies through mergers (see Chapters 8 and 9). As noted above, the pricing expertise of investment bankers is continuously exercised (or tested) in the performance of their dealer activities. Further, those tests are intimately related to marketing skills (for example, institutional sales) and risk-taking capacity (capital available to finance the inventory of securities). Most special-bracket firms perform these functions in a number of secondary markets as well as in the primary (new-issues) market where they lead syndicates.

New Issues Pricing

Setting a price on a new issue is similar to setting a futures price: the flotation process is not completed until some time hence—that is, when securities trade on their own without syndicate support. That time can be shortly after the issue date if

---

[9]The final bargain struck for a private placement probably includes some opportunity-cost factor for avoiding flotation risk. To some extent, this may be encompassed in the rights of holders of privately placed issues to trade these securities prior to maturity either among each other or back to the issuer. There is no neat way of estimating the cost of such options in private placements.

market prices rise for any reason or if the new issue has been underpriced (see below for further discussion of underpricing).

Many new issue transactions, however, don't close out in a short period, and syndicates may be maintained for more than a week (although rarely) if markets move down or if, for any other reason, the issue won't sell. All the securities in the underwriting must be sold at the same price (to issuer, to the public) as long as the syndicate is maintained. This means that in terms of the new issue price relative to prices on other securities, the new issue will appear more expensive to buy the longer it takes to close out the syndicate.

If the security were clearly underpriced relative to the market, syndicates would not have to be maintained for longer than minutes or hours regardless of whether the issue adds to the securities already in the market ("seasoned issuer") or whether it is an IPO. To price an initial offering, a substitute must be found for a trading history of existing stock, or earlier bond issues, by examining comparable companies to develop a general valuation model for the new securities. Once that valuation is done, the final price adjustments are then made for futurity— that is, the price risks associated with a lengthy flotation period. The next section examines the valuation process and futurity adjustments. Recall the types of new stock flotations offered: A *general cash* offer is a flotation to the market at large as contrasted with a *preemptive rights offer,* which is made to current stockholders. General cash offers, in turn, may be sold to underwriters at a firm price; many rights offers are supported by a process that is clearly an insurance-type of underwriting called a standby.

Valuation of an IPO

The IPO of a firm involves either (1) raising funds for executives (owners) selling off a share of the firm for cash to diversify their *own* wealth and/or (2) raising funds to expand the scale of the firm's operations. Depending on when in the firm's history the IPO occurs, reason (1) or (2) predominates, and at its earliest stage, reason (1) may involve financing the industrial implementation of a technological advance or scientific breakthrough. The valuation process thus may start with something as intangible as the financial marketing of an idea. Or in a conventional financial analysis, an investor may decide to participate in the further development of a well-established concern.

In a technical sense, then, a valuation (price per share) that is the equivalent of the present value of the future stream of dividends must be placed on a security some time before any initial dividend may be paid or even expected. In many cases, there may be no history of market valuation to go by. Nevertheless, a price must be set.

At the next stage of corporate development, when a company is well established, setting a price on a new issue still remains an exercise in futures pricing. With the proceeds of the new issue, the firm will not only be larger but may be different (in assets, outputs, financial characteristics) than before. Finally, the price must be set some time before trading can begin. These time lags are:

1. The SEC lag until the issue is declared effective for trading.
2. The flotation lag—that is, until the issue is all sold.

The SEC lag is at present about two days or less assuming the prospectus contains no significant technical errors and the backlog at the SEC is no greater than average.

The second time lag—the flotation lag—reflects the problem of scale: not only is the stock traded for the first time, but a large quantity must be sold at one offering. The mechanism for setting a price in that large-scale context implies the involvement of a dealer rather than a broker. And the aftermath of the large-scale trade carries marketing and inventory implications for the dealer. Leaving these aside for the moment, let's first consider the typical spreadsheets used by corporate finance departments to set reasonable parameters for new-issue pricing.

VALUING INFORMATICS: A CASE STUDY

The exercise below is an attempt to place a valuation on a cash offer, using data from comparable firms to set the new-issue price. As the cover of the Informatics prospectus indicates (Fig-

FIGURE 14–1
Informatics Prospectus

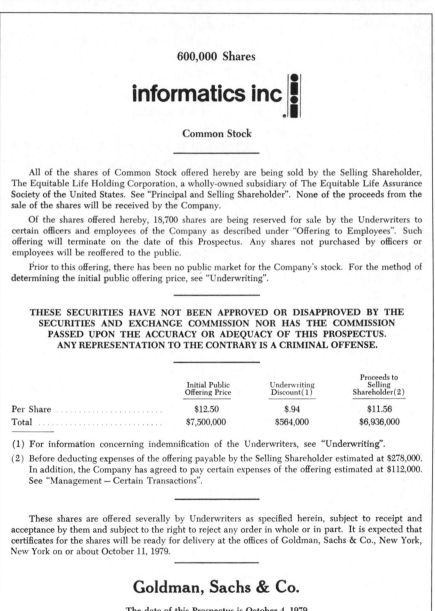

600,000 Shares

informatics inc.

Common Stock

All of the shares of Common Stock offered hereby are being sold by the Selling Shareholder, The Equitable Life Holding Corporation, a wholly-owned subsidiary of The Equitable Life Assurance Society of the United States. See "Principal and Selling Shareholder". None of the proceeds from the sale of the shares will be received by the Company.

Of the shares offered hereby, 18,700 shares are being reserved for sale by the Underwriters to certain officers and employees of the Company as described under "Offering to Employees". Such offering will terminate on the date of this Prospectus. Any shares not purchased by officers or employees will be reoffered to the public.

Prior to this offering, there has been no public market for the Company's stock. For the method of determining the initial public offering price, see "Underwriting".

THESE SECURITIES HAVE NOT BEEN APPROVED OR DISAPPROVED BY THE SECURITIES AND EXCHANGE COMMISSION NOR HAS THE COMMISSION PASSED UPON THE ACCURACY OR ADEQUACY OF THIS PROSPECTUS. ANY REPRESENTATION TO THE CONTRARY IS A CRIMINAL OFFENSE.

	Initial Public Offering Price	Underwriting Discount(1)	Proceeds to Selling Shareholder(2)
Per Share	$12.50	$.94	$11.56
Total	$7,500,000	$564,000	$6,936,000

(1) For information concerning indemnification of the Underwriters, see "Underwriting".

(2) Before deducting expenses of the offering payable by the Selling Shareholder estimated at $278,000. In addition, the Company has agreed to pay certain expenses of the offering estimated at $112,000. See "Management — Certain Transactions".

These shares are offered severally by Underwriters as specified herein, subject to receipt and acceptance by them and subject to the right to reject any order in whole or in part. It is expected that certificates for the shares will be ready for delivery at the offices of Goldman, Sachs & Co., New York, New York on or about October 11, 1979.

Goldman, Sachs & Co.

The date of this Prospectus is October 4, 1979

FIGURE 14–1
(continued)

PROSPECTUS SUMMARY

The following summary is qualified in its entirety by more detailed information and consolidated financial statements appearing elsewhere in this Prospectus. Unless the text indicates otherwise, all share and per share information in this Prospectus gives effect to the recapitalization of the Company which became effective on October 1, 1979 as described under "Management — Certain Transactions" and in Note 6 of Notes to Consolidated Financial Statements.

THE COMPANY

Informatics, Inc. provides a variety of computer-related products and services to both private industry and government. The business of the Company includes the design, development, marketing and maintenance of proprietary computer programs, the furnishing of professional services, consisting principally of programming, system development and facilities management, and the furnishing of information processing services, including timesharing and data management and analysis.

The Common Stock offered hereby may involve special risks. See "Certain Factors".

THE OFFERING

600,000 shares of Common Stock are being sold by the Selling Shareholder (The Equitable Life Holding Corporation). After the offering, the Selling Shareholder will own approximately 63% of the Company's Common Stock and 97% of the Company's Preferred Stock, and will possess approximately 83% of the voting power of the Company's capital stock with respect to the election of directors.

SELECTED FINANCIAL INFORMATION

	1974	1975	1976	1977	1978*	1978*	1979*
						Six Months Ended June 30,	
	(In thousands, except share and per share amounts)					(Unaudited)	
INCOME STATEMENT DATA:							
Revenues	$ 20,527	$ 38,982	$ 58,743	$ 74,768	$ 92,507	$ 41,908	$ 52,970
Income (loss) from continuing operations before extraordinary item	(1,300)	(4,365)	(1,865)	620	1,497	85	935
Net income (loss)	(1,398)	(4,468)	(1,905)	940	2,703	153	1,492
Income (loss) from continuing operations before extraordinary item per common share	(.68)	(2.28)	(.98)	.16	.58	.02	.38
Net income (loss) per common share	(.73)	(2.33)	(1.00)	.31	1.15	.04	.65
Weighted average number of common shares outstanding	1,910,622	1,914,045	1,912,708	2,140,348	2,118,396	2,131,427	2,080,873

*As explained under "Management's Discussion and Analysis of the Consolidated Statements of Operations", reported results have been affected by certain costs incurred in connection with an acquisition and reorganization in 1974. Such costs have made the comparison of results for the first half and second quarter of 1979 with the corresponding periods of 1978 more favorable than a comparison giving effect to the elimination of these costs. The effect of these costs was to reduce per share income from continuing operations by $.48 to the reported $.58 per share for 1978, by $.17 to the reported $.02 per share for the first six months of 1978 and by $.03 to the reported $.38 per share for the first six months of 1979. After giving effect to the elimination of these costs, income from continuing operations before income taxes declined $84,000, or approximately 8%, in the second quarter of 1979 compared with the second quarter of 1978.

	December 31, 1978	June 30, 1979
		(Unaudited)
BALANCE SHEET DATA:		
Working capital	$ 7,945,000	$ 8,537,000
Total assets	40,025,000	39,566,000
Total debt	10,341,000	10,860,000
Total liabilities	28,299,000	26,672,000
Deficit	6,906,000	5,414,000
Shareholders' equity	11,726,000	12,894,000

3

FIGURE 14-2

(DOLLARS IN MILLIONS)

	INFORMATICS, INC. ESTIMATED 12/31/78	APPLIED DATA RESEARCH 12/31/77	AUTOMATIC DATA PROC 6/30/77	BRADFORD NATIONAL CORP 6/30/78	COMPUTER SCIENCES CORP 6/30/78
CAPITALIZATION					
SHORT TERM DEBT	$ 4,789	$0.1	$2.0	$135.8	$57.2
LONG TERM DEBT	$ 6,934 36.1	$0.9 14.1%	$9.2 6.9%	$10.8 17.6%	$57.2 57.0%
PREFERRED STOCK (LIQ VAL)	69 0.3	0.0 0.0	0.0 0.0	0.0 0.0	0.0 0.0
COMMON EQUITY	12,197 63.6	5.5 85.9	124.8 93.1	50.7 82.4	43.1 43.0
TOTAL CAPITALIZATION	$19,200 100.0%	$6.4 100.0%	$134.0 100.0%	$61.5 100.0%	$100.3 100.0%
COMMON SHARES OUTSTANDING	608,000	1,306,000	14,867,000	4,044,000	12,913,000
NET SALES/NET INC/NET MARGIN	12/31/78 = 1978	12/31/77 = 1977	6/30/77 = 1977	12/31/77 = 1977	3/31/78 = 1977
1973	$ N/A $ N/A N/A	$7 $0.5 6.6%	$102 $9.2 9.0%	$41 $2.3 5.6%	$147 $1.1 0.7%
1974	29,560 (1,344) N/A	8 0.5 6.1	130 12.0 9.3	50 2.0 4.1	177 3.6 2.1
1975	38,982 (4,392) N/A	10 0.3 3.1	163 14.3 8.8	57 4.0 7.0	220 7.2 3.3
1976	58,743 (1,882) N/A	13 1.0 7.4	199 18.7 9.4	66 3.2 4.9	235 11.6 5.0
1977	74,768 570 0.8%	17 1.8 10.5	245 23.3 9.5	94 3.5 3.8	277 13.9 5.0
1978	90,400 1,834 2.0	- -	- -	- -	- -
COMPOUND GROWTH/AVG MAR (1973-77)	32.2% N/A	24.7% 6.8%	24.5% 9.2%	23.1% 5.1%	17.2% 3.2%
EPS (FD)/DPS/PAYOUT RATIO					
1973	$ N/A .00 N/A	$0.32 0.00 0%	$0.70 0.00 0%	$0.56 $0.00 0%	$0.08 $0.00 0%
1974	1.04 .00 0%	0.16 0.00 0	0.82 0.05 5	0.50 0.15 15	0.26 0.00 0
1975	(6.97) .00 0	0.82 0.00 0	0.96 0.10 9	1.00 0.20 25	0.51 0.00 0
1976	(.08) .00 0	1.30 0.00 3	1.22 0.21 16	0.79 0.20 23	0.81 0.00 0
1977	1.99 .00 0	1.26 0.08 6	1.58 0.28 17	0.88 0.20 19	0.97 0.00 0
1978	4.08 .00 0	- 0.16 -	1.84 0.43 23	1.03 0.20 -	1.04 0.00 0
NEXT YR EST/IND ANN RATE	4.08 .00 0	2.20 -	2.20 0.52 24	1.25 -	1.25 0.00 0
COMPOUND GROWTH/AVG PAY (1973-77)	40.7% N/A	42.0% -%	22.6% 9%	2.4% 13%	68.6% -%
INTERIM EPS (THIS YR/LAST YR)	N/A N/A	6 MONTHS JUN $0.51 $0.56	12 MONTHS JUN $1.84 $1.58	6 MONTHS JUN $0.55 $0.40	3 MONTHS JUN $0.28 $0.21
MARKET RANGE (CALENDAR YR)	N/A	AMEX	NYSE	AMEX	NYSE
1977	N/A	9.625 - 5.125	30.50 - 21.50	10.625 - 7.50	9.875 - 6.75
1978	N/A	17.50 - 7.875	36.375 - 23.00	13.75 - 6.75	17.00 - 8.00
10/6/78	N/A	14.125	32.875	10.75	14.375
P/E RATIO					
1977	N/A N/A	7.7 4.1	16.6 11.7	10.3 7.3	9.5 6.5
1978	N/A N/A	14.0 6.3	19.8 12.5	13.3 6.6	16.3 7.7
LATEST 12 MONTHS EPS	N/A	11.3	17.9	10.4	13.8
NEXT YR EST EPS	N/A	-	14.9	-	11.5
TANG BOOK VAL/MKT AS A % BOOK	N/A	$4.20 336.6%	$6.69 491.4%	$7.95 135.2%	$2.73 526.6%
DIVIDEND YIELD	0.0%	1.1%	1.6%	1.9%	0.0%
CERTAIN RATIOS (LT'ST FISC YR)					
PRE TAX MARGIN	3.9%	17.9%	18.7%	5.9%	9.4%
TAX RATE	48.0%	41.1%	49.3%	36.3%	46.8%
NET MARGIN	2.0%	10.5%	9.5%	3.8%	5.0%
ASSET TURNOVER (AVG)	N/A	2.1x	1.6x	0.2x	2.0x
RETURN ON ASSETS (AVG)	N/A	21.7%	15.4%	0.7%	9.8%
TOTAL LEVERAGE (AVG)	N/A	1.8x	1.4x	10.8x	3.7x
RETURN ON EQUITY (AVG)	N/A	39.2%	20.9%	7.5%	36.4%

FIGURE 14-2 (continued)

(DOLLARS IN MILLIONS)

	INFORMATICS, INC. ESTIMATED 12/31/78	ELECTRONIC DATA SYSTEMS 6/30/78	LOGICON INC. 3/31/78	NATIONAL CSS INC. 5/31/78	TYMSHARE INC. 3/31/78
CAPITALIZATION					
SHORT TERM DEBT	$ 4,789	$0.9	$0.0	$0.7	$3.5
LONG TERM DEBT	$ 6,934 36.1	$2.6 2.6%	$0.0 0.0%	$6.9 29.4%	$15.6 26.4%
PREFERRED STOCK (LIQ VAL)	69 0.3	0.0 0.0%	0.0 0.0%	0.0 0.0%	0.0 0.0%
COMMON EQUITY	12,197 63.6	97.6 97.4%	8.1 100.0%	16.6 70.6%	43.5 73.6%
TOTAL CAPITALIZATION	$19,200 100.0%	$100.2 100.0%	$8.1 100.0%	$23.5 100.0%	$59.1 100.0%
COMMON SHARES OUTSTANDING	608,000	12,828,000	888,000	2,174,000	4,348,000
NET SALES/NET INC/NET MARGIN	12/31/78 = 1978	6/30/78 = 1977	3/31/78 = 1977	2/28/78 = 1977	12/31/77 = 1977
1973	$ N/A $ N/A N/A	$ 114 $15.3 13.4%	$23 $0.7 2.9%	$24 $1.6 6.7%	$40 $2.3 5.8%
1974	29,560 (1,344) N/A	119 14.6 12.3%	33 0.9 2.7%	33 1.8 5.6%	53 3.4 6.5%
1975	38,982 (4,392) N/A	129 13.6 10.5%	32 0.8 2.5%	36 2.2 6.1%	64 5.0 7.7%
1976	58,743 (1,882) N/A	157 16.4 10.5%	28 1.3 4.6%	42 3.2 7.7%	82 6.7 8.2%
1977	74,768 570 0.8%	211 19.7 9.3%	33 0.8 2.5%	49 3.9 7.9%	101 8.0 7.9%
1978	90,400 1,834 2.0%	–	–	–	–
COMPOUND GROWTH/AVG MAR (1973-77)	32.2% N/A	16.5% 11.2%	6.3% 3.1%	19.8% 6.8%	26.5% 7.2%
EPS (FD)/DPS/PAYOUT RATIO					
1973	$ N/A $ N/A 0%	$1.28 – 0%	$0.50 .00 0%	$0.72 .00 0%	$0.58 .00 0%
1974	1.04 .00 0	1.21 .25 22%	0.78 .00 0	0.84 .00 0	0.85 .00 0
1975	(6.97) .00 0	1.10 .50 48	0.98 .00 0	0.95 .00 5	1.19 .00 0
1976	.08 .00 0	1.54 .60 48	1.41 .00 0	1.41 .08 11	1.55 .00 0
1977	1.99 .00 0	1.90 .72 49	1.68 .00 0	1.68 .20 13	1.82 .00 0
1978	4.08 .00 0	– –	1.82 .00 0	1.82 .23 14	2.04 .00 0
NEXT YR EST/IND ANN RATE	4.08 .00	0.84	2.25 .00	2.25 .32	2.40 .00
COMPOUND GROWTH/AVG PAY (1973-77)	40.7% N/A	30.3% 44%	16.5% 0%	23.8% 3%	36.1% 0%
INTERIM EPS (THIS YR/LAST YR)	N/A N/A		$0.37 $0.30	$0.53 $0.39	$1.33 $1.11
			3 MONTHS JUN	3 MONTHS MAY	6 MONTHS JUN
MARKET RANGE (CALENDAR YR)	N/A	NYSE	AMEX	AMEX	NYSE
1977	N/A N/A	– –	17.625 – 7.25	18.00 – 9.50	23.625 – 14.00
1978	N/A N/A	24.875 – 14.625	19.50 – 11.00	36.00 – 15.375	34.375 – 17.00
10/6/78	N/A N/A	21.375	15.75	29.375	28.00
P/E RATIO					
1977	N/A N/A	– –	17.8 7.3	9.9 5.2	11.6 6.9
1978	N/A N/A	16.3 9.6	19.7 11.1	19.8 8.4	16.9 8.3
LATEST 12 MONTHS EPS	N/A	14.0	15.9	16.1	13.7
NEXT YR EST EPS	N/A	11.3	–	13.1	11.7
TANG BOOK VAL/MKT AS A % BOOK	N/A	$7.61 280.9%	$9.14 172.3%	$6.70 438.7%	$8.33 334.0%
DIVIDEND YIELD	0.0%	3.9%	0.0%	1.1%	0.0%
CERTAIN RATIOS (LTST FISC YR)					
PRE TAX MARGIN	3.9%	15.4%	4.6%	15.3%	15.6%
TAX RATE	48.0%	39.4%	46.0%	48.5%	49.3%
NET MARGIN	2.0%	9.3%	2.5%	7.9%	7.9%
ASSET TURNOVER (AVG)	N/A	1.7x	2.5x	1.6x	1.6x
RETURN ON ASSETS (AVG)	N/A	16.2%	6.2%	12.4%	12.4%
TOTAL LEVERAGE (AVG)	N/A	1.3x	1.8x	2.2x	1.8x
RETURN ON EQUITY (AVG)	N/A	21.3%	11.3%	26.9%	22.7%

FIGURE 14–2 (concluded)

FOOTNOTES:

APPLIED DATA RESEARCH :

    EARNINGS ARE STATED BEFORE EXTRAORDINARY ITEM OF $ -0.1 MILLION OR $ -0.11 PER SHARE IN 1974
    EARNINGS ARE STATED BEFORE EXTRAORDINARY ITEM OF $ 0.2 MILLION OR $ 0.16 PER SHARE IN 1975
    EARNINGS ARE STATED BEFORE EXTRAORDINARY ITEM OF $ 0.4 MILLION OR $ 0.29 PER SHARE IN 1976
    EARNINGS ARE STATED BEFORE DISCONTINUED OPERATIONS OF $ -0.1 MILLION OR $ -0.10 PER SHARE IN 1975
    EARNINGS ARE STATED BEFORE DISCONTINUED OPERATIONS OF $ -0.1 MILLION OR $ -0.11 PER SHARE IN 1977
    AVG INVENTORY METHOD USED SINCE 1974

AUTOMATIC DATA PROC :

    FIFO INVENTORY METHOD USED SINCE 1973

BRADFORD NATIONAL CORP :

    EARNINGS ARE STATED BEFORE EXTRAORDINARY ITEM OF $ 0.0 MILLION OR $ 0.01 PER SHARE IN 1973
    EARNINGS ARE STATED BEFORE EXTRAORDINARY ITEM OF $ 0.1 MILLION OR $ 0.03 PER SHARE IN 1974
    EARNINGS ARE STATED BEFORE EXTRAORDINARY ITEM OF $ 0.1 MILLION OR $ 0.02 PER SHARE IN 1975
    EARNINGS ARE STATED BEFORE EXTRAORDINARY ITEM OF $ 0.3 MILLION OR $ 0.06 PER SHARE IN 1977

COMPUTER SCIENCES CORP :

    EARNINGS ARE STATED BEFORE EXTRAORDINARY ITEM OF $ 3.0 MILLION OR $ 0.23 PER SHARE IN 1976

ELECTRONIC DATA SYSTEMS :

    NO APPLICABLE FOOTNOTES

LOGICON INC :

    FIFO INVENTORY METHOD USED SINCE 1973

NATIONAL CSS INC :

    EARNINGS ARE STATED BEFORE EXTRAORDINARY ITEM OF $ 0.2 MILLION OR $ 0.10 PER SHARE IN 1973

TYMSHARE INC :

    EARNINGS ARE STATED BEFORE EXTRAORDINARY ITEM OF $ 0.3 MILLION OR $ 0.08 PER SHARE IN 1973
    EARNINGS ARE STATED BEFORE EXTRAORDINARY ITEM OF $ 0.2 MILLION OR $ 0.03 PER SHARE IN 1974
    EARNINGS ARE STATED BEFORE EXTRAORDINARY ITEM OF $ 0.1 MILLION OR $ 0.03 PER SHARE IN 1975
    FIFO INVENTORY METHOD USED SINCE 1973

CAPITALIZATION	RANGE FOR COMPANIES IN THIS REPORT	MEDIAN FOR COMPANIES IN THIS REPORT	MEAN FOR COMPANIES IN THIS REPORT
STOCKHOLDERS' EQUITY			
AS A % OF CAPITALIZATION	100.0% – 50.1%	83.9%	81.1
PAYOUT RATIO			
LATEST YEAR	28.1 – 0.0	9.5	11.1
AVG OVER 5 YEARS	25.8 – 0.0	3.1	6.4
PROFITABILITY			
NET MARGIN (LATEST YEAR)	14.9 – 2.1	8.4	7.9
NET MARGIN (5 YEAR AVERAGE)	11.8 – 2.0	6.8	6.9
RETURN ON AVG ASSETS (LATEST YEAR)	21.8 – 4.0	10.6	11.6
RETURN ON AVG EQUITY (LATEST YEAR)	29.9 – 13.9	18.8	19.3
COMPOUND ANNUAL GROWTH RATES			
NET SALES	48.0 – 8.1	17.2	21.1
NET INCOME	72.7 – 5.0	27.0	30.7
EARNINGS PER SHARE	61.3 – 5.7	29.8	28.6
DIVIDENDS PER SHARE	31.3 – 31.3	31.3	31.3
MARKET DATA			
P/E RATIO ON LATEST 12 MO. EPS	12.2X – 11.9X	12.0X	12.0
P/E RATIO ON NEXT YR EST EPS	19.7 – 11.6	11.9	14.4
MARKET AS A % OF BOOK	645.4% – 194.2%	252.3%	322.3
DIVIDEND YIELD	2.4 – 0.0	1.3	1.2

ure 14–1), the initial offering made on October 4, 1979 carried a price to the public of $12.50 per share (and proceeds to the selling shareholders of $11.56 per share). The $12.50 price to public represents a multiple of about 11 times the reported income per share for 1978; a comparison of these data with the spreadsheet data used by the underwriters in pricing the issue (shown in Figure 14–2) indicate that the issue price is right in line with market experience (compare price-earnings ratios for mean and median of comparable firms on pp. 262–63). Some other comparisons (e.g., sales growth rate), to be sure, show somewhat better results for Informatics but that suggests that, at new-issue, those better results may have helped to move up the P/E multiple to the mean industry level.

	Year-End		Six Months Ended June 30	
Per Share	1978	1979	1979	1980
Net income	$1.15	$2.03	$0.65	$0.81
Change in net income	$0.88		$0.16	
Percent change	80%		25%	

The sale of the new issue went so well that in less than one year the selling shareholder (a subsidiary of Equitable Life Assurance Society) saw the stock trade on National Association of Security Dealers Automated Quotation System (NASDAQ) at a price above $20 per share. Consequently, on September 18, 1980, Equitable Life Holdings sold another 1,267,250 shares at a price between the bid/ask quotation (20½ and 20¾) on the close of the preceding day. At that time, market data and spreadsheets tended to confirm the pricing of the issue. This suggests that the pricing process for this firm appears to be less traumatic than it might be in other cases. Because the selling stockholder is a major institutional client, that issuer may be more knowledgeable about capital markets than many other IPO clients (see Figure 14–3).

FIGURE 14–3

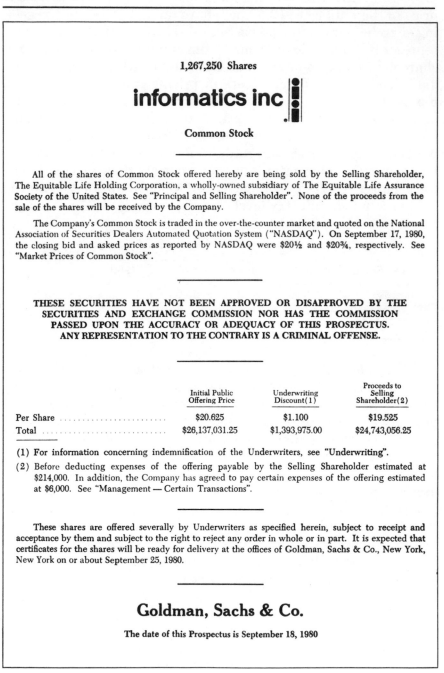

1,267,250 Shares

informatics inc

Common Stock

All of the shares of Common Stock offered hereby are being sold by the Selling Shareholder, The Equitable Life Holding Corporation, a wholly-owned subsidiary of The Equitable Life Assurance Society of the United States. See "Principal and Selling Shareholder". None of the proceeds from the sale of the shares will be received by the Company.

The Company's Common Stock is traded in the over-the-counter market and quoted on the National Association of Securities Dealers Automated Quotation System ("NASDAQ"). On September 17, 1980, the closing bid and asked prices as reported by NASDAQ were $20½ and $20¾, respectively. See "Market Prices of Common Stock".

THESE SECURITIES HAVE NOT BEEN APPROVED OR DISAPPROVED BY THE SECURITIES AND EXCHANGE COMMISSION NOR HAS THE COMMISSION PASSED UPON THE ACCURACY OR ADEQUACY OF THIS PROSPECTUS. ANY REPRESENTATION TO THE CONTRARY IS A CRIMINAL OFFENSE.

	Initial Public Offering Price	Underwriting Discount(1)	Proceeds to Selling Shareholder(2)
Per Share	$20.625	$1.100	$19.525
Total	$26,137,031.25	$1,393,975.00	$24,743,056.25

(1) For information concerning indemnification of the Underwriters, see "Underwriting".

(2) Before deducting expenses of the offering payable by the Selling Shareholder estimated at $214,000. In addition, the Company has agreed to pay certain expenses of the offering estimated at $6,000. See "Management — Certain Transactions".

These shares are offered severally by Underwriters as specified herein, subject to receipt and acceptance by them and subject to the right to reject any order in whole or in part. It is expected that certificates for the shares will be ready for delivery at the offices of Goldman, Sachs & Co., New York, New York on or about September 25, 1980.

Goldman, Sachs & Co.

The date of this Prospectus is September 18, 1980

Avoidance of Flotation Risks: Management's Point of View

Corporations that are expanding rapidly have opportunities to make real investments (with positive net present values) in excess of their internal funds currently available for investment. They will raise outside funds as long as internal rates of return on the new projects exceed the firm's cost of capital. At the margin, however, some projects are necessarily more sensitive to unforeseen rises in cost of capital (that is, flotation risk); and, for all new projects, an unforeseen rise in the cost of capital has the same impact as an unforeseen rise in business risk on expected net present value. Alternatively, an unforeseen rise in the firm's cost of capital could be interpreted as a new tax on new investment. If that "tax" threatens to make the new investment unattractive—that is, carry negative net present value—the new issue may be postponed or canceled.

In view of the foregoing arguments, consider the following propositions:

1. Most corporations that sell a new issue come to market only occasionally; their experience with flotation risks will be limited.
2. Economies of scale with respect to fixed costs abound in new flotations; as a result, ventures into the capital markets are necessarily concentrated into fewer, rather than more frequent, new issues.
3. The chief financial officer (CFO) may be induced to be satisficing rather than maximizing corporate net worth (in connection with flotations). He may feel (probably correctly) that the sale of an issue at a better-than-anticipated price will not generate as much *credit* for him as a failed issue will raise *doubts* about his abilities and promotability. This induces managerial risk avoidance in flotations. In other words, it raises corporate management's demand to shift incidence of flotation risk.
4. Suppose that the decision to sell a new issue is made by a mostly outside board of directors. Aside from their prior responsibilities with due diligence, they have now added a fiduciary responsibility regarding new-issue *timing*.

Their demand for insurance protection will not be reduced.

Summing up, economies of scale limit the number of trips
to market, and the fewer the trips to market, the thinner management's experience. Risk avoidance in new-issue pricing and
in flotation risks generally leads, in turn, to calls for "the experts." Beyond finding another handy group to blame if things
go wrong, the CFO may also conceive of the new-issue underwriting process as a useful insurance scheme that limits the
variance of net present value—or risk—as much as possible
from the cost-of-capital side.

"Privileged Subscription" for Rights Issues and Standby "Insurance"

Most articles of incorporation give shareholders preemptive
rights to new-issue stock subscriptions. This provision reflects
the common-law practice of reserving to current owners—that
is, stockholders—rights associated with their property (common
stock), including a potentially valuable opportunity to acquire
new stock.

Most preemptive rights are presented to current stockholders as the "right" (hence the name) to acquire new shares in
some proportion to their present holdings at a preferential price.
Since only present owners benefit from such "underpricing," the
nominal price set on rights offers—however low the price might
be—does *not* affect stockholder value or any other aspect of ownership status. These offerings must be registered with the SEC
(like any other new-money issue), and the prospectus, like any
other, states the volume of funds to be raised, the price per
share, the purpose of the flotation, and so on. The rights issued
to each stockholder may be in the form of warrants (for example,
the holder can use five warrants to buy one share of additional
stock at $50 within 20 days of the offering date). Rights may be
exercised, sold, or thrown away; they have value only if the market price at the end of the subscription period is above the exercise price. Assume that the market price on the exercise date
is $52 per share. Most often, a subscription agent is named to

receive the rights for the purchase of new stock or for resale by those not exercising their rights. Finally, most of these options (for these are, indeed, call options) are exercised by holders at the end of the subscription period because only by then will it be clear and certain (that is, risk will approach zero) that holders can buy $52 market-price stock at the bargain price of $50.

From the point of view of the issuing corporation and, more specifically, the CFO, this is a desirable and useful result. But to avoid flotation risk (or waiting risk as defined earlier), many corporations even have rights issues underwritten by an investment banking firm on a *standby* arrangement. This means that the underwriter *will not* buy the issue on subscription day if the issue is a success. Instead, the issuing firm pays a standby fee (1 percent of the value of the issue is customary). For that premium (or, in effect, the equivalent to the firm of a *standby put option*), the underwriter stands ready to buy any unsubscribed shares at the subscription price less an additional *take-down discount* (or fee) of 2.5 percent.[10]

If everything works out as planned, the fees paid to the underwriter are the equivalent of an insurance premium. The fees insure against the vagaries of a market where the price might drop below $50 per share and where the standby call option in effect covers flotation risk as defined. That risk is the possibility that the stock market will decline so far—say, below $50 per share—during the subscription period as to make the put option (rights) worthless (out of the money). In fact, the cost of the standby insurance can be calculated as a pay-as-you-go proposition by a set of steps that move the security issuer into a fully hedged ("certainty equivalent") position.

Assume that most current owners—that is, rights holders—will wait until the exercise date to proffer their rights. By the exercise date the stock price has fallen through $50 per share to, say, $48 per share. At that point, the standby put option is invoked, and the corporation sells the shares to the underwriter

---

[10]That last option will also be exercised by the underwriter to the extent that subscribers ignore their valuable rights and do not exercise them. Typically, the underwriter's profits in such transactions are split 50/50 with the issuer.

at $50 per share less the following fees: ½-point standby fee (1 percent) + 1¼-point take-down discount (2.5 percent), leaving the issuer proceeds of 48¼ per share—¼ point better than the current market price. And the risks of an even lower market price as well as all other transaction costs of selling new shares are progressively shifted to the underwriter.

To consider that problem from the issuer's point of view, start with the assumption that the stock issue to be sold had a par value of $20 million (at a $50 exercise price on 400,000 shares). The worst-case scenario then gives the corporation fully hedged minimum proceeds of $20 million less $700,000 [400,000 shares (0.01 + 0.025)($50) = $700,000]—all from owners of the firm. The net proceeds then come to $19.3 million.[11]

If the price on exercise day is above 48¼, the proceeds to the firm will be higher, reaching a maximum of $19.8 million (all from owners of firm) at the exercise price of $50. If the projects for which the new funds are needed require a minimum of $19.3 million cash, then the fully hedged position, having shifted the flotation risk to the underwriter, becomes a rational policy. If on the other hand, the cost of the hedge is too high or if the issuer can afford to be less risk averse, a rational decision might be made not to underwrite the stock issue. Nevertheless, some 70 percent of rights offers are underwritten.

There is a demand for risk shifting to the underwriter even among the do-it-yourself issuers that use preemptive rights offerings. From a stockholder's point of view, that flotation cost can be avoided if the rights offering is priced very substantially—say, 25 percent—below the current market price. In a narrow stockholder's viewpoint, there should be no concern whatever no matter how low the new stock price is set because each stockholder will maintain the same proportionate ownership share. Even if the stockholders *sell* their rights, an efficient

---

[11]Note that the spread between the stock price at the announcement date ($52 per share) and the ultimate floor price ($48) came to $4, or nearly 8 percent of the exercise price. Adding to that spread the 1 percent standby fee and the 2.5 percent take-down discount, a total spread of about 10 percent (typically assumed) is obtained. But the standby arrangements reach their maximum spread only if market decline raises costs to the maximum.

market will price that value appropriately. Why, then, are some 70 percent of new-rights offerings underwritten at significant expense, while using only a modest price discount below market?

The question really being asked here is: Why is the tradeoff between a substantial price discount as in insurance premium (that is, presumably costless to the stockholder) foregone in favor of a costly underwriting (standby) premium associated with a lesser price discount? One possible (and plausible) explanation could be management's fear that the market might misperceive the large discount as an information signal rather than as a flotation-insurance mechanism. This is a generally unexplored area of agency theory where management may prefer easier (even if more expensive) stockholder relations and a consequently higher cost of capital.

This proposition, finally, should be kept conceptually separate from the more general aspect of the payment of a flotation-related insurance fee if that payment appears to have been a "useless" expense. Such a payment can appear useless if the offering goes well and if the underwriting support is unnecessary because of a rise in market prices. But that is the nature of all insurance fees. If the accident insured against does not occur, the payments seem unnecessary. A rational corporate decision to use insurance *before* the coverage period is like any other capital budgeting decision. If it appears to carry positive net present value when made, the decision should be judged accordingly.

SOME CONCLUSIONS:
UNDERWRITING AND ITS RISKS

There have been several instances in which underwriters for even the highest quality issues have taken losses. Just prior to the beginning of the 1980s, in October 1979, IBM floated a $1 billion bond issue that was priced just prior to the weekend in which the Fed, as an anti-inflationary move, shifted policy. (Some have referred to that event as the Saturday night massacre.) The underwriters in the issue took heavy losses.

Likewise, in a well-publicized 1987 flotation that featured a

FIGURE 14–4

BP The British Petroleum Company p.l.c.

42,150,000 Instalment Payment American Depositary Shares

The several US Underwriters are hereby offering (the "Offer") Instalment Payment ADSs, each of which, upon full payment of instalments, will represent twelve Ordinary Shares of The British Petroleum Company p. l. c. ("BP"). The US Underwriters purchased 40,000,000 of the Instalment Payment ADSs offered hereby as part of an International Offer outside the United Kingdom and to institutions in the United Kingdom (the "International Offer") made by The Lords Commissioners of Her Majesty's Treasury of the United Kingdom ("HM Treasury"). The US Underwriters committed to purchase such Instalment Payment ADSs on October 15, 1987 at a price of £1.20 per Ordinary Share for the first instalment (£14.40 per Instalment Payment ADS), less the underwriting discount, and as required by their agreement with HM Treasury and others, the US Underwriters are initially making a public offering of the Instalment Payment ADSs at that price.

Since October 16, 1987, the price of BP's Ordinary Shares has declined substantially. In light of the current adverse market conditions, the initial offer described above is being immediately followed by an Offer by the US Underwriters at the price set forth below, which is less than the price paid by them to HM Treasury. The public offering price may be changed from time to time. Current market conditions may have an adverse effect on the market price of the Instalment Payment ADSs. The Bank of England will make an offer to purchase partly paid Ordinary Shares for a limited period beginning no later than November 6, 1987 at £0.70 per partly paid Ordinary Share ($1.20 at the exchange rate prevailing on October 30,1987). See "The Combined Offer — Bank of England Offer". Such offer will be made available to holders of Instalment Payment ADSs, subject to necessary regulatory approvals.

The Offer is part of the Combined Offer described herein which included the International Offer and an offering (the "Fixed Price Offer") to the general public in the United Kingdom, to eligible UK employees of the BP Group and to existing holders of Ordinary Shares and ADSs at a price of £1.20 per Ordinary Share for the first instalment (£14.40 per Instalment Payment ADS). Because of current market conditions, substantially all of the Ordinary Shares so offered were purchased by underwriters or sub-underwriters at the foregoing price per Ordinary Share. In light of current market conditions, it has been determined not to proceed with the offer previously made to holders of ADSs and holders of Ordinary Shares whose registered addresses are in the United States, and the 2,150,000 Instalment Payment ADSs offered to such holders have been included in the Instalment Payment ADSs offered hereby. See "The Combined Offer — Market Conditions".

BP will receive proceeds of approximately £1.5 billion in connection with its sale to HM Treasury of new Ordinary Shares for sale in the Combined Offer. With respect to the Combined Offer, N M Rothschild & Sons Limited and S. G. Warburg & Co. Ltd. have acted as financial advisers to HM Treasury and BP, respectively.

The US Underwriters have paid to HM Treasury the first instalment of £14.40 per Instalment Payment ADS. The amounts of the second and final instalments will be the US dollar equivalent of £12.60 and £12.60, respectively, based on the then prevailing exchange rates and will be payable by holders of Instalment Payment ADSs. See "Description of American Depositary Receipts" and "Description of Interim Rights".

ADSs are listed on the New York Stock Exchange ("NYSE") and Ordinary Shares are listed on The Stock Exchange, London. The last reported sale price of the ADSs on the NYSE on October 29, 1987 was $55¾ per ADS. See "Market Price Information" for recent market prices for ADSs and Ordinary Shares. Instalment Payment ADSs have been authorized for listing on the NYSE and the underlying Ordinary Shares have been authorized for listing on The Stock Exchange, London. If The Bank of England purchases a sufficiently large number of partly paid Ordinary Shares pursuant to the offer described under "The Combined Offer — Bank of England Offer", the Instalment Payment ADSs could be delisted from the NYSE.

THESE SECURITIES HAVE NOT BEEN APPROVED OR DISAPPROVED BY THE SECURITIES AND EXCHANGE COMMISSION NOR HAS THE COMMISSION PASSED UPON THE ACCURACY OR ADEQUACY OF THIS PROSPECTUS. ANY REPRESENTATION TO THE CONTRARY IS A CRIMINAL OFFENSE.

	Price to Public(1)	Underwriting Commission	Proceeds to HM Treasury(2)(3)
Per Instalment Payment ADS:			
Initial Payment	$17.25	$0.719	$23.987
Second Instalment (due on August 30, 1988)	$21.62	—	$21.618
Final Instalment (due on April 27, 1989)	$21.62	—	$21.618
Total per Instalment Payment ADS	$60.49	$0.719	$67.223
Total	$2,549,653,500	$30,305,850	$2,833,449,450

(1) The amounts set forth in the table have been translated at the exchange rate prevailing on October 30, 1987, the date of this Prospectus, which is applicable only to the initial payment. The actual US dollar amount of the second and final instalments will depend on the exchange rates at the dates of such instalments. Accordingly, the total amount payable in US dollars with respect to each Instalment Payment ADS may be different from the price shown above. The second and final instalments must be accompanied by an additional payment in respect of UK stamp duty reserve tax at the rate then applicable (currently 1½ percent). An amount of $0.259 per Instalment Payment ADS is also payable in addition to the initial payment reflecting a portion of UK stamp duty reserve tax paid by the US Underwriters in respect of the initial payment.
(2) Before deduction of estimated expenses of $6,650,000 attributable to the offering in the United States (including $1,800,000 to be paid to the US Underwriters as reimbursement of certain expenses), of which $4,407,208 will be paid by HM Treasury and $2,242,792 will be paid by BP.
(3) Reflects amount per Instalment Payment ADS paid by US Underwriters to HM Treasury under the International Offer Agreement.

The Instalment Payment ADSs are offered severally by the US Underwriters, as specified herein, subject to receipt and acceptance by them and subject to their right to reject any order in whole or in part. It is expected that the Instalment Payment ADSs will be ready for delivery at the offices of Goldman, Sachs & Co., New York, New York on or about November 6, 1987.

Goldman, Sachs & Co.

Morgan Stanley & Co.
Incorporated
Salomon Brothers Inc

Shearson Lehman Brothers Inc.

The date of this Prospectus is October 30, 1987.

similarly exquisite exercise in bad timing, a large syndicate priced the privatization of a British Petroleum (BP) stock issue on Thursday, October 15, 1987—that is, two business days prior to Black Monday. And, following British practice, the flotation process was not really started until *after* that date (the prospectus is dated October 30, 1987). Accordingly, the pricing box on the BP prospectus looks as if it were set up backwards: the proceeds to be paid to the issuer (Her Majesty's Treasury) were $2,833 million, or $283 million *more* than the $2,550 million paid by the public. The loss suffered by the four underwriters is not a trivial sum even if a share of it was offset by hedging.[12] Finally, in any environment of volatile rates, these risks exist even if the underwriters stop using the British timing schedule for new issues.

---

[12]See discussion of Morgan Stanley income statement for 1987 (Chapter 4) for additional information.

15

NEW ISSUE UNDERWRITING OF STOCKS AND BONDS: ANOTHER APPLICATION OF OPTIONS THEORY

This chapter explores the concept of securities underwriting further, taking as a model the notion of the flotation process as a put option. Using that concept, the Black/Scholes (B/S) model is evaluated as a representation of a new issue flotation "premium." The model is then used to value changes in flotation cost—or changes in put-option *premium* costs—as Rule 415 has changed the process by reducing flotation risk.

THE BLACK/SCHOLES MODEL AS AN UNDERWRITING PROCESS

The Black/Scholes model of option pricing develops an equilibrium solution for option premiums by substituting the value of underlying securities for option value.[1] By adjusting the components of the Black/Scholes substitution model, the new-issues process for stocks and bonds may also be modeled. The following are the necessary adjustments:

1. For option "premium," read "gross spread."
2. For "exercise price," read "proceeds to company."

---

[1]This presentation is based in part on Sharpe's *Investments*, 2nd ed., Prentice-Hall, Inc., Englewood Cliffs, N.J., 1981, Chap. 6. -

3. For "exercise price, plus premium," read "price to public."
4. For "value of dividends," read "accrued interest" (for bonds only).

With respect to the B/S assumptions, there appears to be a good fit (with one exception to be noted) in the actual conditions for a new issue underwriting. These assumptions and conditions are listed in Table 15–1.

The last item appears well within the boundaries established for the B/S model. Even though the prices on the prospectus (to public, to firm) are fixed, these prices must be seen relative to the market environment and in only one way: if mar-

TABLE 15–1

Assumptions, Black/Scholes	Terms and Conditions, Underwriting
1. No transaction cost, no differential taxes.	1. No commissions, no immediate tax affect.
2. Borrowing and lending, at same rate, are unrestricted.	2. New stock issue will not produce dividends; underwriters receive no funds and will not pay funds until deal closes five days after trading begins.* (No funds change hands during syndicate period.)
3. Short-term risk-free rate of interest is known and constant through time.	3. If issue sells quickly, assumption is not relevant. If issue sells slowly, underwriters will need financing only for unsold portion of their own shares *after* syndicate deal closes.
4. Short sales with full use of proceeds are not restricted.	4. Price support operations, including short sales, are permitted during syndicate period.
5. Trading takes place continuously through time.	5. Trading takes place continuously through time.
6. The movement of the stock price can be described by a diffusion process.	6. The price to the public (as well as the price to the issuer) is fixed by prospectus for the syndicate period (or until the sale is completed if the issue goes out the window).

*For a new bond issue, accrued interest is charged (to the buyer) and paid at same rate; the borrowing-lending condition is satisfied.

ket-environment prices move down, and move down substantially, the issues becomes unattractive, and the syndicate will
break up eventually. From the underwriters' point of view, the
flotation is a loser.

If, on the other hand, market prices rise, the issue will sell
out quickly at the price to public stated on the prospectus ("go
out the window"), and the securities will then trade in secondary
markets; the subsequent capital gains accrue to buyers rather
than to syndicate members. Accordingly, from the point of view
of syndicate members, the flotation process implies a limited
possibility of gain and some downside risk. They do it because
the flotation gains (and other benefits) outweigh the potential
for loss.

The B/S security replication model can now be restated as a
flotation proxy. Consider that the underwriting syndicate buys
the stock (which it is obligated to do as the offering becomes
effective); the financing assumption of the B/S model is not necessary since no cash to pay for the stock (or bonds) needs to
change hands prior to the closing of the underwriting deal (this
typically occurs five working days later). As soon as the underwriting is declared effective by the SEC, it is open for trading,
and syndicate members will sell to the public at the new-issue
price. In fact, the syndicate has written a costless call (to the
public) at that price. The "premium equivalent" for the call has
been paid by the issuer (the gross spread). This produces the
combination of the syndicate (1) stock purchase and (2) call that
constitute the equivalent of a "synthetic put" option.

The foregoing uses the option valuation model only as an
analog. The model helps by focusing analysis on the valuation
of the underwriting service cost. No option is written or purchased in any syndicate deal; the foregoing suggests how the
pricing of the gross spread and some other factors in such deals
can be interpreted *as if* an option had been written.

As Figure 15–1 indicates, the two top charts describe the
situation of the syndicate as evaluated by the B/S model:

1. The syndicate is committed to buy the new stock; *its* cost
   (at closing) is the proceeds per share to the company. We
   assume that all out-of-pocket costs are reimbursed by the
   company.

FIGURE 15–1
Syndicate's Position in a Black/Scholes Setting

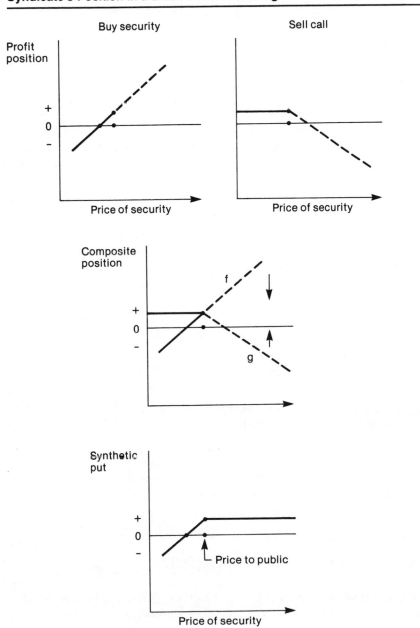

2. The published prospectus shows two prices per share:
   a. The proceeds to the company.
   b. The (higher) price to the public.

The difference between (a) and (b) is the gross spread—that is, the gross revenue to the syndicate. In effect, the syndicate sells a call to the public at the price to public, and the (implicit) option premium is paid by issuer as the gross spread.

In the third chart, called composite position, we show the two parts of the model that are *not relevant* to the syndicate flotation, namely, the situation when the stock price rises above the price to the public. At that time, the issue sells out immediately at the price to public. Line f (stock valuation) and line g (call valuation) exactly offset. As a result, they are shown as broken lines.

In the fourth chart, the situation as seen by a syndicate participant is called a synthetic put precisely because that is the situation in which the syndicate operates.

Thus are illustrated (1) the substitution process of the B/S model and (2) the resultant option value.

Consider now that the new issue spread in a flotation is a straightforward put premium, as indicated earlier, and is set equal to the gross spread. The syndicate will earn the premium only if the public buys at the price stated on the prospectus. If the offering will not sell out at that price, the syndicate will earn less than the premium as average sale price (after close of deal) declines below the price to the public. At "break-even" (on an option value when the premium is equal to zero), the syndicate will be out of pocket an amount equal to expenses plus foregone opportunity earnings on resources employed. At prices below that point, losses will rise dollar for dollar per share (or bond) as the price falls below stated proceeds to company.

UNDERWRITING AS A PUT OPTION

The purchase of a standby (put) option for a rights issue of a new stock has the purpose of hedging flotation risks. The rights issue is a special case where the firm is dealing mainly with its own owners but where it may still feel it remains potentially exposed to severe downward pricing risks that might affect all markets. *All* underwritings (rights or cash, stocks or bonds) incorporate a put option for the issuer. And as noted, the volatility of market prices, when perceived as a dimension of risk, may induce issuers to have their new issues underwritten. By the same token, the valuation of the underwriting spread (as a put option) is also sensitive to price volatility.

Volatility

Figure 15–2 examines the price environment of a market for a security for which a current option price—as distinct from current spot price—is established with a contract date set for the near future (say, an issue date one month hence). Point X is the execution price. It could represent the consensus of market expectations of the spot prices anticipated in the market for maturity of the contract one month away. If market prices are expected to be relatively stable, the range of strike prices on put and call options on the two sides of the futures price would be described between points A and B, which are relatively close to X. Conversely, if the market is expected to be volatile, the range

FIGURE 15–2
Volatility Examined

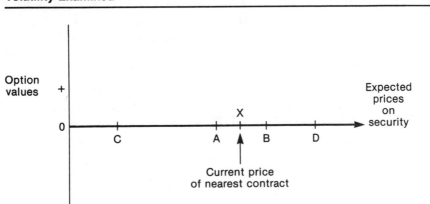

of strike prices widens to the points between C and D. With greater volatility, the premiums for puts and calls will rise substantially, especially as more extreme strike prices are covered. This occurs partly because insurance against smaller declines and partly because greater rate volatility usually is accompanied by higher interest rates (that is, carrying costs). Recall, finally, that a new offering has a fixed sales price so that increases in price will not benefit the issuer.

Insurance Components of New-Issue Flotations

From the issuer's point of view, insurance coverage against a large drop in the bond (or stock) price on the new issue *before pricing* is essential because, if the issue is sold below a certain price, it implies a rise in the firm's cost of capital. In turn, that possibility may raise the risk that the real investment financed by the proceeds from the new issue may carry a negative net present value and should therefore *not* be undertaken. Because the firm that can sell bonds nearly always has the option of financing at short term, it might look on, say, bank loans as a temporary expedient, anticipating consolidation of those bank loans subsequently through a bond issue (when long-term rates have receded). That willingness to pay current short rates that are higher than long rates[2] could be seen as an opportunity cost for insurance (or option) payments to hold current long rates at present levels. In another sense, current short rates may also represent a boundary condition, setting a limit to the price charged for providing a flotation hedge against flotation risk. (Such insurance fees in the form of options or in higher short rates are, however, more likely to be paid the higher the level and the greater the anticipated volatility of future rates.) From the point of view of the bond issuer, how can such insurance be purchased? The shift to the shelf-registration process does just that and is, in effect, equivalent to reducing premiums on a put option.

---

[2]Higher rate volatility frequently occurs when yield curves have a negative slope, that is, when short rates are higher than long.

Put Option Valuation

The syndicate is in a position where it sells a put (only one strike price) as long as the syndicate is maintained. That strike price is the price to the public. If it is set at a discount to market price, as shown in Figure 15–3, that implies only a reduction of risk to the syndicate, not a rise in return. Indeed, if the market price does not recede to the level of the price to public, so that the syndicate's offering is sold out right away since it represents (now) a special bargain, the issuer's management will raise some incisive questions regarding pricing with the lead manager. In turn, the lead manager will be besieged with all kinds of requests for more securities in the "hot" new issue. In all of the postmortems of an excessively successful offering, the syndicate manager will point out that he got no more than the (bargain) price to the public for each security sold, and the issuer knows only too well that all he got was the (still lower) price to the company.

Conversely, suppose that the market declines sharply during the syndicate period to, say, price X. At that point, the put option value is clearly out of the money since, ultimately, the syndicate will break up at a price *below* that paid to the issuer. To be sure, not all securities may have been sold at price X; on the other hand, to the extent that syndicate expenses chew up a share of the gross spread, the syndicate loss (per security) may

FIGURE 15–3
Put Option Values for Syndicate Operations: Underpricing

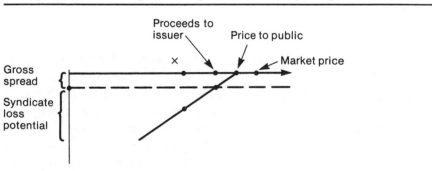

be greater than what has to be a minimum syndicate-loss measure.

As can be seen from the preceding, such market-loss accidents can occur even if, ex ante syndicate trading, the issue was underpriced. In fact, what the preceding may illustrate equally well is that if the issue was priced "at the market," a rise in market prices during the syndicate period will produce the same out-the-window flotation result as an underpriced issue. To be sure, if asked about that resemblance to underpricing results, the syndicate manager can point to the rise in prices *during* the flotation period and to the equality of the market price and the offer price at close of day preceding the flotation. This type of analysis works only for large cash stock offers. For initial public offerings (IPOs), secondary trading information prior to flotation is at best partial and unrepresentative, and for the major share of new flotations, namely bond issues, secondary trading data are too fragmentary to be helpful. And getting back to the cash stock offers, to the extent that these (for public utilities or under Rule 415) are priced by competitive underwritings, the underpricing issue will not be a relevant one.

CALCULATION OF PUT PREMIUM

Let's now consider the issuer's position in two interest-rate (or capital-market) environments:

1. Low price variance.
2. Volatile price variance.

Low Price Variance

Figure 15–4A examines case 1. The frequency distribution of security prices in the time period around the new flotation has a small variance; this is, when the flotation is announced and if the mean value is set at the price paid by the public, it appears there is but a small chance (perhaps 1:5) that the last security will be sold out of the syndicate at a price below that paid to the company. Under those circumstances, the issuing firm does not

FIGURE 15–4
Payoff to Syndicate as an Option Premium

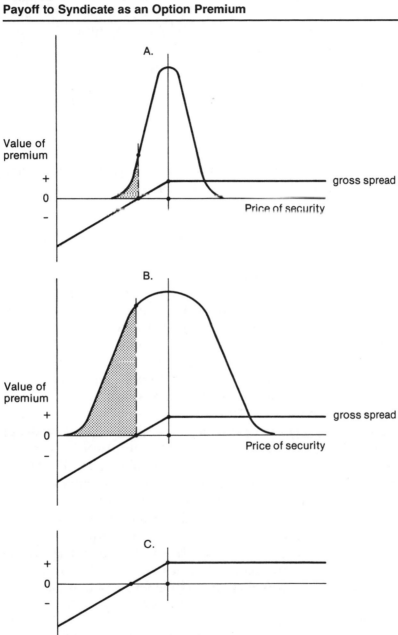

have too much of a problem waiting out a period of say, 21 days during which the SEC examines the prospectus, indenture, and so forth before declaring the issue effective for trading. If, in addition, low volatility prices are associated with low interest rates, as they usually are, the two variables that typically raise the cost of an option premium will be at low levels. This implies that the cost-of-waiting risk is low when variance is low.

High Price Variance

Figure 15–4B illustrates a flotation in a high-variance price (rate) environment. It assumes that gross spreads are the same and that the new issue price paid by the public is the same, but now the probability that the market price during syndicate operations may fall below the price paid to the company is nearly 1:1. Moreover, the cost of the option (or gross spread), which has been held constant, necessarily has to finance a higher rate (carrying) cost if any securities remain unsold after new issue closing. Does this mean that the insurance feature has now fallen in cost? Not necessarily, for the higher price volatility is generally a feature of a high interest rate environment which, by itself, tends to discourage new long-term flotations. In other words, the cost side of the gross spread may be squeezed somewhat by greater competition among underwriters for the lesser volume of new merchandise. But beyond this market effect is the *policy* effect of SEC changes that led to a shortening of waiting period.[3] The first of these changes was the shift to S-16 "instant bond issue" flotations; the second, the shelf registration (Rule 415) mechanics. Under both changes, the effectiveness period between the corporation's decision to go and sale of new issue was cut back to about 2 days from the prior 21 days, and this cut in option duration *of time to maturity* was equivalent to a reduction in flotation risk. In more direct language, the probability in a volatile environment of prices falling substantially is far less for a two-day period than it is for a three-week period.

---

[3]For discussion of these policy changes, see Chapter 16.

Figure 15–4C only traces through the put option cost, indicating that the greater the variance, everything else the same, the higher cost of the option premium. Recall, finally, that the B/S option valuation formula shows a rise in value with (1) the product of time to maturity and the interest rate and (2) the product of variability of the security and time to maturity.

Moving from High Variance to Low Variance

Suppose the environment for flotation of new issues is conditioned to competition in a period of high price variance. Suppose further that the markets perceive a reduction in risk—that the variance of price fluctuation (that is, price volatility) begins to recede. In this environment, the flotation risks are reduced, and competion among investment bankers will squeeze gross spreads closer to the now lower cost of the insurance premium. Further, an understanding of the lessened variance-related risks to underwriters would enable issuers to bargain more effectively for a narrower gross spread even if they continue to use shelf-registration mechanics for new stocks. The fact that underwriters were aware of the lessened variance of all markets (in mid-1985) is shown by Figure 15–5, prepared by Salomon Brothers.

Returning to Figure 15–4, the market change to lower volatility in 1985 has shifted the risk-analysis replication from the middle panel back to the upper panel. Chapter 17 discusses how that change in risk perception, along with shelf registration, has changed the syndicate game. Suffice it to say that the sharp reduction in risk perception among underwriters can help explain the sharp reduction in the number of underwriters participating in each syndicate to the ultimate minimum, namely, the bought deal where the lead underwriter is the sole underwriter and the syndicate consists of one investment banking firm. If risk is less, syndicate diversification can be less, and in that fashion, even a thin spread of about one fourth of 1 percent for the issue can be made to work for the single underwriter.

This contraction of syndicate size is the counterpart to the collapse of the time delay from the leisurely two- to three-week

FIGURE 15–5

Price Volatility in the Debt and Equity Markets (Annualized Percentage Change, Trend Adjusted, Based on Closing Prices of Previous 60 Days)

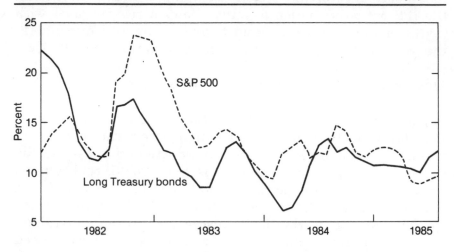

time span needed to organize the large syndicates of the 1960s.[4] The following discussion of a typical large new syndicate flotation of the 1960s shows that the problems and concerns of flotation managers remain the same.

PRICING NEW ISSUES AND SYNDICATE MANAGEMENT: THE GOOD OLD DAYS

In many respects, the new issues flotation process is thought to be the quintessential function of investment banking. However, other financial industries also float new issues. Commercial banks do so for corporate private placements, for publicly issued bonds of state and local governments and authorities, and for the federal government. Financial industries compete for new

---

[4]Among the other changes brought about by shelf registration is the virtual elimination of regional investment bankers in routine syndicate operations.

issues business. Insurance companies and investment banking firms also offer private placements and new issue flotations of state and local governments. Nevertheless, the investment banking industry has become associated with, at least, the competitively priced corporation flotation process.

Bidding Mechanics in the 1960s: A Case Study

The following section describes the competitive bidding process for a new AT&T bond issue.[5] Because that issue was very large for the time ($100 million), the pricing decision was made by members of a large underwriting group acting as a syndicate. Each member had been tentatively assigned a share of the new issue. The pricing decision, to be successful, had to better that of a strong rival syndicate.

Preparation for a Large Issue

When a corporation planned a large financing in the 1960s, it announced its intention some time before scheduling the issue to warn other issuers to stay out of the way and to prepare the capital market. In line with this practice, AT&T announced its intention to borrow $100 million several months before the date of actual issue. The early announcement gave potential investors, such as insurance companies, pension funds, and bank trust accounts, the opportunity to adjust their financial commitments to make room, if they wished, for sizable chunks of the issue. At the same time, other potential corporate borrowers were made aware that the AT&T underwriting would bring special pressures on the market, making it unwise to schedule other sizable flotations around that period.

A light calendar of flotations, then, made possible a more eager participation in the underwriting by syndicate members because their overall market commitments during the flotation

---

[5]The following is taken from E. Bloch, "Pricing a Corporate Bond Issue: A Look behind the Scenes," *Federal Reserve Bank of New York Monthly Review,* October 1961.

period would have been less. And the better the demand for bonds among syndicate members, the stronger their bid would be and the lower the borrowing cost to the borrowing firm. In the underwriting of the AT&T issue, two competing syndicates were formed. One of the groups, managed by X Investment Bank, consisted of more than 100 investment firms, and the competing syndicate, led by Y Investment Bank, was about as sizable.

Managing such large syndicates was the business of about a half-dozen large investment banking houses. Only the largest among them had the capital, the manpower, and the market contacts necessary to propose the proper price for a large offering. If a given house, acting as syndicate manager, wins what the market considers a fair share of the bidding competitions in which it participates, it gains in a number of ways. Not only is its prestige enhanced—which helps in managing future syndicates—but the house that continuously proves the high quality of its market judgment may be more successful in attracting negotiated financings. This concern for the future tends to intensify present competition among managing underwriters.

But while the half-dozen syndicate leaders were rivals, they were also potential allies because a grouping of underwriters exists only for a given flotation and the next offering on the market will involve a different group. During the preparation for the AT&T issue, two of the major firms in the rival syndicate led by Y Investment Bank knew they would be associated with X Investment Bank in a large secondary stock offering within two weeks. Because of the shifting associations and combinations of firms from syndicate to syndicate, current associates in an underwriting insist on conserving their independence of action, and this has an important bearing on the pricing process, as we shall see below.

The first informal price meeting on the forthcoming issue took place at X Investment Bank two days before the actual bidding date set for the issue. Fifteen senior officers of X Investment Bank actively engaged in trading and underwriting met to discuss pricing recommendations that would win the issue and at the same time find ready acceptance in the market. The terms of the new issue were discussed in light of current market factors, and each pricing suggestion was, in effect, an answer to a double-barreled question. First, how attractive was the issue in terms of quality, maturity, call provisions, and other features, and, second, how receptive was the market at this time? Among the factors discussed as leading to a lower yield was the new bonds' Aaa rating, while factors leading to a higher yield included the lack of call protection and the large size of the issue.

The preliminary discussion of the offering price then shifted to the "feel of the market." Even the proponents of a relatively high yield recognized that the final bid should be closer to current market yields on similar securities, owing to the relatively light calendar of forthcoming new corporate flotations. Another sign pointing to aggressive bidding was a relatively light dealer inventory of corporate securities. The discussion of competitive demands for funds was not confined to the corporate-securities market, however, but extended to the markets for municipal and Treasury issues. Here the picture was mixed. The light calendar of forthcoming municipal issues was cited by proponents of a lower yield, while those in favor of a higher yield pointed to expectations of a relatively heavy volume of Treasury financing. Finally, the discussion moved on to assess the possibility of changes in significant market rates such as the prime loan rate and Federal Reserve bank discount rates during the flotation period. It was agreed that the likelihood of such changes during the financing period was small. Each of the officers of X Investment Bank then independently set down his opinion of the proper pricing of the issue (the combination of coupon rate and price offered the borrower) and the reoffering "spread" (the difference between the bid price and the reoffering price to the public).

The majority of the 15 members of the group agreed that the new bonds should carry a rate of 4¼ percent to the borrower with the bonds priced at par and with a reoffering spread of about $7 per $1,000 bond.[6] One member of the group thought

---

[6]These rate numbers may look small, but the spread is not that different from more recent experience.

that a lower yield might be needed to win the bid, and two or three others indicated yields higher than 4¼ percent. The aggressiveness of X Investment Bank's price ideas can be judged from the fact that newspaper comment on the likely level for the winning bid on the day of this meeting indicated a yield in the neighborhood of 4.30 percent.

Marketing Strategy

Simultaneously, assessments of the market for the purpose of establishing a proper bid for the issue were under way in the offices of the allied syndicate members. The comparison of various opinions of the "best" bid of the syndicate took place a day later, the day before the actual opening of the bids by the borrower. This was the preliminary price meeting, to which each firm in the syndicate was invited. At the meeting, each participant firm named the price it was willing to pay for the number of bonds tentatively assigned in the underwriting.[7] The poll of the 100-odd allied syndicate members revealed far less aggressiveness (that is, willingness to accept a low yield) by the smaller firms than was shown by the syndicate manager. Relatively few ideas were at 4¼ percent, while one of the "major underwriters" (that is, a firm tentatively assigned $3 million of bonds or more) put his offering yield at 4.35 percent, and a small firm went as high as 4.40 percent.

In this particular underwriting, X Investment Bank seemed quite eager to win the bid, partly because of its optimistic appraisals of the state of the bond market and partly because it is the syndicate manager's responsibility to push for a winning bid and to exercise the proper persuasion to carry his syndicate along. Syndicate managers are particularly concerned with prestige because, rightly or wrongly, the market apparently does not attach nearly so much significance to membership as to leadership in a losing syndicate.

---

[7]In this meeting, as in the final meeting, a number of security measures were taken to prevent a leak of information to the competing syndicate.

This factor explains the paradox that the followers, rather than the manager, may be more responsible for the failure to win a bid for lack of aggressiveness, even though the market tends to place the blame on the manager. But smaller syndicate mem-. bers may be reluctant participants at lower yields because their commitment of funds for even a relatively small portion of a large underwriting may represent a larger call (or contingent liability) against the small firm's capital than it does for a bigger firm. Even though the larger firm's capital may be as fully employed as that of the smaller firm in its total underwriting business, the commitment of a large portion of capital for a single underwriting may make the smaller firm more hesitant to take that particular marketing risk.

• In preparing for the final price meeting, the syndicate manager held the first of a number of behind-the-scenes strategy sessions. At these meetings, some basic decisions were made about ways and means of holding the syndicate together. During the final price meeting, any firm believing that the market risk of the proposed group bid was too great (that the yield was too low to sell well) had the right to drop out of the syndicate. Conversely, syndicate members who liked the group bid could raise the extent of their participation. Of course, if many syndicate members drop out, particularly major underwriters, too much of a burden is placed on the remaining members, and the result is, in effect, to veto the proposed bid. The aggressive manager thus is placed squarely in the middle of a tug-of-war. If his bid is too aggressive and carries a relatively low yield, the syndicate may refuse to take down the bonds; if the bid is too cautious and carries too high a yield, the syndicate may lose the bidding competition to the rival group. This conflict was resolved at the final price meeting.

Syndicate Tactics

On the morning of the day on which the final bids were made to the borrower, officers of the syndicate manager held their final conference to decide on their own share of the underwriting. In effect, a manager who believes in an aggressive bid puts up or shuts up by his willingness to absorb a greater share of the total underwriting as firms drop out of the syndicate at lower yields. A manager's strong offer to take more bonds may induce a number of potential dropouts to stay at a lower yield, partly because their share of the flotation won't be raised by a given number of dropouts since the manager is picking up the pieces. But beyond the arithmetic effect, a strong offer may have a psychological impact, and some reluctant participants may decide that the manager knows more than they do and that his willingness to raise his share at a given yield is his way of backing the strength of his judgment.

This psychological downward push on yields may be small, but sometimes even a tiny difference can mean the difference between success and failure. For example, in late 1959, the winning syndicate for a $30 million competitive utility issue bid $\frac{1}{100}$ of a cent more per $1,000 bond than the losing syndicate—*$3 more for the whole $30 million issue!*[8]

Another important factor in holding the syndicate together is the strength of the "book" for the new issue. The book is a compilation of investor interest in the new bonds. This interest may have been solicited or unsolicited and may have gone directly to X Investment Bank or to other members of the syndicate from institutional investors. Thus the book is a sample of market strength. All the interest in the book is tentative since no lender would commit funds for an issue of unknown yield. Nevertheless, it is impossible to exaggerate the importance of a large book to an aggressive syndicate manager in holding his group together at the lowest possible yield. Because reluctant participants in an underwriting are particularly concerned about the selling risk, the larger the book, the more reassured they will feel at any given rate. Put another way, the better the book, the more bonds a firm will take at a given rate, thus absorbing more dropouts. Indeed, the size of the book was consid-

---

[8]At times, tie bids are received. On September 12, 1961, two underwriters bid identical amounts, down to the last $\frac{1}{100}$ of a penny per $1,000 bond, for a $3 million issue of municipal bonds. Such tie bids are as rare as a golfer's hole in one, however.

ered so important that the final price meeting on the AT&T underwriting was interrupted a number of times by the latest indications of interest in the issue.

The Final Price Meeting

As a means of preventing information leaks, representatives of the firms attending the final price meeting were locked in a room. The meeting was opened by a vice president of X Investment Bank with a brief review of the good state of the book—about half the issue had tentatively been spoken for. He had derived further encouragement for an aggressive bid from the healthy state of the bond market. Thus he proposed to make his bid at the 4¼ percent rate agreed on at the X Investment Bank preliminary meeting two days earlier.

The immediate reaction to this statement was a chorus of moans. Apparently, the book was not sufficiently broad to carry the doubters along with the first bid, nor did the manager indicate any other action that would have made his proposal more acceptable. When the group was polled, large and small dropouts cut the $100 million underwriting by about a third. The failure to carry the syndicate at the first go-round was later attributed by some X Investment Bank people to the fact that three dropouts occurred among the first set of major underwriters polled (the eight largest firms, each of which had been tentatively assigned $3 million of bonds). And in the second set ($2 million assigned to each firm), another few had fallen by the wayside.

Thus a new bid proposal had to be presented to the group. Following another behind-the-scenes consultation of the senior officers of the managing underwriter, a 4⅜ percent coupon with a price above par was proposed with a bid yield of 4.27 percent. Amid continued grumbling of the majority of the members of the meeting, this was readily accepted by nearly every firm.

Judging that they might have leaned over too far in the direction of their reluctant followers, the officers of the syndicate manager consulted once again and decided to present a somewhat more aggressive bid to the syndicate. In the third proposal, the bid price on the 4⅜ coupon was upped by 20 cents per $1,000 bond. The underwriters, still grumbling, were polled again and, following a few minor dropouts, approved the new price. The final allocation of the bonds differed relatively little from the tentative original allocation except that the manager picked up the allotments of the dropouts by adding about $3 million to his own commitment. By this time only a few minutes were left until the formal opening of the competitive bids by AT&T. The final coupon and price decisions were telephoned to the syndicate's representative at the bidding, who formally submitted the bid to AT&T.

Promptly at 11:30 A.M. the doors of the price committee meeting were thrown open, and within 30 seconds of that time, the news was shouted from the trading room that the X Investment Bank bid had lost. The difference in the bid prices between the two syndicates came to a little more than $1 per $1,000 bond.

The bonds were released for trading by the Securities and Exchange Commission at around 4 P.M. and were quickly snapped up by market investors. At X Investment Bank the feeling of gloom hung heavy, particularly since the first bid offered to the price meeting would have won the issue.

Would a better X Investment Bank book have carried the defecting major underwriters along on the first bid? Should the manager have been willing to take more bonds to carry the group along in the first recommendation which would have won the issue? And would market acceptance of that bid have been as good as that accorded the actual winning bid of Y syndicate? These postmortems were bound to be inconclusive, and the unremitting pressures of the underwriting business soon cut them short. Within the next several days, a number of other securities were scheduled to come to market. Tomorrow was another day and another price meeting.

To syndicate participants in the 1980s, the foregoing will appear almost quaint in the leisurely pacing of the pricing process and its modest rate levels. Today, the availability of shelf-registration issues to corporations forces lead underwriters to come up with a bid for a new issue in as many hours as it used to take days a generation earlier. However, the earlier experience provides a slow-motion replay of the motivation of syndicate managers and the love-hate relationship between them and other syndicate participants.

PART IV

POLICY ISSUES

16

FULL DISCLOSURE
AND SECURITIES REGULATION:
THE CHANGE TO
SHELF REGISTRATION

One of the many ironies that turn up in studies of regulatory policy is that any regulatory shift is likely to have two effects: (1) the one intended by the change and (2) the one not foreseen by the regulators. Of the two, the second is frequently the most significant.

The Securities Act of 1933[1] and the Securities Exchange Act of 1934[2] provide separate, although related, regulatory disclosure systems. The first act (to be called Securities Act) requires the registration of new issues and disclosure of relevant information regarding the issuer corporation and prohibits misrepresentation and fraud related to the new security. The second act (to be called Exchange Act) extended the same disclosure principles to secondary-market trading and required the registration of national exchanges as well as of brokers and dealers for the purpose of self-regulation. Since 1934 both acts have been administered by the Securities and Exchange Commission (SEC), a quasi-judicial agency of the U.S. government.[3]

Federal securities legislation of all types relies heavily on

---

[1]15 U.S.C. 577a et seq.
[2]15 U.S.C. 578a et seq.
[3]Initially, securities regulation was a state function that began in 1911 with the passage of the first "Blue Sky laws." Resulting variances were brought into some degree of order by the proposal (as late as 1956) of the Uniform Securities Acts.

the principles of (1) *full disclosure* and (2) *self-regulation*. The first of these is reflected in the publication of data for the use of investors. Each firm whose securities are traded publicly is expected to publish its balance sheet and operating data within a specified time after completion of its fiscal period. Further, if a new-money issue is to be sold, these data (specific to the company) as well as other data specific to the new issue must be presented to potential buyers. As a result, virtually all firms with securities listed on exchanges publish audited annual reports and 10-K statements on a routine basis as well as new issue prospectuses when a new issue is to be sold. In support of the self-regulatory principle, the SEC has delegated to the various exchanges its power to control trading practices for securities listed on those exchanges while retaining the final authority to supplement, alter, or reject an exchange's rules and regulations.

The SEC has delegated similar powers to the National Association of Securities Dealers (NASD), a private trade association of over-the-counter dealers and traders.[4] The SEC manages policy changes (like most other bureaucracies) by suasion and discussion rather than fiat; when these methods prove ineffective, the SEC acquires quasi-judicial powers to discipline violators. And in the end, not only is the SEC a creature of the Congress, but major changes can be made by legislation, such as the advent of negotiated commissions for trades on the NYSE.[5]

FULL DISCLOSURE

The disclosure process refers to new issues as well as to trading in secondary markets. It is a fact of financial life that the largest issuers of new-money securities are also those firms whose securities trade in large volume on secondary markets. Full disclo-

---

[4]Similar statutes have been enacted by Congress to permit self-regulation of futures and option markets.

[5]That change was mandated by the Security Act Amendments of 1975.

sure under the Exchange Act, which provides investors in existing securities with up-to-date and audited information on these stocks and bonds, suggests that there is little need to repeat the same information when the same issuers place *new* securities on the market. Any review of prospectuses[6] up to 1981 shows that such documents largely duplicate accounting information already disclosed in annual reports and 10-Ks. The combination of the two disclosure systems or, in practical terms, the incorporation by reference—rather than reprinting—of annual reports and 10-K data into a prospectus was seen as an efficiency move as far back as 1966, when Milton Cohen suggested integrating the two reporting systems.[7]

Subsequent to Cohen's seminal article, the SEC established two sets of study groups whose recommendations produced a sequence of modest policy changes to simplify new-issue registration documents. In 1967, the SEC took its first small step toward integrating the two systems adopting Form S-7, a somewhat shorter registration form than the S-1 form it replaced. The S-7 form relied on the availability of some information contained in Exchange Act filings, but it did not permit any reporting by reference.[8] In 1970, the SEC adopted Form S-16 (following the issuance of the Wheat Report) which permitted issuers who qualified for Form S-7 to register certain *secondary* distributions by *incorporation by reference* of information contained in Exchange Act reports.[9]

This apparent breakthrough in combining the two reporting systems is not as profound a change as implied by the issuance of a special SEC ruling. For secondary trades, the citation by *reference* is just repetition of information previously published under the Exchange Act. And as Table 16–1 indicates, the num-

---

[6]Required by the Securities Act of 1933.

[7]Milton Cohen, "'Truth in Securities' Revisited," *Harvard Law Review* 79 (1966), p. 1340. The SEC commissioned two reports to examine the disclosure systems. (1) *Disclosure to Investors: A Reappraisal of Administrative Policies under the 1933 and 1934 Acts, 1969* (called the Wheat Report); and (2) *Report of the Advisory Committee on Corporate Disclosure to the Securities and Exchange Commission,* 95th Congress, First Session, 451 (Comm. Print 1977).

[8]SEC Release No. 4886, November 1967.

[9]SEC Release No. 5117, December 1970.

TABLE 16–1

Large-Scale Trades on the NYSE by Secondaries and Blocks, 1972, 1981, and 1986 (In Number of Transactions and by Thousands of Shares Traded)

Year	NYSE Secondaries and Other Special Methods		NYSE Block Trades		Percent of Block Trades in Total NYSE Trading Volume
	Number of Trades	Number of Shares Traded	Number of Trades	Volume of Shares	
1972	154	64,067	31,207	766,406	18.5%
1981	34	14,351	145,564	3,771,442	31.8
1986	13	20,570	665,587	17,811,335	49.9

Source: New York Stock Exchange, *NYSE Fact Book 1987* (New York: 1987), pp. 15, 71.

ber and volume of formal secondary distributions had declined quite sharply by the end of the 1970s to about one fifth of that in the early 1970s. By contrast, block trades became the method of choice for distributing large (secondary) trades in the 1970s. For example, in 1986 block trades at about 17.8 billion shares constituted nearly one half of all of the trading volume done on the NYSE, while secondaries (at a mere 20 million shares) barely exceeded $\frac{1}{10}$ of 1 percent.

SHORT-FORM REGISTRATIONS

Following the recommendations of the Advisory Committee on Corporate Disclosure,[10] the SEC in 1978 produced a more significant change by making Form S-16 available to the same qualified issuer for *primary* (or new-money) offerings in firm-commitment underwritings.[11] The mere availability of the short-form registration statement was only a beginning, however. What made that form most useful to issuers was, paradoxically enough, the sharp rise in interest rates as well as the even

---

[10]*Report of the Advisory Committee on Corporate Disclosure to the Securities and Exchange Commission,* 95th Congress, First Session, 451 (Comm. Print 1977).

[11]SEC Release No. 5923, April 1978.

FIGURE 16–1
Interest-Rate Volatility: 1955–1983

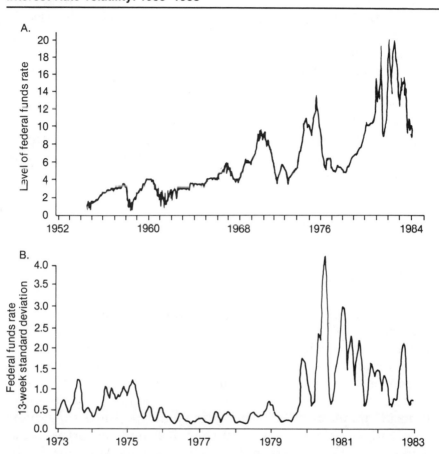

Source: Federal Reserve Bank of Chicago.

greater rise in rate volatility that occurred shortly thereafter. As
the charts in Figure 16–1 indicate, the most sensitive short-term
rates (Federal funds rates as published by the Federal Reserve
Bank of Chicago)[12] not only reached all-time highs in the 1980s
but also showed a substantial rise in variability per unit of time.

[12]Federal Reserve Bank of Chicago, *Economic Perspectives,* January–February
1983, p. 11.

These increases in rate fluctuations were replicated in bond issues, thereby producing much greater bond-price changes per unit of time than previously experienced. In part, the rise in short-term rates in early 1980 reflected a shift in corporate borrowing (or demand for funds) toward short maturities to avoid locking in record interest rates on bonds. And when, in the aftermath of the 1980 recession, a large volume of that short debt was refinanced at lower long-term rates, the S-16 registration form—called instant bond issues—gave corporations the equivalent of a costless two-day put as compared to the earlier three- to four-week delay (in the put) for the SEC to permit a new bond issue to become effective.

PERSPECTIVES ON THE PROSPECTUS UNDER RULE 415

In the context of the recent policy changes for broker–dealer firms, it is interesting to compare the regulation of depository-type institutions. Banking supervisors (the Controller of the Currency, FDIC, and the Federal Reserve) send examiners into each bank institution about once each year to perform *confidential* reviews of past performance and current lending practices. By contrast, the securities industry, its member firms, and its products (whether new-money issues or secondary offerings) are subject to public disclosure, including data specific to the issuers (corporations, states, public authorities, and so forth). New-money securities issued under Rule 415 may now satisfy the public-disclosure provisions of the Securities Act by including Exchange Act information by reference only.

However, some additional changes were associated with the shelf-registration process, such as a sharp reduction in the time delay before a new issue might be sold. In a narrow sense, there is an analogy between the SEC's internal staff review of information presented in a new-issue prospectus before the issue becomes effective (or is permitted to be sold) and the bank examination process. One critic of that process observed that SEC staff efforts involved, in their reviews of full disclosure, ". . . filtering out everything but objective facts, as if the investor could not focus a suitable skepticism on estimates of value or projections of future earnings."[13] Kripke goes further in suggesting that the prospectus, which was to have been the "primary document intended by the statute to inform the investor . . . has been a negativistic, pessimistic document, lacking in forward looking information which can affect securities prices and sales."[14] In short, Kripke believes that the potential investor does not refrain from reading a prospectus because of its boilerplate language and legalese (as is frequently argued by others) but because the thorough drycleaning efforts of the SEC staff have robbed the document of any information that cannot be absolutely sustained by 20/20 hindsight—or found in previously published documentation.

So why all the fuss over shelf registrations and the shortened time for an offering to become effective?

UNDERWRITER LIABILITY AND DUE DILIGENCE

The best answer is that the full-disclosure provisions of the Securities Act attach parallel liability to the experts (e.g., lawyers, accountants, issuers, and investment bankers). Section 11 of the Securities Act imposes absolute liability on the issuer (for example, the corporation) for securities registered under the act for "material misstatements in and omissions from registration statements"[15] and, going beyond this, it imposes a liability on new issue underwriters (as well as some others) based on a negligence standard with respect to disclosure of "material information."[16]

---

[13]H. Kripke, *The SEC and Corporate Disclosure* (New York: Harcourt Brace Jovanovich, 1979), p. 14.

[14]Ibid., p. 15. Kripke argues further, ". . . the [SEC] staff is fearful that the investor will misconceive the probabilities of expectations, and therefore most registration statements contain repeated warnings that 'there can be no assurance' that an expectation will be borne out."

[15]Section 11(a).

[16]*Ernst and Ernst* vs. *Hochfelder,* 425 U.S. 185, 208 (1976).

Thus both the corporate issuer and the investment banker are liable for selling securities on the basis of erroneous or omitted information. The rationale for this provision of the act is two-fold:

1. To set up an adversarial relationship between the issuer and the investment banker to provide the investing public with the best possible information set.[17] "The act seeks not only to secure accuracy in the information that is volunteered to investors but also, and perhaps more especially, to compel the disclosure of significant matters which were heretofore rarely, if ever disclosed."

2. To enforce (1) by making lack of "due diligence" costly to the underwriter. From the investment banker's point of view, he would be relieved of liability under the statute if he could demonstrate that he had fought the good fight; that "he had, after reasonable investigation, reasonable ground to believe, and did believe, at the time such part of the registration statement became effective, that the statements therein were true and that there was no omission to state a material fact required to be stated or necessary to make the statements therein not misleading."[18]

If the investment banker can demonstrate that he followed due diligence in investigating the issuer-client's representations (rather than accepting them at face value), he has a *procedural* defense against negligence suits by investors.

However, neither the SEC nor the courts have offered specific guidelines for investment bankers in conducting such investigations, and the court has indicated that the investment banker's investigation (and verification of the issuer's statements) are matters of judgment that vary with the circum-

---

[17]As cited in *Escott vs. Leasco Data Processing Equipment Corp.*, 332 F. Supp. 544, 567 (1971). Citation is from Shulman, "Civil Liability and the Securities Act," *Yale Law Journal* 43 (1933), p. 227.

[18]Sect 11(b)(3) of Securities Act.

stances of the issuer.[19] Perhaps such uncertainty, along with the fear of potential negligence suits, was designed to encourage investment bankers to press their issuers to a high, rather than a low, disclosure standard.[20]

Suppose that the time lag between a corporation's decision to sell a new issue and its offer for resale by an underwriter has been collapsed from five weeks to two days and that the new-issue prospectus is reduced to boilerplate summary language. For companies with an Aaa or Aa rating, such a cursory review of available data, given substantial and continuous company research by outsiders, may be sufficient. Yet, as the following section suggests, investors use historical accounting data (from annual reports, 10-Ks, prospectuses, and so forth) only as a base from which to form expectations.

CAPITAL-MARKET EFFICIENCY: HOW RELEVANT?

Capital-market efficiency in the finance literature is discussed almost exclusively in terms of equilibrium stock prices. Research papers suggest that the secondary stock market is quite efficient with respect to:

1. Information contained in stock prices prior to date examined by analyst.
2. Publicly available information regarding company.
3. All information.[21]

From this most writers have concluded that returns in excess of the risk-free rate can be earned only by an investor's acceptance of systematic (that is, market), or undiversifiable, risk.

---

[19]In *Escott vs. Bar Chris Construction Corp.* (332 F. Supp. at 582).

[20]Full-disclosure standards are not universally accepted as the means of regulating securities markets. For a generally negative view, see G. Benston, "Required Disclosure and the Stock Market: An Evaluation of the Securities Exchange Act of 1934," *American Economic Review* 63 (1973), no. 1, pp. 132–55.

[21]This information hierarchy is contained in E. Fama, "Efficient Capital Markets: A Review of Theory and Empirical Work," *Journal of Finance,* May 1970, p. 383.

Capital-market efficiency is thus comparable to a response to "stale news."[22] For a market to be considered efficient, the current price of, say, IBM stock takes account of last year's earnings and necessarily reflects that figure. Last year's IBM earnings per share is a number readily and cheaply available from IBM's annual report, 10-K, and other sources.

With respect to this year's earnings, the situation is quite different. Many securities analysts and institutional and private investors spend substantial time and effort researching and forecasting this year's (and further-out years') IBM earnings, knowing that the further away, the more erroneous their estimates are likely to be. The more at variance each announcement of actual earnings is from the (consensus) anticipations, the greater the market's response to the (then newly stale) news.

In effect, the substantial amount of work done on stock-market efficiency reflects both the ready availability of price and trading volume data collected for long periods of time for many New York Stock Exchange (NYSE)-listed firms and the related research designs that developed a number of statistically testable hypotheses. (Summaries of the literature are available in a number of sources.[23]) The statistical inference techniques employed by scholars in this field boil down to a rejection of the hypothesis that the markets are *not* efficient. Because many articles examine different facets of market efficiency, it is convenient to discuss the issue under three headings:

1. Weak form.
2. Semistrong form.
3. Strong form.

Briefly put, the weak form rejects the hypothesis that stock selection can be enhanced by analyzing past stock-price behav-

---

[22]For further discussion, see K. Garbade, *Securities Markets* (New York: McGraw-Hill, 1982), esp. pp. 236ff. The earlier discussion of SEC staff reviews of prospectus language basically refers to improving accuracy in presenting the most recent of stale news, while "due diligence" by the investment banker could be said to refer, by the same standards, to accuracy of stale news immediately prior to a new-issue flotation (or in legalese, "material new information").

[23]See, for example, Garbade, *Securities Markets,* Chap. 13; and Lorie and Hamilton, *The Stock Market* (Homewood, Il.: Richard D. Irwin, 1973), Chap. 4.

ior (technical analysis); the semistrong form rejects the hypothesis that present prices do not reflect all publicly available information (that is, stale news) regarding each company. The strong form considers the hypothesis that those with insider information can, consistently and often, use it to produce superior investment results. Here the studies suggest that insiders make gains prior to release of publicly available information; at least, that insider trades are particularly well timed in relation to market behavior. Thus the strong form of the efficient-market hypothesis is generally rejected. To sum up, the efficient-market hypothesis represents a series of tests by which to reject the proposition that NYSE stock prices *do not* efficiently reflect publicly available information

It is important to recall this research literature in spite of its more cumbersome language (based on statistical inference) because these probabilistic judgments should not be collapsed into possibly misleading, albeit simpler, positive statements (such as the markets *are* efficient). One cannot assert the truth (or error) of the weak or semistrong or strong form of the efficient-market hypothesis. One can only argue that the evidence supporting their validity is persuasive and that the investment community is in general, but not necessarily unanimous, agreement on this.

BOND SHELF ANNOUNCEMENTS AND MARKET-EFFICIENCY HYPOTHESIS

The major volume of shelf-registration issues are bond issues not stock issues (see introduction to Part III). In part this follows from the nature of U.S. corporate finance where much more new equity value is created by retained earnings than by net new stock flotations. Even if there were no decline in the equity/debt ratio,[24] that particular by-product of U.S. dividend payout policy ensures a continuing preponderance of new-money debt financ-

---

[24]Since the ratio *has* been declining secularly, that change will further raise the ratio of new debt to new-equity flotations.

ing over new stock flotations. Under these conditions, the efficient-markets hypothesis will apply *not* to the lion's share of new flotations, namely new debt financings, but to the much lesser (albeit important) volume of new-equity issues. M. Weinstein studied the price behavior of newly issued corporate bonds, following some problems with earlier studies that referred mainly to differences in coupon yield between new and seasoned issues or between new issues and bond-price indexes. Weinstein's study contrasts new-issue yields (which he found underpriced) and the adjustment of new-issue yields to market and yields to be completed within one month. He does not give his sources of data for market yields; they are probably NYSE bond prices, which are subject to all the problems suggested above. Moreover, the period covered (1962–74) is one of relatively greater rate stability than more recent experience.[25]

In addition, the question may be raised whether the efficient-markets hypothesis applies with the same force to new-issue stock pricing as it does to secondary-market trading. One major difference has to be relative supply. In the new-issue case, each new flotation raises the volume by some proportion to outstanding shares. That rate of increase may be decided by each firm's management on the basis of parameters that may or may not be the same as that of other firms or from one time in history to another. In secondary trading, on the other hand, market participants are involved in the same playing field at the same time (each sale is also a purchase). The perceived need to use an investment banker for virtually every new issue, while market mechanics including most large block trades are routine, suggests a distinction with a difference.

Taking this argument still another step, consider Commissioner Thomas's arguments in her dissent to the temporary Rule 415 extension.[26] She specifically objected to the use of the shelf-registration process for new primary equity offerings.[27] Her objections were twofold: (1) The foreshortened offer period would

---

[25]See M. Weinstein, "The Seasoning Process of New Corporate Bond Issues," *Journal of Finance,* December 1978, p. 1334.

[26]SEC Release No. 6423, September 2, 1982.

[27]Commissioner Thomas does not object to existing rules that permit shelf registration for *secondary* equity issues.

reduce opportunities to build nationwide syndicates, thereby cutting out regional dealers and making the industry less effective. And (2) individual investors would not receive timely enough information to make decisions ". . . because in non-Rule 415 offerings, the underwriters are selected before a filing [and] the underwriters' due diligence can begin early in the process, and the resulting give-and-take among the parties and their counsel should produce a higher-quality disclosure document than one prepared unilaterally by the issuer."[28]

The second objection suggests that Commissioner Thomas does not expect the efficient-markets hypothesis, cited by those commissioners voting in support of Rule 415, to work within the markets for which most supporting evidence is available, namely, the stock market.[29] None of the commissioners distinguished between the evidence developed (1) for empirical research on the efficient-markets hypothesis (this covered mainly secondary-market equity trading) and (2) its policy application, pro or con, to primary equity markets. Worse still, all the commissioners broadly assumed that the general and bland presumption of "efficiency" applies to the largest part of the primary markets, namely, new *bond* issues. The small amount of evidence in the literature on bond-market efficiency at best leaves open the question of whether efficiency in those markets is even comparable to that of stock markets.

There are understandable reasons for the absence of market-efficiency studies for secondary bond trading. Almost the entire bond market consists of institutional trading, mainly among principals and over the counter. Therefore, there is little empirical evidence on, say, corporate bond transactions (or on municipals or foreign issues, and so forth) in secondary markets even though trading volume is heavy. Nearly all bond traders consider the volume of daily trading in corporate bonds alone (1984)

---

[28]SEC Release No. 6423.

[29]In Commissioner Thomas's discussion of debt offerings, on the other hand, she refers to commission discussion and industry testimony that debt issues without notice "periods" are acceptable because the issuing companies ". . . are widely followed by financial analysts, and therefore, under the efficient-market theory, it is reasonable to assume that information about these companies is generally available." ("Debt Offerings by S-3 Issuers," SEC Release No. 6423, September 2, 1982, under No. 6.)

to be about $4 billion.[30] But because many trades involve swaps and because the merchandise traded is continuously changing (many AA and AAA firms *each* have some tens or dozens of bond series outstanding), even a cross-sectional study involves horrendous data-discovery and analytical problems.[31]

On the other hand, a good record of trading data and of some inventory figures for government securities and the dealers in that market is available, as are some price and volume data. As a result, most nongovernment bond traders use the market for governments as a *numeraire* data set. This permits pricing and trading in high-quality nongovernment securities to proceed as if there were a continuous information and trading system in each issue. The fact that pricing and trading can take place by using the equivalent of an indexing system attests to traders' ingenuity and flexibility. That substitution mechanism, likewise, suggests how difficult it would be to develop efficiency studies based on actual bond trades (either on a cross-section or a time-series basis).[32] Or put another way, the fact that traders use index (or government securities) data as substitute data indicates that the corporate-bond market does not have direct data available in usable form.

COULD RATING AGENCIES PROVIDE A SUBSTITUTE FOR EFFICIENCY HYPOTHESIS?

Some might argue that new bond flotations are carefully examined by bond-quality rating agencies, such as Moody's and Standard & Poor's, and that professionals in these agencies provide risk evaluations for new and existing issues, while the data pro-

---

[30]The data of bond trades recorded on the NYSE floor—about $7 billion for *a year* (par value in 1982)—thus represents no more than one or two *days'* worth of over-the-counter trading.

[31]For example, AT&T *alone* has nearly two dozen separate bond and note issues outstanding, not counting any of its operating subsidiaries.

[32]Moreover, any such empirical analysis should encompass not only publicly issued (and occasionally traded) corporates but the large volume of private placements as well.

duced by government securities markets can continue to serve as a proxy for current returns and expected returns. Does this mean that the legal concept of public disclosure and the adversarial relationship between issuer and investment banker and the agency conflicts between corporate management and stockholders are to be surrendered to rating agencies? Will these agencies then be subject to investor damage suits (under Section 11 of the Securities Act) if material information was not properly evaluated? Will quality assessments even be possible as a practical procedure (or at reasonable cost) in such a case?

New bond flotations are carefully watched by the bond-quality rating agencies, and some may argue that professionals in those rating agencies provide another evaluation act regarding new or material information. It probably should not be argued with equal force that the rating agencies may provide something like the due diligence of investment bankers since they do not carry the same liability as does the issuer, the directors of the issuer, or even the investment banker.[33] If rating agencies had a greater legal responsibility at new issue, their more intense and continuous involvement with the issuer (to protect themselves against damage suits) might be a conflict of interest with regard to rating independence and neutrality.

---

[33]Section 11(a) of the Securities Act [15 U.S.C. 577 K (a)]. Section 11 of the act attempts to protect the investor by setting up a *purposely* adversarial relationship between issuer and the investment banker.

17

SHELF REGISTRATION OF BOND ISSUES: THE CURRENT SITUATION

With the experience of shelf financing still new (in fall 1982), the majority of Securities and Exchange Commission (SEC) commissioners argued that the "experiment" (i.e., "temporary" Rule 415) should be continued. For most of the summer and fall of 1982 and 1983, the financial markets were rising in price and receding somewhat in volatility compared to the preceding period since October 1979. How would the markets (and issuers) respond should a more hostile environment return? To examine this issue, let's look at the problem of waiting out a 21-day (as opposed to a 1- or 2-day) effectiveness period in a volatile market.

THE SHIFT IN RISK

To assess the shift in the incidence of risk, consider, first, the problem of a single corporation placing one issue of new bonds in the market prior to Rule 415. Proceeds will be used for expanding plant and equipment and related corporate purposes. The company's chief financial officer (CFO) feels the bond issue will be acceptable only if the interest rate is low enough so that, in view of the risk adjusted cash flows of the new project, the project will yield a positive net present value.

    The CFO is well through the new-issue preliminaries, due-diligence meetings, and so on, and is currently sweating out the waiting period before the new issue becomes effective. He has always been aware of market volatility, but now, when he reads the papers, he lives and dies as interest rates fall and rise. Until the new issue becomes effective, he still has one option—he can cancel the deal altogether if he feels that some intermediate rise in rates has significantly shifted the odds and pushed the project into negative net present value territory. If his peers in his industry are turning to shorter-term financing, he faces all the more pressure to cancel the issue. Arguing *against* cancellation is the fact that all the new-issue costs already incurred must be paid. And, as indicated elsewhere, these costs are substantial.[1] Finally, even if the new issue is canceled and short-term financing substituted, the fact that the new loan comes at a time when rates are higher does not help present value estimates either.

All else the same, the more volatile the bond market, the less predictable the cost and, hence, the more costly the funds that are raised in it. Bond issues can be sold at rates so high that their proceeds will be invested in projects with low or even negative net present value. Even the cancellation (formal or informal) of a number of issues because of these uncertainties necessarily adds to effective flotation costs.

At best, the as yet unpriced but announced bond issue was in the past subject to the vagaries of the bond market while the SEC and the lead underwriters reviewed the prospectus. But a single issue could have produced a more generic "waiting risk." Suppose that, in a volatile market, a company perceived a temporary "window of opportunity"—that is, a temporary market decline in yields. A bond issue was announced, a syndicate formed, and a preliminary prospectus sent to the SEC. However, in the three- to four-week waiting period, other firms in a similar situation also brought out their issues with the result that the "window" slammed shut, and bond prices began to fall. Thus the very perception of an opportunity could cancel it out before the bond sale became effective.

Conversely, when bond sales were pressed on the market as

---

[1]The problem is complicated further by concerns about relationships with the syndicate's lead investment banking firm, although in a crunch, the syndicate will have bigger things to worry about.

bond prices were declining, the competition for new-issue placements was less, whatever the wait. The risk asymmetry in a
volatile market is clear: if the market is perceived as relatively
receptive, issuer competition makes it less so; if the market is
unreceptive, lack of competition will not improve receptivity.
Thus market volatility imposed unpredictable waiting risks on
new issues equal to the eventual yield of the bonds waiting to be
made effective by the SEC staff. And with a longer waiting period, these risks were borne mainly by the issuer.

Now consider the shortened S-16 registration process which
could be completed in two days. In spring 1980, a bond market
rally developed, and bond financings hit record highs in June
and July. Then the market rally began to reverse, partly because
of a flood of new offerings. As yield volatility *up* began to replace
yield volatility *down,* bond issuers began to perceive the risk
reduction implicit in speeding up every element of the new-issue
process, including the underwriting arrangements. Issuers expected lead underwriters (under Form S-16) to come up with
firm price bids for a new issue within hours of a request.

Issuers under the S-16 registration form enjoyed over time
a reduction in risk-adjusted waiting costs even if ex post underwriting spreads *did not change!* On the other hand, lead investment bankers asked to make bids on new issues, especially as
temporary windows get crowded, were exposed to price-change
risks for a *longer* period than previously. Consider the underwriter's waiting period under the old three- to four-week waiting
period. Once the issue's nonprice terms were decided and the
issue's effectiveness period neared its close, the issue could be
placed on the market immediately, or overnight at the latest.
Under the 415 rules, the issuer requests a bid, and the lead underwriter makes an offer that is accepted within, say, three
hours. The price risks of a firm offer are shifted to the underwriter and the syndicate for the next 45 hours. The issuer is now
exposed for, at most, the three-hour period of waiting out his bid
request that he can reject in any case.

Given this downstream shift in price risk in the issuing process (not to mention increased due-diligence risks), why do lead
underwriters step up to bid? To retain the prestige associated
with being a leader (or special-bracket) firm in the syndicate

game, underwriters must maintain a high profile by managing a large volume of new offerings. For such firms the risk-adjusted proceeds of new underwritings would now be less even if the underwriting spreads did not change! To that extent, the foreshortened new issue process has helped the issuers not only to reduce risks but also to shift at least a share of the waiting risks forward from the borrowing firm to the investment banker.

The pressure to compete in the underwriting area and the reduction in risk-adjusted returns also spread competitive forces to other financial services. The result is a shift to "transactional finance"—that is, the breakdown of long-term professional relationships between a given corporation and a specific investment banker. The shift to "instant new issues" with the S-16 form helped sharpen competitive pressures in the industry and served as a transitional instrument to the shelf-registration process.

SHELF REGISTRATION: CURRENT SUPPLY PROBLEMS

Major-bracket underwriters could protect themselves against market vagaries over the two-day effectiveness period by using financial satellite markets (financial futures, among others). The special-bracket firm that engages in continuous bidding for new issues could secure an automatic dollar averaging of volatility costs (unanticipated rises in rate after a successful bid) and gains (unanticipated rate drops). Unfortunately, however, the asymmetries of flotation agreement prohibit this. Because of the crowding effects of windows, a flood of new issues would tend to reduce the benefits of unanticipated gains.

HEDGING

From the point of view of investment bankers, the greatest difficulties are encountered when the inventory of unsold bonds grows (because prices are dropping as rates rise). To make life more difficult, inventory carrying costs move up with the general rise in rates. Thus the investment banker faces the same hedging problem as other commodity dealers, namely, that inventories tend to surge as prices fall. Of course, sales at prices below cost—that is, at a capital loss—may be made to cut losses and/or the certainty of rising carrying costs.[2] Accordingly, syndicate managers may use the classic short hedge of commodity traders (or farmers). For example, in the expectation of declining prices, the investment banker could decide to sell 10-year Treasury bond futures (take a position) on some proportion of his anticipated average unsold inventory. Some do so. Others emphasize dealing with each bond syndicate on its own terms. For lead underwriters, this practice at least appears to carry the advantage of relating risks and returns to each flotation and simultaneously integrating those results with the accounting of expenses to the syndicate membership.

Consider the unusual combination of items that are priced jointly on the face of a prospectus: first, the price to the company and, second, the price to the public. The difference between the two is, of course, the underwriting discount. This means that, as long as the syndicate agreement is in force, no sales to the public may be made at a price different from that set on the prospectus—the equivalent of placing a put-option price on each new stock or bond.

There are, however, two uncertainties: (1) The maturity period of the in-the-money options cannot be known because expiration is coterminous with the conclusion of a successful syndicate. Such deals may sell very quickly—within a day or less—especially if market prices are expected to move up more. (2) If market prices move down far enough, the put-option equivalent becomes an out-of-the-money option to the underwriters

---

[2]The question of carrying cost relates only in part to financing an undesired rise in inventory. Because all bonds are sold with accrued interest, the direct carrying cost may be largely offset by such interest accruals. However, the following factors make the offset less than perfect: (1) As rates rise, so do all carrying costs. (2) In bond bear markets (with negative yield curves), short-term carrying costs may be higher than the accrued interest rate per unit of time (although that differential is helped by the tax deductibility of higher carrying costs).

as soon as the bond price falls more than the algebraic total of: (*a*) share of gross spread less (*b*) expenses charged. The maturity period of that option (or syndicate) will be determined when the syndicate breaks its price-maintenance agreement, and this may take weeks. Finally, the actual loss may be greater than an option premium or its theoretical equivalent because there is no limit to the size of the price drop at the point of the syndicate's breakup.

The hedging process thus may be divided into in-the-money and out-of-the-money strategies. In-the-money strategies are simple because they involve a community of interest between the issuing company and its underwriters. The company places its issue at an agreed price; the latter collects its spread (the premium) very quickly and at no further risk. Indeed, for many new stock issues, a "Green Shoe" option on the face of the prospectus is customary (the corporation grants the underwriters the option of acquiring up to 15 percent more shares than indicated in the prospectus at the same terms as the new issue prices).[3] Many prospectuses carry the notation that the Green Shoe option is exercisable for 30 days from issue date "solely for the purpose of covering overallotments." The community of interest between syndicate and issuer involves the company issuing 15 percent more shares than indicated in the original offering *and at the same price.* For the underwriters, the advantage lies in the fact that if, in its market stabilization transactions, the syndicate manager had taken a short position in a rising market, that position could be covered by the Green Shoe option at the offering price as opposed to a more expensive market price.

On the other hand, in a falling market, the attempt to place the new offering may involve overallotments to syndicate participants as a way to encourage sales efforts. Of course, if a market drop is correctly foreseen, the only way an acceptable bid can be made to the issuer is for the lead manager to accept an unusually large proportion of the offering himself. Such a situation

---

[3]This option was first used in an offering by the Green Shoe Co., and the name stuck.

implies that overallotments to other syndicate members represent smaller shares of the total offering. The question of aggressive bidding and related risks was discussed in Chapter 15.

DOING A DEAL

Assume a corporation registers a 415-type offering with the SEC. The issuer has completed virtually all decision-making on nonrate issues. For a bond issue, this involves security factors (for example, debenture issue or mortgage bond, sinking fund, maturity and/or call protection). In fact, the issue is ready to go except for some fine-tuning on nonrate aspects (if required) and the interest rate/issue price decision. Since the major practical purpose of the 415 exercise is to give issuers the chance to catch interest-rate dips,[4] a go decision by an issuer may involve a request for bids from two or more special-bracket firms. In effect, what occurs is a speeded-up version of the competitive bidding process described earlier.

On the other hand, some corporations who maintain long-term relationships with a specific investment banking firm then negotiate the terms (including contract rate and price) of the new issue with that firm.

However the price is decided, once it is agreed to by the issuing corporation and the purchasing syndicate, the investment bankers in effect agree to buy the new issue and will own it until they sell it to the public. Syndicates sell issues for an amount higher than the proceeds to the company; the difference is the underwriting discount and commission or underwriting spread.

Once the terms, conditions, and all the other features of a new bond issue are set up, a *registration statement* is filed with the SEC, as well as a *preliminary prospectus* that discloses material relevant to any prospective buyer, with the exception of

---

[4]Or at least avoid unanticipated rate surges.

final price and contract rate.[5] The registration statement, filed with the SEC, becomes effective, and a *final prospectus* is issued as soon as, in the opinion of the SEC, there has been adequate disclosure to the public. Because nonrate terms of previously registered shelf issues are well known in the markets and large issuers' activities are closely followed by security analysts, the waiting period for shelf-registered issues may be as short as two days. As the prospectus copy shows, however, (see Figure 17–1) the SEC does not take a position with regard to investment merits of the issue or the reasonableness of the offering price or yield. As noted above, while the issue is in the process of being sold by the syndicate, the risk that the price of the issue may fall—conceivably even below the price paid to the borrowing firm—is borne entirely by the investment banking members of the syndicate.

While the red-herring prospectus is outstanding and during the actual selling period of the new issue, the lead manager runs the book. This means that prior to the final price setting the lead manager keeps a record of indications of interest of potential buyers. Once the issue goes effective the lead manager maintains a record of actual sales to new buyers by members of the syndicate and by members of the selling group. If a portion of the new issue remains unsold because market interest rates are rising, the syndicate manager can stabilize the new issue's price and market by standing ready to make purchases at or above the offering price. The syndicate manager may take a short position in the issue, and the price pegging may be continued for a time or stopped.[6] In most cases, the underwriters' agreement that establishes the syndicate limits the amount of stabilizing purchases that can be made. Syndicate members want to have

---

[5]Because of the printing on the preliminary prospectus is colored in red, it is often called the red-herring prospectus.

[6]The following appears in every prospectus: "In connection with this offering, the underwriters may overallot or effect transactions which stabilize or maintain the market price of the securities offered hereby at a level above that which might otherwise prevail in the open market. Such stabilizing, if commenced, may be discontinued at any time."

FIGURE 17–1

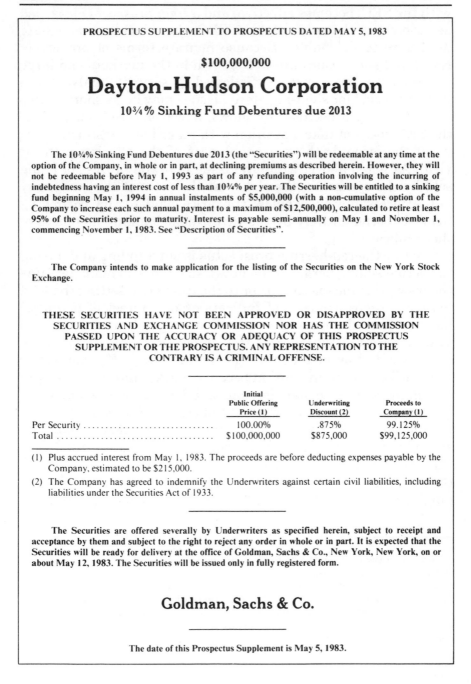

PROSPECTUS SUPPLEMENT TO PROSPECTUS DATED MAY 5, 1983

$100,000,000

Dayton-Hudson Corporation

10¾% Sinking Fund Debentures due 2013

The 10¾% Sinking Fund Debentures due 2013 (the "Securities") will be redeemable at any time at the option of the Company, in whole or in part, at declining premiums as described herein. However, they will not be redeemable before May 1, 1993 as part of any refunding operation involving the incurring of indebtedness having an interest cost of less than 10¾% per year. The Securities will be entitled to a sinking fund beginning May 1, 1994 in annual instalments of $5,000,000 (with a non-cumulative option of the Company to increase each such annual payment to a maximum of $12,500,000), calculated to retire at least 95% of the Securities prior to maturity. Interest is payable semi-annually on May 1 and November 1, commencing November 1, 1983. See "Description of Securities".

The Company intends to make application for the listing of the Securities on the New York Stock Exchange.

THESE SECURITIES HAVE NOT BEEN APPROVED OR DISAPPROVED BY THE SECURITIES AND EXCHANGE COMMISSION NOR HAS THE COMMISSION PASSED UPON THE ACCURACY OR ADEQUACY OF THIS PROSPECTUS SUPPLEMENT OR THE PROSPECTUS. ANY REPRESENTATION TO THE CONTRARY IS A CRIMINAL OFFENSE.

	Initial Public Offering Price (1)	Underwriting Discount (2)	Proceeds to Company (1)
Per Security	100.00%	.875%	99.125%
Total	$100,000,000	$875,000	$99,125,000

(1) Plus accrued interest from May 1, 1983. The proceeds are before deducting expenses payable by the Company, estimated to be $215,000.

(2) The Company has agreed to indemnify the Underwriters against certain civil liabilities, including liabilities under the Securities Act of 1933.

The Securities are offered severally by Underwriters as specified herein, subject to receipt and acceptance by them and subject to the right to reject any order in whole or in part. It is expected that the Securities will be ready for delivery at the office of Goldman, Sachs & Co., New York, New York, on or about May 12, 1983. The Securities will be issued only in fully registered form.

Goldman, Sachs & Co.

The date of this Prospectus Supplement is May 5, 1983.

some control over the share of the offering and the costs allotted to them (see below for further discussion).

Underwriting Spreads and Discounts

The difference between the price paid by the public and the proceeds to the company is the underwriting discount or spread; frequently that number is referred to as the gross spread. In recent years and for most significant bond issues, the gross spread has been less than 1 percent of the issue ($10 on a $1,000 bond). To that sum the underwriter adds some out-of-pocket expenses (for legal fees, due-diligence meetings, and so on) which appear on the front page of the prospectus as "expenses payable by the Company."[7]

Out of the gross spread, the lead underwriter customarily collects a management fee of 20 percent. If the bond issue comes to $100 million, the management fee to the lead underwriter is $200,000. Syndicate members selling directly to the public then get, in the aggregate, about $8 per bond so sold. Dealers who are *not* syndicate members but are part of the selling group get a share of the spread called the selling concession. Table 17–1 illustrates a preliminary distribution of the gross spread. Note that only $785,000 of the $1 million spread is accounted for. The manager earns an (implicit) management fee for selling 30,000 bonds directly to public. In fact, he collects an additional $140,000 (or the equivalent of an additional 70,000 bonds' worth). The manager and syndicate members split the $2.50 underwriters' discount for the 30,000 bonds distributed by the selling group members in proportion to their original subscription stated in the prospectus (say, in a 30 percent manager/70 percent member proportion). The selling group is committed only to sell the securities without committing its capital to risk taking. Put differently, if the bond market were to drop the price of the new bond to, say, $985, the cost of the $5 net loss per bond *plus*

---

[7]These nonmarket costs such as printing, due-diligence meetings, and legal fees to outside counsel are not trivial and may come to between ¼ to ½ of 1 percent of the proceeds of a new issue.

TABLE 17–1
Preliminary Distribution of Gross Spread

	Management Fee	Underwriter Discount	Sales Concession	Bonds Sold to Public	Direct Income
Manager	$2.00	$2.50	$5.50	30,000	$300,000
Syndicate member	—	2.50	5.50	40,000	320,000
Group member	—	—	5.50	30,000	165,000
Total					$785,000

the added expenses incurred by the manager in stabilizing the issue would also be shared on 30/70 ratio between the manager and the syndicate membership.

Reallowance

Reallowance is a share of the selling concession (usually less than 50 percent of the sum—say $2 per bond in this case) paid to members of the syndicate or of the selling group for the sale of bonds to the public over and above those acquired from the manager. A reallowance is paid to the firm that actually makes the sale, but the balance of the spread is retained by the member who agreed to release the bonds.

The manager is the ultimate and final payer of all of these amounts—only he has all the data since he runs the book. Figure 17–2 indicates the distribution of the bonds as set by the Underwriting Agreement; the lead underwriter for the Dayton-Hudson Corporation, Goldman, Sachs & Co., took down $37.5 million of the $100 million issue. The next largest set of underwriters are the major special-bracket firms: First Boston, Merrill Lynch, Morgan Stanley, and Salomon Brothers, all of which took $3.5 million each. Goldman, Sachs will treat these firms as well as it wants to be treated by them when they run the book in another offering.

FIGURE 17–2

UNDERWRITING

Subject to the terms and conditions set forth in the Underwriting Agreement, the Company has agreed to sell to each of the Underwriters named below, and each of the Underwriters, for whom Goldman, Sachs & Co. are acting as representatives, has severally agreed to purchase, the principal amount of Securities set forth opposite its name below.

Underwriters	Principal Amount
Goldman, Sachs & Co.	$ 37,500,000
Bear, Stearns & Co.	2,500,000
A. G. Becker Paribas Incorporated	2,500,000
Blyth Eastman Paine Webber Incorporated	2,500,000
Alex. Brown & Sons	1,500,000
Dain Bosworth Incorporated	2,500,000
Dillon, Read & Co. Inc	2,500,000
Donaldson, Lufkin & Jenrette Securities Corporation	2,500,000
Drexel Burnham Lambert Incorporated	2,500,000
A. G. Edwards & Sons, Inc.	1,500,000
The First Boston Corporation	3,500,000
E. F. Hutton & Company Inc.	2,500,000
Kidder, Peabody & Co. Incorporated	2,500,000
Lazard Freres & Co.	2,500,000
Merrill Lynch, Pierce, Fenner & Smith Incorporated	3,500,000
Morgan Stanley & Co. Incorporated	3,500,000
Oppenheimer & Co., Inc.	1,500,000
Piper, Jaffray & Hopwood Incorporated	2,500,000
Prudential-Bache Securities Inc.	2,500,000
L. F. Rothschild, Unterberg, Towbin	2,500,000
Salomon Brothers Inc	3,500,000
Shearson/American Express Inc.	2,500,000
Smith Barney, Harris Upham & Co. Incorporated	2,500,000
Thomson McKinnon Securities Inc.	1,500,000
Wertheim & Co., Inc.	2,500,000
Dean Witter Reynolds Inc.	2,500,000
Total	$100,000,000

Under the terms and conditions of the Underwriting Agreement the Underwriters are committed to take and pay for all of the Securities, if any are taken.

The Underwriters propose to offer the Securities in part directly to retail purchasers at the initial public offering price set forth on the cover page of this Prospectus Supplement, and in part to certain securities dealers at such price less a concession of 0.50% of the principal amount. The Underwriters may allow, and such dealers may reallow, a concession not to exceed 0.25% of the principal amount to certain brokers and dealers. After the Securities are released for sale to the public, the offering price and other selling terms may from time to time be varied by the representatives.

LEGAL OPINIONS

The validity of the Securities offered hereby is being passed upon for the Company by Faegre & Benson, 3400 IDS Center, Minneapolis, Minnesota 55402, and for the Underwriters by Sullivan & Cromwell, 125 Broad Street, New York, New York 10004, who may rely on Faegre & Benson as to matters of Minnesota law.

S-6

BOUGHT DEALS, PREMARKETED DEALS, AND COMPETITIVE BIDS, CIRCA 1985

For some bond flotations in mid-1985, gross spreads substantially narrowed. The first sample below, Norwest Financial, Inc. (see Figure 17–3) shows a gross spread of 0.268, or slightly above ¼ of 1 percent. The description of the underwriting agreement in the prospectus (see Figure 17–4) names Merrill Lynch as the *sole* underwriter, and Merrill Lynch "proposes initially to offer part of the notes directly to the public at the offering price . . . and part to dealers at a price that represents a concession not in excess of .2 of 1 percent of the principal amount." Under the latter circumstance, Merrill Lynch would keep no more than 0.068 percent of the gross spread, which comes to about .23 percent. Such bought deals with tight spreads have become commonplace under Rule 415.

Under that same rule, the negotiated deal arrangement has been developed. In this arrangement, notes are marketed to syndicate members and by them to clients (Figure 17–5).

Finally, the Citicorp note (see Figure 17–6) was bid for competitively and, even though the gross spread was not especially thin (compare the 0.6 of 1 percent with the Norwest issue of 0.268), the syndicate certainly was—the manager carrying more than 80 percent of the total.

However, if all the major firms engage in deals like these (that is, with the manager carrying half the deal or more and with very short syndicates), deal diversification will simply involve fewer firms. For the firms that manage those deals, effective diversification among the deals still exists as long as sufficient capital is available to the major firms. Rule 415 has forced, quite inadvertently, many smaller and regional firms out of the syndicate game. On the other hand, major underwriting firms have felt the need to build their capital positions because they need to buy larger proportions of more issues and on short notice. Likewise, the pressure to build capital may also be responsible, at least in part, for the drive of more firms to switch from partnership to corporate organization.

SYNDICATE RISK MANAGEMENT AND HEDGING

The syndicate manager and all syndicate members by necessity operate with price control on the upside. As long as the syndicate is maintained, they may not make sales at prices higher than the price to the public stated in the prospectus. If an unanticipated rise in security prices occurs after the new issue is priced and before the syndicate's distribution is complete, the syndicate will experience a reduction in risk but no increase in revenues; it only benefits because it sells out its long positions more rapidly. If, in order to support the new issue price, the syndicate manager took a short position in the issue prior to the unforeseen price surge, he may have to cover the short (1) at a higher market price (that is, potentially at a loss) or (2) by exercising the Green Shoe option, if one was written into the prospectus. In case (1), he would reduce his gross flotation revenue by the extent of the net cost of the short cover.[8] In case (2), the aggregate revenue from the flotation would rise by somewhat less than 10 percent for the syndicate as a whole if, as is typical, the Green Shoe option is equal to 10 percent of the new issue and the short-cover operations carried some costs.

Suppose that market prices do not move up but move down. Instead of having the new issue go out the window, the flotation process now is slow going in the face of declining market prices. For all syndicate members, unsold inventories of the new issue rise to levels higher than desired.[9] This result involves, first, the acceptance of greater-than-before inventory price risks on larger inventories. Second, investment bankers (like all financial firms) carry a high-leverage capital structure; that is, they manage on a narrow base of equity capital. Charges against the cap-

---

[8]At the least, there would be an opportunity cost in that total revenues would be less than: (a) the share of gross spread (per security sold) times (b) the number sold by managers, syndicate members, or others.

[9]Suppose that, in order to place some of the new issue with institutional investors, syndicate members engage in preferential swap transactions. This could work as follows. They place a premium bid with an institution on security X taken in a swap for new issue Y; their report to the syndicate shows only as a Y transaction.

FIGURE 17–3

PROSPECTUS SUPPLEMENT

(To Prospectus dated December 28, 1983)

 FINANCIAL

$50,000,000

Norwest Financial, Inc.

9⅞% Senior Notes 1990 Series due June 15, 1990

Interest payable June 15 and December 15, commencing December 15, 1985.

The Notes are redeemable on or after June 15, 1989 at the option of the Company, in whole or in part, without premium.

THESE SECURITIES HAVE NOT BEEN APPROVED OR DISAPPROVED BY THE SECURITIES AND EXCHANGE COMMISSION NOR HAS THE COMMISSION PASSED UPON THE ACCURACY OR ADEQUACY OF THIS PROSPECTUS SUPPLEMENT OR THE PROSPECTUS TO WHICH IT RELATES. ANY REPRESENTATION TO THE CONTRARY IS A CRIMINAL OFFENSE.

	Price to Public(1)	Underwriting Discount	Proceeds to Company(1)(2)
Per Note	99.88%	.268%	99.612%
Total	$49,940,000	$134,000	$49,806,000

(1) Plus accrued interest, if any, from July 18, 1985.

(2) Before deducting expenses payable by the Company estimated at $50,000.

The Notes are offered for delivery on or about July 18, 1985, subject to prior sale, when, as and if delivered to and accepted by Merrill Lynch, Pierce, Fenner & Smith Incorporated. Merrill Lynch, Pierce, Fenner & Smith Incorporated reserves the right to withdraw, cancel or modify such offer and to reject orders in whole or in part.

Merrill Lynch Capital Markets

The date of this Prospectus Supplement is July 2, 1985.

FIGURE 17–4

UNDERWRITING

Under the terms of and subject to the conditions contained in an Underwriting Agreement dated July 2, 1985, Merrill Lynch, Pierce, Fenner & Smith Incorporated has agreed to purchase the Notes and the Company has agreed to sell the Notes to Merrill Lynch, Pierce, Fenner & Smith Incorporated.

Merrill Lynch, Pierce, Fenner & Smith Incorporated proposes initially to offer part of the Notes directly to the public at the public offering price set forth on the cover page hereof and part to dealers at a price which represents a concession not in excess of .20 of 1% of the principal amount. Merrill Lynch, Pierce, Fenner & Smith Incorporated may allow and such dealers may reallow a concession not in excess of .125 of 1% of the principal amount, to certain other dealers. After the initial public offering, the public offering price and such concessions may be changed.

The Underwriting Agreement provides that the Company will indemnify Merrill Lynch, Pierce, Fenner & Smith Incorporated against certain civil liabilities, including liabilities under the Securities Act of 1933, as amended, or contribute to payments Merrill Lynch, Pierce, Fenner & Smith Incorporated may be required to make in respect thereof.

S-4

FIGURE 17–5

$125,000,000

The Stop & Shop Companies, Inc.

10¾% Notes Due 1995

Interest Payable January 15 and July 15

The Notes may not be redeemed prior to July 15, 1992. On and after that date, the Notes are redeemable at the option of the Company, in whole or in part, at 100% of the principal amount thereof plus accrued interest to the redemption date. The Notes, which mature on July 15, 1995, are not entitled to any mandatory redemption or sinking fund provisions. See "Description of Notes."

Application has been made to list the Notes on the New York Stock Exchange.

THESE SECURITIES HAVE NOT BEEN APPROVED OR DISAPPROVED BY THE SECURITIES AND EXCHANGE COMMISSION NOR HAS THE COMMISSION PASSED UPON THE ACCURACY OR ADEQUACY OF THIS PROSPECTUS. ANY REPRESENTATION TO THE CONTRARY IS A CRIMINAL OFFENSE.

	Price to Public	Underwriting Discounts and Commissions (1)	Proceeds to Company (2)
Per Note	99.75%	.70%	99.05%
Total	$124,687,500	$875,000	$123,812,500

(1) The Company has agreed to indemnify the Underwriters with respect to certain liabilities, including liabilities under the Securities Act of 1933. See "Underwriting."
(2) Before deducting certain expenses payable by the Company estimated at $265,000.

The Notes are offered by the several Underwriters named herein subject to prior sale, to withdrawal, cancellation or modification of the offer without notice, to delivery to and acceptance by the Underwriters, and to certain further conditions. It is expected that delivery of the Notes will be made at the office of Shearson Lehman Brothers Inc., New York, New York, on or about July 16, 1985.

Shearson Lehman Brothers Inc.

July 9, 1985

FIGURE 17–5 (continued)

indemnity satisfactory to it before it enforces the Indenture or the Notes. Subject to certain limitations, holders of a majority in principal amount of the Notes may direct the Trustee in its exercise of any trust or power. The Trustee may withhold from Noteholders notice of any continuing default (except a default in payment) if it determines that withholding notice is in their interests. The Company is required to file periodic reports with the Trustee as to the absence of default.

Directors, officers, employees or stockholders of the Company will not have any liability for any obligations of the Company under the Notes or the Indenture or for any claim based on, in respect of, or by reason of such obligations or their creation. Each Noteholder by accepting a Note waives and releases all such liability. The waiver and release are part of the consideration for the issue of the Notes.

The Trustee

The First National Bank of Boston (the "Bank") will act as Trustee under the Indenture. Under an existing line of credit and a revolving loan agreement, the Company has available to it up to $70,000,000 from the Bank. The maximum principal amount outstanding under the line of credit since February 2, 1985 was $11,000,000. No borrowings are currently outstanding under the line of credit or the revolving loan agreement. The Bank also serves as the Transfer Agent for the Company's Common Stock and provides other customary commercial banking and fiduciary services for the Company. See also the note under "Capitalization."

UNDERWRITING

The Underwriters, represented by Shearson Lehman Brothers Inc. (the "Representative"), have severally agreed, subject to the terms and conditions contained in the Underwriting Agreement, a copy of which is filed as an exhibit to the Registration Statement, to purchase from the Company the Notes offered hereby. The names of the several Underwriters and the principal amount of Notes to be purchased by each of them are as follows:

Underwriter	Principal Amount of Notes
Shearson Lehman Brothers Inc.	$ 44,900,000
The First Boston Corporation	4,500,000
Goldman, Sachs & Co.	4,500,000
Merrill Lynch, Pierce, Fenner & Smith Incorporated	4,500,000
Morgan Stanley & Co. Incorporated	4,500,000
Salomon Brothers Inc	4,500,000
Bear, Stearns & Co.	3,400,000
Alex. Brown & Sons Incorporated	3,400,000
Dillon, Read & Co. Inc.	3,400,000
Donaldson, Lufkin & Jenrette Securities Corporation	3,400,000
Drexel Burnham Lambert Incorporated	3,400,000
E. F. Hutton & Company Inc.	3,400,000
Kidder, Peabody & Co. Incorporated	3,400,000
Lazard Frères & Co.	3,400,000
PaineWebber Incorporated	3,400,000
Prudential-Bache Securities Inc.	3,400,000
L. F. Rothschild, Unterberg, Towbin	3,400,000
Smith Barney, Harris Upham & Co. Incorporated	3,400,000
Wertheim & Co., Inc.	3,400,000
Dean Witter Reynolds Inc.	3,400,000
A. G. Edwards & Sons, Inc.	2,000,000
Oppenheimer & Co., Inc.	2,000,000
Prescott, Ball, Turben	2,000,000
Thomson McKinnon Securities Inc.	2,000,000
Tucker, Anthony & R. L. Day, Inc.	2,000,000
	$125,000,000

12

FIGURE 17–6

$150,000,000

CITICORP ✚

11% Subordinated Notes Due August 1, 1995

Interest on the Subordinated Notes (the "Notes") is payable semiannually on February 1 and August 1, commencing February 1, 1986. The Notes will be subordinate and junior in right of payment to all Senior Indebtedness (as defined in the Prospectus) of Citicorp. The Notes are redeemable on and after August 1, 1990, at the option of Citicorp, in whole or in part, at their principal amount plus accrued interest.

THESE SECURITIES HAVE NOT BEEN APPROVED OR DISAPPROVED BY THE SECURITIES AND EXCHANGE COMMISSION NOR HAS THE COMMISSION PASSED UPON THE ACCURACY OR ADEQUACY OF THIS PROSPECTUS SUPPLEMENT OR THE PROSPECTUS. ANY REPRESENTATION TO THE CONTRARY IS A CRIMINAL OFFENSE.

	Price to Public(1)	Underwriting Discount	Proceeds to Citicorp(1)(2)
Per Note	99.55%	.60%	98.95%
Total	$149,325,000	$900,000	$148,425,000

(1) Plus accrued interest, if any, from July 30, 1985.

(2) Before deduction of expenses payable by Citicorp.

The Notes are offered severally by the Underwriters as specified herein subject to receipt and acceptance by them and subject to their right to reject orders in whole or in part. It is expected that the Notes will be ready for delivery at the offices of Goldman, Sachs & Co., New York, New York, on or about July 30, 1985.

Goldman, Sachs & Co.

The date of this Prospectus Supplement is July 23, 1985.

FIGURE 17–6 (*continued*)

SUPPLEMENTAL DESCRIPTION OF NOTES

The Notes offered hereby will be limited to $150,000,000 aggregate principal amount and will mature on August 1, 1995. The Notes will be subordinate and junior in right of payment to all Senior Indebtedness (as defined in the Prospectus) of Citicorp. The Notes will bear interest from July 30, 1985 at the rate per annum shown on the front cover of this Prospectus Supplement, payable semiannually on February 1 and August 1 of each year, commencing February 1, 1986, and at maturity, to the person in whose name the Note (or any Predecessor Note) is registered at the close of business on the January 15 and July 15 next preceding such Interest Payment Date. The Notes will be issued in denominations of $1,000 or any integral multiple thereof.

The Notes offered hereby will not be subject to redemption prior to August 1, 1990. On and after such date they will be subject to redemption upon not less than 30 nor more than 60 days' notice by mail at any time, in whole or in part, at the election of Citicorp, at a redemption price equal to their principal amount plus accrued interest to the date of redemption If less than all the Notes are to be redeemed, Notes will be selected by the Trustee by such method as it shall deem fair and appropriate and which may provide for selection for redemption of portions of the principal amount of any Note of a denomination larger than $1,000.

Reference is made to the Prospectus for a description of other terms of the Notes.

UNDERWRITING

Subject to the terms and conditions set forth in the Underwriting Agreement, Citicorp has agreed to sell to each of the Underwriters named below, and each of the Underwriters, for whom Goldman, Sachs & Co. are acting as Representatives, has severally agreed to purchase, the principal amount of Notes set forth opposite its name:

Underwriter	Principal Amount
Goldman, Sachs & Co.	$122,200,000
Alex. Brown & Sons Incorporated	2,700,000
Daiwa Securities America Inc.	2,700,000
Drexel Burnham Lambert Incorporated	2,700,000
E. F. Hutton & Company Inc.	2,700,000
Keefe, Bruyette & Woods, Inc.	2,700,000
Kidder, Peabody & Co. Incorporated	3,500,000
The Nikko Securities Co. International, Inc.	2,700,000
Nomura Securities International, Inc.	2,700,000
M. A. Schapiro & Co., Inc.	2,700,000
Yamaichi International (America), Inc.	2,700,000
Total	$150,000,000

Citicorp has been advised by the Representatives that the several Underwriters propose initially to offer the Notes to the public at the public offering price set forth on the cover page of this Prospectus Supplement and to certain dealers at such price less a concession not in excess of .375% of the principal amount of the Notes. Underwriters may allow and such dealers may reallow a concession not in excess of .125% of such principal amount. After the initial public offering, the public offering price and such concessions may be changed.

Citicorp has agreed to indemnify the Underwriters against certain civil liabilities, including liabilities under the Securities Act of 1933.

See "Plan of Distribution" in the Prospectus for further information regarding the distribution of the Notes offered hereby.

S-8

ital base because of larger security inventories (or eventual capital losses) constrain firms' decision making and/or risk taking.
With stronger expectations of market-price declines (or greater
future risks), risk avoidance may become stronger or more
widely held.

Tactics

Accordingly, lead underwriters may resort to two types of actions
to offset risk in flotations. *Tactical* actions refer to the specific
flotation itself. The Green Shoe option is the most useful tactic
in an unanticipated up market. In a volatile market with little
strong direction, overallotment by the managing underwriter is
probably the best marketing device. The managing underwriter
offers added securities to syndicate members of the selling group
with the expectation that they will put forth a strong sales effort
just because they have a chance to earn whatever share of the
spread to which they are entitled and for a larger volume of securities. If, in the process, they place more securities by accepting more swaps at relatively attractive prices to the buyer of the
new issue, they would be no more than fine-tuning the bid/ask
spread while selling at the fixed price to the public.

In the flotation of new equity issues, syndicate members
may engage in what appear to be counterproductive actions,
namely, selling into the syndicate manager's support bid in the
market. Of course, even a relatively small firm that is an occasional syndicate member would never want to appear to be foul-
ing the nest in this manner. It would hide the action by using a
broker's broker (or more than one) to hide its identity. In turn,
the syndicate manager, by keeping all the facts of actual syndicate sales and support operations to himself, tries to prevent
information leaks regarding slow sales to keep such defections
to a minimum. Large syndicate participants who are special-
bracket firms (or those in the next bracket who frequently run
syndicates), although tempted, may fear retaliatory actions by
their peers if such actions are even suspected.

In turn, even the syndicate participants who do not expect
to be managing syndicates are constrained from engaging in
such self-protective actions too frequently. They know that

cycles of slim stock offerings in down markets (when the temptation to bail out is strongest) are followed by surges in stock flotations in bull markets. Thus responsible syndicate behavior safeguards the prestige of syndicate participants and the occasional appearance in tombstone ads. In addition, it assures the small firm (and, even more important, its customers) of continuously available new merchandise. Because this process helps the distribution process generally, lead managers, in turn, may be constrained from disciplining syndicate members too obviously.

Strategy

The group of special-bracket firms and all other important syndicate managers have the problem of temporarily becoming buyers of last resort for the offerings they manage. This proposition implies that they will be accumulating securities at those times when markets are less receptive or most unpredictable. For the major underwriters for whom maintenance of market share in the new-offering game is important, an accumulation of unsold securities when markets are difficult or uneasy may be implied. Moreover, the compulsion to maintain market share does not permit the luxury of making too many bids too far away from the markets. Inevitably, some inventories accumulate.

Suppose an underwriter wants to hedge a $1 million *undesired* inventory bond position. Even for a significant investment banking firm this would not be an unusually large or small amount considering that, as new issue syndicates break up and positions are liquidated, new flotations are taken in. The hedge could be an offset to a revolving excess inventory.

Now suppose that, in a skittish market, nearby Treasury bond futures are trading at $65.[10] For a hedge value of 10 contracts of $100,000 par each, these constitute a market value of $650,000 with a par value of $1 million (for 8 percent U.S. gov-

---

[10]The following data are taken from F. H. Trainer, Jr., "The Uses of Treasury Bond Futures in Fixed-Income Portfolio Management," *Financial Analysts Journal*, January–February 1983, pp. 28–29.

ernments with a maturity of about 15 years). Assuming a $20,000 initial margin requirement, the short sale of 10 bond futures contracts is equivalent to a short sale of $650,000 long governments on 97 percent margin. If market prices fall so that price quotations on futures decline from $65 to $64 (or by 1½ percent) the value of the 10 contracts (short) would rise by $10,000, a cash value that may be withdrawn from the account.

The cash value of the undesired $1 million inventory in the syndicate will probably have declined by the same amount that, if it were marked to market, would have reduced the firm's available capital by $10,000. If the cash gain from the futures short position is deposited into the firm's capital, the decline is exactly offset. Of course, there is a commission fee for this hedging transaction. Using the preceding transaction, the bid/ask spread per contract plus commission per round trip is about ²⁄₃₂ of a point or approximately ¹⁄₁₀ of 1 percent. (The round-trip cost for 10 contracts would therefore be about $650.)

Finally, the question arises whether the breadth and depth of the futures market is great enough to accommodate hedging significant flotations volume. Suppose that the total volume of syndicate hedging was not 10 bond contracts but 1,000. For example, in 1987, the total daily trading volume of Treasury bond futures contracts averaged about 263,000 contracts. That meant a short hedging position for 1,000 industry contracts came to less than ½ of 1 percent of daily trading volume, an amount not likely to raise price variances in futures market.[11]

Other Syndicate Games—An Example

Prior to the pricing of an initial public offering (IPO), the managing underwriter gets indications of interest from institutional buyers and other major clients that add up to the full number of shares expected to be sold (1 million shares) plus the Green Shoe option (another 150,000 shares). The price range discussed with the client and known to the syndicate as well as the institutions

---

[11]On October 19, 1987, when the New York Stock Exchange traded about $20 billion of stock, the Chicago Board of Trade traded some $50 billion of Treasury bond futures.

was $9 to $11 per share. At that price range, the manager has a number of indications that the stock will be held by buyers if he can price it within the range.

Assume that the market experiences a sinking spell—the most-recent Fed report on the money supply raises fears of an impending rise in the discount rate. The managing underwriter is still committed to produce the shares for the buyers if they ask for them after pricing, but he now feels that the institutions, in view of bearish market price expectations, may prefer to trade the stock, rather than hold it. There may even be opinions in the syndicate department that some of the institutions may now be free riders in the deal rather than just traders.

The manager might go back to the client for permission to lower the price range by $1 (to $8–$10) in view of the chillier market climate. But the client had been attracted to the underwriter because *his* range ($9–$11) was better than that of another underwriter with whom the client had previously considered the deal. The client could argue that he was being played for a sucker by the second underwriter's higher price just to get the business. After all, he could argue, the M1, M2, and M3 reports of the Fed are often substantially revised, and the manager should know the vagaries of prices in the markets since that is his business. What should the manager do?

The manager decides to continue with the offering as originally proposed ($9–$11 per share), but the greater price uncertainty in the marketplace requires more underwriting support. The manager knows the size of the demand in his book while he continues to evaluate the quality of that demand. He provides that added support by taking a naked short position in the market. (This short position is in addition to the covered short represented by the Green Shoe option.) As a result, the manager adds to the perceived market demand for the stock (which stands in the book in the form of indications of interest at 1,150,000 shares) another "synthetic" 150,000 market-share demand, which constitutes his naked short.

If he covers the naked short at a below-market price (because expectations of continued market-price declines are fulfilled), he will have helped to support the price and acted in his fiduciary function with respect to the issuer. If the market rises, the short cover will be more expensive, and the syndicate's expenses rise. As a result, the syndicate will produce a lesser return to its members but will have successfully sold the deal.[12]

In point of fact, the naked short is another aspect of the underwriting-insurance process. It is a premium paid on the equivalent of an accident policy. That policy is designed to cover the reduction in cash proceeds—the accident—that might have been brought about by an unfortunate timing event in the economy at large. And even though the premium paid adds to costs, these costs are spread over the syndicate as a whole.

SUMMARY AND SOME NEW THOUGHTS ON AGENCY COSTS

The syndicate tactics indicated earlier reduce the riskiness of placing a particular issue with the public at the least time delay (overallotment) and least cost (Green Shoe option). Such tactics are designed to place the maximum portion of the offering with the public at the price fixed in the syndicate; these mechanisms could reduce the "unique" or "specific" risks of flotation per issue.

So much for specific flotations. The active syndicate participants in volatile markets and under the shelf registration rule will face continuous requests to place new issue bids at short notice. A clustering of such opportunities at times of temporary rate drops also reflects a risk clustering of surges of inventories of unsold securities priced above the current market. From the point of view of portfolio management (of unsold inventory), there is an unexpected result:

1. Portfolio structure (by securities) is *not* determined by the portfolio manager but by random issue of new secu-

---

[12]On the other hand, the higher price per share on the issue will probably mean somewhat better underwriting revenues to the syndicate. In part, this offsets the higher short-cover costs.

rities (at the option of issuers) and the macroeconomic policies that affect reception.

2. Proportions of securities in portfolio are *not* based on low risk/high return tradeoff but by something more random that may approach its reverse if interest-rate volatility carries an upward bias. Under these circumstances, co-variance of returns may become more positive, and portfolio variance may be rising.

To offset the rising systematic risk of unanticipated portfolio surges, short positions in futures markets may be established and maintained. In part, this procedure permits gross new issue spreads to be maintained (even though systematic risk may be rising) as long as the transaction cost of developing a short hedge is relatively low. Another reason for the relative stability of gross spreads even as rising rate volatility raises portfolio risks is the economics of capital budgeting that reduces the volume of flotations (long-term) as rates rise and the cost of capital to the issuer rises.[13] Rising competition among underwriters for the lesser volume of new product (such as new securities) also holds down the size of potential inventories of unsold issues. Inevitably, then, the short hedge in the futures market becomes more attractive the greater the perceived systematic risk.

Agency Costs

The foregoing discussion could be reinterpreted as representing a special case of agency theory. Jensen and Meckling define an agency relationship as ". . . a contract under which one or more persons [the syndicate participant(s)[14]] engage another person (the agent) to perform some service on their behalf which involves delegating some decision-making authority to the agent. If both parties to the relationship are utility maximizers, there

---

[13]In part also, corporations with an inelastic demand for funds will find short-term financing substitutes.

[14]In the original article, that person is called the principal(s).

is good reason to believe that the agent will not always act in the best interests of the principal. The *principal* can limit divergences from his interest by establishing appropriate incentives for the agent and by incurring monitoring costs designed to limit the aberrant activities of the agent."[15]

In some interesting ways, the foregoing approach could be reversed. The relatively free hand given lead managers, their monopoly control over the information set (the book), and their use of syndicate tactics makes *managers* the agents of syndicate members. That point, as well as potential future role reversals among the syndicate members (where all the majors are syndicate managers as well as members some of the time), suggests that agency theory, when applied to syndicates, should be discussed in terms of "double agency."[16] Still, under Rule 415 the foregoing application of agency theory applies to the interrelationship among the syndicate members *only* and *not* to the relationship between the corporate (or other) issuers and the investment bankers. Once the corporation has sold the issue, it becomes the syndicate's risk and selling problem.

Monitoring costs may be small and monitoring itself quite effective in those cooperative enterprises where each member has a chance to be chairperson—that is, the monitor—some of the time. To the extent that one effect of Rule 415 has been the shorter syndicate and much heavier participation by managing underwriters, leading to the bought deal, monitoring costs are substantially reduced because nearly all syndicate members are now major underwriters. In fact, each syndicate member is sooner rather than later in a lead managership position. If major participants represent a small number acting in a well-defined market, information regarding performance ex post is available quickly, and the ability to retaliate is continuously present. For the few smaller firms left, behavior such as shirking or anti-

---

[15]M. C. Jensen and W. H. Meckling, "Theory of the Firm: Managerial Behavior and Ownership Structure," *Journal of Financial Economics* 3 (1976), p. 308, (italics in original).

[16]Jensen and Meckling also point out that agency costs "arise in any situation involving cooperative effort" (p. 309).

group behavior can be controlled by threats—or only the fear—that future syndicate allocations will be still further reduced. The fact that the small number of major participants are always in the same markets and competing to win bids for the same merchandise helps enforce discipline among them.

The agency problem, as proposed by Jensen and Meckling and Jensen and Fama, is based on a long-term separation in which the segregation of risk bearing and corporate managerial decision making is fixed (although it cannot be perfectly specified) in spite of the uncertainties in which these relationships obtain. On the other hand, the reality of continued role reversals in the syndicate game provides a built-in remedy to the agency problem. Finally, the disclosure and underwriter liability provisions of the Securities Act of 1933 (Section 11)[17] offer potential direct remedies to corporate and other issuers if collusion is suspected in a given flotation. In any case, substitute flotation methods, including private placements, are always available if an issuer wants to assess alternative flotation costs.

---

[17]For further discussion see Chapter 16.

18

INVESTMENT BANKERS AND THEIR CLIENTS: INSTITUTIONALIZATION TAKES COMMAND

Electronic trading has created a revolution in financial markets by breaking the barriers of scale, time, and space. At the trading level, broker–dealers have an increasing need for a large capital base. Only the largest investment banking firms will have the capacity to act as counterparts—that is, as dealers—for the increasingly larger trades done continuously by the world's largest institutional clients. This chapter will detail the following dimensions to institutionalization:

1. Those involved in large-scale trading generally.
2. Block trading.
3. Merger-related activities.

LARGE-SCALE TRADING: INVESTMENT BANKERS AS DEALERS

With the electronic marvels of instant communication came the demand to transfer vast sums just as quickly. Finding two large transactors who want to do exactly opposite sides of a single trade at the same time becomes less probable the larger the trade and the shorter the decision lag. And yet, high-speed communications are perhaps more likely to trigger professional and institutional-sized transactions than retail trades.

Until the late 1950s, the auction markets of the New York Stock Exchange (NYSE) easily accommodated just about all transactions in common stock of listed firms, and floor trading arrangements were functionally related to the large number of generally offsetting small-scale orders. In that sense, the specialist system could readily absorb temporary price fluctuations and small random retail imbalances of supply and demand.

During the 1960s and 1970s, the stock market *became increasingly institutionalized.*[1] At that time, substantial upheavals occurred in both the broker–dealer industry and the NYSE and other exchanges because institutional-type trading could not be made to work in an essentially retail-type marketplace. For example, in the late 1960s, the NYSE could not cope with a transaction volume of 13 to 15 million shares *per day* and had to close one day a week to catch up with the paperwork. In addition, some 100 firms were forced to leave the industry due to insufficient capital or insufficient capacity to deal with the transactions' volume, size, or record keeping. General dissatisfaction with some trading practices finally led to congressional action in providing investor insurance, the Securities Investor Protection Corporation (SIPC), and negotiated commissions.[2]

In the 1970s, the information network developed by and for institution-sized traders[3] led them to seek mechanisms away from the floor to trade positions. This meant that a dealer network had to be developed to serve the contra side; the participants were called block traders—the "upstairs" traders (as contrasted symbolically to "floor traders"). Of course, some block traders could provide a search process—that is, a large-scale brokerage function—where the equivalent of a "private placement" of a large secondary trade was done for a commission fee. The dozen or so investment banking firms that manage private

---

[1]See for example, the multivolume report by the SEC, *Institutional Investor Study Report* 82d Congress, First Session, U.S. Government Printing Office (Washington, D.C.: 1971).

[2]For a more complete discussion, see E. Bloch and R. H. Schwartz, eds., *Impending Changes for Securities Markets* (Greenwich, CT: JAI Press, 1979).

[3]Access to Dow Jones and Reuters news wires is much too costly for retail traders but not for institutions.

placements or public syndicates also have the facilities to do block trades effectively.

The investor side of block trading is based on growing institutionalization of the savings process. The development of pension funds and their encouragement by legislation such as Employee Retirement Income Security Act of 1974 (ERISA) helped increase labor force demands for deferred lifetime compensation. Governmental efforts and institutional arrangements designed to keep the process honest probably contributed too. In more recent years, Keogh and Individual Retirement Account (IRA) plans for middle-income individuals further added to the institutionalization of savings in firms that were not necessarily financial intermediaries with tightly constrained asset regulations.

When all the foregoing is multiplied by income growth related to rapid inflation and to the demand for portfolio performance to maintain the real value of capital, it is easy to explain how large amounts of funds began to accumulate and how fund managers at times wished to make substantial trades on short notice. Thus institutionalization of savings led to institutionalization of trading, and this required development of trading and risk-taking services on a large scale and at short notice.

Within the investment banking community the capacity to trade on a large scale is done by what Securities and Exchange Commission (SEC) reports call national full-line firms and large investment banking houses, many of which are also the special-bracket firms that manage most of the major flotations (see Chapter 3). A synergistic relationship clearly exists between the skills and capacities required to do large-scale trading in secondary markets and syndicate management in primary markets. What, then, does it take to be a dealer in institutional-sized transactions, or a special-bracket firm? Why do some firms that are large in terms of assets or in trading activity not move to become special-bracket firms? Is it lack of competition or oligopolistic collusion?

Posing the question of whether there is competition (or its restraint) in the industry is not useful because the more fundamental problem is which firms have the ability continuously to be a *dealer* on a large scale. This requires the capacity to perform efficiently several not necessarily complementary services:

1. Secondary sales *in size*.
2. Pricing close to the market (that is, relatively high price with small commission charge).[4]
3. Accepting inventory risks.

The first item, size, is the most fundamental aspect of special-bracket investment banking. It involves the capacity to find buyers for large blocks of stock or a large proportion of a bond issue and skill in setting prices that clear the market without leaving too large a residual to be inventoried. Adding in the narrowing of equity trading commissions (following May 1, 1975) results in a market environment in which the intermediary is expected to accept more risk for less return on some transactions while trading in size. Further, the willingness to make bids on a continuing basis for large-scale offerings at close-to-market prices is necessary to maintain membership in the club. All these members, by proving they belong by offering continuous large-scale *secondary* trading capacity, will, in consequence, be asked to make bids as lead underwriters for new issues as well. Two nearly inconsistent capacities are thus required to serve institutional investors:

1. Size.
2. Agility.

Size

The size criterion alone would qualify a number of additional broker–dealer firms to belong to the SEC's groups of national full line or large investment banks. Why don't they? One possible answer is that although the New York-based and the NYSE regionals do participate in virtually the same markets as in-

---

[4]As we shall indicate below, the unit charge for commissions tends to drop with size.

vestment banking firms (and even at comparable *aggregate* volume), their average transaction size is closer to retail sized than wholesale sized. This difference in emphasis by the more retail-oriented firms, even those deemed to be large in total assets and in equity capital, involves them only occasionally with large-scale trades. In fact, they do their business with a somewhat different clientele than the more institution-oriented firms even though the merchandise traded may be the same for all.

In that sense, then, the difference between wholesale and retail is an analog to the block trader in IBM stock and the retail broker in IBM. Both use the same merchandise trading at similar prices. The big difference is that for all practical purposes trade execution takes place in two separate markets even though the consolidated NYSE tape prints virtually all block transactions.[5]

As a proxy for this proposition, consider the impact of negotiated commissions (since May Day 1975) on both small-sized and large-scale traders as developed by an SEC study.[6] As shown by the bottom charts in Figure 18–1, commissions on large-scale trades for institutional accounts dropped by about 50 to 60 percent between 1975 and 1981, individual commissions fell by less. Commissions on small-sized trades (200 shares or less) dropped about 20 percent for institutions, while individuals were charged about the same at the beginning and the end of the period for trading fewer than 200 shares. Finally, institutions always paid less commission (as a share of the total trade) than did individuals, and the relative cost difference was greater the *smaller* the transaction size. Moreover, comparing transaction costs at the beginning and end of the period studied shows that, for institutions, these costs have receded for all transactions. However, for individuals, transactions costs in the 1980s at the low-sized end are slightly higher than in 1975, while at the upper end they are slightly lower. The market power of institutions has clearly dominated the establishment of transactions costs; this is borne out

---

[5]For further discussion of block trading see below.

[6]SEC Directorate of Economic and Policy Analysis, "Commission Rate Trends, 1975–1981" (Washington, D.C.: July 7, 1982), p. 5.

FIGURE 18–1
Effective Commission Rates versus Order Size, April 1975 and 4th Quarter 1981

A. Commissions as a percent of principal value

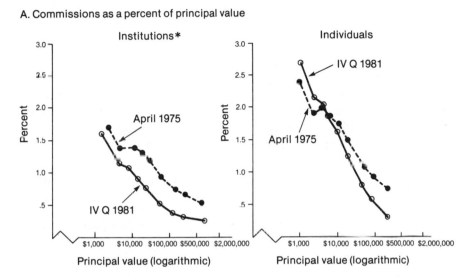

B. Commission cents per share

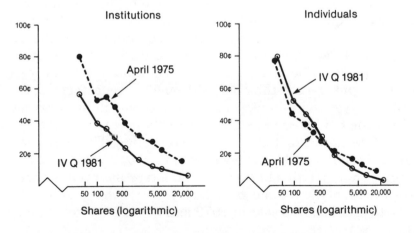

*Where institutional and individual customers cannot be precisely identified, COD business is defined as institutional and all other business as individual.

Source: U.S. Securities and Exchange Commission. Directorate of Economic and Policy Analysis, Survey of Commission Charges on Brokerage Transactions.

especially by direct comparison on the cost/principal value basis shown in the top chart in Figure 18–1.

Agility

The element of the institutional trading process most difficult to illustrate is the ability to place large blocks of securities with institutional buyers without market dislocation. The bond markets, be they for U.S. governments or corporate or foreign issues, are largely institutional and over the counter.[7] As a result, little bond-trading information relevant to institutional transactions[8] is available; we infer the institutionalization of these markets from the structural changes in equity trading.

Table 18–1 indicates the two major methods of institutional trading performed through the NYSE:

1. Organized secondary offerings and other special methods.
2. Block trades.

The first set of secondaries indicated in Table 18–1 uses the full panoply of mechanics that makes such offerings similar to a new issue: a formal prospectus is written, a syndicate of investment bankers is formed, and all other requirements of the securities act (as amended) are met. Block trades, on the other hand, are much simpler. A single investment banker (usually) is asked for a bid, and if that bid is deemed satisfactory by the seller,[9] the investment banker takes the responsibility to resell the shares he bid for or place those not sold in inventory.

The data shown in Table 18–1 are revealing. Through 1975, the annual volume of blocks sold came to about three quarters of a billion shares (half a billion in 1974, a recession year). Starting with 1976, block volume grew each year, reaching more than one fourth of all shares sold in 1979 and about 50 percent since 1983.

---

[7]Tax-exempt issues are somewhat less institutionalized, however.

[8]The information regarding bond trading on organized exchanges refers to only a tiny fraction of total transactions.

[9]Nearly all block trades are sales.

TABLE 18-1
Large-Scale Trades on the NYSE by Secondary Offerings and by Block Trades, 1972–1986 (In Number of Transactions and by Thousands of Shares Traded; % of Total NYSE Volume)

| Year | Secondary Offerings | | Block Trades | | |
	Number of Transactions	Shares	Number of Trades	Shares	% of NYSE Volume
1972	154	65,067	31,207	766,406	18.5
1973	174	33,160	29,233	721,356	17.8
1974	57	7,243	23,200	549,387	15.6
1975	73	21,257	34,420	778,610	16.6
1976	69	20,341	47,632	1,001,254	18.7
1977	49	10,685	54,275	1,183,924	22.4
1978	34	11,285	75,036	1,646,905	22.9
1979	26	9,559	97,509	2,164,726	26.5
1980	34	18,611	133,597	3,311,132	29.2
1981	34	14,351	145,564	3,771,442	31.8
1982	72	39,047	254,707	6,742,481	41.0
1983	67	61,049	363,415	9,842,080	45.6
1984	24	21,180	433,427	11,492,091	49.8
1985	8	21,309	539,039	14,222,272	51.7
1986	13	20,570	665,587	17,811,335	49.9

Source: New York Stock Exchange, *NYSE Fact Book 1987* (New York: 1987).

This proposition bears out the general point that the market organization of the NYSE and other exchanges is not necessary to block trading. Further, those wholesale methods crossed on the retail floor, namely, secondary offerings and other special methods, are no longer a significant factor, while the more or less informal and quick-acting upstairs deals are currently the method of choice for large-scale transactions. In fact, there is an analog here of instant secondaries—that is, block trades—to instant bond issues institutionalized by Rule 415 shelf registrations. And large upstairs block dealers and major lead underwriters for bonds tend to be the same firms.

A Case Study

These arguments were brought out in almost textbook fashion by the second-largest block trade executed on the NYSE up to 1983, a deal that produced about $130 million for the seller.

One of the most confusing and complex takeover–merger deals ever attempted involved, among others, Martin Marietta, the Bendix Corporation, and Allied Corporation (see Chapter 8). The outcome, after much sound and fury, was a takeover of Bendix by Allied. In the Bendix takeover, Allied Corporation acquired a huge block of stock (previously bought by Bendix) of RCA Corporation (5.4 million shares of common and 145,600 shares of preferred) that represented about 7.2 percent of RCA's ownership. Allied did not wish to acquire RCA or even a minority interest in that company—to the contrary, in early 1983, it wanted to reduce the substantial debt ($2.4 billion) it had taken on to finance the Bendix acquisition

In late February 1983,[10] Allied "retained Oppenheimer & Co., Inc., for financial advice and assistance" but also talked to many other of the largest investment bankers "all of whom were interested in handling the RCA transaction." One of these firms (Lehman Brothers) proposed an underwriting-type deal for the sale of the block because one of the Lehman partners sat on the RCA board, and, in the opinion of legal advisers, a registered deal with SEC approval would be required. This would involve a two-day delay.

Allied decided not to delay. On Wednesday, March 30, the actual transaction crossed the tape as a block at $23.75 per share at 3:22 P.M., a few hours after Salomon Brothers had made a bid for the stock and a few weeks after Oppenheimer had attempted (unsuccessfully) to work the block. According to *The New York Times* (March 31, 1983), "John Gutfreund, Salomon's chairman, said that the investment house offered to buy the block without having lined up any customers, but strictly on the basis of its recent conviction that the public and institutional

---

[10]The following is based on "The Story Behind The Deal," *Investment Dealer Digest*, April 12, 1983.

appetite for good-quality equities is much greater than we perceived it to be. He said that Salomon had agreed to buy the stock from Allied at 3:15 . . . and, after a blaze of phone calls by its 300-strong sales force, had resold all the common shares by 3:30."

The story further explained that about 90 percent of the buyers were domestic financial institutions, of which none took more than 500,000 shares.

The following client relationships may have been influenced by Salomon's move:

1. Salomon's power as an effective mover of large blocks was clearly enhanced.
2. Its service to Allied in so doing, by providing immediate liquidity to enable Allied to pay down its debt (partly raised to finance the takeover), emphasized point 1.
3. Last—and not least—to RCA the successful dispersion of a large minority position without a major price change helped to reinforce that firm's independence while, at the same time, *not* raising its cost of capital.

In *The New York Times,* industry analysts speculated, "Salomon may have earned about $2 million in commissions for its 15 minutes work." Strictly speaking, this is not an accurate statement since Salomon made most of its fee from the bid/ask spread of about 25 cents per share on the block trade. Moreover, the compensation was for risk taking (the risk that during the trade the price would not recede by more than the ¼ point spread) rather than for Salomon's work of making "a blaze of phone calls." Indeed, in the postmortems on the deal, the *Investment Dealers Digest* quoted an unnamed investment banker to the effect that a trading decision involving over 5 million shares of a firm (RCA) that had "experienced sustained earnings disappointments" included, of course, a sizable capital risk, "especially when you are talking about a risk bid in an open market when everyone is talking [on March 30, 1983] about a market correction."

Competitive forces in the market may take the form not only of providing a cheaper price to win an issue. As this study suggests, there may be competition in risk taking by the *size of the transaction,* with pricing determined essentially in a parallel (retail) market. The shift away from organized secondary transactions to block trades reflects growing institutionalization or, in operative terms, the demand by potential sellers to execute a trade.

OTHER INSTITUTIONAL DEMANDS

Beyond the block traders that the institutions use to transact in scale, they have engaged in "basket-trading" using the Designated Order Turnaround (DOT) system on the NYSE as a counterpart to index arbitrage, or as a part of portfolio insurance (see Chapter 5). As the discussion in preceding section suggested, block trades can be "shopped" by the dealer. On the other hand, basket trading (of a set of stocks designed to replicate an index) has to be done instantaneously to serve its purpose. Whereas the former places emphasis on a dealer's capacity to deal, the latter puts pressure on the *market's* liquidity. But as Chapter 5 indicated, equity market and derivative market dislocation also places pressure on all market makers. As the Brady commission pointed out, there is, indeed, one market.

MANAGEMENT CONFLICTS
FOR INSTITUTIONS

Increasingly, the country's wealth is managed by institutions such as insurance companies, pension funds, and bank trust departments. It is that large-scale accumulation of wealth that naturally leads to accumulation of large-scale portfolios. In turn, these large portfolios have been adjusted by large-scale trades.

In the half century since the appearance of Berle and Means's work which emphasized the split between corporate control and ownership, its influence has spread to legislation (for example, the Securities Act of 1933 and the Securities and

Exchange Act of 1934) and a huge volume of academic work has been generated.[11] One of the best-known academic versions explores agency theory—the conflicts of interest between management and ownership. Fama and Jensen,[12] in a recent recasting of the theory, examined managerial efficiency in decision making by "decomposing" strategic decision making from operations management. In that version, a distinction is made between (1) decision initiation and implementation and (2) decision control through monitoring and choices made among proposals presented. Their argument concludes that, in modern complex organizations, these two functions will be separated. This line of analysis suggests that the internal organization of large and complex organizations is not only important but has a bearing on their economic performance as well.

The argument may be pushed further on the ownership side. The emphasis here is on the proposition that the management of wealth has undergone a split between ownership and management. Decisions regarding institutional portfolios are made by managers of wealth with minimal participation by the owners of wealth. This characteristic of wealth holding can be most readily assessed by a survey of pension funds.[13] By 1980 aggregate assets of *private* plans alone exceeded $400 billion, and *annual* contributions came to $70 billion (about 6 percent of annual wages and salaries).

The growth of these plans, with the related incentives for growth, is not unlike the agency theory story itself. Just as Berle and Means presented their insight into the separation of ownership and management from a long focus dating back to the

---

[11]See, for example, Jensen & Meckling, "Theory of the Firm: Managerial Behavior Agency Costs and Ownership Structure," *Journal of Financial Economics* 3 (1976), pp. 305–60; and R. H. Coase, "The Nature of the Firm," *Economica* 4 (1937).

[12]E. F. Fama and M. Jensen, "Separation of Ownership and Control," *Journal of Law and Economics,* June 1983, pp. 301–26.

[13]The following is based on two important contributions to the literature by Alicia H. Munnell: (1) *The Economics of Private Pensions* (1982 Washington, D.C.: The Brookings Institution); and (2) "Who Should Manage the Assets of Collectively Bargained Plans," Federal Reserve Bank of Boston, *New England Economic Review,* July–August 1983.

18th century, so the theory of employer-financed pension plans has been related by Alicia Munnell to ". . . unilaterally provided gratuities that employers offered long-service employees in order to induce them to retire."[14] At present such paternalism has become institutionalized through the tax system because the tax code treats employer contributions more favorably than employee contributions.[15] In effect, this leads to a tax-induced preference for deferred wages to be invested by the employer prior to disbursement to employees, and hence pension plans tend to be *employer* controlled. In turn, that control is sometimes turned over to others, who then succeed to the managment of wealth. The major industries that perform wealth-management services are life insurance companies, private pension funds, state and local government employee funds, and other insurance firms.

Table 18–2 indicates how levels of holdings in credit market instruments and in equities have grown in the 1980s among institutional investors. In the markets for credit instruments, life insurance companies maintain a position equal to about one half of the holdings shown. Indeed, the rise in holdings between 1981 and 1987 for each of the institutions and for the subtotal represents about a doubling of holdings. In the area of equities, the subtotal for the institutions indicates a rise greater than twofold despite rather low holdings among the life companies, and despite the post-crash valuation adjustments for all holders.

Finally, the memo account at the bottom of Table 18–2 indicates the annual share of the *acquisition* by financial institutions of credit market instruments. That last memo item shows a near-doubling in the annual purchase programs (as a share of total purchases of all investors) between the first year and the last. Moving to the assessment of the share of institutional *equity* holdings, we find that in 1982 the $414 million so held (out of a total of $1720 million; see Table in Conclusion to Part I)

---

[14]Munnell, "Who Should Manage the Assets," ibid., p. 20.

[15]Employer contributions and the income earned on them remain untaxed until benefits are distributed to the beneficiary. Conversely, employee contributions may be taxed at the source.

TABLE 18–2

Institutional Investors by Levels of Holdings in Credit Markets and in Equities, 1981–1987 (In Billions of Dollars and Percent)

	1981	1982	1983	1984	1985	1986	1987
Life insurance companies							
Corporate equities	$ 46	$ 53	$ 62	$ 60	$ 72	$ 83	$ 84
Credit market instruments	414	457	509	563	639	726	816
Private pension funds							
Corporate equities	219	262	314	309	393	456	459
Credit market instruments	179	204	234	256	283	303	364
State and local government employee funds							
Corporate equities	48	60	90	96	120	150	179
Credit market instruments	172	195	211	246	269	300	320
Other insurance							
Corporate equity	32	39	48	45	57	68	72
Credit market instruments	132	137	139	150	181	218	252
Subtotals: institutions							
Corporate equities	$345	$414	$ 514	$ 510	$ 642	$ 757	$ 794
Credit market instruments	$897	$993	$1,093	$1,215	$1,372	$1,547	$1,752
For credit instruments Memo A/C (in %)							
Annual share taken by all institutions	11.0	3.8	6.6	11.6	13.3	14.5	19.5

Source: Federal Reserve Flow of Funds and Salomon Brothers.

355

constituted about 24 percent of total. By 1987, that share had grown to 27 percent. The question now arises: If the growth of managed pension funds (and other institutionalized assets) keeps rising, how does the separation of wealth management from wealth ownership affect pension fund governance?

There is, in fact, a curious detachment between "ownership" and management in the context of pensions. Considering pensions as deferred wages (and deferred wages *are* wages), the future pension beneficiary is the "owner" and the current portfolio manager is the "manager." There are two dimensions to this type of separation:

1. The *space* separation of the owner–worker from the policy making (within constraints) of the wealth manager and the added separation of the worker–beneficiary from the corporate official in deciding on:
   a. The portfolio manager.
   b. Change in the portfolio manager.
   c. Changes in the financial management of pension policies.
2. The *time dimension* that separates the current, usually automatic, purchase by the worker of a portfolio management service from the pension manager and the eventual receipt of pension benefits based on unknown intermediate rates of return.

The diffuseness of that financial principal–agent relationship is blurred further by the fickleness of the connection between corporate trusteeship and its capacity to change agents (called portfolio managers). Some people may also have the misapprehension that the pension corpus representing deferred wages is the employer's contribution and thus not the employee–owner's money, causing further psychological barriers to effective monitoring, control, and so forth. If anything, the availability of the federal Pension Benefit Guaranty Corporation insurance scheme, because it provides a financial backstop, may, by offering psychological comfort, serve to diffuse further the owner–manager relationship.

AGENCY THEORY:
IMPLICATIONS FOR TRADING

Suppose that pension-fund managers, trust managers, and other wealth managers begin to see that they manage an increasingly large portion of the country's wealth for the actual owners. To an increasing extent, they then become aware that they are a larger share of the financial market. To paraphrase Pogo, they will have met the market and discover that the market is them. They may even find that simply buying the market may be the only policy by which they can achieve at least average performance.

From this it follows that as their portfolios grow larger, wealth administrators have more rationale to acquire securities from large firms almost exclusively. This must be so for two reasons: (1) When buying more at one time (than on average) as employment rises, most pension funds would be in the market with a strong, predictable cash flow. (2) Likewise, markets can more readily absorb sell surges without excessively large price declines if sales occur in the more widely distributed security issues of large firms. Put slightly differently, the need to make very large amounts of purchases or sales at any one time forces these large institutions to acquire securities in the largest firms even if they wish to achieve only average performance. Recall that institutions pay the lowest commission charges (Figure 18–1) and that they carry enough market power to get competitive-bid price equivalents for block trades. Nevertheless, their concern regarding their performance, and their awareness of market power also helps to explain the demand for portfolio insurance (as discussed in Chapter 5). At least up to the 1987 crash, that mechanism offered a chance of avoiding all trading costs and risks.

For the wealth managers, in turn, the portfolio management of a significant portion of the stock of many of the largest and best-known corporations may make them the largest single owners—at least by proxy—in the original agency context. If a number of institutional investors achieve that position but find it unacceptable to participate in corporate governance, we may have still another and unforeseen split in the ownership–management or agency relationship.[16] If the institutions maintain voting neutrality, it may take a substantially *smaller* share of outside stockholders or takeover interests to achieve a controlling ownership position in even the largest firms. That is to say, the higher proportion of institutional ownership that does *not* participate in corporate policy decisions, the lower the proportion of ownership it takes to control even large corporations.

This seeming digression illustrates elements of investment institutionalization to which an important and different application of agency theory may be applied. Given the focus on investment banking, the shift to large-scale activities by investment banking firms in making markets was the necessary counterpart to financial institutionalization. What made that shift technologically feasible was the data-processing revolution which (1) generated enormous scale economies for large transactions and (2) provided further scale economies for information. The direction of that change was supported by tax subsidies to individuals shifting funds to institutional pension management as well as into IRAs and Keogh plans (a *demand-side* phenomenon).

Further evidence supporting that proposition is the growth of large-scale *equity* trades (block trades) reported by the NYSE (see Table 18–1).

As shown by the last line of the table, block trades—the indicator for institutional activity—reached one half of NYSE volume in 1986. Since most block trades are arranged away from the floor, if the relative growth in that area continues at the present rate, the volume of institutional equity trading away from the floor may exceed that done on the floor. That would, of course, make the volume of NYSE stock trading more dealer than auction oriented.

---

[16]Pension fund managers may have several conflicts of interest in voting their shares: (1) If they do not vote with management, they may lose the pension account. (2) If they vote with management, a political question may be raised regarding a few pension managers "controlling" the corporate universe. For a general discussion of this issue, see SEC, *Staff Report on Corporate Accountability,* Senate Committee on Banking, 96th Congress, Second Session (1980).

MERGERS AND PENSION
FUND MANAGEMENT

Part II discussed the investment banking firms' participation in mergers and takeovers. At this point it is useful to discuss what appears to be a side issue, namely, the participation of pension fund managers in corporate governance—another unforeseen byproduct of the current merger wave and institutionalization.

Under ERISA, the manager of a pension fund is supposed to make decisions solely to benefit the interest of pension beneficiaries. Because one of the few good bets in merger analysis is that the largest share of GAIN (see Chapter 8) accrues to the *target* firm, pension-fund managers have tended to vote proxies *against* antitakeover amendments. An article in *Institutional Investor*[17] clearly indicates that up to the early 1980s many firms (and their CEOs) put strong pressure on pension managers to vote *with* the management of target firms. In the words of the article, "Institutional investors generally oppose antitakeover amendments because they would rather sell shares to acquirers at healthy premiums" (p. 145). Of course, such sales also improve the manager's performance rating. The article suggests that antitakeover resolutions are now being passed by wide margins even though in 1985 institutions owned about 75 percent of NYSE-listed stocks. The explanation offered was that a nonfavorable (to management) vote of a large pension-fund holding can be identified and that an implicit, or even explicit, threat to take away the management of the pension fund appears to be sufficient to induce compliance with corporate policy rather than with fiduciary responsibility.[18] Since the mid 1980s, some major independent and public employee funds have voted their proxies *against* antitakeover resolutions, thereby taking a *GAIN* when it came their way. On the other hand, corporate in-house pension managers or pension managers hired by corporate management have been under pressure to side with management. To offset

---

[17]"The Proxy Pressure on Pension Managers," *Institutional Investor,* July 1985, pp. 145–47.

[18]Ibid., p. 147.

that pressure, the U.S. Department of Labor in 1988 wrote a policy statement emphasizing the fiduciary duties of pension trustees to beneficiaries.

Institutionalization has led to the need for large-scale trading and large-scale investing—and to potential large-scale conflicts of interest. The agency conflict now interposes not one but *two* layers of management between the owners (that is, beneficiaries) and the firm's policies. It appears that monitoring even by presumptive U.S. government regulators (the Department of Labor) has been slow in becoming more effective. Institutionalization that interposes several layers of equity management between the largely anonymous owners and the corporation's management group has produced a profound change in agency relationships. One could deal with the overly simple assumption of individual owner and individual manager by the usual request for more research. The knowledgeable players in the merger, takeover, and risk arbitrage games are doing exactly that research as applied to individual firms in the marketplace (see Part II). In effect, that research may provide the most effective, if "hidden-hand," type of monitoring left in the age of institutionalization. And taking this argument one last step, even the possibility of a takeover may help to concentrate the minds of the managements of many listed firms.

CONCLUSION TO PART IV

INSTITUTIONALIZATION AND THE ONE-MARKET CONCEPT

In the *Brady Report* cited at length in Chapter 5, the market break of October 19, 1987 was attributed in large part to the failure of the markets for stock, stock index futures, and stock options "to act as one [market]."[1] An important linkage of these markets is based on the financial instruments and trading strategies deriving from the increased institutionalization of holding equities. As a way of avoiding excessively large, or too frequent, trading of large blocks of stock, and in pursuit of *average* performance, institutional investors have turned to "portfolio insurance." According to the Brady Report "Portfolio insurance theory assumes that it would be *infeasible* to sell huge volumes of stock on the exchange in short periods of time with only a small price impact. These institutions came to believe that the futures market offered a separate haven of liquidity sufficient to allow them

---

[1] See *Report of the Presidential Task Force on Market Mechanisms,* New York, January 1988, p. VI. (This source is referred to as the *Brady Report* throughout.)

to liquidate huge positions over short periods of time with minimal price displacement."[2] As Chapter 5 indicated, that belief proved illusory in October 1987.

The *Brady Report* also argues that the *market makers* that provided portfolio insurance and other hedge vehicles ". . . routinely hedge their positions by trading in two markets. For example market makers in the S&P 100 option hedge by using the S&P 500 futures contract, and some NYSE specialists also hedge . . . with futures contracts."[3]

The other hedging mechanism discussed by the *Brady Report,* namely, index arbitrage (sometimes called "program trading") also is used as an example linking ". . . the stock and index futures markets. Faced with increasingly chaotic markets in October [1987], portfolio insurers, to the extent possible, abandoned their reliance on the futures market to execute their strategies and switched to selling stocks directly. . . ."[4]

There is little need to repeat here the discussion in Chapter 5 of the 1987 market break. The point made here is that it was the institutionalization of the financial markets that pushed many of the institutional changes that, ultimately, raised the demand for hedging services. The magnitude of that demand change provided incentives for the linkages of the basic security markets, and the markets for derivative instruments.

As institutionalization grows, the demand by large investors for market-making services will grow more than proportionately. This is so for the following reasons: In markets with rising prices, market-making services will be provided by a growing number of dealers. Conversely, in a down market, or a down market made more skittish by large selling waves of institutional-sized blocks, fewer market makers will be willing to deal in scale, thereby further widening the amplitude of price variance. At that time, the investment bankers who can survive, and even thrive, in that high-variance environment will be the industry leaders.

---

[2]Op. cit., pp. 55–56. Emphasis supplied.
[3]Op. cit., p. 55.
[4]Ibid.

19

HOW THE INDUSTRY IS CHANGING (AGAIN)

As predicted in the first edition, no last word may ever be written about the investment banking industry. Consider the behavior of a set of firms whose service to their clients derives from the capacity to make markets where none is immediately available. Such firms will maximize their value by a continuous search for innovative securities and new markets.

Many of the preceding chapters have focused on these innovations. The incentive to innovate arises from a market maker's perception of a market inefficiency. By developing an improvement, the innovative firm increases its rate of return. The prospect of higher rates of return also encourages the activities of the imitator-firm(s) and, between them, these firms develop the new market. Necessarily, the new markets induce changes in the ways of doing business among the market makers themselves.

This proposition is illustrated in Figure 19–1. The model used is that of the mortgage market in which the innovation was the refinancing of residential mortgages by a variety of mortgage backs. In panel (a) the wide price (or rate) spread between A_m (ask) and B_m (bid) represents the cost of the market inefficiency of trading whole loans, that is, trading the actual residential mortgage. (For further discussion of this inefficiency see Chapter 7.) Panel (c) indicates the miniscule transaction rate of whole loans relative to the eventual volume of mortgage backs when these appear. With the first mortgage back issue, the innovative security can trade with a lower ask price, and a higher

FIGURE 19–1
Market Innovation

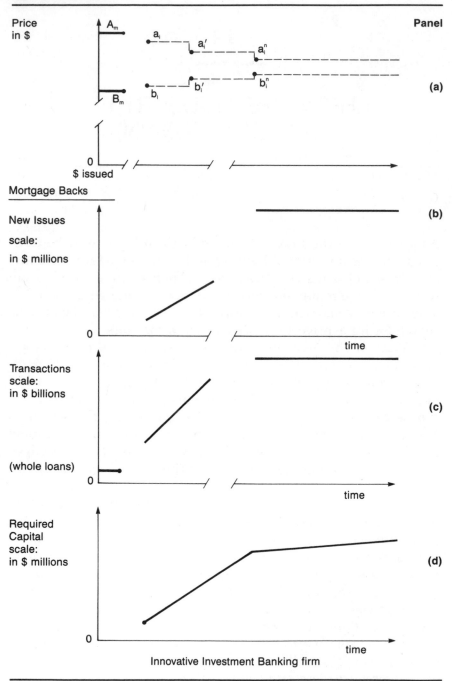

Panel

Price in $

A_m

a_i

a_i'

a_i^n

b_i

b_i'

b_i^n

B_m

(a)

0

$ issued

Mortgage Backs

New Issues
scale:
in $ millions

(b)

0

time

Transactions
scale:
in $ billions

(c)

(whole loans)

0

time

Required
Capital
scale:
in $ millions

(d)

0

time

Innovative Investment Banking firm

bid price, that is, with a narrower spread ($a_i - b_i$) in panel (a). That spread is still wide enough for the innovator to do well even though he now has to set some capital aside to support the rising volume of new issues, and of secondary trading.

As his competitors become his imitators, the bid/ask price narrows still further, that is, the market becomes more competitive and more efficient. That very rise in efficiency permits additional imitators to enter just because each individual transacting firm will have to face less risk owing to the deepening of the market itself. As a result, a rapidly growing market implies less spread for traders, but also more volume, and a less than proportionate rise in required capital.[1] Aggregate volume rises as long as rates of return to human and financial capital remain appropriate to the risk taken: the limits on growth in panels (b) and (c) are based in part on a ratio that relates the returns from bid/ask spreads (panel a) to required level of capital (panel d). That ratio declines *both* because b/a spreads go down (to b^n/a^n), and the need for dealer capital rises.

A number of additional examples could be cited. In Chapters 4 and 6 the junk bond innovation produced by Drexel Burnham was shown to be imitated by other special-bracket firms, thereby developing a substitute for the commercial banks' commercial and industrial loans. In Chapter 6 the support by Drexel to the *secondary* market for junk bond issues was shown to be accompanied by a progressive increase in new issue imitation by other special-bracket firms. Ultimately, that set of actions by Drexel Burnham helped to move that same firm to industry leadership. Other examples could be cited, including (1) the rise and fall of stock index arbitrage as it was conducted by major investment bankers for institutional investors and (or) their own account (Chapter 5) and (2) the intermediation of interest rate (and foreign exchange) swaps to the point where it is now a routine activity dominated by commercial banks.

---

[1]Please note the scale difference in panels b, c, d: The new-issue scale is in *m*illions of dollars; the trading scale is in *b*illions of dollars; and the required capital per investment banker is in *m*illions of dollars.

INSTITUTIONAL INVESTORS

Chapter 18 considered the customers making use of the new marketplaces, namely, the financial institutions. The expansion in the number and size of institutional clients was a necessary condition for the expansion of the marketplace. It is a fact that the elimination of market inefficiencies (e.g., in the mortgage market) also improves the rates of return of the clients, that is, of the institutional investors. Higher bids and lower ask prices cut their transaction costs, thereby raising rates of return. As a result there were enormous increases in all aspects of trading: the rise in scale of the average secondary trade was mentioned, as was the acceleration in the speed with which routine deals had to be executed to have any chance of success in the fiercely competitive marketplace.

Previously, in the early 1980s, the markets experienced a sharp rise in interest rate levels along with a surge in rate volatility that set historical records. To deal with this rise in *issuer* risk the Securities and Exchange Commission (SEC) permitted major corporate security issuers to move to instant security flotations—that is, to shelf registration (Chapter 16). For investment bankers, the demands made by institutional sellers in the secondary markets, and by corporate issuers in the primary markets, forced them to deal on a previously unknown scale. Deals also had to be done with the much faster reaction speed that the new information and execution technology made not only possible, but essential.

INCREASING FINANCIAL AND HUMAN CAPITAL

This increase in the ante for participation in all of the major financial markets sharply raised investment banking risks. To deal with larger risks required a parallel increase in capitalization of the market makers themselves. Their own corporate finance people could show that the vast new demand for financial capital would have to be met by new sources of funds. Unlike the partnerships in which senior personnel had grown up, the corporate form would give the firms better access to large amounts of capital. At the same time, the vast increase in the scale, and in the number of mergers, acquisitions, and takeovers stressed investment banking capacity in other ways: for example, the practice of providing bridge loans to bidder firms tended to encumber up to a third of a major investment banker's equity (see Part II). To be sure, this practice facilitated the consummation of the deal, and helped to keep in house the underwriting of the new issue that financed the deal (and incidentally served to repay the bridge loan). Nevertheless, other parts of the firm might feel the constraints of scarce firm capital being so concentrated.[2] Once again, the demand for financial capital might press these already heavily leveraged firms to raise still more funds.

Further, the need for ever more capacity to develop information, to execute, and to hedge required not only the addition of financial capital and the latest in electronic capacity but an expansion of human capital as well. The major investment banking firms doubled and tripled their employment through the mid-1980s. And these new employees were highly trained professionals who were compensated accordingly. Their activities, in many cases, were devoted to the hedging of ever increasing and complex risks that were related, in many instances, to the very security innovations that the pressure of competition forced each of the major firms to produce.

The added financial capital to support all of the above could, as indicated, be more readily raised by the corporate form. In addition, once the firm was so structured, it also could seek capital support from other U.S. firms, or from foreign firms (Chapter 4). The events of October 1987 created concerns not only with risk and capital capacity but also regarding substitute techniques, namely, the ability of hedging techniques to deal successfully with heightened asset volatility.

---

[2]The added risks taken on with the large-scale bridge loans for mega-takeover deals have, in May 1988, been dealt with by an old investment banking method, namely, syndication. In the $6¾ billion takeover of Federated Department Stores by Campeau Corp., *First Boston* "syndicated" the bridge loan of $2.1 billion with *Paine Webber* and *Dillon, Read*. (See "Talking Deals" by James Sterngold, *New York Times,* May 5, 1988, p. D-2.)

ORGANIZATIONAL CHANGES

Some further changes were occurring inside the industry, notably a change of internal organization. Recall that through the mid-1980s the large, powerful trading firm with multiple capacities appeared to be the dominant form: it could underwrite instant new issues; trade on a large institutional scale at a moment's notice; innovate new securities; and be a major player in the game of corporate control all at the same time. In a period when rapid growth in size was accompanied by rising profits and bonuses, whatever internal strains might have existed were, if not hidden, at least covered by the avalanche of profitable deals and the frantic 14-hour days and 7-day weeks it took to close one deal before racing to the next one.

Once that rate of activity slowed, so did the money avalanche. And once some losses began to appear—months before the all-too-convenient date of October 19, 1987—so did the internal stresses reveal themselves. Wall Street firms had undergone such ups and downs before, as indicated in Chapter 5. The difference this time was that all the firms were now so much larger. That quantitative difference became a qualitative one as well because the change from partnership to corporate form was more than a financial or a legal one. Prior to the mid-1980s, informal control systems through direct personal contacts were feasible, and directly involved as control agents the partners who had a direct investment in the firm. But in 1987 and later, in the corporate form, the stockholders demanded attention. And the chief executive officer (CEO) of the firm was made to feel responsible.

The CEO was faced with the following problems: How to control the deal flow, the flood of complex transactions, expenses? How to control the esoteric new tools of hedging, the innovative issues, and the computer systems dealing with all of the above? How to deal with a professional and deal-driven staff of 5,000 or more, many of whom were not known personally to the senior managers? In many firms a new control bureaucracy had to be organized, and was given a good deal of authority. Contrast this with the old partnership form where each partner at the least knew everyone in his own department, and knew and understood what each professional was doing. In the new, post-1986 regime, the control bureaucracy could easily be identified with staff reductions and lower bonuses. This cut into the authority of the division heads, many of whom were former partners. The CEO today has to attempt to control the new, larger, more complex system in which his department heads may feel that their power bases are being chopped away by a mindless control bureaucracy. Here two management systems conflict. And the result is that the multi-service investment banking firms begin to multiply by fission: senior personnel leave to organize specialized boutiques.

CRISIS MANAGEMENT

Still another byproduct of the tougher times that began in 1987 was the actual disappearance of some firms. The most spectacular of these was the absorption of E. F. Hutton by Shearson Lehman American Express. This is not the place to discuss that event aside from suggesting that when market competition gets tougher, the less effective participants in the marketplace are the first to disappear. In short, it is market pressure rather than an internal industry problem that forces the most severe change in particular firms; firm failure may be a firm-related control problem rather than an industry-wide management failure.

The tougher competition that began early in 1987 was industry-wide (see Chapters 4 and 5). Rates of return to equity for all members of the New York Stock Exchange (NYSE) (which reflect primarily returns to investment banking industry) showed their sharpest year-to-year decline in 1986 to 1987, as shown in Table 19–1.

These industry data contain a substantial irony: the very success of investment bankers that led to their tripling of (mainly equity) capital in the mid-1980s placed a fixed component into their capital structure. Further, suppose that a shortfall of revenues is associated with a perception of increased risk in the firm's positions [such as, e.g., losses in mortgage strip positions, or the perception that high-return transactions in merger and acquisition (M&A)-type activities encumber large

TABLE 19–1
Returns to Equity, All NYSE
Members, 1983–87 (In Percent)

	Before Tax	After Tax
1987	5	NM
1986	29	16
1985	29	15
1984	13	4
1983	37	19

NM, not meaningful.

Source: NYSE.

amounts of firm capital for bridge loans]. Then the possibility of reducing capital size in line with lessened activity may not be advisable or even feasible. As a result, returns to equity plummet.

TOWARD A FINANCE ECOLOGY

The notion of a finance ecology is implicit in the activities of a set of market makers that takes over when the organized markets cannot produce the services required. A simple example of that is the block trading activity (relative to trading on NYSE) of investment bankers. Going beyond these market-supplementing activities, the typical full-service investment banking firm had become a trader, dealer, and market maker in each of the world's major markets by the late 1980s. On a worldwide basis, investment bankers were integrating several financial markets through such mechanisms as swaps or even index arbitrage. And they were doing this in competition, as well as through cooperation, with other investment bankers.

The paradigm of this form of cooperative competition is the new-issue syndicate: in that one-time organization, competitors join for one deal only; the syndicate members may be on opposite sides in another deal. Still, each is an insurance scheme to minimize the risks of distributing the one issue. Similarly, the marketplace for innovative securities becomes, because of the actions of the imitators, a systematic mechanism for spreading risk and improving efficiency for market makers and investors. Together the market participants trade and interact as each other's financial environment: they form an ecology.

THE FIRST CHANGE:
FROM PARTNERSHIP TO CORPORATION

The foregoing has emphasized the macro side or market-based mechanisms that have changed the size and the structure of most full-service investment bankers. Consider now the micro side: most of the firms shifted from a partnership to a corporate form when the size of the deals done, and the number of deals increased early in the 1980s. Further, the new electronic technology permitted—and shelf registration required—faster execution, with consequent increases in risk. As a result, the major investment bankers doubled and tripled their financial and human capital during the early and mid-1980s.

It is important to recall that the transition from the smaller scale, lower volume, and lesser/volatility of the 1970s was accompanied by the change in organization from partnership to corporation for most of the major investment bankers. In the 1980s the rise in risks, and the need to acquire more capital required most of the firms to switch their organizational structure. In that sense, form followed function.

Another element in the change to the corporate form was the development, especially after 1986, of internal control mechanisms and systems that senior management used increasingly as firms doubled and tripled in size, but especially as the firms' rates of return came under pressure after 1986. A significant number of the entrepreneurial groups in some full-service firms—notably in M&A departments—then felt that the control bureaucracies were constraining the most profitable parts of the firm. This negative response to the firm's attempt at organized control, and a positive response to the opportunity to do M&A

deals on their own, induced a number of these individuals to form some two dozen boutiques in the period following the mid-1980s: the form evolved with the function.

THE CHALLENGE:
HOW TO CONTROL CHANGE

Since the large-scale wave of personnel dismissals in 1987–88, the internal reorganizations and the moves toward expense controls, several investment banking firms have engaged in self-studies and in hiring consultants to assess damage and to learn from mistakes. In retrospect, the prior overhiring, over-expansion, and the lack of strategic planning have been pointed to as the obvious errors that hindsight readily reveals. In like fashion, expansion into new markets is seen as a correctible excess: the helter-skelter rush to pre-bang London has been pictured as a lemming-like rush to (over)seas.

I would like to propose a more useful—albeit a not necessarily more comforting—assessment of that process. Fundamental to the following is the proposition that the investment-banking industry has virtually no fixed costs, not even the "fixed" variable costs implicit in a stable payroll. This tends to minimize the management infrastructure even after the organization of a control bureaucracy. And with minimal management manpower there tends to be minimal strategic planning. This has been pointed to as a major flaw and a major factor in the industry's excessive boom/bust cycles.

But this ain't necessarily so. The traditional, horizontal management structure of the industry—the partner (or managing director) surrounded by "his" traders—can move fast when prices move, and that structure can move fast into *new markets* when that move is important. That flexibility carries a cost. That cost is, from one viewpoint, the mere opportunism of a firm moving, helter skelter. From another viewpoint it is a quick and profitable response to a market opportunity.

I propose that we forgo the adjectives and, instead, attempt in a more functional approach to understand what's going on.

And what's going on is that we have an industry that has made a specialty of making markets where other firms with higher fixed cost ratios may fear to move. That is why I believe it is useful to consider that form follows function, and even more broadly in a macro context the notion of a "finance ecology."

Consider the organizational structure of a newly formed boutique to do, say, leveraged buyouts. Assume that the boutique can get all of the capital-type financing it needs from outside investors (individual and institutional). Assume further that required operational and underwriting functions are "rented" from other full-service firms. The boutique, consisting of a few partners and of a support staff of between 50 and 100 professionals can then be seen as a replica of the old entrepreneurial, horizontally organized partnership. In that type of single-purpose organization there is very little need for a management or planning group, or even a control infrastructure.

For the full-service firms on the other hand, the individual components such as the M&A department, syndicate department, mortgage backs, etc., etc., are each to be seen at any one time as potentially more important or less important (relative to the other internal departments). As the markets change, or as opportunities for innovations change, the full-service firms have to control and to reallocate resources and capital on the way to maximizing corporate value. The excess return opportunities to innovators in financial markets depend (1) on early discovery of market opportunities and (2) on the reaction pattern and reaction speed of competing market makers. "Strategic" planning for future and as yet *un*perceived opportunities, and for the related reaction patterns of competitors, appears to be an exercise in the realms of uncertainty and hope. A more realistic management program would attempt to assess and control current activities and capital needs. Based on that experience, a forecast of the firm's optimum size and capital could then be developed.[3]

---

[3]A case in point is the *Morgan Stanley* secondary stock issue of Friday, May 13, 1988. About 2.2 million shares of previously restricted stock were sold by Morgan executives. Of that total, 1.2 million shares were repurchased by Morgan Stanley. As a result, *less* stock will be outstanding while the stock *float* will have been raised.

CHANGE AS NORM

The boutiques and the full-service firms are organized to fill different needs, even though the M&A parts of both do the same things. By broadening the micro view to the macro, to the notion of a finance ecology, I want to underline that a relatively free financial market permits quick adjustments of the food chain equivalents (the securities) and of the competing organisms within it (the investment bankers and their clients). The freedom to innovate, to change, and to trade and hedge at relatively low cost will ensure that the participants will be able to adjust quickly. In a relatively free financial market, change not only becomes the norm with respect to security prices or types, but it also becomes a way of life for its participants. The decisions made by management as the new opportunities beckon may be to expand more or less, but the bottom line results will not be solely the product of the firm's own decisions, but will also reflect the competitive responses of other firms. Nor is the environmental unpredictability limited to competitors among investment bankers: For example, a June 1988 decision by the U.S. Supreme Court may have the effect of broadening competitive powers of U.S. *commercial* banks under the Glass Steagall Act. And the Congress may make even more substantial changes in the Glass Steagall Act by legislative action.

As with any other ecological system the mechanism of mutual adaptation is partly a random process. This is so because so much depends on the unknown behavior of competitors at some uncertain time in the future when the environment turns more competitive or more favorable. Consider a time when conditions for expansion look good, and when a refusal to expand may subject the firm to a nearly certain comparative reduction in client access *now,* and cuts off the higher returns available *now.* Consider further the position of a major multipurpose trading firm serving mainly institutional clients. That firm's management may believe that it will lose market share among institutional clients if it is not represented in a sufficiently wide set of capital markets, including new and innovative markets. That set of commitments distinguishes the major trading firm (from the specialty boutiques). If its management wishes to maintain market share on those terms, its scope for planning may then be restricted to a short-term or *tactical* planning effort.

Surrounding any ecological system (in which everyone's future value is explicitly made a function of the competitive interaction among participants) there is one last variable: the climate in which the finance ecology develops is conditioned by taxation and regulation. To a significant degree, the investment banker's freedom to innovate was able to grow because of the climate of deregulation. If there should be greater regulatory (or tax) constraints, fewer innovations would be worth developing. Further, transaction costs would probably be higher. By the industry thus being constrained to primarily routine transactions, strategic planning would then become feasible. It would also be a lot less important.

SUGGESTIONS FOR
FURTHER READING

The material covered by this book was restricted to U.S. firms and to their major activities as market makers. For this reason, I have avoided extensive coverage of *municipal securities, money market* issues, and *futures, options,* and *foreign exchange* markets. The decision to limit this book was made because many investment banking firms have not been important players in some of these markets and have dropped out of others. In addition, there are very good books available on each of these subjects. I offer the following suggestions as sources for further reading.

INVESTMENT BANKING BACKGROUND

Corrected Opinion of Harold R. Medina, in United States of America, Plaintiff *v.* Henry S. Morgan, Harold Stanley, et. al., Defendants, Filed February 4, 1954. (This document of some 400 pages is an excellent text covering the history and background of U.S. investment banking up to 1950.)

S. L. Hayes, A. M. Spence, D. V. P. Marks, *Competition in the Investment Banking Industry,* Harvard University Press, Cambridge, MA, 1983.

J. P. Williamson, ed., *The Investment Banking Handbook,* J. Wiley, New York, 1988.

FINANCIAL MARKETS

K. Garbade, *Securities Markets,* McGraw Hill, New York, 1982.

S. Levine, ed., *The Financial Analyst's Handbook,* 2nd ed., Dow Jones-Irwin, Homewood, IL, 1988.

R. A. Schwartz, *Equity Markets,* Harper & Row, New York, 1988.

R. Lamb, S. P. Rappaport, *Municipal Bonds,* 2nd ed., McGraw Hill, New York, 1987.

I. Walter, *Global Competition in Financial Services,* Ballinger, Cambridge, MA, 1988.

E. I. Altman, S. A. Nammacher, *Investing in Junk Bonds,* Wiley, New York, 1986.

J. Cox, M. Rubinstein, *Options Markets,* Prentice Hall, Englewood Cliffs, 1985.

S. Figlewski, *Hedging With Financial Futures,* Ballinger, Cambridge, MA, 1986.

R. C. Ferrara, M. M. Brown, J. H. Hall, *Takeovers—Attack and Survival,* Butterworth Legal Publishers, Stoneham, MA, 1987.

M. Stigum, *The Money Market,* rev. ed., Dow Jones-Irwin, Homewood, IL, 1983.

CORPORATE FINANCE, INVESTMENTS, AND PORTFOLIO ANALYSIS

The following books provide further reading in corporate decision making and the decision making of the financial institutions that constitute the major traders in capital markets.

R. A. Brealey, S. C. Myers, *Principles of Corporate Finance,* 3rd ed., McGraw Hill, New York, 1988.

E. J. Elton, M. J. Gruber, *Modern Portfolio Theory and Investment Analysis,* 3rd ed., Wiley, New York, 1987.

W. F. Sharpe, *Investments,* 3rd ed., Prentice Hall, Englewood Cliffs, 1985.

COMMON INVESTMENT BANKING AND FINANCIAL MARKET TERMS[1]

Accrued interest   Interest due from the issue or from the last coupon date to the present on an interest-bearing security. The buyer of the security pays the quoted dollar price plus accrued interest.

Acquired or target firm   The firm that is bought in a merger or acquisition.

Active   A market in which there is much trading.

Add-on rate   A specific rate of interest to be paid (in contrast to the rate on a discount security, such as a Treasury bill, that pays *no* interest).

Adjustable Rate Mortgage (ARM)   A type of mortgage in which the interest rate is periodically adjusted as market rates change.

After-tax real rate of return   Money after-tax rate of return minus the inflation rate.

Agencies   Federal agency securities.

Agent   A firm that executes orders for or otherwise acts on behalf of another (the principal) and is subject to its control and authority. The agent may receive a fee or a commmission.

All-in cost   Total costs, explicit and other. Example: In a swap the all-in rate to a fixed income payer *plus* the pro rata share of flotation costs added to the rate.

All or none (AON)   Requirement that none of an order be executed unless all of it can be executed at the specified price.

---

[1]This glossary is adapted in part from the glossary in Marcia L. Stigum and Rene O. Branch, Jr., *Managing Bank Assets and Liabilities* (Homewood, IL: Dow Jones-Irwin, 1983), pp. 397–418.

Annual report   A yearly report to shareholders containing financial statements (balance sheets, income statement, source and application, and funds statement), auditor's statement, president's letter, and various other information.

Arbitrage   Strictly defined, buying something where it is cheap and selling it where it is dear; for example, a bank buys three-month CD money in the U.S. market and sells three-month money at a higher rate in the Eurodollar market. In the money market, arbitrage often refers: (1) to a situation in which a trader buys one security and sells a similar security in the expectation that the spread in yields between the two instruments will narrow or widen his profit; (2) to a swap between two similar issues based on an anticipated change in yield spreads; and (3) to situations where a higher return (or lower cost) can be achieved in the money market for one currency by utilizing another currency and swapping it on a fully hedged basis through the foreign exchange market.

Arrearage   An overdue payment as in passed preferred dividends. If cumulative, arrearage must be made up before common dividends are resumed.

Asked price   The price at which securities are offered.

Auditor's statement   A letter from the auditor to the company and its shareholders in which the accounting firm certifies the propriety of the methods used to produce the firm's financial statements.

Away   A trade, quote, or market that does not originate with the dealer in question; for example, "the bid is 98–10 away (from me)."

Back up   (1) When yields rise and prices fall, the market is said to back up. (2) When an investor swaps out of one security into another of shorter current maturity (such as out of a two-year note into an 18-month note), he is said to back up.

Bank discount rate   Yield basis on which short-term noninterest-bearing money market securities are quoted. A rate quoted on a discount basis understates bond equivalent yield. That must be calculated when comparing return against coupon securities.

Bank line   A line of credit granted by a bank to a customer.

Bank wire   A computer message system linking major banks. It is used not for effecting payments but as a mechanism to advise the receiving bank of some action that has occurred, such as the customer's payment of funds into that bank's account.

Bankers' acceptance (BA)   A draft or bill of exchange accepted by a bank or trust company. The accepting institution guarantees payment of the bill.

Basis   (1) The number of days in the coupon period. (2) In commodities jargon, basis is the spread between a futures price and some other price. Money market participants talk about spread rather than basis.

Basis point   One one hundredth of 1 percent.

Basis price   The price expressed in terms of yield to maturity or annual rate of return.

Bear market   A declining market or a period of pessimism when declines in the market are anticipated. (A way to remember: "bear down.")

Bearer security   A security whose owner is not registered on the books of the issuer. A bearer security is payable to the holder.

Best-efforts basis   Securities dealers do not underwrite a new issue but sell it on the basis of what can be sold.

Bid price   The price offered for securities. (Demand price)

Bills   Government debt securities issued on a discount basis by the U.S. Treasury for periods of one year or less (Treasury bills).

Black/Scholes formula   An option pricing formula based on the assumption that a riskless hedge between an option and its underlying stock should yield the riskless return. Black/Scholes asserts that option value is a function of the stock price, striking price, stock return volatility, riskless interest rate, and option term.

Block   A large amount of securities, normally much more than what constitutes a round lot in the market in question. On the NYSE, a trade of 10,000 or more shares.

Bond   A debt obligation (usually long term) in which the borrower promises to pay a set coupon rate until the issue matures, at which time the principal is repaid. Some bond issues are secured by a mortgage on a specific property, plant, or piece of equipment. See also **Debenture.**

Bond anticipation notes (BANs)   Issued by states and municipalities to obtain interim financing for projects that will eventually be funded long term through the sale of a bond issue.

Bond swap   A technique for managing a bond portfolio by selling some bonds and buying others; may be designed for taxes, yields, or trading profits (also called asset swap).

Book-entry securities   The Treasury and federal agencies have moved to a book-entry system in which securities are not represented by engraved pieces of paper but are maintained by financial institutions in computerized records of the securities they own as well as those they are holding for customers. In the case of other securities for which there is a book-entry system, engraved securities do exist somewhere in quite a few instances. These securities do not move from holder to holder but are usually kept in a central clearinghouse or by another agent.

Book value   The value at which a debt security is shown on the holder's balance sheet. Book value is often acquisition cost ± amortization/accretion, which may differ markedly from market value. It can be further defined as "tax book," "accreted book," or "amortized book" value.

Bracketing   The group of underwriters in a syndication. The major investment banking firms come first, but they can be elsewhere. Other brackets are determined by participating underwriters' size and capacity to place securities.

Bridge financing   Interim financing of one sort or another.

Broker   A broker brings buyers and sellers together for a commission paid by the initiator of the transaction or by both sides; he does not position. In the money market, brokers are active in markets in which banks buy and sell money and in interdealer markets.

Broker call-loan rate or call-loan rate   The interest rate charged by banks for loans brokers use to support their margin loans to customers. The customer's margin loan rate is usually scaled up from the broker call-loan rate.

Bull market   A period of optimism when increases in market prices are anticipated. (A way to remember: "bull ahead.")

Buy-back   Another term for a repurchase agreement.

Calendar   List of new bond issues scheduled to come to market soon.

Call money   Interest-bearing bank deposits that can be withdrawn on 24-hours notice. Many Eurodeposits take the form of call money.

Call protection   An indenture provision preventing a security (usually a bond or preferred stock) from being redeemed earlier than a certain time after its issue. Thus a 20-year bond might not be callable for the first 5 years after its issue.

Callable bond   A bond that the issuer has the right to redeem prior to maturity by paying some specified call price.

Capital Asset Pricing Model (CAPM) A theoretical relationship that explains returns as a function of the risk-free rate and market risk.

Carry The interest cost of financing securities held. (See also **Negative carry** and **Positive carry.**)

Cash flow Reported profits (after tax) plus depreciation, depletion, and amortization.

Cash market Traditionally, this term has been used to denote the market in which commodities were traded, for immediate delivery, against cash. Since the inception of futures markets for T bills and other debt securities, a distinction has been made between the cash markets in which these securities trade for immediate delivery and the futures markets in which they trade for future delivery.

Cash settlement In the money market, a transaction is said to be made for cash settlement if the securities purchased are delivered against payment in Fed funds on the same day the trade is made.

Cathode-ray tubes (CRTs) Used to display market quotes.

Certificate of deposit (CD) A time deposit with a specific maturity evidenced by a certificate. Large-denomination CDs are typically negotiable.

CHIPS The New York Clearing House's computerized Clearing House Interbank Payments System. Most Euro transactions are cleared and settled through CHIPS rather than over the Fed wire.

Circle Underwriters, actual or potential as the case may be, often seek out and "circle" retail interest in a new issue before final pricing. The customer circled has basically made a commitment to purchase the note or bond or to purchase it if it comes at an agreed-on price. In the latter case, if the price is other than that stipulated, the customer supposedly has first offer at the actual price.

Clear A trade carried out by the seller delivering securities and the buyer delivering funds in proper form. A trade that does not clear is said to fail.

Clearing house In the options or futures market, the corporation that is responsible for matching buyers and sellers and for ensuring that traders fulfill their performance obligations.

Clearinghouse funds Payments made through the New York Clearing House's computerized Clearing House Interbank Payments System. Clearinghouse debits and credits used to be settled in Fed funds on the first business day after clearing. Since October 1981, these debits and credits have been settled on the same day in Fed funds.

Collateral   An asset pledged to assure repayment of debt.

Collateralized mortgage obligation (CMO)   One of several classes of bonds (short-term to long-term) issued against a pool of mortgages as collateral. Bond debt service is financed from mortgage payments.

Commercial paper   An unsecured promissory note with a fixed maturity of no more than 270 days. Commercial paper is normally sold at a discount from face value.

Commissions   Fees charged by brokers for handling securities trades.

Committed facility (line of credit)   A legal commitment undertaken by a bank to lend to a customer.

Competitive bid   (1) A bid tendered in a Treasury auction for a specific amount of securities at a specific yield or price. (2) Issuers such as municipalitites and public utilities often sell new issues by asking for competitive bids from at least two syndicates.

Compound interest   Returns are compounded by reinvesting one period's income to earn additional income the following period. Thus at 9 percent compounded annually, $100 will yield $9 the first year. In the following year, the 9 percent will be computed on $109 for a return of $9.81. In the third year the principal will have grown to $118.81 (100 + 9 + 9.81), and another 9 percent will add about $10.62. This process continues with the interest being applied to a larger and larger principal. Compounding may take place annually, as above, or more frequently.

Compound value   The end-period value of a sum earning a compounded return.

Confirmation   A memorandum to the other side of a trade describing all relevant data.

Consortium banks   A merchant banking subsidiary set up by several banks that may or may not be of the same nationality. Consortium banks are common in the Euromarket and are active in loan syndication.

Convertible bond   A bond containing a provision that permits conversion to the issuer's common stock at some fixed exchange ratio.

Corporate bond equivalent   See **Equivalent bond yield.**

Corporate taxable equivalent The rate of return required on a par bond to produce the same after-tax yield to maturity that the premium or discount quoted would.

Country risk See **Sovereign risk.**

Coupon (1) The annual rate of interest on the bond's face value that a bond's issuer promises to pay the bondholder. (2) A certificate attached to a bond evidencing interest due on a payment date.

Cover Eliminating a short position by buying the securities shorted.

Covered interest arbitrage Investing dollars in an instrument denominated in a foreign currency and hedging the resulting foreign exchange risk by selling the proceeds of the investment forward for dollars.

Credit risk The risk that an issuer of debt securities or a borrower may default on his obligations or that payment may not be made on the sale of a negotiable instrument. (See **Overnight delivery risk.**)

Cross hedge Hedging a risk in a cash market security by buying or selling a futures contract for a different but similar instrument.

Current coupon A bond selling at or close to par; that is, a bond with a coupon close to the yield currently offered on new bonds of similar maturity and credit risk.

Current issue In Treasury bills and notes, the most recently auctioned issue. Trading is more active in current issues than in off-the-run issues.

Current maturity Current time to maturity on an outstanding note, bond, or other money market instrument; for example, a five-year note one year after issue has a current maturity of four years.

Current yield Coupon payments on a security as a percentage of the security's market price.

Cushion bonds High-coupon bonds that sell at only a moderate premium because they are callable at a price below that at which a comparable noncallable bond would sell. Cushion bonds offer considerable downside protection in a falling market.

Day trading Intraday trading in securities for profit as opposed to investing for profit.

Dealer A dealer, as opposed to a broker, acts as a principal in all transactions, buying and selling for his own account.

Dealer loan Overnight, collateralized loan made to a dealer financing his position by borrowing from a money market bank.

Debenture   A bond secured only by the general credit of the issuer.

Debt-to-equity ratio   The ratio of the dollar amount of debt outstanding to the value of equity outstanding.

Debt leverage   The amplification in the return earned on equity funds when an investment is financed partly with borrowed money.

Debt securities   IOUs created through loan-type transactions—commercial paper, bank CDs, bills, bonds, and other instruments.

Default   Failure to make timely payment of interest or principal on a debt security or to otherwise comply with the provisions of a bond indenture.

Demand line of credit   A bank line of credit that enables a customer to borrow on a daily or an on-demand basis.

Designated Order Turnaround System   (DOT, sometimes called SuperDot) is an electronic order-routing system through which member firms of NYSE transmit orders directly to post where security is traded; after execution, report is returned electronically to member firm.

Direct paper   Commercial paper sold directly by the issuer to investors.

Direct placement   Selling a new issue not by offering it for sale publicly but placing it with one or several institutional investors.

Discount basis   See **Bank discount rate.**

Discount bond   A bond selling below par.

Discount paper   See **Discount securities.**

Discount rate   The rate of interest charged by the Fed to member banks that borrow at the discount window. The discount rate is an add-on rate.

Discount securities   Non-interest-bearing money market instruments that are issued at a discount and redeemed at maturity for full face value; for example, U.S. Treasury bills.

Discount window   A facility provided by the Fed enabling member banks to borrow reserves against collateral in the form of governments or acceptable paper.

Disintermediation   The investing of funds that would normally have been placed with a bank or other financial intermediary directly into debt securities issued by ultimate borrowers; for example, into bills or bonds.

Distributed   After a Treasury auction, there will be many new issues in dealers' hands. As those securities are sold to retail, the issue is said to be distributed.

Diversification   Dividing investment funds among a variety of securities offering independent returns.

Divestiture or spinoff   The disposal of some part of a firm's operations in the form of a newly created company.

DM   Deutsche (German) marks.

Documented discount notes   Commercial paper backed by normal bank lines plus a letter of credit from a bank stating that it will pay off the paper at maturity if the borrower does not. Such paper is also referred to as LOC (letter of credit) paper.

Dollar bonds   Municipal revenue bonds for which quotes are given in dollar prices. Not to be confused with U.S. Dollar bonds, a common term of reference in the Euro bond market.

Dollar price of a bond   The percentage of face value at which a bond is quoted.

Don't know (DK, DKed)   "Don't know the trade"—a street expression used whenever one party lacks knowledge of a trade or receives conflicting instructions from the other party (for example, with respect to payment).

Due bill   An instrument evidencing the obligation of a seller to deliver securities sold to the buyer. Occasionally used in the bill market.

Dun & Bradstreet   A firm that rates the creditworthiness of many borrowers and generates financial ratios on many industry groups.

Duration   The weighed average (present value) rate of return of a bond's principal and interest.

Dutch auction   An auction in which the lowest price necessary to sell the entire offering becomes the price at which all securities offered are sold. This technique has been used in Treasury auctions.

Earnings per common share (EPS)   The net income of a company—minus any preferred dividend requirements—divided by the number of outstanding common shares.

Effective (or going effective)   The SEC has finished examination of the offering statement and will permit the deal to take place.

Efficient-market hypothesis The theory that the market correctly prices securities in light of the known relevant information. In its weak form, the hypothesis implies that past price and volume data (technical analysis) cannot be profitably used in stock selection. The semistrong form implies that no superior analysis of public data can improve stock selection consistently. In the hypothesis' strong form, even inside (nonpublic) information is thought to be reflected accurately in prices.

Eligible bankers' acceptances In the BA market an acceptance may be referred to as eligible because it is acceptable by the Fed as collateral at the discount window and/or because the accepting bank can sell it without incurring a reserve requirement.

Employee Retirement Income Security Act (ERISA) A 1974 federal law that protects workers' pension funds.

Equity Net worth; assets minus nonequity liabilities. The stockholder's residual ownership position.

Equivalent bond yield The annual yield on a short-term, non-interest-bearing security calculated so as to be comparable to yields quoted on coupon securities.

Equivalent taxable yield The yield on a taxable security that would leave the investor with the same after-tax return he would earn by holding a tax-exempt municipal; for example, for an investor taxed at a 50 percent marginal rate, equivalent taxable yield on a muni note issued at 3 percent would be 6 percent.

Euro bonds Bonds issued in Europe outside the confines of any national capital market. A Euro bond may or may not be denominated in the currency of the issuer.

Euro CDs CDs issued by a U.S. bank branch or foreign bank located outside the United States. Almost all Euro CDs are issued in London.

Euro lines Lines of credit granted by banks (foreign or foreign branches of U.S. banks) for Eurocurrencies.

Eurocurrency deposits Deposits made in a bank or bank branch that is not located in the country in whose currency the deposit is denominated. Dollars deposited in a London bank are Eurodollars; German marks deposited there are Euromarks.

Eurodollars U.S. dollars deposited in a U.S. bank branch or a foreign bank outside the United States.

Exchange rate *See* **Foreign exchange rate.**

Exempt securities   Instruments exempt from the registration requirements of the Securities Act of 1933 or the margin requirements of the Securities and Exchange Act of 1934. Such securities
include governments, agencies, municipal securities, commercial
paper, and private placements.

Expected value   The mean, or average, value of a random variable.

Extension swap   Extending maturity through a swap; for example,
selling a two-year note and buying one with a slightly longer current maturity.

Face value   The maturity value of a bond or other debt instrument;
sometimes referred to as the bond's par value.

Fail   A trade is said to fail if on settlement date either the seller fails
to deliver the securities in proper form or the buyer fails to deliver
the funds in proper form.

Fed (The Federal Reserve System)   The federal government
agency that exercises monetary policy through its control over
banking system reserves.

Fed funds   See **Federal funds.**

Fed wire   A computer system linking member banks to the Fed; used
for making interbank payments of Fed funds and for making de-
liveries of and payments for Treasury and agency securities.

Federal credit agencies   Agencies of the federal government set up
to supply credit to various classes of institutions and individuals;
for example, S&Ls, small business firms, students, farmers, farm
cooperatives, and exporters.

Federal Deposit Insurance Corporation (FDIC)   A federal institution that insures bank deposits, currently up to $100,000 per
deposit.

Federal funds   (1) Non-interest bearing deposits held by member
banks at the Federal Reserve. (2) Used to denote "immediate available" funds in the clearing sense.

Federal funds rate   The rate of interest at which Fed funds are
traded. This rate is influenced by the Federal Reserve through
open-market operations.

Federal Home Loan Banks (FHLB)   The institutions that regulate
and lend to savings and loan associations. The Federal Home Loan
Banks play a role analogous to that played by the Federal Reserve
banks vis-à-vis member commercial banks.

Federal Reserve Board of Governors   The governing body of the

Federal Reserve System. The seven members are appointed by the president for long and staggered terms.

Firm   Refers to an order to buy or sell that can be executed without confirmation for some fixed period.

Fixed dates   In the Euromarket the standard periods for which Euros are traded (one month to a year) are referred to as the fixed dates.

Fixed pricing   The way an IPO is priced. The night before the offering the managing underwriters price the deal. The underwriters up to a certain time after the deal is priced each have the right to reject being an underwriter.

Fixed-rate loan   A loan on which the rate paid by the borrower is fixed for the life of the loan.

Flat trades   (1) A bond in default trades flat; that is, the price quoted covers both principal and unpaid accrued interest. (2) Any security that trades without accrued interest.

Floating-rate note   A note that pays an interest rate tied to current money market rates. The holder may have the right to demand redemption at par on specified dates.

Floating supply   The amount of securities believed to be available for immediate purchase; that is, in the hands of dealers and investors available for sale.

Flotation   The initial sale of a security.

Flotation cost   The total cost of issuing a new security.

Flower bonds   Government bonds that are acceptable at par in payment of federal estate taxes when owned by the decedent at the time of death.

Footings   A British expression for the bottom line of an institution's balance sheet; total assets equal total liabilities plus net worth.

Foreign bond   A bond issued by a nondomestic borrower in the domestic capital market.

Foreign exchange rate   The price at which one currency trades for another.

Foreign exchange risk   The risk that a long or short position in a foreign currency might, due to an adverse movement in the relevant exchange rate, will have to be closed out at a loss. The long or short position may arise out of a financial or commercial transaction.

Forward Fed funds Fed funds traded for future delivery.

Forward market A market in which participants agree to trade some commodity, security, or foreign exchange at a fixed price at some future date.

Forward rate The rate at which forward transactions in some specific maturity are being made; for example, the dollar price at which DM can be bought for delivery three months hence.

Free reserves Excess reserves minus member bank borrowings at the Fed.

Full-coupon bond A bond with a coupon equal to the going market rate and consequently selling at or near par.

Futures market A market in which contracts for future delivery of a commodity or a security are bought and sold; the organized exchange on which contracts are traded.

Gap A mismatch between the maturities of a bank's assets and liabilities.

Gapping Mismatching the maturities of a bank's assets and liabilities, usually by borrowing short and lending long.

General obligation bond Municipal securities secured by the issuer's pledge of its full faith, credit, and taxing power.

General partner A partner with unlimited liability.

Give up The loss in yield that occurs when a block of bonds is swapped for another block of lower-coupon bonds. Can also be applied to the sharing of commission income by one broker with another (pre-1975).

Glass–Steagall Act A 1933 federal act requiring the separation of commercial and investment banking.

Go-around When the Fed offers to buy securities, to sell securities, to do repos, or to do reverses, it solicits competitive bids or offers, as the case may be, from all primary dealers. This procedure is known as a go-around.

Golden parachute A very generous termination agreement for upper management; takes effect if control of the firm shifts.

Good delivery A delivery in which everything—endorsement, any necessary attached legal papers, and so on—is in order.

Government National Mortgage Association (GNMA) A government agency that provides special assistance on selected types of mortgages. Its securities are backed both by its mortgage portfolios and by the general credit of the government.

Governments Negotiable U.S. Treasury securities.

Green Shoe Overallotment option granted by the company to the managing underwriter to purchase an additional 10 to 15 percent of the offering if needed. This option has to be exercised less than eight days after the deal. For IPOs there is a Green Shoe option in almost every deal. This gives the manager extra flexibility in creating the proper environment for the offering.

Greenmail The practice of acquiring a large percentage of a firm's stock and then threatening to take over the firm unless management buys you out at a premium.

Gross spread The difference between the price that the issuer receives for its securities and the price that investors pay for them. This spread equals the selling concession plus the management and underwriting fees.

Haircut Wall Street jargon for ratio of equity capital (relative to borrowed funds) required of members of organized exchanges. That ratio rises with the riskiness of the assets held. The ratio is set by self-regulating organizations for their members.

Handle The whole-dollar price of a bid or offer is referred to as the handle. For example, if a security is quoted 101-10 bid and 101-11 offered, 101 is the handle. Traders are assumed to know the handle, so a trader would quote that market to another by saying he was at 10-11. (The 10 and 11 refer to 32nds.)

Hedge To reduce risk (1) by taking a position in futures equal and opposite to an existing or anticipated cash position or (2) by shorting a security similar to one in which a long position has been established.

Hedge ratio In the futures or options market, the number of contracts to trade per unit of a spot position in order to offset the price variability in the spot position.

Histogram A bar chart displaying a probability distribution in which the assigned probabilities add up to 100 percent.

Hit A dealer who agrees to sell at the bid price quoted by another dealer is said to hit that bid.

In the box This means that a dealer has a wire receipt for securities indicating that effective delivery on them has been made. This jargon is a holdover from the time when Treasuries took the form of physical securities and were stored in a rack.

Indenture of a bond   A legal statement spelling out the obligations of the bond issuer and the rights of the bondholder.

Insider   A person with material knowledge about the operation of a firm.

Insider trading   Buying or selling by persons having access to non-public information relating to the company in question.

Institutional pot   That portion of the underwriting that has been set aside to satisfy the demands from major institutional investors.

Interest rate exposure   Risk of gain or loss to which an institution is exposed due to possible changes in interest-rate levels.

IPO   Initial public offering.

Joint account   An agreement between two or more firms to share risk and financing responsibility in purchasing or underwriting securities.

Junk bonds   High-risk bonds carrying high yields that have below investment grade credit ratings or are in default.

Lettered stock   Newly issued stock sold at a discount to large investors prior to a public offering of the same issue. Lettered stock buyers agree not to sell their shares for a prespecified period. SEC Rule 144 restricts such sales (sometimes called "restricted" stock).

Leverage   See **Debt leverage.**

Leveraged lease   The lessor provides only a minor portion of the cost of the leased equipment, borrowing the rest from another lender.

Lifting a leg   Closing out one side of a long-short arbitrage before the other is closed.

Line of credit   An arrangement by which a bank agrees to lend to the line holder during some specified period any amount up to the full amount of the line.

Liquidity   A liquid asset is one that can be converted easily and rapidly into cash without a substantial loss of value. In the stock or money markets a security is said to be liquid if the spread between the bid and asked prices is narrow, and reasonable size can be done at those quotes.

Liquidity diversification   Investing in a variety of maturities to reduce the price risk to which holding long bonds exposes the investor.

Liquidity risk   In banking, the risk that monies needed to fund may not be available in sufficient quantities at some future date. Implies an imbalance in committed maturities of assets and liabilities.

London Interbank Offered Rates (LIBOR)   Rate on Eurodollar deposits traded between banks. There is a different LIBOR rate for each deposit maturity. Different banks may quote slightly different LIBOR rates because they use different reference banks.

Long   (1) Owning a debt security, stock, or other asset. (2) Owning more than one has contracted to deliver.

Long bonds   Bonds with a long current maturity.

Long coupons   (1) Bonds or notes with a long current maturity. (2) A bond in which one of the coupon periods, usually the first, is longer than the others or longer than standard.

Long hedge   The purchase of a futures contract to lock in the yield at which the person stands ready to buy and sell.

Make a market   A dealer is said to make a market when he quotes bid and offered prices at which he stands ready to buy and sell (i.e., price making).

Manager bills and delivers   The managing underwriter actually confirms the securities sold on behalf of the other underwriters and delivers the new stock for those underwriters. The buyer only receives one piece of paper rather than 100 different pieces of paper with orders on them.

Manager and co-manager   The manager's responsibility is to control the books, road shows, and prospectus. The co-manager might only have one responsibility and that is to sell X amount of stock.

Margin   Borrowing to finance a portion of a securities purchase. The Fed regulates the extent of margin borrowing by setting the margin rate (according to Regulations T and U). If a 60 percent rate is set, $10,000 worth of stock may be purchased with up to $4,000 of borrowed money. Only listed and some large OTC companies' securities qualify for margin loans.

Margin call   The demand from a broker for an investor to deposit additional margin funds with a broker.

Marginal tax rate   The tax rate that would have to be paid on an additional dollar of taxable income earned.

Market value   The price at which a security is trading and could presumably be purchased or sold.

Marketability   A negotiable security is said to have good marketability if there is an active secondary market in which it can easily be resold.

Mark-to-market Practice of recomputing equity position in a margin account (stock or futures) on a daily basis. May also refer to bond valuation as rates change.

Merchant bank A British term for a bank that specializes not in lending out its own funds but in providing various financial services such as accepting bills arising out of trade, underwriting new issues, and providing advice on acquisitions, mergers, foreign exchange, and portfolio management. In U.S. usage also includes bridge loans in takeover deals.

Merger or acquisition The combination of two or more firms, with the result being a single independent company.

Mismatch A mismatch between the interest rate maturities of a bank's assets and liabilities. See also **Gap** and **Unmatched book.**

Money market The market in which short-term debt instruments (such as bills, commercial paper, and bankers' acceptances) are issued and traded.

Money market (center) bank A bank that is one of the nation's largest and consequently plays an active and important role in every sector of the money market.

Money market fund A mutual fund that invests solely in money market instruments.

Money rate of return The annual money return as a percentage of asset value.

Money supply definitions currently used by the Fed
M-1: Currency plus demand deposits and other checkable deposits.
M-2: M-1 plus overnight RPs and money market funds and savings and small (less than $100,000) time deposits.
M-3: M-2 plus large time deposits and term RPs.

Mortgage-backed security A debt instrument representing a share of, for example, GNMA pass-throughs, or backed by FNMA bonds; a pool of mortgages.

Mortgage bond A bond secured by a lien on property, equipment, or other real assets.

Multicurrency clause Such a clause on a Euro loan permits the borrower to switch from one currency to another on a rollover date.

Municipal (muni) notes   Short-term notes issued by municipalities in anticipation of tax receipts, proceeds from a bond issue, or other revenues.

Municipals   Securities issued by state and local governments and their agencies.

Naked position   A long or short position that is not hedged.

National Association of Security Dealers (NASD)   The self-regulator of the OTC market and umbrella group for all broker-dealers.

National Association of Security Dealers Automated Quotations (NASDAQ)   The name applied to stock quotation machines of NASD.

National banks   National banks are federally chartered banks that are subject to supervision by the Comptroller of the Currency. State banks, in contrast, are state chartered and state regulated.

Negative carry   The net cost incurred when the cost of carry exceeds the return from the securities being financed.

Negotiable certificate of deposit   A large-denomination (generally $1 million) CD that can be sold but cannot be cashed in before maturity.

Negotiable order of withdrawal (NOW) accounts   These amount to checking accounts on which depository institutions (banks and thrifts) may pay a rate of interest.

Negotiated sale   A situation in which the terms of an offering are determined by negotiation between the issuer and the underwriter rather than through competitive bidding by underwriting groups.

New-issues market   The market in which a new issue of securities is first sold to investors.

New money   In a Treasury refunding, the amount by which the par value of the securities offered exceeds that of those maturing.

Noncompetitive bid   In a Treasury auction, bidding for a specific amount of securities at the price, whatever it may turn out to be, equal to the average price of the accepted competitive bid.

Nonperforming loan   A loan on which interest is not paid as it accrues. Since banks are examined only periodically, a nonperforming loan may or may not be classified.

Note   Coupon issues with a relatively short original maturity are often called notes. Muni notes, however, have maturities ranging from a month to a year and pay interest only at maturity. Treasury notes are coupon securities that have an original maturity of up to 10 years.

Odd lot   Less than a round lot.

Off-balance-sheet financing   Financing that does not appear on the balance sheet. See **Swaps.**

Off-the-run issue   In Treasuries and agencies, an issue that is not included in dealer or broker runs. With bills and notes, normally only current issues are quoted.

Offer   Price asked by a seller of securities.

One-sided (one-way) market   A market in which only one side, the bid or the asked, is quoted or firm.

Open book   See **Unmatched book.**

Open repo   A repo with no definite term. The agreement is made on a day-to-day basis, and either the borrower or the lender may choose to terminate. The rate paid is higher than on an overnight repo and is subject to adjustment if rates move.

Opportunity cost   The cost of pursuing one course of action measured in terms of the forgone return offered by the most-attractive alternative.

Option   (1) **Call option:** A contract sold for a price that gives the holder the right to buy from the writer of the option, over a specified period, a specified amount of securities at a specified price. (2) **Put option:** A contract sold for a price that gives the holder the right to sell to the writer of the contract, over a specified period, a specified amount of securities at a specified price.

Original maturity   The maturity at issue. For example, a five-year note has an original maturity at issue of five years; one year later it has a current maturity of four years.

Over-the-counter (OTC) market   Market created by dealer trading as opposed to the auction market prevailing on organized exchanges.

Overnight delivery risk   A risk brought about because differences in time zones between settlement centers require that payment or delivery on one side of a transaction be made without knowing until the next day whether funds have been received in account on the other side. Particularly apparent where delivery takes place in Europe for payment of dollars in New York.

Pac-Man defense   A tactic used to avoid takeover by attempting to take over the attacking firm.

Paper   Money market instruments, commercial paper, and other.

Paper gain (loss)   Unrealized capital gain (loss) on securities held in portfolio, based on a comparison of current market price and original cost.

Par   (1) Price of 100 percent. (2) The principal amount at which the issuer of a debt security contracts to redeem that security at maturity, *face value.*

Par bond   A bond selling at par (usually $1,000 per bond).

Pass-through   A mortgage-backed security on which payment of interest and principal on the underlying mortgages are passed through to the security holder by an agent.

Paydown   In a Treasury refunding, the amount by which the par value of the securities maturing exceeds that of those sold.

Pay-up   (1) The loss of cash resulting from a swap into higher-price bonds. (2) The need (or willingness) of a bank or other borrower to pay a higher rate to get funds.

Pension fund   A fund created for the purpose of paying pensions to retired employees.

P/E ratio   The stock price relative to the most recent 12-month earnings per share.

Pickup   The gain in yield that occurs when a block of bonds is swapped for another block of higher-coupon bonds.

Picture   The bid and asked prices quoted by a broker for a given security.

Placement   A bank depositing Eurodollars with or selling Eurodollars to another bank is often said to be making a placement.

Plus   Dealers in governments normally quote bids and offers in 32nds. To quote a bid or offer in 64ths, they use pluses; for example, a dealer who bids 4 + is bidding the handle plus $4/32 + 1/64$, which equals the handle plus 9/64.

Point   (1) 100 basis points = 1 percent. (2) One percent of the face value of a note or bond. (3) In the foreign exchange market, the lowest level at which the currency is priced. Example: One point is the difference between sterling prices of $1.8080 and $1.8081.

Poison pill   An antitakeover defense in which a new diluting security is issued to existing shareholders if control of the firm is about to shift.

Portfolio   The collection of securities held by an investor.

Position   (1) To go long or short in a security. (2) The amount of securities owned (long position) or owed (short position).

Positive carry   The net gain earned when the cost of carry is less than the return on the securities being financed.

Preemptive rights   Shareholder rights to maintain their proportional share of their firm by subscribing proportionally to any new stock issue.

Premium   (1) The amount by which the price of an issue being traded exceeds the issue's par value. (2) The amount that must be paid in excess of par to call or refund an issue before maturity. (3) In money market parlance, the fact that a particular bank's CDs trade at a rate higher than others of its class or that a bank has to pay up to acquire funds.

Premium bond   A bond selling above par.

Prepayment   A payment made ahead of the scheduled payment date.

Present value   The value of a future sum or sums discounted by the appropriate discount rate, or factor (D.F.).

Presold issue   An issue that is sold out before the coupon announcement.

Price risk   The risk that a debt security's price may change due to a rise or fall in the going level of interest rates.

Prime rate   The rate at which banks lend to their best (prime) customers. The all-in cost of a bank loan to a prime credit equals the prime rate plus the cost of holding compensating balances.

Principal   (1) The face amount or par value of a debt security. (2) A person who acts as a dealer buying and selling for his own account. (3) An officer of an investment banking firm.

Private placement   An issue that is offered to a single or a few investors as opposed to being publicly offered. Private placements do not have to be registered with the SEC.

Project notes (PNs)   Issued by municipalities to finance federally sponsored programs in urban renewal and housing. They are guaranteed by the U.S. Department of Housing and Urban Development.

Prospectus   A detailed statement prepared by an issuer and filed with the SEC prior to the sale of a new issue. The prospectus gives detailed information on the issue's conditions and the company's financing.

Put   See **Option.**

Put bond   A bond with an indenture provision allowing it to be sold back to the issuer at a prespecified price.

Rate risk   In banking, the risk that profits may decline or losses occur because a rise in interest rates forces up the cost of funding fixed-rate loans or other fixed-up assets.

Ratings   An evaluation given by Moody's, Standard & Poor's, Fitch, or other rating services of a security's credit worthiness.

Real market   The bid and offer prices at which a dealer could do size. Quotes in the brokers' market may reflect not the real market but pictures painted by dealers playing trading games.

Reallowance   On a new issue distribution, members of the NASD may buy and sell from each other at the reallowance concession. NASD members are able to buy and sell securities at a discount from one another.

Red herring   A preliminary prospectus containing all the information required by the Securities and Exchange Commission except the offering price and coupon of a new issue.

Refunding   Redemption of securities by funds raised through the sale of a new issue.

Registered bond   A bond whose owner is registered with the issuer.

Registration statement   A statement that must be filed with the SEC before a security is offered for sale. The statement must contain all materially relevant information relating to the offering. A similar type of statement is required when a firm's shares are listed.

Regular-way settlement   In the money and bond markets, the regular basis on which some security trades are settled is that delivery of the securities purchased is made against payment in Fed funds on the day following the transaction.

Regulation Q   A Fed rule that limits interest rates that bank and thrifts can pay on certain types of deposits/investments. Deregulation has largely eliminated the regulation's effect.

Regulation T   A Fed rule that governs credit to brokers and dealers for security purchases.

Regulation U   A Fed rule that governs margin credit limits.

Reinvestment rate   (1) The rate at which an investor assumes interest payments made on a debt security can be reinvested over the life of that security. (2) The rate at which funds from a maturity or sale of a security can be reinvested. Often used in comparison to give-up yield.

Relative value The attractiveness—measured in terms of risk, liquidity, and return—of one instrument relative to another or for a given instrument of one maturity relative to another.

Reopen an issue The Treasury, when it wants to sell additional securities, will occasionally sell more of an existing issue (reopen it) rather than offer a new issue.

Repo See **Repurchase agreement.**

Repurchase agreement (RP or repo) A holder of securities sells these securities to an investor with an agreement to repurchase them at a fixed price on a fixed date. The security buyer in effect lends the seller money for the period of the agreement, and the terms of the agreement are structured to compensate him for this. Dealers use RP extensively to finance their positions. Exceptiion: When the Fed is said to be doing RP, it is lending money; that is, increasing bank reserves.

Reserve requirements The percentages of different types of deposits that member banks are required to hold on deposit at the Fed, or in currency.

Retail Individual and institutional customers as opposed to dealers and brokers.

Revenue anticipation notes (RANs) These are issued by states and municipalities to finance current expenditures in anticipation of the future receipt of nontax revenues.

Revenue bond A municipal bond secured by revenue from tolls, user charges, or rents derived from the facility financed.

Reverse See **Reverse repurchase agreement.**

Reverse repurchase agreement Most typically, a repurchase agreement initiated by the lender of funds. Reverses are used by dealers to borrow securities they have shorted. Exception: When the Fed is said to be doing reverses, it is borrowing money; that is, absorbing reserves.

Revolver See **Revolving line of credit.**

Revolving line of credit A bank line of credit on which the customer pays a commitment fee and can take down and repay funds according to his needs. Normally the line involves a firm commitment from the bank for a period of several years.

Right A security allowing shareholders to acquire new stock at a prespecified price over a prespecified period. Rights are generally issued proportional to the number of shares currently held and are normally exercisable at a specified price, usually below the current market. Rights usually trade in a secondary market after they are issued.

Risk The degree of uncertainty of the return on an asset.

Risk arbitrage Taking offsetting positions in the securities of an acquisition candidate and its would-be acquirer.

Roll over Reinvest funds received from a maturing security in a new issue of the same or a similar security.

Rollover Most term loans in the Euromarket are made on a rollover basis, which means that the loan is periodically repriced at an agreed spread over the appropriate, currently prevailing LIBOR rate.

Round lot In the money market, round lot refers to the minimum amount for which dealers' quotes are good. This may range from $100,000 to $5 million, depending on the size and liquidity of the issue traded. On the NYSE, this is 100 shares.

RP See **Repurchase agreement.**

Rule 415 An SEC rule allowing shelf registration of a security which may then be sold at issuer's decision without separate registrations of each part.

Run A run consists of a series of bid and asked for quotes for different maturities. Dealers give to, and ask for runs from, each other.

Running the books, or book-running manager The manager who has total control over an offering (usually appears on the upper left of the list of underwriters in a tombstone advertisement).

S&L See **Savings and loan association.**

Safekeep For a fee, banks will safekeep (that is, hold in their vault, clip coupons on, and present for payment at maturity) bonds and money market instruments.

Sale repurchase agreement See **Repurchase agreement.**

Savings and loan association A federal- or state-chartered institution that accepts savings deposits and invests the bulk of the funds thus received in mortgages.

Savings deposit An interest-bearing deposit at a savings institution that has no specific maturity.

Scale A bank that offers to pay different rates of interest on CDs of varying maturities is said to post a scale. Commercial paper issuers also post scales.

Seasoned issue An issue that has been well distributed and trades well in the secondary market.

Secondary distribution A large public securities offering made outside the usual exchange or OTC market (often underwritten). Those making the offering wish to sell more of the security than they believe can be easily absorbed by the market's usual channels. A secondary offering spreads out the period for absorption.

Secondary market The market in which previously issued securities are traded

Sector A group of securities that are similar with respect to maturity, type, rating, and/or coupon.

Securities and Exchange Commission (SEC) An agency created by Congress to protect investors in securities transactions by administering securities legislation.

Selling concession The portion of the gross spread that brokers receive for selling underwritten securities.

Selling group Those firms that are not members of the underwriting group who want to participate on a registered distribution.

Serial bonds A bond issue in which maturities are staggered over a number of years.

Settle See **Clear.**

Settlement date The date on which a trade is cleared by delivery of securities against funds. The settlement date may be the trade date or a later date.

Shell branch A foreign branch—usually in a tax haven—which engages in Eurocurrency business but is run out of a head office.

Shop In street jargon, a money market or bond dealership.

Shopping Seeking to obtain the best bid or offer available by calling a number of dealers and/or brokers.

Short A market participant assumes a short position by selling a security he does not own. The seller makes delivery by borrowing the security sold or reversing it in. (See also **Short sale.**)

Short bonds Bonds with a short current maturity.

Short book See **Unmatched book.**

Short coupons   Bonds or notes with a short current maturity.

Short hedge   The sale of a futures contract to hedge, for example, a position in cash securities or an anticipated borrowing need.

Short sale   The sale of securities not owned by the seller in the expectation that the price of these securities will fall or as part of an arbitrage. A short sale must eventually be covered by a purchase of the securities sold.

Sinking fund   Indentures on corporate issues often require that the issuer make annual payments to a sinking fund, the proceeds of which are used to retire randomly selected bonds in the issue. Another type of sinking fund permits the issuer to retire the bond by a market purchase.

Size   Large in size, as in "size offering" or "in there for size." What constitutes size varies with the sector of the market.

Sovereign risk   The special risk, if any, that attaches to a security (or deposit or loan) because the borrower's country of residence differs from that of the investor's. Also referred to as country risk.

Specialist   An exchange member who makes a market in listed securities.

Spot market   The market for immediate as opposed to future delivery. In the spot market for foreign exchange, settlement is two business days ahead.

Spot rate   The price prevailing in the spot market.

Spread   (1) The difference between bid and asked prices on a security. (2) The difference between yields on or prices of two securities of differing sorts or differing maturities. (3) In underwriting, the difference between the price realized by the issuer and the price paid by the investor. (4) The difference between two prices or two rates. What a commodities trader would refer to as the basis.

Spreading   In the futures market, buying one futures contract and selling a nearby one to profit from an anticipated narrowing or widening of the spread over time.

Stabilization   Maintaining an orderly market at or below the offering price. A managing underwriter can be a buyer of the deal's stock in, for example, a cold market. This helps to stabilize the price of the stock. One other way of stabilizing the price of the stock is by going short.

Stop-out price   The lowest price (highest yield) accepted by the Treasury in an auction of a new issue.

Street The brokers, dealers, and other knowledgeable members of the financial community; from the Wall Street financial community.

Subject Refers to a bid or offer that cannot be executed without confirmation from the customer.

Subordinated debenture The claims of holders of this issue rank after those of holders of various other unsecured debts incurred by the issuer.

Swap (1) In securities, selling one issue and buying another. (2) In foreign exchange, buying a currency spot and simultaneously selling it forward. (3) In liability swaps, exchanging fixed for variable liabilities (in banks these are carried off the balance sheet).

Swap rate In the foreign exchange market, the difference between the spot and forward rates at which a currency is traded.

Swing line See **Demand line of credit.**

Switch British English for a swap; that is, buying a currency spot and selling it forward.

Syndicate A group of investment bankers organized to underwrite a new issue or secondary offering.

Tail (1) The difference between the average price in Treasury auctions and the stop-out price. (2) A future money market instrument (one available some period hence) created by buying an existing instrument and financing the initial portion of its life with a term RP.

Take (1) A dealer or customer who agrees to buy at another dealer's offered price is said to take that offer. (2) Eurobankers speak of taking deposits rather than buying money.

Take-out (1) A cash surplus generated by the sale of one block of securities and the purchase of another; for example, selling a block of bonds at 99 and buying another at 95. (2) A bid made to the seller of a security that is designed (and generally agreed) to take him out of the market.

Takeover bid A tender offer designed to acquire a sufficient number of shares to achieve working control of the target firm.

Taking a view A London expression for forming an opinion as to where interest rates are going and acting on it.

Tax anticipation bills (TABs) Special bills that the Treasury occasionally issues. They mature on corporate quarterly income tax dates and can be used at face value by corporations to pay their tax liabilities.

Tax anticipation notes (TANs)   Issued by states or municipalities to finance current operations in anticipation of future tax receipts.

Target firm   See **Acquired firm.**

Technical condition of a market   Demand and supply factors affecting price, in particular the net position—long or short—of dealers.

Tender offer   An offer to purchase a large block of securities made outside the general market in which the securities are traded (exchanges, OTC).

Term bonds   A bond issue in which all bonds mature at the same time.

Term Fed funds   Fed funds sold for a period of time longer than overnight.

Term loan   A loan extended by a bank for more than the normal 90-day period. A term loan might run five years or more.

Term RP (repo)   RP borrowings for a period longer than overnight, may be 30, 60, or even 90 days.

Thin market   A market in which trading volume is low and in which consequently bid and asked quotes are wide and the liquidity of the instrument traded is low.

Tight market   A tight market, as opposed to a thin market, is one in which volume is large, trading is active and highly competitive, and spreads between bid and ask prices are narrow.

Time deposit   An interest-bearing deposit at a savings institution that has a specific maturity.

Trade date   The date on which a transaction is initiated. The settlement date may be the trade date or a later date.

Trade on top of   Trade at a narrow or no spread in basis points to some other instrument.

Treasury bill   A non-interest-bearing discount security issued by the U.S. Treasury to finance the national debt. Most bills are issued to mature in three months, six months, or one year.

Trustee   A bank or other third party which administers the provisions of a bond indenture or of an asset portfolio.

TT&L account   A Treasury tax and loan account at a bank.

Turnaround Securities bought and sold for settlement on the same day.

Turnaround time The time available or needed to effect a turnaround.

Two-sided market A market in which both bid and asked prices, good for the standard unit of trading, are quoted.

Two-way market A market in which both a bid and an asked price are quoted.

Underwriter A dealer who purchases new issues from the issuer and distributes them to investors. Underwriting is one function of an investment banker.

Variable-price security A security, such as stocks and bonds, that sells at a fluctuating, market-determined price.

Variable-rate CDs Short-term CDs that pay interest periodically on *roll* dates; on each roll date the coupon on the CD is adjusted to reflect current market rates.

Variable-rate loan Loan made at an interest rate that fluctuates with the prime. (See also **Floating rate note.**)

Venture capital Risk capital extended to start-up or small going concerns.

Visible supply New muni bond issues scheduled to come to market within the next 30 days.

Warrants Certificates offering the right to purchase stock in a company at a specified time over a specified period.

When-issued trades Typically there is a lag between the time a new bond is announced and sold and the time it is actually issued. During this interval, the security trades "wi"—"when, as, if issued."

Wi When, as, if issued. See **When-issued trades.**

Wi wi T bills trade on a wi basis between the day they are auctioned and the day settlement is made. Bills traded before they are auctioned are said to be traded wi wi.

Wire house An exchange member electronically linked to an exchange.

Without If 70 were bid in the market and there was no offer, the quote would be "70 bid without." The expression *without* indicates a one-way market.

Yankee bond A foreign bond issued in the U.S. market, payable in dollars, and registered with the SEC.

Yield curve   A graph showing, for securities that all expose the investor to the same credit risk, the relationship at a given point in time between yield and current maturity. Yield curves are typically drawn using yields on governments of various maturities.

Yield to maturity   The rate of return yielded by a debt security held to maturity when both interest payments and the investor's capital gain or loss on the security are taken into account.

Zero coupon   A security sold at a discount whose interest rate is determined by a rise in value per unit of time; its maturity value equals par.

INDEX